THE HEART

Sir Ernest Shackleton is regarded as perhaps the greatest of all Antarctic explorers. Born in 1874 in County Kildare, he was apprenticed in the Merchant Navy and became a junior officer under Scott during the 1901–04 expedition to the South Pole. In 1907 he led his own expedition on the whaler *Nimrod*, coming within ninety-seven miles of the South Pole, the feat for which he was knighted. The events of that expedition are chronicled in *The Heart of the Antarctic*, his first book. His heroic reputation was made during the ill-fated *Endurance* expedition, during which he lead his men to safety after being marooned for two years on the polar ice. His second book, *South*, is his recounting of that expedition. He died in 1922 during his fourth Antarctic expedition and was buried in the whaler's cemetery on South Georgia Island in the South Atlantic.

THE HEART
OF THE
ANTARCTIC

The Farthest South Expedition
1907–1909

by

Sir Ernest Shackleton, CVO

PENGUIN BOOKS

PENGUIN BOOKS

Published by the Penguin Group
Penguin Books Ltd, 27 Wrights Lane, London W8 5TZ, England
Penguin Putnam Inc., 375 Hudson Street, New York, New York 10014, USA
Penguin Books Australia Ltd, Ringwood, Victoria, Australia
Penguin Books Canada Ltd, 10 Alcorn Avenue, Toronto, Ontario, Canada M4V 3B2
Penguin Books (NZ) Ltd, Private Bag 102902, NSMC, Auckland, New Zealand

Penguin Books Ltd, Registered Offices: Harmondsworth, Middlesex, England

First published in two volumes by William Heinemann 1909
This popular edition published in one volume by William Heinemann 1910
Published in the United States of America by Signet 2000
Published in Penguin Books 2000

3

THE HEART
OF THE
ANTARCTIC

The Farthest South Expedition
1907–1909

EXPLORATIONS AND SURVEYS
OF THE EXPEDITION

Ross Sea

MAGNETIC SOUTH POLE AREA
Elevation: 7,260 ft.

Mt. Bellingshausen

Drygalski Ice Barrier Tongue

Ross Island

Cape Royds
(location of the winter camp)

Mt. Erebus

McMurdo Sound

B Depot

Ross Ice Barrier
Mean height 150 feet

Shackleton's route

Scott's farthest south

Beardmore Glacier

Shackleton's farthest south
(88°23' Latitude, 162° Longitude)

SOUTH POLE

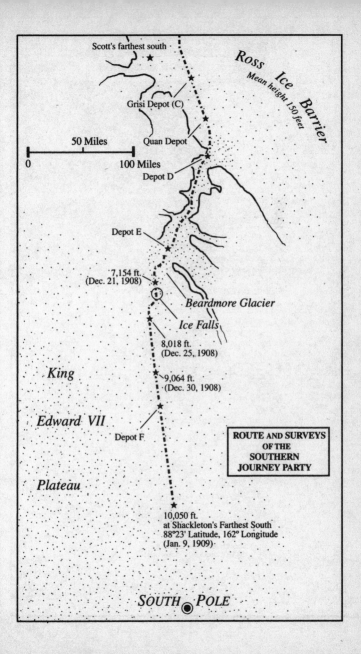

Scott's farthest south

Ross Ice Barrier
Mean height 150 feet

Grisi Depot (C)

Quan Depot

50 Miles

0   100 Miles

Depot D

Depot E

7,154 ft.
(Dec. 21, 1908)

Beardmore Glacier

Ice Falls

8,018 ft.
(Dec. 25, 1908)

King

9,064 ft.
(Dec. 30, 1908)

Edward VII

Depot F

Plateau

10,050 ft.
at Shackleton's Farthest South
88°23' Latitude, 162° Longitude
(Jan. 9, 1909)

**ROUTE AND SURVEYS
OF THE
SOUTHERN
JOURNEY PARTY**

SOUTH ● POLE

PREFACE

THE scientific results of the expedition cannot be stated in detail in a single volume. Some of the more important features of the geographical work were as follow.

We passed the winter of 1908 in McMurdo Sound, twenty miles north of the *Discovery* winter quarters. In the autumn a party ascended Mount Erebus and surveyed its various craters. In the spring and summer of 1908 to 1909, three sledging parties left winter quarters; one went south and attained the most southerly latitude ever reached by man, and another reached the South Magnetic Pole for the first time; while a third surveyed the mountain ranges west of McMurdo Sound.

The Southern Sledge-Party planted the Union Jack in latitude 88° 23' South, within one hundred geographical miles of the South Pole. This party of four ascertained that a great chain of mountains extends from the 82nd parallel, south of McMurdo Sound, to the 86th parallel, trending in a southeasterly direction; that other great mountain ranges continue to the south and southwest, and that between them flows one of the largest glaciers in the world, leading to an inland plateau, the height of which, at latitude 88° South, is over 11,000 ft. above sea level. This plateau presumably continues beyond the geographical South Pole, and extends from Cape Adare to the Pole.

The journey made by the Northern Party resulted in the attainment of the South Magnetic Pole, the position of which was fixed, by observations made on the spot and in the neighborhood, at latitude 72° 25' South, longitude 155° 16' East. The first part of this journey was made along the coastline of Victoria Land, and many new peaks, glaciers, and ice tongues were discovered, in addition to a couple of small islands. The whole of the coast traversed was carefully triangulated, and the existing map was corrected in several respects.

The survey of the western mountains by the Western Party added to the information of the topographical details of that part of Victoria Land, and threw some new light on its geology.

The discovery of forty-five miles of new coastline extending from Cape North, first in a southwesterly and then in a westerly direction, was another important piece of geographical work.

I should like to tender my warmest thanks to those generous people who supported the expedition in its early days. Miss Dawson Lambton and Miss E. Dawson Lambton made possible the first steps toward the organization of the expedition, and assisted afterward in every way that lay in their power. Mr. William Beardmore (Glasgow), Mr. G. A. McLean Buckley (New Zealand), Mr. Campbell McKellar (London), Mr. Sydney Lysaght (Somerset), Mr. A. M. Fry (Bristol), Colonel Alexander Davis (London), Mr. H. H. Bartlett (London), and other friends contributed liberally toward the cost of the expedition.

I also wish to thank those friends who guaranteed a large part of the necessary expenditure, and the Imperial Government for the grant of £20,000, which enabled me to redeem those guarantees.

Overseas Britain showed a sympathetic interest. I am indebted to the Government of the Commonwealth of Australia for a contribution of £5000. The New Zealand Government gave me £1000; and also agreed to pay half the cost of towing the *Nimrod* as far as the Antarctic Circle. Indeed the kindness and generosity of Australasians will remain one of the happiest memories of the "British Antarctic Expedition, 1907." My indebtedness to various firms in the matter of supplies has been acknowledged in Chapter VIII.

I have drawn on the diaries of various members of the expedition to supply information regarding events that occurred while I was absent on journeys. Professor T. W. Edgeworth David narrates the incidents of the Northern Journey.

In regard to the management of the affairs of the expedition during my absence in the Antarctic, I would like to acknowledge the work done for me by my brother-in-law, Mr. Herbert Dorman, of London; by Mr. J. J. Kinsey, of Christchurch, New Zealand; and by Mr. Alfred Reid, the manager of the expedition, whose work throughout has been as arduous as it has been efficient.

Finally, let me say that to the members of the expedition, whose work and enthusiasm have been the means of securing the measure of success recorded in these pages, I owe a debt of gratitude that I can hardly find words to express. I realize very fully that without their faithful service and loyal cooperation under conditions of extreme difficulty success in any branch of our work would have been impossible.

ERNEST H. SHACKLETON

PREFACE TO SECOND EDITION

The publication of this edition of "The Heart of the Antarctic" calls for a word or two from me.

Owing to the necessity of recording all that occurred during our stay in the Antarctic and the inclusion of much scientific matter, the first edition attained proportions that made it, not only expensive to publish, but placed the book out of reach of the ordinary reader.

In this edition the narrative embraces all matters of general public interest. Judging by the way in which the public has shown its interest in the doings of the Expedition, I feel that the time has come for the issue of an account of our Work in Antarctic, less bulky in form and at a lower price.

I hope that the following pages will convey to readers a good idea of the work of our Expedition in the Far South: and, as a last word, I wish to thank all English speaking people all the world over for the keen interest taken in the efforts of our members to extend the general knowledge of that portion of the Imperial Dominion round about the Pole.

E.H.S.

CONTENTS

CHAPTER I

The Expedition

Inception and Preparation: Food supply: Equipment: The
Nimrod: Hut for Winter Quarters: Clothing: Ponies, Dogs,
and Motorcar: Scientific Instruments: Miscellaneous
Articles of Equipment

MEN go out into the void spaces of the world for various
reasons. Some are actuated simply by a love of adventure, some have the keen thirst for scientific knowledge,
and others again are drawn away from the trodden paths
by the "lure of little voices," the mysterious fascination
of the unknown. I think that in my own case it was a
combination of these factors that determined me to try
my fortune once again in the frozen south. I had been
invalided home before the conclusion of the *Discovery*
expedition, and I had a very keen desire to see more of
the vast continent that lies amid the Antarctic snows and
glaciers. Indeed the stark polar lands grip the hearts of
the men who have lived on them in a manner that can
hardly be understood by the people who have never got
outside the pale of civilization. I was convinced, moreover, that an expedition on the lines I had in view could
justify itself by the results of its scientific work. The *Discovery* expedition had brought back a great store of information, and had performed splendid service in several
important branches of science. I believed that a second
expedition could carry the work still further. The *Discovery* expedition had gained knowledge of the great
chain of mountains running in a north and south direction from Cape Adare to latitude 82° 17' South, but
whether this range turned to the southeast or eastward
for any considerable distance was not known, and therefore the southern limits of the Great Ice Barrier plain
had not been defined. The glimpses gained of King Edward VII Land from the deck of the *Discovery* had not
enabled us to determine either its nature or its extent,
and the mystery of the Barrier remained unsolved. It

1

was a matter of importance to the scientific world that
information should be gained regarding the movement
of the ice sheet that forms the Barrier. Then I wanted
to find out what lay beyond the mountains to the south
of latitude 82° 17' and whether the Antarctic continent
rose to a plateau similar to the one found by Captain
Scott beyond the western mountains. There was much
to be done in the field of meteorology, and this work
was of particular importance to Australia and New
Zealand, for these countries are affected by weather conditions that have their origin in the Antarctic. Antarctic
zoology, though somewhat limited, as regarded the range
of species, had very interesting aspects, and I wanted to
devote some attention to mineralogy, apart from general
geology. The aurora australis, atmospheric electricity,
tidal movements, hydrography, currents of the air, ice
formations and movements, biology and geology, offered
an unlimited field for research, and the dispatch of an
expedition seemed to be justified on scientific grounds
quite apart from the desire to gain a high latitude.

The difficulty that confronts most men who wish to
undertake exploration work is that of finance, and in this
respect I was rather more than ordinarily handicapped.
The equipment and dispatch of an Antarctic expedition
means the expenditure of very many thousands of
pounds, without the prospect of any speedy return, and
with a reasonable probability of no return at all. I drew
up my scheme on the most economical lines, as regarded
both ship and staff, but for over a year I tried vainly to
raise sufficient money to enable me to make a start. I
secured introductions to wealthy men, and urged to the
best of my ability the importance of the work I proposed
to undertake, but the money was not forthcoming, and
it almost seemed as though I should have to abandon
the venture altogether. I persisted, and toward the end
of 1906 I was encouraged by promises of support from
one or two personal friends. Then I made a fresh effort,
and on February 12, 1907, I had enough money promised
to enable me to announce definitely that I would go
south with an expedition. As a matter of fact, some of
the promises of support made to me could not be ful-
filled, and I was faced by financial difficulties for some

time; but when the Governments of Australia and New Zealand came to my assistance, the position became more satisfactory.

In the *Geographical Journal* for March 1907 I outlined my plan of campaign, but this had to be changed in several respects at a later date owing to the exigencies of circumstances. My intention was that the expedition should leave New Zealand at the beginning of 1908, and proceed to winter quarters on the Antarctic continent, the ship to land the men and stores and then return. By avoiding having the ship frozen in, I would render the use of a relief ship unnecessary, as the same vessel could come south again the following summer and take us off. "The shore party of nine or twelve men will winter with sufficient equipment to enable three separate parties to start out in the spring," I announced. "One party will go east, and, if possible, across the Barrier to the new land known as King Edward VII Land, follow the coast-line there south, if the coast trends south, or north if north, returning when it is considered necessary to do so. The second party will proceed south over the same route as that of the southern sledge party of the *Discovery;* this party will keep from fifteen to twenty miles from the coast, so as to avoid any rough ice. The third party will possibly proceed westward over the mountains, and, instead of crossing in a line due west, will strike toward the magnetic pole. The main changes in equipment will be that Siberian ponies will be taken for the sledge journeys both east and south, and also a specially designed motorcar for the southern journey. . . . I do not intend to sacrifice the scientific utility of the expedition to a mere record-breaking journey, but say frankly, all the same, that one of my great efforts will be to reach the southern geographical pole. I shall in no way neglect to continue the biological, meteorological, geological and magnetic work of the *Discovery.*" I added that I would endeavor to sail along the coast of Wilkes Land, and secure definite information regarding that coastline.

The program was an ambitious one for a small expedition, no doubt, but I was confident, and I think I may claim that in some measure my confidence has been justified. Before we finally left England, I had decided that if possible I would establish my base on King Edward VII Land instead of at the *Discovery* winter quarters in McMurdo Sound, so that we might break entirely new ground. The narrative will show how completely, as far as this particular matter was concerned, all my plans were upset by the demands of the situation. The journey to King Edward VII Land over the Barrier was not attempted, owing largely to the unexpected loss of ponies before the winter. I laid all my plans very carefully, basing them on experience I had gained with the *Discovery* expedition, and in the fitting out of the relief ships *Terra Nova* and *Morning,* and the Argentine expedition that went to the relief of the Swedes. I decided that I would have no committee, as the expedition was entirely my own venture, and I wished to supervise personally all the arrangements.

When I found that some promises of support had failed me and had learned that the Royal Geographical Society, though sympathetic in its attitude, could not see its way to assist financially, I approached several gentlemen and suggested that they should guarantee me at the bank, the guarantees to be redeemed by me in 1910, after the return of the expedition. It was on this basis that I secured a sum of £20,000, the greater part of the money necessary for the starting of the expedition, and I cannot express too warmly my appreciation of the faith shown in me and my plans by the men who gave these guarantees, which could be redeemed only by the proceeds of lectures and the sale of this book after the expedition had concluded its work. These preliminary matters settled, I started to buy stores and equipment, to negotiate for a ship, and to collect around me the men who would form the expedition.

The equipping of a polar expedition is a task demanding experience as well as the greatest attention to points of detail. When the expedition has left civilization, there is no opportunity to repair any omission or to secure any article that may have been forgotten. It is true that the explorer is expected to be a handy man, able to contrive dexterously with what materials he may have at hand; but makeshift appliances mean increased difficulty and added danger. The aim of one who undertakes to organize such an expedition must be to provide for every contingency, and in dealing with this work I was fortunate in being able to secure the assistance of Mr. Alfred Reid, who had already gained considerable experience in connection with previous polar ventures. I appointed Mr. Reid manager of the expedition, and I found him an invaluable assistant. I was fortunate, too, in not being hampered by committees of any sort. I kept the control of all the arrangements in my own hands, and thus avoided the delays that are inevitable when a group of men have to arrive at a decision on points of detail.

The first step was to secure an office in London, and we selected a furnished room at 9 Regent Street, as the headquarters of the expedition. The staff at this period consisted of Mr. Reid, a district messenger and myself, but there was a typewriting office on the same floor, and the correspondence, which grew in bulk day by day, could be dealt with as rapidly as though I had employed stenographers and typists of my own. I had secured estimates of the cost of provisioning and equipping the expedition before I made any public announcement regarding my intentions, so that there were no delays when once active work had commenced. This was not an occasion for inviting tenders, because it was vitally important that we should have the best of everything, whether in food or gear, and I therefore selected, in consultation with Mr. Reid, the firms that should be asked to supply us. Then we proceeded to interview the heads of these firms, and we found that in nearly every instance we were met with generous treatment as to prices, and with ready cooperation in regard to details of manufacture and packing.

FOOD SUPPLIES

Several very important points have to be kept in view in selecting the food supplies for a polar expedition. In the first place the food must be wholesome and nourishing in the highest degree possible. At one time that dread disease scurvy used to be regarded as the inevitable result of a prolonged stay in the ice-bound regions, and even the *Discovery* expedition, during its labors in the Antarctic in the years 1902–4, suffered from this complaint, which is often produced by eating preserved food that is not in a perfectly wholesome condition. It is now recognized that scurvy may be avoided if the closest attention is given to the preparation and selection of food stuffs on scientific lines, and I may say at once that our efforts in this direction were successful, for during the whole course of the expedition we had not one case of sickness attributable directly or indirectly to the foods we had brought with us. Indeed, beyond a few colds, apparently due to germs from a bale of blankets, we experienced no sickness at all at the winter quarters.

In the second place the food taken for use on the sledging expeditions must be as light as possible, remembering always that extreme concentration renders the food less easy of assimilation and therefore less healthful. Extracts that may be suitable enough for use in ordinary climates are of little use in the polar regions, because under conditions of very low temperature the heat of the body can be maintained only by use of fatty and farinaceous foods in fairly large quantities. Then the sledging foods must be such as do not require prolonged cooking, that is to say, it must be sufficient to bring them to the boiling point, for the amount of fuel that can be carried is limited. It must be possible to eat the foods without cooking at all, for the fuel may be lost or become exhausted.

More latitude is possible in the selection of foods to be used at the winter quarters of the expedition, for the ship may be expected to reach that point, and weight is therefore of less importance. My aim was to secure a large variety of foods for use during the winter night. The long months of darkness impose a severe strain on any men unaccustomed to the conditions, and it is desirable to relieve the monotony in every way possible. A variety of food is healthful, moreover, and this is especially important at a period when it is difficult for the men to take much exercise, and when sometimes they are practically confined to the hut for days together by bad weather.

All these points were taken into consideration in the selection of our food stuffs. I based my estimates on the requirements of twelve men for two years, but this was added to in New Zealand when I increased the staff. Some important articles of food were presented to the expedition by the manufacturers: and others, such as the biscuit and pemmican, were specially manufactured to my order. The question of packing presented some difficulties, and I finally decided to use "Venesta" cases for the food stuffs and as much as possible of the equipment. These cases are manufactured from composite boards prepared by uniting three layers of birch or other hard wood with waterproof cement. They are light, weatherproof, and strong, and proved to be eminently suited to our purposes. The cases I ordered measured about two feet six inches by fifteen inches, and we used some 2500 of them. The saving of weight, as compared with an ordinary packing case, was about four pounds per case, and we had no trouble at all with breakages, in spite of the rough handling given our stores in the process of landing at Cape Royds after the expedition had reached the Antarctic regions.

I decided to take food supplies for the shore party for two years; and some additions were made after the arrival of the *Nimrod* in New Zealand.*

I arranged that supplies for thirty-eight men for one year should be carried by the *Nimrod* when the vessel went south for the second time to bring back the shore party. This was a precautionary measure in case the *Nimrod* should get caught in the ice and be compelled to spend a winter in the Antarctic, in which case we would still have had one year's provisions in hand.

EQUIPMENT

After placing some of the principal orders for food supplies, I went to Norway with Mr. Reid in order to

*See p. 23.

secure the sledges, fur boots and mits, sleeping bags, ski, and some other articles of equipment. I was fortunate, on the voyage from Hull to Christiania, in making the acquaintance of Captain Pepper, the commodore captain of the Wilson Line of steamers. He took a keen interest in the expedition, and he was of very great assistance to me in the months that followed, for he undertook to inspect the sledges in the process of manufacture. He was at Christiania once in each fortnight, and he personally looked to the lashings and seizings as only a sailor could. We arrived at Christiania on April 22, and then learned that Mr. C. S. Christiansen, the maker of the sledges used on the *Discovery* expedition, was in the United States. This was a disappointment, but after consultation with Scott-Hansen, who was the first lieutenant of the *Fram* on Nansen's famous expedition, I decided to place the work in the hands of Messrs. L. H. Hagen and Company. The sledges were to be of the Nansen pattern, built of specially selected timber, and of the best possible workmanship. I ordered ten twelve-foot sledges, eighteen eleven-foot sledges and two seven-foot sledges. The largest ones would be suitable for pony haulage. The eleven-foot ones could be drawn by either ponies or men, and the small pattern would be useful for work around the winter quarters and for short journeys such as the scientists of the expedition were likely to undertake. The timbers used for the sledges were seasoned ash and American hickory, and in addition to Captain Pepper, Captain Isaachsen and Lieutenant Scott-Hansen, both experienced Arctic explorers, watched the work of construction on my behalf. Their interest was particularly valuable to me, for they were able in many little ways hardly to be understood by the lay reader to ensure increased strength and efficiency. I had formed the opinion that an eleven-foot sledge was best for general work, for it was not so long as to be unwieldy, and at the same time was long enough to ride over sastrugi and hummocky ice. Messrs. Hagen and Company did their work thoroughly well, and the sledges proved all that I could have desired.

The next step was to secure the furs that the expedition would require, and for this purpose we went to

Drammen and made the necessary arrangements with Mr. W. C. Möller. We selected skins for the sleeping bags, taking those of young reindeer, with short thick fur, less liable to come out under conditions of dampness than is the fur of the older deer. Our furs did not make a very large order, for after the experience of the *Discovery* expedition I decided to use fur only for the feet and hands and for the sleeping bags, relying for all other purposes on woollen garments with an outer covering of windproof material. I ordered three large sleeping bags, to hold three men each, and twelve one-man bags. Each bag had the reindeer fur inside, and the seams were covered with leather, strongly sewn. The flaps overlapped about eight inches, and the head of the bag was sewn up to the top of the fly. There were three toggles for fastening the bag up when the man was inside. The toggles were about eight inches apart. The one-man bags weighed about ten pounds when dry, but of course the weight increased as they absorbed moisture when in use.

The foot gear I ordered consisted of eighty pairs of ordinary finnesko, or reindeer fur boots, twelve pairs of special finnesko and sixty pairs of ski boots of various sizes. The ordinary finnesko is made from the skin of the reindeer stag's head, with the fur outside, and its shape is roughly that of a very large boot without any laces. It is large enough to hold the foot, several pairs of socks, and a supply of sennegrass, and it is a wonderfully comfortable and warm form of foot gear. The special finnesko are made from the skin of the reindeer stag's legs, but they are not easily secured, for the reason that the native tribes, not unreasonably, desire to keep the best goods for themselves. I had a man sent to Lapland to barter for finnesko of the best kind, but he only succeeded in getting twelve pairs. The ski boots are made of soft leather, with the upper coming right round under the sole, and a flat piece of leather sewn on top of the upper. They are made specially for use with skis, and are very useful for summer wear. They give the foot plenty of play and do not admit water. The heel is very low, so that the foot can rest firmly on the ski. I bought five prepared reindeer skins for repairing, and a supply of repairing gear, such as sinew, needles, and waxed thread.

I have mentioned that sennegrass is used in the finnesko. This is a dried grass of long fiber, with a special quality of absorbing moisture. I bought fifty kilos (110.25 lb.) in Norway for use on the expedition. The grass is sold in wisps, bound up tightly, and when the finnesko are being put on, some of it is teased out and a pad placed along the sole under the foot. Then when the boot has been pulled on more grass is stuffed around the heel. The grass absorbs the moisture that is given off from the skin, and prevents the sock freezing to the sole of the boot, which would then be difficult to remove at night. The grass is pulled out at night, shaken loose, and allowed to freeze. The moisture that has been collected congeals in the form of frost, and the greater part of it can be shaken away before the grass is replaced on the following morning. The grass is gradually used up on the march, and it is necessary to take a fairly large supply, but it is very light and takes up little room.

I ordered from Mr. Möller sixty pairs of wolfskin and dogskin mits, made with the fur outside, and sufficiently long to protect the wrists. The mits had one compartment for the four fingers and another for the thumb, and they were worn over woollen gloves. They were easily slipped off when the use of the fingers was required, and they were hung round the neck with lampwick in order that they might not get lost on the march. The only other articles of equipment I ordered in Norway were twelve pairs of skis, which were supplied by Messrs. Hagen and Company. They were not used on the sledging journeys at all, but were useful around the winter quarters. I stipulated that all the goods were to be delivered in London by June 15, 1907.

The *Nimrod*

Before I left Norway I paid a visit to Sandyfjord in order to see whether I could come to terms with Mr. C. Christiansen, the owner of the *Bjorn*, a ship specially built for polar work, which would have suited my purposes most admirably. She was a new vessel of about 700 tons burthen and with powerful triple-expansion engines, better equipped in every way than the forty-year-old *Nimrod,* but I found that I could not afford to buy her, much as I would have wished to do so.

When I returned to London I purchased the *Nimrod,* which was then engaged on a sealing venture, and was expected to return to Newfoundland within a short time. The ship was small and old, and her maximum speed under steam was hardly more than six knots, but on the other hand, she was strongly built, and quite able to face rough treatment in the ice. Indeed, she had already received a good many hard knocks in the course of a varied career. She was inspected on my behalf and pronounced sound, and, making a fairly rapid passage, arrived in the Thames on June 15. I must confess that I was disappointed when I first examined the little ship, to which I was about to commit the hopes and aspiration of many years. She was much dilapidated and smelled strongly of seal oil, and an inspection in dock showed that she required caulking and that her masts would have to be renewed. She was rigged only as a schooner and her masts were decayed, and I wanted to be able to sail her in the event of the engine breaking down or the supply of coal running short. I had not then become acquainted with the many good qualities of the *Nimrod,* and my first impression hardly did justice to the plucky old ship.

I proceeded at once to put the ship in the hands of Messrs. R. and H. Green, of Blackwall, the famous old firm that had built so many of Britain's "wooden' walls," and that had done fitting and repair work for several other polar expeditions. She was docked for the necessary caulking, and day by day assumed a more satisfactory appearance. The signs of former conflicts with the ice floes disappeared, and the masts and running gear were prepared for the troubled days that were to come. Even the penetrating odor of seal oil ceased to offend after much vigorous scrubbing of decks and holds, and I began to feel that after all the *Nimrod* would do the expedition no discredit. Later still I grew really proud of the sturdy little ship.

Quarters were provided on board for the scientific staff of the expedition by enclosing a portion of the after hold and constructing cabins which were entered by a steep ladder from the deck house. The quarters were certainly small; for some reason not on record, they were known later as "Oyster Alley."

As the *Nimrod,* after landing the shore party with stores and equipment, would return to New Zealand it was necessary that we should have a reliable hut in which to live during the Antarctic night until the sledging journeys commenced in the following spring.

THE HUT

The hut would be our only refuge from the fury of the blizzards, and in it would be stored many articles of equipment as well as some of the food. A hut measuring (externally) thirty-three feet by nineteen feet by eight feet to the eaves was specially constructed, to my order, by Messrs. Humphreys of Knightsbridge. After being erected and inspected in London, it was shipped in sections.

It was made of stout fir timbering of best quality in walls, roofs, and floors, and the parts were all morticed and tenoned to facilitate erection in the Antarctic. The walls were strengthened with iron cleats bolted to main posts and horizontal timbering, and the roof principals were provided with strong iron tie rods. The hut was lined with match boarding, and the walls and roof were covered externally first with strong roofing felt, then with one-inch tongued and grooved boards, and finally with another covering of felt. In addition to these precautions against the extreme cold the four-inch space in framing between the match boarding and the first covering of felt was packed with granulated cork, which assisted materially to render the wall non-conducting. The hut was to be erected on wooden piles let into the ground or ice, and rings were fixed to the apex of the roof so that guy ropes might be used to give additional resistance to the gales. The hut had two doors, connected by a small porch, so that ingress and egress would not mean the admission of a draft of cold air; and the windows were double, in order that the warmth of the hut might be retained. There were two louvre ventilators in the roof, controlled from the inside. The hut had no fittings, and we took little furniture. I proposed to use cases for the construction of benches, beds, and other necessary articles of internal equipment. The hut was to be lit with acetylene gas, and we took a generator, the necessary piping, and a supply of carbide.

The cooking range we used in the hut was manufactured by Messrs. Smith and Wellstrood, of London, and was four feet wide by two feet four inches deep. It had a fire chamber designed to burn anthracite coal continuously day and night and to heat a large superficial area of outer plate, so that there might be plenty of warmth given off in the hut. The stove had two ovens and a chimney of galvanized steel pipe, capped by a revolving cowl. It was mounted on legs.

CLOTHING

Each member of the expedition was supplied with two winter suits made of heavy blue pilot cloth, lined with Jaeger fleece. A suit consisted of a double-breasted jacket, vest and trousers, and weighed complete fourteen and three-quarter pounds. The underclothing was secured from the Dr. Jaeger Sanitary Woollen Company.

An outer suit of windproof material is necessary in the polar regions, and I secured twenty-four suits of Burberry gaberdine, each suit consisting of a short blouse, trouser overalls and a helmet cover. For use in the winter quarters we took four dozen Jaeger camel hair blankets and sixteen camel hair triple sleeping bags.

PONIES, DOGS, AND MOTORCAR

I decided to take ponies, dogs, and a motorcar to assist in hauling our sledges on the long journeys that I had in view, but my hopes were based mainly on the ponies. Dogs had not proved satisfactory on the Barrier surface, and I had not expected my dogs to do as well as they actually did. I felt confident, however, that the hardy ponies used in Northern China and Manchuria would be useful if they could be landed on the ice in good condition. I had seen these ponies in Shanghai, and I had heard of the good work they did on the Jackson-Harmsworth expedition. They are accustomed to hauling heavy loads in a very low temperature, and they are hardy, sure footed, and plucky. I noticed that they had been used with success for very rough work during the Russo-Japanese War, and a friend who had lived in Siberia gave me some more information regarding their capabilities.

I therefore got into communication with the London manager of the Hong Kong and Shanghai Bank (Mr. C. S. Addis), and he was able to secure the services of a leading firm of veterinary surgeons in Shanghai. A qualified man went to Tientsin on my behalf, and from a mob of about two thousand of the ponies, brought down for sale from the northern regions, he selected fifteen of the little animals for my expedition. The ponies chosen were all over twelve and under seventeen years of age, and had spent the early part of their lives in the interior of Manchuria. They were practically unbroken, about fourteen hands high, and of various colors. They were all splendidly strong and healthy, full of tricks and wickedness, and ready for any amount of hard work over the snow fields. The fifteen ponies were taken to the coast and shipped by direct steamer to Australia. They came through the test of tropical temperatures unscathed, and at the end of October 1908 arrived in Sydney, where they were met by Mr. Reid and at once transferred to a New Zealand bound steamer. The Colonial Governments kindly consented to suspend the quarantine restrictions, which would have entailed exposure to summer heat for many weeks, and thirty-five days after leaving China the ponies were landed on Quail Island in Port Lyttelton, and were free to scamper about and feed in idle luxury.

I decided to take a motorcar because I thought it possible, from my previous experience, that we might meet with a hard surface on the Great Ice Barrier, over which the first part, at any rate, of the journey towards the south would have to be performed. On a reasonably good surface the machine would be able to haul a heavy load at a rapid pace. I selected a 12–15 horsepower New Arrol-Johnston car, fitted with a specially designed air-cooled four cylinder engine and Simms Bosch magneto ignition. Water could not be used for cooling, as it would certainly freeze. Round the carburetor was placed a small jacket, and the exhaust gases from one cylinder were passed through this in order that they might warm the mixing chamber before passing into the air. The exhaust from the other cylinders was conveyed into a silencer that was also to act as a foot warmer. The frame of the car was of the standard pattern, but the manufacturers had taken care to secure the maximum of strength, in view of the fact that the car was likely to experience severe strains at low temperature. I ordered a good supply of spare parts in order to provide for breakages, and a special nonfreezing oil was prepared for me by Messrs. Price and Company. Petrol was taken in the ordinary tins. I secured wheels of several special patterns as well as ordinary wheels with rubber tires, and I had manufactured wooden runners to be placed under the front wheels for soft surfaces, the wheels resting in chocks on top of the runners. The car in its original form had two bracket seats, and a large trough behind for carrying stores. It was packed in a large case and lashed firmly amidships on the *Nimrod,* in which position it made the journey to the Antarctic continent in safety.

I placed little reliance on dogs, as I have already stated, but I thought it advisable to take some of these animals. I knew that a breeder in Stewart Island, New Zealand, had dogs descended from the Siberian dogs used on the Newnes-Borchgrevink expedition, and I cabled to him to supply as many as he could up to forty. He was only able to let me have nine, but this team proved quite sufficient for the purposes of the expedition, as the arrival of pups brought the number up to twenty-two during the course of the work in the south.

SCIENTIFIC INSTRUMENTS

The equipment of a polar expedition on the scientific side involved the expenditure of a large sum of money and I felt the pinch of necessary economies in this branch. I was lent three chronometer watches by the Royal Geographical Society. I bought one chronometer watch, and three wardens of the Skinners' Company gave me one which proved the most accurate of all and was carried by me on the journey toward the Pole.

The Geographical Society was able to send forward an application made by me for the loan of some instruments and charts from the Admiralty, and that Department generously lent me the articles contained in the following list:

3 Lloyd-Creak dip circles.
3 marine chronometers.
1 station pointer, 6 ft.
1 set of charts, England to Cape and
    Cape to New Zealand.
1 set of Antarctic charts.
1 set of charts from New Zealand through
    Indian Ocean to Aden.
1 set of charts, New Zealand to Europe *via* Cape Horn.
12 deep-sea thermometers.
2 marine standard barometers.
1 navy-pattern ship's telescope.
1 ship's standard compass.
2 azimuth mirrors (Lord Kelvin's type).
1 deep-sea sounding machine.
3 heeling error instruments.
1 3-in. portable astronomical telescope.
1 Lucas deep sea sounding machine.

I placed an order for further scientific instruments with Messrs. Cary, Porter and Company, Limited, of London.

Amongst other instruments that we had with us on the expedition was a four-inch transit theodolite, with Reeve's micrometers fitted to horizontal and vertical circles. The photographic equipment included nine cameras by various makers, plant for the darkroom, and a large stock of plates, films, and chemicals. We took also a moving picture camera in order that we might place on record the curious movements and habits of the seals and penguins, and give the people at home a graphic idea of what it means to haul sledges over the ice and snow.

MISCELLANEOUS

The miscellaneous articles of equipment were too numerous to be mentioned here in any detail. I had tried to provide for every contingency, and the gear ranged from needles and nails to a Remington typewriter and two Singer sewing machines. There was a gramophone to provide us with music, and a printing press, with type, rollers, paper, and other necessaries, for the production of a book during the winter night. We even had hockey sticks and a soccer ball.

CHAPTER II

The Staff of the Expedition

The Members of the Expedition:
Nimrod leaves East India Docks,
July 30: In the Solent, August 3–5

THE *personnel* of an expedition of the character I proposed is a factor on which success depends to a very large extent. The men selected must be qualified for the work, and they must also have the special qualifications required to meet polar conditions. They must be able to live together in harmony for a long period without outside communication, and it must be remembered that the men whose desires lead them to the untrodden paths of the world have generally marked individuality. It was no easy matter for me to select the staff, although over four hundred applications arrived from persons wishing to join the expedition. I wanted to have two surgeons with the shore party, and also to have a thoroughly capable biologist and geologist, for the study of these two branches of science in the Antarctic seemed to me to be of especial importance. After much consideration I selected eleven men for the shore party. Three of them only, Adams, Wild, and Joyce, had been known to me previously, while only Wild and Joyce had previous experience of polar work, having been members of the *Discovery* expedition. Every man, however, was highly recommended, and this was the case also with the officers whom I selected for the *Nimrod*.

THE MEMBERS OF THE EXPEDITION
SHORE PARTY
ERNEST H. SHACKLETON, commander.
PROFESSOR T. W. EDGEWORTH DAVID. F.R.S., director of the scientific staff.
LIEUTENANT J. B. ADAMS, R.N.R., meteorologist.
SIR PHILIP BROCKLEHURST, Bart., assistant geologist.
BERNARD DAY, motor expert.

ERNEST JOYCE, in charge of dogs, sledges, etc.
DR. A. F. MACKAY, surgeon.
DOUGLAS MAWSON, D.Sc., B.E., physicist.
BERTRAM ARMYTAGE, in charge of ponies.
DR. E. MARSHALL, surgeon, cartographer.
G. E. MARSTON, artist.
J. MURRAY, biologist.
RAYMOND PRIESTLEY, geologist.
W. ROBERTS, cook.
F. WILD, in charge of provisions.

Before leaving New Zealand I was able to add to the strength of the staff:

Professor Edgeworth David, F.R.S., of Sydney University, consented to accompany us as far as the winter quarters, with the idea of returning in the *Nimrod,* but I persuaded him eventually to stay in the Antarctic, and his assistance in connection with the scientific work, and particularly the geology, was invaluable.

Dr. Mawson (lecturer in mineralogy, etc., at the Adelaide University) joined us as physicist.

SHIP'S STAFF
LIEUTENANT R. G. ENGLAND, R.N.R., captain.
JOHN K. DAVIS, chief officer, later captain.
A. L. A. MACKINTOSH, second officer.
A. E. HARBORD, auxiliary second officer.
H. J. L. DUNLOP, chief engineer.
W. A. R. MICHELL, surgeon.
ALFRED CHEETHAM, third officer and boatswain.
W. D. ANSELL, steward.
J. MONTAGUE, cook.
E. ELLIS
H. BULL
S. RICHES   } A.B.s.
J. PATON
W. WILLIAMS
G. BILSBY, carpenter
[LIEUTENANT F. P. EVANS, R.N.R., was appointed captain for the second voyage to the Antarctic.]

The work of preparation made rapid progress, and as the end of July approached the stores and equipment were stowed away on board the *Nimrod* in readiness for the voyage to New Zealand. The final departure for the south was to be made from Lyttelton, at which I felt sure, from former experience, that I should receive every assistance from the authorities.

Early in July we exhibited at a room in Regent Street samples of our stores and equipment, and some thousands of people paid us a visit. The days were all too short, for scores of details demanded attention; but there were no delays, and on July 30, 1907, the *Nimrod* sailed from the East India Docks on the first stage of the long journey to New Zealand. Most of the members of the shore staff, including myself, intended to make this journey by mail steamer, but I left the docks with the *Nimrod,* intending to travel as far as Torquay.

We anchored for the first night at Greenhithe. Next morning, after landing Mr. Reid at Tilbury in order that he might return to London for letters, we proceeded on our way down channel. When Mr. Reid reached London, he found a telegram from the King's equerry, commanding the *Nimrod* to visit Cowes in order that their Majesties the King and Queen might inspect the ship and equipment on Sunday, August 4. Mr. Reid had some difficulty in delivering this message to me, but the Admiral superintendent at Sheerness kindly despatched a tug which overtook the *Nimrod* off Ramsgate. On August 1 we stopped for an hour off Eastbourne to enable some supporters of the expedition to pay us a farewell visit, and then proceeded to the Solent, where we anchored.

CHAPTER III

Royal Visit to the *Nimrod*

In the Solent: The *Nimrod* visited by Royal Party:
Her Majesty Queen Alexandra presents a Union Jack
to the Commander of the Expedition Torquay,
August 6: *Nimrod* arrives: August 7, The *Nimrod*
sails for Lyttelton, via St. Vincent and Cape Town:
Arrival at Lyttelton, November 23, 1907

COWES, *Aug. 4.*

THEIR Majesties King Edward and Queen Alexandra,
their Royal Highnesses the Prince of Wales, the Princess
Victoria, Prince Edward and the Duke of Connaught,
came on board and inspected the *Nimrod,* an honor
which was greatly appreciated by the members of the
expedition.

The royal party showed much interest in some of the
equipment for the southern journey. The picture shows
His Majesty the King examining the sledges, etc.

Her Majesty Queen Alexandra graciously entrusted
me with a Union Jack to be carried on the southern
journey; His Majesty King Edward graciously conferred
on me the Victorian Order.

The *Nimrod* sailed for Torquay early on the following
morning, and arrived there on August 6. We drank success to the expedition at a farewell dinner that evening,
and on the morning of Wednesday, August 7, the ship
sailed for New Zealand, and after calling at St. Vincent
and Capetown, arrived at Lyttelton on November 23,
the voyage having occupied three months and a half. Mr.
Reid reached Australian waters a month ahead of the
Nimrod, in order to make the necessary arrangements
and meet the Manchurian ponies, and I arrived early in
December to arrange for leaving Lyttelton on January
1, 1908.

CHAPTER IV

Lyttelton to the Antarctic Circle

Final Preparations at Lyttelton: Enthusiastic send-off:
In tow of the *Koonya* for 1510 miles:
Getting through the Pack-ice: Ross Sea
reached January 17

THE final preparations at Lyttelton during the month of
December involved a great deal of work, but by Decem-
ber 31 all was in readiness for a start on New Year's
Day.

The Postmaster General of the Dominion had printed
off for us a small issue of special stamps, and had constituted me a postmaster during my stay in the Antarctic.

The ponies were enjoying their holiday on Quail Island, and it was necessary that they should be broken
to handling and sledge hauling. Mr. C. Tubman undertook this work, with the assistance of Dr. Mackay, and
there were some exciting moments on the island. All the
ponies had names, and we finally took away from New
Zealand ten animals known as "Socks," "Queen,"
"Grisi," "Chinaman," "Billy," "Zulu," "Doctor,"
"Sandy," "Nimrod," and "Mac" respectively.

The quarters of the scientific staff on board the *Nimrod* were certainly small, in fact there was just room for
the bunks and nothing else. As the day of departure
approached and the scientists brought their personal belongings, Oyster Alley reached a state of congestion that
can hardly be imagined.

The ponies were to be carried on deck, and ten stout
stalls were built for them. The motorcar was enclosed in
a large case and made fast with chains on the after hatch
whence it could be transferred easily on to the ice when
the occasion arose. The deck load was heavy and included cases of maize, tins of carbide for the manufacture of acetylene gas, a certain quantity of coal and the
sledges. The *Nimrod* was low in the water as a result,
and when we left Lyttelton the little ship had only three

feet six inches of freeboard. Some live sheep presented to us by New Zealand farmers were placed on board the *Koonya,* the steamer which was to tow the *Nimrod* to the south. Messrs. Nathan and Co., of Wellington, presented the expedition with sixty-eight cases of "Glaxo" dried milk, 192 lb. of New Zealand butter, and two cases of New Zealand cheese. Several other acceptable gifts were received before we sailed.

I had been anxious to have the *Nimrod* towed south in order to save coal. The ship could not take in a large quantity of coal after our provisions and equipment had been placed on board, for she was considerably overloaded, and it was important that there should be enough coal to take the ship through the ice and back to New Zealand, and also to provide for the warming of the hut during the winter. The Government of the Dominion consented to pay half the cost of the tow, and Sir James Mills, chairman of the Union Steamship Company, offered to pay the other half. The *Koonya,* a steel built steamer of about 1100 tons, was chartered and placed under the command of Captain F. P. Evans. The wisdom of this selection was proved by after events. The pressure of work at this time was tremendous, and I owed a very great deal to the assistance and advice I received from Mr. J. J. Kinsey, of Christchurch. Before my departure I placed the conduct of the affairs of the expedition in New Zealand in his hands.

December 31, 1907. The stores and equipment were now on board and were as complete as we could make them, and I had written my final letters, both business and personal. The ponies and the dogs were to be placed on board the *Nimrod* early the following morning.

January 1, 1908, arrived at last! Warm, fine, and clear broke the morning of our last day in civilization. Before sunset we were to sever all ties with the outer world and more than a year must elapse ere we could look again on the scenes familiar to ordinary daily life. For me this day brought a feeling of relief, after all the strenuous work of the previous year, though the new work I was entering upon was fraught with more anxiety and was more exacting than any that had gone before. We all looked forward eagerly to our coming venture, for the glamour of the unknown was with us and the South was calling.

My personal belongings were gathered out of the chaos of papers and odds and ends in my office at the hotel; I knew that the legacy of unanswered letters, requests for special stamps, and the hundred and one things that collect under such circumstances would be faithfully administered by Mr. Reid. Orders had been given to Captain England to have all in readiness for casting off at 4 P.M., and early in the afternoon most of us were on board. It was Regatta day and Lyttelton was crowded with holiday makers, many thousands of whom had come to see the *Nimrod*. All day the deck of our little vessel was thronged by the general public, who evinced the greatest interest in everything connected with the ship and her equipment. Naturally the ten ponies, now safely housed in their stalls on the forward deck, were a special attraction. Our nine dogs also claimed a share of attention, although it was a gymnastic feat to climb through the supports of the pony structure, stretching across the decks, in order to reach the forecastle, where the dogs lay panting in the hot sun. To the uninitiated the number and size of the beams belonging to the pony structure seemed excessive, but we knew we might encounter heavy weather which would tax their strength to the utmost. The *Nimrod* was deep in the water, for every available corner had been stowed with stores and coal and, if we could have carried it, we would have added at least another fifty tons to our two hundred and fifty; but the risk was too great. Indeed I was somewhat anxious as to the weather she might make, though I knew she was a good sea boat and had great confidence in her. There were many whose criticisms were frankly pessimistic as to our chances of weathering an Antarctic gale; and as I stood on deck I could hear the remarks of these Job's comforters. Such criticisms, however, did not disturb us, for we had confidence in the ship.

Oyster Alley was crammed with the personal belongings of at least fourteen of the shore party; it was the temporary resting place for many of the scientific instruments, so that both ingress and egress were matters of extreme difficulty. The entrance to this twentieth-century

Black Hole was through a narrow doorway and down a ladder, which ushered one into almost complete darkness, for the doorway was practically filled up with cases, and the single narrow deck light generally covered by the feet of sightseers. The shore party's fourteen bunks were crammed with luggage, which also occupied the whole of the available floor space. It was in this uncomfortable place that the spirit of romance, the desire for the wind whitened Southern Seas, and the still whiter wastes of the silent Antarctic, grew stronger in the heart of George Buckley, as he sat there talking over the days and doings before us, longing for a share in the work, even though he might only go as far as the Antarctic circle. He knew that time would not permit him to do more than this. Suddenly he jumped up, came to me, and asked if I would take him as far as the ice. I was only too glad to consent, for his interest in the expedition showed that his heart was in our venture, and his personality had already appealed to us all. It was 2 P.M. when the decision was made, and the *Nimrod* was to sail at 4 P.M. He managed to catch a train to Christchurch, dashed into his club, gave his power of attorney to a friend; slung his toothbrush and some underclothing into a bag; struggled through one seething crowd at Christchurch Station and another at the wharf, and arrived on board the *Nimrod*, a few minutes before sailing time equipped for the most rigorous weather in the world with only the summer suit he was wearing: surely a record in the way of joining a Polar expedition!

Time was passing quickly, it was nearing four o'clock and all our party were on board save Professor David. I had seen him earlier in the afternoon, struggling along the crowded wharf, bending under the weight of one end of a long iron pipe, a railway porter attached to the other. This precious burden, he had informed me, when it was safely on board, was part of the boring gear to be used in obtaining samples of ice from the Great Ice Barrier; he had found it at the railway station, where it had been overlooked. Doubtless he was having a last skirmish round in case there was anything else that had been left, and just as I was getting anxious, for I did not want to delay the departure of the ship, he appeared.

His arms were filled with delicate glass apparatus and other scientific paraphernalia. As he was gingerly crossing the narrow gangway he was confronted by a stout female, of whom the Professor afterwards said: "She was for the shore, let who would be for the Pole." They met in the middle of the gangway. Hampered by the things he was carrying, the Professor could not move aside; he was simply charged down by superior weight, and clutching his precious goods, fell off the gangway on to the heads of some of our party. Wonderful to relate nothing was broken.

At one minute to four orders were given to stand by the engines, at 4 P.M. the lines were cast off from the wharf and the *Nimrod* moved slowly ahead. Cheer after cheer broke from the watching thousands as we moved towards the harbor entrance, with the Queen's flag flying at the fore and our ensign dipping farewell at the stern. The cheering broke out afresh as we passed the United States magnetic survey ship *Galilee*. She also was engaged in a scientific mission, but her lines were laid in warmer climes and calmer seas. Hearty as was this send off, it seemed mild compared to that which we received on passing the pier-head lighthouse. The air trembled with the crash of guns, the piercing steam whistles and sirens of every steamship in the port; and a roar of cheering from the throats of the thirty thousand people who were watching the little black hulled barque moving slowly towards the open sea. With our powerful ally, the *Koonya,* steaming in front, and on each side passenger boats of the Union Company carrying some six or seven thousand persons, we passed down the Roads, receiving such a farewell and "Godspeed" from New Zealand as left no man of us unmoved. The farewells were not over, for we were to receive one more expression of goodwill, and one that came nearer to the hearts of those of us who were sailors than any other could. Lying inside the Heads were three of His Majesty's ships of the Australian Squadron, the flagship *Powerful,* the *Pegasus* and the *Pioneer.* As we steamed past the last-named her crew mustered on the forecastle head and gave us three hearty cheers; we received the same from the *Pegasus* as we came abeam of her, our party of thirty-nine returning the cheers as we passed each ship in turn. Then we drew abreast of the flagship and from the throats of the nine hundred odd bluejackets on board her we got a ringing farewell, and across the water came the sound of her band playing "Hearts of oak are our ships," followed by "Auld Lang Syne." We responded with three cheers and gave another cheer for Lady Fawkes, who had taken a kindly interest in the expedition.

Shortly after passing the *Powerful,* we stopped to pick up our tow-line from the *Koonya,* but before doing this we transferred to the tug-boat *Canterbury* the few personal friends who had accompanied some of the members of the expedition down the harbor. We then came close up to the stern of the *Koonya* and hauled in the 4-in. wire cable she was to tow us with. A 4-in. wire is measured not as 4 in. diameter, but 4 in. circumference, and is made of the finest steel. We passed a shackle through the eye at the end of this wire and shackled on to the free ends of both our chain cables. We then let out thirty fathoms of each cable, one on each side of the bow, and made the inner ends fast round the foremast in the 'tween decks. This cable acted as a "spring," to use a nautical term; that is to say, it lessened the danger of the wire snapping if a sudden strain were put upon it, for the cable hung down in the water owing to its weight, even when the ship was being towed at seven or eight knots. This operation being completed we signaled the *Koonya* to go ahead and we were soon in the open sea. There was a slight breeze and a small choppy sea. Before we had been under way for an hour water began to come in at the scupper holes and through the wash ports. This looked ominous to us, for if the *Nimrod* was going to be wet in such fine weather, what was she going to be like when we got a southerly gale! She moved through the water astern of *Koonya* like a reluctant child being dragged to school; she seemed to have no vitality of her own. This was due to her deeply loaded condition, and more especially to the seven tons of cable and the weight of the wire on her bows dragging her nose down into the sea. No Antarctic exploring ship had been towed to the ice before, but it meant the saving of coal

to us for a time when the tons saved in this manner
might prove the salvation of the expedition.

Night came down on us, and the last we saw of New
Zealand was a bold headland growing fainter and fainter
in the gathering gloom. The occupants of Oyster Alley,
after a somewhat sketchy meal in the wardroom, were
endeavoring to reduce the chaos of their quarters into
some sort of order. The efforts of some of the scientific
staff were interrupted at times by sudden attacks of seasickness, and indeed one would not have been surprised
if the seafaring portion of the staff had also succumbed,
for the atmosphere of the alley, combined with the peculiar motion of the ship, was far from pleasant. A few of
the members of the party preferred to sleep on deck in
any odd corner they could find, and one man in particular was so overcome by the sea that for three days and
nights he lay prostrate amongst the vegetables and cases
of butter and carbide, on the unused fore bridge of the
ship. He seemed to recover at mealtimes, and as his lair
was just above the galley, he simply appeared from
under his sodden blankets, reached down his hand, and
in a plaintive voice asked for something to fill the yawning cavern that existed in his interior. Professor David
was given Dr. Michell's cabin, the latter taking up his
abode in Oyster Alley. The cabin measured about 5 ft.
10 in. by 3 ft., and as the Professor had nearly a quarter
of a ton of scientific instruments, books, and cameras,
one can imagine that he had not much room for himself.
The wardroom of the *Nimrod* was about 12 ft. long and
8 ft. broad, and as there were twenty-two mouths to feed
there three times a day, difficulties were present from
the beginning of the voyage. Dunlop's cabin came into
service as the largest overflow dining room, for it accom-
modated three people. Davis and Mackintosh each
found room for another hungry explorer in his cabin.
When the food arrived it was passed along to the outside
dining rooms first. Then people in the main room were
served. All went well that first night out, for there was
comparatively little movement, but later on the story of
an ordinary meal became a record of adventure. I took
up my quarters in the captain's cabin, and fluctuated
between the bunk and the settee for a resting place, until

the carpenter made me a plank bed about four inches off the deck. We did not know that we were not to take our clothes off for the next two weeks, but were to live in a constant state of wetness, wakefulness, and watchfulness until the *Nimrod* arrived in the neighborhood of the winter quarters.

Bad weather was not long delayed. As the night of January 1 wore on, the wind began to freshen from the southwest, and the following morning the two vessels were pitching somewhat heavily and steering wildly. The *Koonya* signaled us to veer, that is, to slack out thirty more fathoms on each of our two cables, and with great difficulty we managed to do this. The ship was pitching and rolling, flinging the cables from one side of the deck to the other, and with our forty-year-old windlass it was no light task to handle the heavy chains. Then I felt one of the first real pinches of the stringent economy that had to be practiced from the inception of the expedition. How I wished for the splendid modern gear of the *Discovery,* the large, specially built vessel that we had on the previous expedition. During the afternoon the wind and sea increased greatly, and the *Nimrod* pitched about, shifting everything that could be moved on deck. The seas began to break over her, and we were soon wet through, not to be properly dry again for the next fortnight. The decks were flooded with heavy seas, which poured, whitecapped, over the side, and even the topsail yards were drenched with the spray of breaking waves. Life lines were stretched along the deck, and it was a risky thing to go forward without holding on.

Our chief anxiety was the care of the ponies, and looking back now to those days, it remains a matter of wonder to me how they survived the hardships that fell to their lot. That night I arranged for a two-hour watch, consisting of two members of the shore staff, to be always in attendance on the ponies. The pony shelter had five stalls on the port side and five on the starboard side of the deck, with the fore hatch between them. The watch keepers named this place "The Cavalry Club," and here in the bleak and bitter stormy nights, swept off their feet every now and then by the seas washing over the fore hatch, the members of the shore party passed many a bad quarter of an hour. They bore all the buffeting and discomfort cheerfully, even as those men of old, who "ever with a frolic welcome took the thunder and the sunshine." Night in the pony stables was a weird experience with inky blackness all round, save only where the salt-encrusted hurricane lamp, jerking to and fro, made a glimmer of light. The roar of the tempest rose into a shriek as the wind struck the rigid rigging, the creaking and swaying of the roof of the stable and the boat skids, which partly rested their weight on it, seemed to threaten a sudden collapse with each succeeding and heavier roll, and the seas crashed dully as they fell on board. The swirling waters, foam-white in the dim rays of the lamp, rushed through the stable and over the hatch, and even from the bridge far aft, we could hear the frightened whinnies of the animals, as they desperately struggled to keep their feet in the water that flooded the rolling stables. Every now and then some wave, larger and fiercer than the one before, would sweep the decks, tear the mats from under the feet of the ponies, and wash the watch keepers almost under the struggling beasts. When the bulk of the water had passed, the mats were nailed down again with difficulty, and the two watchers resumed their seats on a bag of fodder that had been fastened to the hatch. One can imagine that after a two-hours' watch a rest was welcome. Oyster Alley was wet enough, and the beds were soaking, while the atmosphere was thick and heavy; but these conditions did not prevent the wearied men from falling asleep after wedging themselves into their bunks, lest some extra heavy lurch should send them to keep company with the miscellaneous collection of articles careering up and down the deck of the "Alley."

All during our second night out the weather was so bad, that we kept going slow, having requested the *Koonya* to slacken speed late in the afternoon. Next morning found us plunging, swerving, and rolling in a high sea, with a dull grey stormy sky overhead, and apparently no prospect of the weather becoming settled. We were moving little more than a mile an hour towards the south, and the ship seemed to be straining herself on account of the heavy pull on her bows, and the re-

sulting lack of buoyancy. The weather moderated somewhat in the afternoon, and we signaled the *Koonya* to
"increase speed." By midnight the improvement in the
weather was much more marked. The following morning, January 4, we set loose the carrier pigeon which one
of the New Zealand sailors had brought with him. We
attached a message to the bird, briefly describing our
passage so far, and hoped it would safely accomplish the
three hundred odd miles to the land. On releasing our
messenger it made one or two wide circles round the
ship, and then set off in a beeline towards its home. We
wondered at the time whether any of the albatrosses,
which were now fairly numerous about our stern, especially at meal times, would attack the stranger, and we
heard afterwards that the pigeon had not reached its
home.

The hope that we were going to keep finer weather
was dispelled in the afternoon, for the wind began to
increase and the rising sea to break on board again, and
within a couple of hours we were bearing the full brunt
of another furious gale. The sea-going qualities of the
Nimrod were severely taxed, but the little vessel rose to
the occasion. As the gale increased in vehemence, she
seemed to throw off the lethargy, one might almost say
the sulkiness, which possessed her when she found herself outward bound at the end of a tow line, for the first
time in her strenuous life of forty years. Now that the
tow line, in the fury of the gale, was but of little use
save to steady us, the *Nimrod* began to play her own
hand. It was wonderful to see how she rose to the largest
oncoming waves. She was flung to and fro, a tiny speck
in this waste of waters, now poised on the summit of a
huge sea, whence we got almost a bird's-eye view of the
gallant *Koonya* smashing into the turmoil ahead; now
dipping into the wave valleys, from which all we could
discern of our consort was in very truth "just a funnel
and a mast lurching through the spray."

As the afternoon wore on, those of us who were not
still in the clutches of seasickness watched the grandeur
of the gale. I shall always remember Buckley, who stood
for hour after hour on the *Nimrod*'s poop, reveling in
the clash and strife of the elements. Keen yachtsman

that he was, his admiration was aroused by the way the two ships battled with the storm. Professor David, also, hanging to the dripping rails, was fascinated by the wild scene, and between the gusts we spoke of many things. Somehow or another the conversation turned to one's favorite poets, and it is but natural that, under these circumstances of stress and strain, Browning's verse was often the subject of conversation. Night drew on, sullen and black, our only light the lamp we steered by on the *Koonya*'s mast. We could imagine the stalwart figure of that splendid seaman, Captain Evans, as he stood on his spray-drenched bridge, alert, calm, and keen, doing his best to ease the little ship astern. We had nothing but admiration for the consummate seamanship that anticipated our every need and wish. All that night it blew harder than ever; on the morning of the 5th, I told Captain England to signal the *Koonya* and ask her to pour oil on the water in the hope that it might help us. To a certain extent I think it did, but not enough to prevent the heaviest seas from breaking on board. I thought that the gale had reached its height on the previous day, but certainly this evening it was much stronger. The *Nimrod* rolled over fifty degrees from the perpendicular to each side; how much more than that I cannot say, for the indicator recording the roll of the ship was only marked up to fifty degrees, and the pointer had passed that mark. Let the reader hold a pencil on end on a table, and then incline it fifty degrees one way, and back again till it reaches fifty degrees on the other side, and he will realize the length of arc through which the masts and deck of the *Nimrod* swung. It was only natural, under these circumstances, that the sturdy little ponies had their strength taxed to the utmost to keep their footing at all. It was impracticable to sling them, for they were only half broken, and the attempt to put a sling under one drove it nearly crazy with fright. All we could do was to try and soothe them, and the animals evidently appreciated the human voice and touch. Buckley had a wonderful way with them, and they seemed to understand that he was trying to help them.

Occasionally there were clear patches of sky to the south and east between the squalls. We had sleet for the first time on January 5, and the wind, ranging between west, south, and southwest, was chilly for the height of summer, the temperature being about 46° F. We passed large masses of floating kelp which may have torn from the islands to the southwest of us, for at noon on January 5 we were still north of the fiftieth parallel, a latitude corresponding to the South of England. Our course lay practically south, for I wanted to enter the pack ice somewhere about the 178th meridian east, previous experience having shown that the pack is less dense about that meridian than it is further west. About 9 P.M. that night, during an extra heavy roll, one of the ponies slipped down in its stall, and when the ship rolled the opposite way, turned right over on its back, as it could not regain its footing. We tried everything in our power to get the poor beast up again, but there was no room to work in the narrow stall, and in the darkness and rushing water it would have been madness to have tried to shift the other ponies out of the adjacent stalls in order to take down the partition, and so give the poor animal room to get up itself. We had perforce to leave it for the night, trusting that when daylight came the weather might have moderated, and that with the light we might be able to do more. It speaks wonders for the vitality of the animal that in spite of its cramped position and the constant washing of the cold seas over it during the whole night, it greedily ate the handfuls of hay which were given it from time to time. Every now and then the pony made frantic efforts to get on to its feet again, but without avail, and before the morning its struggles grew weaker and weaker. The morning of January 6 broke with the gale blowing more strongly than ever. There was a mountainous sea running, and at ten o'clock, after having made another futile attempt to get "Doctor," as he was called, on his legs, and finding that he had no strength of his own, I had regretfully to give orders to have him shot. One bullet from a heavy service revolver ended his troubles. During the morning the gale moderated somewhat, and at noon we were in latitude 50° 58' South, and longitude 175° 19' East.

During the afternoon of January 6, the wind increased again, the squalls being of hurricane force, and the wind shifting to between west and northwest. The *Koonya* ahead was making bad weather of it, but was steaming as fast as practicable, for with the wind and sea coming more abeam she was able to make better headway than when she was plunging into a head sea with the weight and bulk of the towing cable and the *Nimrod* astern of her, factors in the situation that made the handling of the steamer very difficult. The temperature of the air that day was up to 49° F., but the sea temperature had dropped to 44°. This continuous bad weather was attributed by some on board to the fact that we had captured an albatross on the second day out. It is generally supposed by seamen to be unlucky to kill this bird, but as we did it for the purposes of scientific collections and not with the wantonness of the "Ancient Mariner," the superstitious must seek for some other reason for the weather. By this time most of the scientific staff had recovered from seasickness, so to employ their time when they were not on pony guard, meteorological observations were taken every hour. There sometimes was an inclination to obtain the temperature of the sea water from the never failing stream which poured over the deck, but to the observers' credit this feeling was sternly suppressed, and the more legitimate and accurate, if less simple means, that of drawing it from over the side, was adopted. It is not at all an easy operation to draw water in this way from the sea when a ship is under way, and in our particular circumstances the observer often got premature knowledge of the temperature by the contents of the bucket, or the top of a sea, drenching him. On this day we began to feel the serious effects of the towing strain on the ship. For days the sailors' quarters below the fore deck had been in a state of constant wetness from the leaking of the fore deck, and the inhabitants of Oyster Alley had come to the conclusion that it might more suitably be named "Moisture Alley." But when Dunlop, the chief engineer, came on the poop bridge that afternoon and reported that the ship was making about three feet of water in an hour, matters assumed a more serious complexion. I had not expected that we would get off scot free, as the ship had to endure a very severe strain, and was old, but three feet of water in an hour showed that she was feeling the effects of the towing very much. It was necessary to rig the hand pump to help the steam pumps to keep the water under, and this became, as the Professor remarked, the occasion for an additional scientific instrument to be used by the shore party. A watch was set to use this pump, and two members of the staff worked it for two hours, or as long as occasion demanded, and at the end of that time were relieved by two more. The weather grew steadily worse, and by midnight the squalls were of hurricane force. Even the mastheads of the *Koonya* disappeared from view at times, and the light we were steering by would only be seen for a few seconds, and would then disappear behind the mounting wall of waters that separated the two ships. A moderate estimate of the height of the waves is forty-two feet. During the squalls, which were accompanied by hail and sleet, the tops of the seas were cut off by the force of the wind and flung in showers of stinging spray against our faces, drenching even the topsail yards of the *Nimrod*. Each green wave rushed at us as though it meant to swamp the ship, but each time the *Nimrod* rose bravely, and, riding over the seemingly overwhelming mass, steadied for a moment on the other side as it passed on, seething and white, baffled of its prey. All night there were squalls of terrific force, and the morning of January 7 brought no abatement of the storm. The seas now came on board with increasing frequency, finding out any odd article that had escaped our vigilance and survived the rolling of the ship. A sack of potatoes was washed on to the deck, and the contents were floating in two or three feet of water. But standing on the poop bridge I heard one of the crew, in no way disheartened, singing, as he gathered them up, "Here we go gathering nuts in May."

At noon we were in latitude 53° 26' South and longitude 127° 42' East. In the afternoon the weather moderated slightly, though there was a heavy, lumpy sea. Albatrosses were becoming much more numerous, especially the sooty species, the death of which, on Shelvoke's voyage, inspired Coleridge's memorable poem. I noticed one, flying low between the two ships, strike its wings against the wire tow-line, which had suddenly emerged from the waves owing to the lift of the *Koonya*'s stern upon a sea. The weather became fairly moderate during the night and remained so next morning, with the wind in the northwest. After the second day out we had shifted the dogs from the forecastle head to the fore bridge, and one of these, in its struggles to get down on to the main deck, strangled itself before we knew that it was in trouble.

There was constant rain during the morning of January 8, but it did not beat the sea down much, and during the evening, with the wind shifting to the south southwest, the gale increased again. It was so bad, owing to the confused sea, that we had to signal the *Koonya* to heave to. We did this with the sea on our starboard quarter. Suddenly one enormous wave rushed at us, and it appeared as though nothing could prevent our decks being swept, but the ship rose to it, and missed the greater part, though to us it seemed as if the full weight of water had come on board. We clung tightly to the poop rails, and as soon as the water had passed over us we wiped the salt from our eyes and surveyed the scene. The sea had smashed in part of the starboard bulwarks and destroyed a small house on the upper deck, pieces of this house and the bulwarks floating out to the leeward; the port wash-port was torn from its hinges, so that water now surged on board and swept away at its own sweet will, and the stout wooden rails of the poop deck, to which we had been clinging, were cracked and displaced, but no vital damage was done. The look of disgust on the faces of the dripping pony watch keepers, as they emerged from the waterlogged "Cavalry Club," was eloquent of their feelings. The galley was washed out and the fire extinguished. This happened more than once, but so pluckily did the members of the cooking department work that never during the whole of this very uncomfortable time had we been without a warm meal. This means far more than one is apt to think, for the galley was only five feet square, and thirty-nine persons blessed with extremely hearty appetites had to be provided for.

In a large measure, this unbroken routine of hot meals, the three oases of what I might call pleasure in the daily desert of discomfort, was due to Roberts, who, besides being assistant zoologist to the expedition, was going to act as cook. Seeing that the ship's staff would have more work to do than they could well carry out in providing for the thirty-nine people on board, he volunteered the first day out to assist the ship's cook, and the result was that we were always provided with fresh bread and hot cocoa and tea. Montague, the ship's cook, was ever at work, though the galley was in a constant state of flood. The stewards, Handcock and Ansell, worked wonders in getting the food across the danger zone between the galley and the wardroom. Ansell, with ten plates in one hand, overlapping one another up his arm, would arrive safely at his destination, though his boots were often filled with water on the way aft. Of course there were times when he was not so successful, and he would emerge from a sea with his clothes, hair, and face plentifully sprinkled with food. As a rule the accidents occurred in the wardroom, after the arrival of the food. The tablecloth, after two or three days, assumed an écru color, owing to the constant upsetting of tea and coffee. Some of the staff had perforce to take their meals standing, from lack of seating accommodation, and the balancing of a plate of soup when the ship was rolling heavily required skill and experience. The meal was generally accompanied by the spurting of seawater through the wardroom door, or through cracks in the skylight, and the water washed to and fro unheeded until the meal was ended, and the indefatigable Ansell turned his attention to it. It was in the wardroom that I salved a small wooden case from the water, and found that it contained a patent mixture for extinguishing fires. The rooms of the ship's officers, opening out of the wardroom, were in a similar state of dampness, and when an officer finished his watch and turned in for a well earned sleep, he merely substituted for clothes that were soaked through, others which were a little less wet.

The water, however, did not damp the spirits of those on board, for nearly every night extemporary concerts were held, and laughter and mirth filled the little wardroom. It is usual on Saturday nights at sea to drink the toasts, "Absent Friends," and "Sweethearts and Wives."

I was generally at this time in the after cabin or on the bridge, and if, as sometimes happened, I had forgotten that particular day, a gentle hint was conveyed to me by Wild or Dunlop starting a popular song, entitled "Sweethearts and Wives," the chorus of which was heartily rendered by all hands. This hint used to bring my neglect to my mind, and I would produce the necessary bottle.

On January 10 we had a clear sky during the morning until about ten o'clock, and then, with a westerly wind, the breeze became heavier, and rain commenced. Most of us that day, taking advantage of the comparative steadiness of the ship, managed to wash our salt encrusted faces and hair; we had become practically pickled during the past week. About midnight we had a light wind from the north northeast, and the almost continuous rain of the previous twelve hours had flattened the sea considerably.

At noon, on January 11, we were in latitude 57° 38' South, and longitude 178° 39' West, and during the day the wind and sea increased again from the northwest. The nature of this particular sea made it necessary for us to keep the ship away, altering our course from south to southeast, and before midnight the gale had reached its now customary force and violence. As I was standing on the bridge at 2 A.M., peering out to windward through a heavy snow squall that enveloped us, I saw, in the faint light of breaking day, a huge sea, apparently independent of its companions, rear itself up alongside the ship. Fortunately only the crest of the wave struck us, but away went the starboard bulwarks forward and abreast of the pony stalls, leaving a free run for the water through the stables. When we left port it was our augean problem how best to clean out the stables, but after the first experience of the herculean waves, the difficulty was to try and stop the flushing of them by every sea that came on board forward, and now not only every wave that fell on board, but the swell of the ocean itself swept the stables clean. This particular sea shifted the heavy starboard whaleboat from its chocks, landing it almost amidships on top of the "Cavalry Club." It swept some of our bales of fodder down on to the main deck, where they mingled with the drums of oil and cases of carbide torn from their lashings. Our latitude at noon was 59° 8' South, and 179° 30' East. The squalls of sleet and snow gave place later to clearer weather with a mackerel sky, which was of special interest to the meteorologists, as indicating the trend of the upper currents of the air.

During the afternoon the strength of the expedition was increased by Possum, one of our dogs, giving birth to six fine puppies. The mother and family were found a warm bed on the engine room skylight, where a number of our cases were stowed. We signaled the happy event to the *Koonya* by flags, and received Captain Evans' congratulations. Signaling by flags was necessarily a somewhat slow operation, especially as the commercial code of signals is not exactly adapted for this particular sort of information, and we could see by the length of time they took to verify each signal that they were at a loss as to the subject matter of our communication, the incident of a birth naturally being farthest removed from their thoughts at such a time. Whenever the weather moderated at all the two ships always held short conversations by flags, and the Commander of the *Koonya* used to make inquiries in particular about the health of the scientific staff.

January 13 brought with it a gentle breeze from the eastward, the heavy leaden sky broke into blue, flecked with light cirrus clouds, and the day seemed warmer and more pleasant than any we had experienced since we left Lyttelton, though the temperature of the air and sea water were down to 34° and 37° F respectively. The warm sun tempted those who had not before been much in evidence on to the poop deck, and the whole vessel began to look like a veritable Petticoat Lane. Blankets, coats, boots, bags that might once have been leather but which now looked like lumps of dilapidated brown paper; pajamas that had been intended to be worn when the owners first came aboard the *Nimrod;* books that had parted with their covers after sundry adventures in dripping Oyster Alley, but whose leaves evinced the strongest disinclination to separate; pillows of pulp that had once been pillows of feathers; carpet slippers, now merely bits of carpet; in short, all the personal belongings of each member of the expedition, including their most sacred Penates and Lares, were lying in a heterogeneous mass on the poop deck, in order that they might dry. A few of us ventured on baths, but it was chilly work in the open air, with the temperature only two degrees above freezing point.

Some of our party, who were old sailors, had not much impedimenta to look after and to dry; the hard-won experience of early days have taught them the lesson that the fewer things you have to get wet, the fewer you have to get dry. Adams in particular observed this rule, for he wore the flannel trousers in which he came on board the ship at Lyttelton through all this weather, allowing them to dry on him after each successive wetting. He fondly clung to them throughout the period we were navigating in the ice, and while working the ship at winter quarters, and would doubtless have worn them on the ascent of Erebus if they had not practically come to pieces.

We were now keeping a sharp lookout for icebergs and pack; we had been steering a little more to the east, as I felt that our delay owing to bad weather would give us little time for navigation if we had to pass through much pack ice, and a few degrees more easting might perhaps give us a more open sea. The meeting with the pack ice was to terminate the *Koonya*'s tow, and that also meant our parting with Buckley, who had endeared himself to every man on board, from able seaman upwards, and had been of the greatest assistance to us in the matter of the ponies. It was due to his prompt action on one occasion that the life of "Zulu" was saved. We decided to give a farewell dinner to our friend that night, and Marston designed special menu cards for the occasion. At noon that day we were in latitude 61° 29' South, longitude 179° 53' East. During the afternoon the weather kept fine and we set some square sail. Occasionally during the bad weather of the previous week we had put "fore and afters" on to try and steady the ship, but the wind had carried them away. The *Koonya* had done the same, with a similar result. Our dinner that night was a great success, and it was early next morning before we turned in.

Next morning, January 14, we sighted our first iceberg,

and passed it at a distance of about two and a half miles. It had all the usual characteristics of the Antarctic bergs, being practically tabular in form, and its sides being of a dead white color. The sight of this, the first sentinel of the frozen south, increased Buckley's desire to stay with us, and it was evident that the thought of leaving our little company was not a pleasant one to him. There was a remarkable belt of clouds across the sky during the morning, and their direction indicated the movement of the upper air, so the Professor and Cotton made several estimates of the height of this belt of cloud to try to determine the lower limit of the higher current. The mean measurements were taken, partly with a sextant and partly with an Abney level, to the edge of the belt of mackerel sky. The result of the observations was that the height of this belt was fixed at about thirteen thousand feet. The belt of cloud was traveling in an east northeast direction at the rate of about fourteen miles an hour. The surface wind, at this time was blowing lightly from the west. Our latitude at noon was 63° 59' South and the longitude 179° 47' West, so we had crossed the 180th meridian.

During the afternoon we passed two more icebergs with their usual tails of brash ice floating out to leeward. The sea had changed color from a leaden blue to a greenish gray. Albatrosses were not nearly so numerous, and of those following the ship the majority were the sooty species. The Cape pigeon and Wilson's petrel were occasionally to be seen, also a small gray-colored bird, which is generally found near the pack, but the name of which I do not know. We called them "ice birds." Another sign of the nearness of the ice was that the temperature of the air and water had dropped to 32° F. Everything pointed to our proximity to the pack, so we signaled the *Koonya* that we were likely to sight the ice at any moment. I also asked Captain Evans to kill and skin the sheep he was carrying for our supplies, as they would be much more easily transported when the time came to cast off. The weather remained fine with light winds during the night.

Next morning it was fairly thick with occasional light squalls of snow, and about 9 A.M. we saw the ice looming up through the mist to the southward. It seemed to stretch from southwest to southeast, and was apparently the forerunner of the pack. Now had come the time for the *Koonya* to drop us, after a tow of 1510 miles—a record in towage for a vessel not built for the purpose. Before the *Koonya* finally cast off from us, she had achieved another record, by being the first steel vessel to cross the Antarctic Circle.

About 10 A.M. I decided to send Captain England across to the *Koonya* with Buckley and the mail. Our letters were all stamped with the special stamp given by the New Zealand Government. The sea was rising again, and the wind increasing, so we lost no time in making the necessary communication by boat between the two ships. During a favorable roll the whale boat was dropped into the water, and Buckley, with his weekend handbag, jumped into her. We gave him three cheers as the boat pushed off on its boisterous journey to the *Koonya*. With his usual forethought, to make matters lighter for the boat's crew, Captain Evans had floated a line astern, attached to a life buoy, and after about twenty-five minutes' hard pulling against wind and sea, the buoy was picked up, and the boat hauled alongside the steamer. I was glad to see the boat coming back again shortly afterward, for the wind kept increasing and the sea was rising every moment, but in a lull, after pouring oil on the water, we hauled the boat up safely.

A thin line had been brought back from the *Koonya*, and at a signal from us Captain Evans paid out a heavier one, which we hauled on board. He then maneuvered his ship, so as to get her as near as possible to us, in order that we might haul the carcasses of the sheep on board. Ten of these were lashed on the line, and by dint of pulling hard, we got them on board. Meanwhile the greater part of our crew were working the old-fashioned windlass, getting in slowly, link by link, the port-towing cable, whilst the *Koonya* took in as much of her wire hawser as she conveniently could. Our heavy line was carried away, owing to a sudden strain, before we received the second installment of water-logged mutton. Captain Evans brought the *Koonya* round our stern, and a heaving line, to which the sheep were attached, was thrown on board, but as soon as we began to haul on it, it broke, and we had the chagrin of seeing our fresh mutton floating away on the billows. It was lost to sight shortly afterward, but we could locate its position by the albatrosses hovering above, doubtless surprised and delighted with this feast.

About a quarter to one Captain Evans signaled that he was going to cut his hawser, for in the rising sea the two vessels were in dangerous proximity to each other. We saw the axe rise and fall, rise and fall again, and the tie was severed. The *Koonya*'s work was done, and the *Nimrod* was dependent on her own resources at last. Our consort steamed round us, all hands on both ships cheering, then her bows were set north and she vanished into a gray, snowy mist, homeward bound. We spent a long afternoon struggling to get on board the one hundred forty fathoms of cable and thirty fathoms of wire that were hanging from our bows. The windlass was worked by means of levers, and all hands were divided into two parties, one section manning the port levers, the other the starboard. All that afternoon, and up to seven o'clock in the evening, they unremittingly toiled at getting the cable in link by link. At last we were able to proceed, and the ship's head was put due south. We prepared to work our way through the floating belt of pack that guards the approach to the Ross Sea. The weather had cleared, and we passed the ice which we had seen in the morning. It was a fairly loose patch of what appeared to be thick land ice. We gradually made our way through similar streams of ice and small hummocky bergs, most of them between forty and fifty feet in height, but a few reaching a hundred feet.

By 2 A.M. on the morning of January 16, the bergs were much more numerous; perhaps they could hardly be classed as bergs, for their average height was only about twenty feet, and I am of opinion, from what I saw later, that this ice originally formed part of an ice-foot from some coastline. None of the ice that we passed through at this time had the slightest resemblance to ordinary pack ice. About 3 A.M., we entered an area of tabular bergs, varying from eighty to one hundred and fifty feet in height, and all the morning we steamed in

beautiful weather with a light northerly wind, through
the lanes and streets of a wonderful snowy Venice.
Tongue and pen fail in attempting to describe the magic
of such a scene. As far as the eye could see from the
crow's nest of the *Nimrod,* the great, white, wall-sided
bergs stretched east, west, and south, making a striking
contrast with the lanes of blue-black water between
them. A stillness, weird and uncanny, seemed to have
fallen upon everything when we entered the silent water
streets of this vast unpeopled white city. Here there was
no sign of life, except when one of the little snow petrels,
invisible when flying across the glistening bergs, flashed
for a moment into sight, as it came against the dark
water, its pure white wings just skimming the surface.
The threshing of our screw raised a small wave astern
of the ship, and at times huge masses of ice and snow
from the bergs, disturbed by the unaccustomed motion,
fell thundering in our wake. Some of these bergs had
been weathered into the fantastic shapes more character-
istic of the Arctic regions, and from peak and spire
flashed out the new caught rays of the morning sun.
Beautiful as this scene was, it gave rise to some anxiety
in my mind, for I knew that if we were caught in a
breeze amidst this maze of floating ice, it would go hard
with us. Already an ominous dark cloud was sweeping
down from the north, and a few flakes of falling snow
heralded the approach of the misty northerly wind. I was
unfeignedly thankful, when, about three in the afternoon, I saw from the crow's nest open water ahead. A
few more turnings and twistings through the devious
water lanes, and we entered the ice free Ross Sea. This
was the first time that a passage had been made into the
Ross Sea without the vessel having been held up by pack
ice. I think our success was due to the fact that we were
away to the eastward of the pack, which had separated
from the land and the Barrier, and had drifted in a
northwest direction. All my experience goes to prove
that the easterly route is the best. Behind us lay the long
line of bergs through which we had threaded our way
for more than eighty miles from north to south, and
which stretched east and west for an unknown distance,
but far enough for me to say without exaggeration that

there must have been thousands of these floating masses of ice. Whence they had come was open to conjecture; it was possible for them to have drifted from a barrier edge to the eastward of King Edward VII Land. If that were so, the barrier must be much lower than the Great Ice Barrier, and also much more even in height, for the vast majority of the bergs we passed were not more than one hundred thirty feet high, and seemed to be of a fairly uniform thickness. The lights and shadows on the bergs to the eastward at times almost gave them the appearance of land, but as they were congregated most thickly in this direction, we did not venture to make closer acquaintance with them. Of one thing I am certain, this ice had not long left the parent barrier or coastline, for there was no sign of weathering or wind action on the sides; and if they had been afloat for even a short period they must infallibly have shown some traces of weathering, as the soft snow was at least fifteen to twenty feet thick. This was apparent when pieces broke off from the bergs, and in one or two cases, where sections had been sheared off the top of particular bergs, evidently by collision with their fellows. There were no indications or signs of embedded rocks or earthy material on the bergs, so I am led to believe that this great mass of ice must have been set free only a short time previously from some barrier edge at no great distance. Our latitude at noon on the 16th was 68° 6' South, and the longitude 179° 21' West.

Before we entered the actual line of bergs a couple of seals appeared on the floe-ice. I did not see them myself, but from descriptions I gathered that one was a crab-eater, and the other a Weddell seal. A few of the Adelie penguins were observed also, and their quaint walk and insatiable curiosity afforded great amusement to our people, the surprise of the birds on seeing the ship was so thoroughly genuine. Marston, our artist, whose sense of the ludicrous is very fully developed, was in ecstasies at their solemn astonishment and profound concern, and at the way they communicated their feelings to one another by flapping their makeshift wings, craning their necks forward with ruffled feathers, and uttering short squawks. Marston's imitation of the penguin was perfect, and he and the rest of us always responded eagerly to the call on deck whenever we were passing a group of these polar inhabitants.

When we were clear of the icebergs a distinct swell was felt coming from the south, and for once the movement of the ocean was welcome to us, for it showed that we might expect open water ahead. I was fairly confident that we had managed to elude the pack, and without doubt for a ship, well found and capable of fair speed, the passage between the bergs on the meridian down which we steered is preferable to the slower progress through the ordinary pack farther west. I doubt if I would, except under similar circumstances, when time and coal were very precious, risk an old vessel like the *Nimrod,* which steams but slowly in this labyrinth of heavy ice, but a faster vessel could make the passage with safety. It may be that in future seasons the Antarctic Ocean in this particular part will be found to be quite ice free, and a later expedition may be able to work more to the eastward, and solve the riddle as to the existence of land in that neighborhood.

It was fortunate that we cleared the ice that afternoon, for shortly afterward the wind increased from the north, and the weather became thick with falling snow. The temperature was just at freezing point, and the snow melted on the decks when it fell. Altogether about an inch of snow fell between 2 P.M. and midnight. We saw no ice until eight o'clock next morning (January 17), and then only one small berg. The wind shifted to the southeast, the sky cleared somewhat, and with an open horizon all round we observed no sign of ice at all.

CHAPTER V

The Attempt to Reach King Edward VII Land

Disappearance of Barrier Inlet: Course to King Edward VII
Land blocked by Ice: Course set for McMurdo Sound:
Arrival at Cape Royds, February 3

WE were now in the Ross Sea, and it was evident that
we had avoided the main pack. Our position at noon
(January 17) was 70° 43' South latitude, and 178° 58'
East longitude. We were now steering a little more westerly, so as to strike the Barrier well to the east of Barrier
Inlet, and also to avoid the heavy pack that previous
expeditions had encountered to the east of meridian 160°
West where the ice has always proved impenetrable. In
the afternoon the wind blew fresh, and the sky became
overcast again, and snow began to fall. This snow differed from that brought by the northerly wind; the
northerly snow had consisted of flakes about a quarter
of an inch in diameter, while that now met with was
formed of small round specks, hard and dry, like sago—
the true Antarctic type. Birds now became more numerous. Large numbers of Antarctic petrels circled around
and around the ship. Their numbers were so great that
as the flights passed close by, the whirring of the wings
could be distinctly heard on board.

Toward evening we began to pass a number of small
floe bergs and pack ice. We could not see very far ahead,
as the weather was thick, so we steered more to the west
to skirt this mass of ice. One berg had evidently been
overturned, and also showed signs of having been
aground. The Adelie penguins had become much more
numerous, and we saw an occasional seal, but too far
off to distinguish the species. During the early hours of
January 18 we passed a few large bergs, and as morning
progressed the wind increased, ranging between south
by west and south by east. The ship was pitching to a
short sea, and as the water coming on board froze on
deck, and in the stables, we made shift to keep it out by

nailing canvas over the gaping holes in the bulwarks. Adams and Mackay were engaged in this very chilly job; Adams, slung in a rope over the side, every now and then got soaked up to the middle when the ship dipped into the sea, and as the temperature of the air was four degrees below freezing point, his tennis trousers were not of much value for warmth in the circumstances. When he got too cold to continue outside, Mackay took his place, and between them they made a very creditable jury bulwark, which prevented the bulk of the water rushing into the stable. The wind continued with a force of about forty miles an hour, up till midday of the 19th, when it began to take off a little, and the sky broke blue to the northeast; the decks were thickly coated with soft ice, and the fresh water pumps had frozen up hard.

We were now reveling in the indescribable freshness of the Antarctic that seems to permeate one's being, and which must be responsible for that longing to go again which assails each returned explorer from polar regions. Our position at noon on January 19 was latitude 73° 44' South and longitude 177° 19' East. The wind had decreased somewhat by midnight, and though the air remained thick and the sky overcast during the whole of the 20th, the weather was better. We passed through occasional masses of floating ice and large tabular bergs, and at noon were in latitude 74° 45' South, longitude 179° 21' East.

On the 21st the weather grew clear, the temperature was somewhat higher, and the wind light. We observed small flights of snow petrels and Antarctic petrels, and saw a single giant petrel for the first time. There were also several whales spouting in the distance. The same sort of weather continued throughout the day, and similar weather, though somewhat clearer, was experienced on the 22nd. On the morning of the 23rd we saw some very large icebergs, and toward evening these increased in number. They were evidently great masses broken off the Barrier. Early in the morning we passed a large tilted berg, yellow with diatoms. On our port side appeared a very heavy pack, in which a number of large bergs were embedded. Our course for these three days was about due south, and we were making good headway under steam.

We were now keeping a sharp lookout for the Barrier, which we expected to see at any moment. A light southeasterly wind blew cold, warning us that we could not be very far away from the ice sheet. The thermometer registered some twelve degrees of frost, but we hardly felt the cold, for the wind was so dry. At 9:30 A.M. on the 23rd a low straight line appeared ahead of the ship. It was the Barrier. After half an hour it disappeared from view, having evidently been only raised into sight as an effect of mirage, but by eleven o'clock the straight line stretching out east and west was in full view, and we rapidly approached it. I had hoped to make the Barrier about the position of what we call the Western Bight, and at noon we could see a point on our starboard, from which the Barrier dropped back. This was evidently the eastern limit of the Western Bight. Shortly after noon we were within a quarter of a mile of the ice face, and exclamations of wonder and astonishment at the stupendous bulk of the Barrier were drawn from the men who had not seen it before.

We slowly steamed along, noting the various structures of the ice, and were thankful that the weather promised to keep fine, for the inlet to which we were bound could not easily have been picked up in thick weather. The height of the Barrier about this point ranged from a hundred and fifty feet to two hundred feet. In the afternoon, about half past one, we passed an opening in the Barrier trending in a southeasterly direction, but its depth was only about three-quarters of a mile. The eastern point had the form of the bows of a gigantic man-of-war, and reached a height of about two hundred thirty feet. It was appropriately called "The Dreadnought."

As we steamed close in to the Barrier, watching carefully for any sign of an opening, we were able to observe accurately the various changes in the ice face. In places the wall was perfectly smooth, clean cut from the top to the water line, in other places it showed signs of vertical cracks, and sometimes deep caverns appeared, which, illuminated by the reflected light, merged from light translucent blue into the deepest sapphire. At times great black patches appeared on the sides of the Barrier in the distance, but as we neared them they were resolved into huge caverns, some of which cut the water line. One was so large that it would have been possible to have steamed the *Nimrod* through its entrance without touching either side or its top by mast or yard. Looking at the Barrier from some little distance, one would imagine it to be a perfectly even wall of ice; when steaming along parallel with it, however, the impression it gave was that of a series of points, each of which looked as though it might be the horn of a bay. Then when the ship came abeam of it, one would see that the wall only receded for a few hundred yards, and then new points came into view as the ship moved on. In some places a cornice of snow overhung the Barrier top, and again in others the vertical cracks had widened so that some portions of the ice wall seemed in immediate danger of falling. The vagaries of light and shadow made appearances very deceptive. One inlet we passed had the sides thrown up in little hummocks, not more than ten or fifteen feet high, but until we were fairly close these irregularities had the appearance of hills.

The weather continued fine and calm. During the voyage of the *Discovery* we had always encountered a strong westerly current along the Barrier, but there was absolutely no sign of this here, and the ship was making a good five knots. To the northward of us lay a very heavy pack, interspersed with large icebergs, one of which was over two miles long and one hundred fifty feet high. This pack ice was much heavier and more rugged than any we had encountered on the previous expedition. Evidently there must have been an enormous breaking away of ice to the eastward for as far as we could see from the crow's nest, to the north and east, this ice continued.

About midnight we suddenly came to the end of a very high portion of the Barrier, and found as we followed around that we were entering a wide shallow bay. This must have been the inlet where Borchgrevink landed in 1900, but it had greatly changed since that time. He describes the bay as being a fairly narrow inlet.

On our way east in the *Discovery* in 1902 we passed an inlet somewhat similar, but we did not see the western end as it was obscured by fog at the time. There seemed to be no doubt that the Barrier had broken away at the entrance of this bay or inlet, and so had made it much wider and less deep than it was in previous years. About half a mile down the bay we reached fast ice. It was now about half past twelve at night, and the southerly sun shone in our faces. Our astonishment was great to see beyond the six or seven miles of flat bay ice, which was about five or six feet thick, high rounded ice cliffs, with valleys between, running in an almost east and west direction. About four miles to the south we saw the opening of a large valley, but could not say where it led. Due south of us, and rising to a height of approximately eight hundred feet, were steep and rounded cliffs, and behind them sharp peaks. The southerly sun being low, these heights threw shadows which, for some time, had the appearance of bare rocks. Two dark patches in the face of one of the further cliffs had also this appearance, but a careful observation taken with a telescope showed them to be caverns. To the east rose a long snow slope which cut the horizon at the height of about three hundred feet. It had every appearance of ice covered land, but we could not stop then to make certain, for the heavy ice and bergs lying to the northward of us were setting down into the bay, and I saw that, if we were not to be beset, it would be necessary to get away at once. All around us were numbers of great whales showing their dorsal fins as they occasionally sounded, and on the edge of the bay ice half a dozen Emperor penguins stood lazily observing us. We named this place the Bay of Whales, for it was a veritable playground for these monsters.

We tried to work to the eastward so as once more to get close to the Barrier which we could see rising over the top of the small bergs and pack ice, but we found this impossible, and so struck northward through an open lead and came south to the Barrier again about 2 A.M. on the 24th. We coasted eastward along the wall of ice, always on the lookout for the inlet. The lashings had been taken off the motorcar, and the tackle rigged to hoist it out directly we got alongside the ice foot, to which the *Discovery* had been moored; for in Barrier Inlet we proposed to place our winter quarters.

I must leave the narrative for a moment at this point and refer to the reasons that made me decide on this inlet as the site for the winter quarters. I knew that Barrier Inlet was practically the beginning of King Edward VII Land, and that the actual bare land was within an easy sledge journey of that place, and it had the great advantage of being some ninety miles nearer to the South Pole than any other spot that could be reached with the ship. A further point of importance was that it would be an easy matter for the ship on its return to us to reach this part of the Barrier, whereas King Edward VII Land itself might quite conceivably be unattainable if the season was adverse. Some of my *Discovery* comrades had also considered Barrier Inlet a good place at which to winter. After thinking carefully over the matter I had decided in favor of wintering on the Barrier instead of on actual land, and on the *Koonya*'s departure I had sent a message to the headquarters of the expedition in London to the effect that, in the event of the *Nimrod* not returning at the usual time in 1908, no steps were to be taken to provide a relief ship to search for her in 1909, for it was only likely under those circumstances that she was frozen in; but that if she did not turn up with us in 1909, then the relief expedition should start in December of that year. The point to which they should first direct their search was to be Barrier Inlet, and if we were not found there, they were to search the coast of King Edward VII Land. I had added that it would only be by stress of the most unexpected circumstances that the ship would be unable to return to New Zealand.

However, the best laid schemes often prove impracticable in polar exploration, and within a few hours our first plan was found impossible of fulfillment. Within thirty-six hours a second arrangement had to be abandoned. We were steaming along westward close to the Barrier, and according to the chart we were due to be abreast of the inlet about 6 A.M., but not a sign was there of the opening. We had passed Borchgrevink's Bight at

1 A.M., and at 8 P.M. were well past the place where Barrier Inlet ought to have been. The Inlet had disappeared, owing to miles of the Barrier having calved away, leaving a long wide bay joining up with Borchgrevink's Inlet, and the whole was now merged into what we had called the Bay of Whales. This was a great disappointment to us, but we were thankful that the Barrier had broken away before we had made our camp on it. It was bad enough to try and make for a port that had been wiped off the face of the earth, when all the intending inhabitants were safe on board the ship, but it would have been infinitely worse if we had landed there whilst the place was still in existence, and that when the ship returned to take us off she should find the place gone. The thought of what might have been made me decide then and there that, under no circumstances, would I winter on the Barrier, and that wherever we did land we would secure a solid rock foundation for our winter home.

We had two strings to our bow, and I decided to use the second at once and push forward toward King Edward VII Land. Just after 8 A.M. on the 24th we turned a corner in the Barrier, where it receded about half a mile, before continuing to the eastward again. The line of its coast here made a right angle, and the ice sloped down to sea level at the apex of the angle, but the slope was too steep and too heavily crevassed for us to climb up and look over the surface if we had made a landing.

We tied the ship up to a fairly large floe, and I went down to England's cabin to talk the matter over. In the corner where we were lying there were comparatively few pieces of floe ice, but outside us lay a very heavy pack, in which several large bergs were locked. Our only chance was to go straight on, keeping close to the Barrier, as a lane of open water was left between the Barrier and the edge of the pack to the north of us. Sights were taken for longitude by four separate observers, and the positions calculated showed us we were not only well to the eastward of the place where Barrier Inlet was shown on the chart, but also that the Barrier had receded at this particular point since January 1902.

About nine o'clock we cast off from the floe and

headed the ship to the eastward, again keeping a few hundred yards off the Barrier, for just here the cliff over-hung, and if a fall of ice had occurred while we were close in the results would certainly have been disastrous for us. I soon saw that we would not be able to make much easting in this way, for the Barrier was now trend-ing well to the northeast, and right ahead of us lay an impenetrably close pack, set with huge icebergs. By 10 A.M. we were close to the pack and found that it was pressed hard against the Barrier edge, and, what was worse, the whole of the northern pack and bergs at this spot were drifting in toward the Barrier. The seriousness of this situation can be well realized by the reader if he imagines for a moment that he is in a small boat right under the vertical white cliffs of Dover; that detached cliffs are moving in from seaward slowly but surely, with stupendous force and resistless power, and that it will only be a question of perhaps an hour or two before the two masses come into contact with his tiny craft between.

There was nothing for it but to retrace our way and try some other route. Our position was latitude 78° 20' South and longitude 162° 14' West when the ship turned. The pack had already moved inside the point of the cliff where we had lain in open water at eight o'clock, but by steaming hard and working in and out of the looser floes we just managed to pass the point at 11:20 A.M. with barely fifty yards of open water to spare between the Barrier and the pack.

I breathed more freely when we passed this zone of immediate danger, for there were two or three hundred yards of clear water now between us and the pack. We were right under the Barrier cliff, which was here over two hundred fifty feet high, and our course lay well to the south of west, being roughly southwest true; so as we moved south more quickly than the advancing ice we were able to keep close along the Barrier, which gradu-ally became lower, until about three o'clock we were abreast of some tilted bergs at the eastern entrance of the Bay of Whales. There was a peculiar light which rendered distances and the forms of objects very decep-tive, and a great deal of mirage, which made things appear much higher than they actually were. This was particularly noticeable in the case of the pack ice; the whole northern and western sea seemed crowded with huge icebergs, though in reality there was only heavy pack. The penguins that we had seen the previous night were still at the same place, and when a couple of miles away from us they loomed up as if they were about six feet high. This bay ice, on which many seals were lying, was cracking, and would soon float away, with one or two large icebergs embedded in it.

Skirting along the seaward edge we came to the high cliff of ice at the westerly end, and passed safely out of the bay at ten minutes to four. We then continued to the westward, still having the heavy pack to the north. One berg that we passed was a temporary resting place for hundreds of Antarctic and snow petrels, and these took flight as we approached. About 6 P.M. the pack ice seemed to loosen somewhat, and by half past seven, from the crow's nest, I could see a lead of open water to the north through the belt of pack, and beyond that there appeared to be a fairly open sea. About eight o'clock the ship's head was put north, and we soon gained a fairly open sea, occasionally having to make detours around the heavier packed floes, though we were able to push aside the lighter pieces. At midnight, our easterly progress was arrested by a line of thick conglomerated pack, and we had to steer north for nearly an hour before we could again set the course easterly. It is remarkable how limited one's horizon is at sea, for from the crow's nest, after passing this belt of pack, there appeared to be open water for an indefinite distance, yet by two o'clock we were up against the rigid ice again. Low pack ice is not visible at any great distance, and one could not trust an appearance of open water, even with the wide horizon obtained from the crow's nest. All night long we followed a zigzag course in the endeavor to penetrate to the east, at times steering due west, practically doubling on our tracks, before we could find an opening which would admit of our pursuing the direction we desired to follow. During the night it had been somewhat cloudy toward the south, but about 3 A.M. it became quite clear over the Barrier, and we saw to our disappointment that we had made hardly any progress to the eastward, for we were at that hour only just abeam of the Bay of Whales. About half past seven in the morning we passed a huge berg, nearly three miles in length and over two hundred feet in height, and at eight o'clock the sea became much more open; indeed, there was no ice in sight to the east at all. It was a bright, sunny morning, and things looked much more hopeful as I left the bridge for a sleep, after having been on deck all night.

When I came up again, just before noon on January 25, I found that my hopes for a clear run were vain. Our noon observations showed that we were well to the north of the Barrier, and still to the westward of the point we had reached the previous morning before we had been forced to turn around. The prospect of reaching King Edward VII Land seemed to grow more remote every ensuing hour. There was high hummocky pack interspersed with giant icebergs to the east and south of the ship, and it was obvious that the whole sea between Cape Colbeck and the Barrier at our present longitude must be full of ice. To the northward the strong ice blink on the horizon told the same tale. It seemed as if it would be impossible to reach the land, and the shortness of coal, the leaky condition of the ship, and the absolute necessity of landing all our stores and putting up the hut before the vessel left us made the situation an extremely anxious one for me. I had not expected to find Barrier Inlet gone, and, at the same time, the way to King Edward VII Land absolutely blocked by ice, though the latter condition was not unusual, for every expedition in this longitude up till 1901 had been held up by the pack; indeed Ross, in this locality, sailed for hundreds of miles to the northward along the edge of a similar pack on this meridian. It is true that we had steam, but the *Discovery,* or even the *Yermak,* the most powerful ice breaker ever built, would have made no impression upon the cemented field of ice.

I decided to continue to try and make a way to the east for at least another twenty-four hours. We altered the course to the north, skirting the ice as closely as possible, and taking advantage of the slightest trend to the eastward, at times running into narrow culs-de-sac in the main pack, only to find it necessary to retrace our way again. The wind began to freshen from the west, and the weather to thicken. A little choppy sea washed over the edges of the floes, and the glass was falling. About five o'clock some heavy squalls of snow came down, and we had to go dead slow, for the horizon was limited at times to a radius of less than one hundred yards. Between the squalls it was fairly clear, and we could make out great numbers of long, low bergs, one of which was over five miles in length, though not more than forty feet high. The waves were splashing up against the narrow end as we passed within a couple of cables' length of the berg, and almost immediately afterward another squall swept down upon us. The weather cleared again shortly, and we saw the western pack moving rapidly toward us under the influence of the wind; in some places it had already met the main pack. As it was most likely that we would be caught in this great mass of ice, and that days, or even weeks, might elapse before we could extricate ourselves, I reluctantly gave orders to turn the ship and make full speed out of this dangerous situation. I could see nothing for it except to steer for McMurdo Sound, and there make our winter quarters. For many reasons I would have preferred landing at King Edward VII Land, as that region was absolutely unknown. A fleeting glimpse of bare rocks and high snow slopes was all that we obtained of it on the *Discovery* expedition, and had we been able to establish our winter quarters there, we could have added greatly to the knowledge of the geography of that region. There would perhaps have been more difficulty in the attempt to reach the South Pole from that base, but I did not expect that the route from there to the Barrier surface, from which we could make a fair start for the Pole, would have been impracticable. I did not give up the destined base of our expedition without a strenuous struggle, as the track of the ship given in the sketch map shows; but the forces of these uncontrollable ice packs are stronger than human resolution, and a change of plan was forced upon us.

After more trouble with the ice we worked into

clearer water and the course was set for McMurdo Sound, where we arrived on January 29, and found that some twenty miles of frozen sea separated us from Hut Point. I decided to lie off the ice foot for a few days at least, and give Nature a chance to do what we could not do with the ship, that is, to break up the miles of ice intervening between us and our goal.

So far the voyage had been without accident to any of the staff, but on the morning of the 31st, when all hands were employed getting stores out of the after hatch, preparatory to landing them, a hook on the tackle slipped and, swinging suddenly across the deck, struck Mackintosh in the right eye. He fell on the deck in great pain, but was able, in a few minutes, to walk with help to England's cabin, where Marshall examined him. It was apparent that the sight of the eye was completely destroyed, so he was put under chloroform, and Marshall removed the eye, being assisted at the operation by the other two doctors, Michell and Mackay. It was a great comfort to me to know that the expedition had the services of thoroughly good surgeons. Mackintosh felt the loss of his eye keenly; not so much because the sight was gone, but because it meant that he could not remain with us in the Antarctic. He begged to be allowed to stay, but when Marshall explained that he might lose the sight of the other eye, unless great care were taken, he accepted his ill fortune without further demur, and thus the expedition lost, for a time, one of its most valuable members.

Whilst waiting at the ice, I thought it as well that a small party should proceed to Hut Point, and report on the condition of the hut left there by the *Discovery* expedition in 1904. I decided to send Adams, Joyce, and Wild, giving Adams instructions to get into the hut and then return the next day to the ship. They started off on their sixteen mile march with plenty of provisions in case of being delayed, and a couple of spades. On their return, Adams reported that they had found the hut practically clear of snow, and the structure quite intact.

On February 3 I decided to wait no longer at the ice face, but to seek for winter quarters on the east coast of Ross Island. About four o'clock we got under way and started toward Cape Barne on the lookout for a suitable landing place. Steaming slowly north along the coast we saw across the bay a long, low snow slope, connected with the bare rock of Cape Royds, which appeared to be a likely place for winter quarters.

About eight o'clock I left the ship in a boat, accompanied by Adams and Wild. Proceeding toward the shore, we used the hand lead at frequent intervals until we came up against fast ice. This covered the whole of the small bay from the corner of Flagstaff Point (as we afterward named the seaward cliff at the southern end of Cape Royds) to Cape Barne to the southward. Close up to the Point the ice had broken out, leaving a little natural dock into which we ran the boat. Adams and I scrambled ashore, crossing a well defined tide crack and going up a smooth snow slope, about fifteen yards wide, at the top of which was bare rock. Hundreds of Adelie penguins were moving to and fro on the top of the slope, and they greeted us with hoarse squawks of excitement.

A very brief examination of the vicinity of the ice foot was sufficient to show us that Cape Royds would be an excellent place at which to land our stores. We therefore shoved off again, and skirting along the ice foot to the south, sounded the bay and found that the water deepened from two fathoms close in shore to about twenty fathoms four hundred yards further south.

After completing these soundings we pulled out toward the ship, which had been coming in very slowly. We were pulling along at a good rate when suddenly a heavy body shot out of the water, struck the seaman who was pulling stroke, and dropped with a thud into the bottom of the boat. The arrival was an Adelie penguin. It was hard to say who was the most astonished— the penguin, at the result of its leap on to what it had doubtless thought was a rock, or we, who so suddenly took on board this curious passenger. The sailors in the boat looked upon this incident as an omen of good luck. There is a tradition amongst seamen that the souls of old sailors, after death, occupy the bodies of penguins, as well as of albatrosses; this idea, however, does not prevent the mariners from making a hearty meal off the breasts of the former when opportunity offers. We arrived on board at 9 P.M., and by 10 P.M. on February 3 the *Nimrod* was moored to the bay ice, ready to land the stores.

Immediately after securing the ship I went ashore, accompanied by the Professor, England, and Dunlop, to choose a place for building the hut. We passed the penguins, which were marching solemnly to and fro, and on reaching the level land, made for a huge boulder of kenyte, the most conspicuous mark in the locality. I thought that we might build the hut under the lee of this boulder, sheltered from the southeast wind, but the situation had its drawbacks, as it would have entailed a large amount of leveling before the foundation of the hut could have been laid. We crossed a narrow ridge of rock just beyond the great boulder, and, turning a little to the right up a small valley, found an ideal spot for our winter quarters. The floor of this valley was practically level and covered with a couple of feet of volcanic earth; at the sides the bedrock was exposed, but a rough eye measurement was quite sufficient to show that there would be not only ample room for the hut itself, but also for all the stores, and for a stable for the ponies. A hill right behind this little valley would serve as an excellent shelter to the hut from what we knew was the prevailing strong wind, that is, the southeaster. A glance at the illustrations will give the reader a much better idea of this place than will a written description, and he will see how admirably Nature had provided us with a protection against her own destructive forces. [Editor's Note: Illustrations deleted due to problems of finding originals and/or quality reproductions.] A number of seals lying on the bay ice gave promise that there would be no lack of fresh meat.

With this ideal situation for a camp, and everything else satisfactory, including a supply of water from a lake right in front of our little valley, I decided that we could not do better than start getting our gear ashore at once. There was only one point that gave me any anxiety, and that was as to whether the sea would freeze over between this place and Hut Point in ample time for us to get across for the southern and western journeys in the following spring. It was also obvious that nothing could be done in the way of laying out depots for the next season's work, as directly the ship left we would be cut off from any communication with the lands to the south of us, by sea and by land, for the heavily crevassed glaciers fringing the coast were an effectual bar to a march with sledges. However, time was pressing, and we were fortunate to get winter quarters as near as this to our starting point for the south.

CHAPTER VI

The Landing of Stores and Equipment
February 3–22, 1908

Blizzard in McMurdo Sound, February 18–21: *Nimrod*
sails for New Zealand, February 22

WE returned to the ship to start discharging our equipment, and with this work commenced the most uncomfortable fortnight, and the hardest work, full of checks and worries, that I or any other member of the party had ever experienced. If it had not been for the whole-hearted devotion of our party, and their untiring energy, we would never have got through the long toil of discharging. Day and night, if such terms of low latitudes can be used in a place where there was no night, late and early, they were always ready to turn to, in face of most trying conditions, and always with a cheerful readiness. If a fresh obstacle appeared there was no time lost in bemoaning the circumstance, but they all set to work at once to remove the obstruction. The first thing to be landed was the motorcar, and after that came the ponies, for it was probable that any day might see the breakup of the bay ice, and there being only two fathoms of water along the shore, as we had ascertained by sounding down the tide crack, the ship could not go very close in. It would have been practically impossible to have landed the ponies in boats, for they were only half broken in, and all in a highly strung, nervous condition. At 10:30 P.M. on February 3 we swung the motor over on to the bay ice, and all hands pulled it up the snow slope across the tide crack and left it safe on the solid ground. This done, we next landed one of the lifeboats, which we intended to keep down there with us. Joyce ran the dogs ashore and tied them up to rocks, all except Possum, who was still engaged with her little puppies. Then followed the foundation pieces of the hut, for it was desirable that we should be safely housed before the ship went north. Meanwhile, the carpenter was busily engaged in unbolting the framework of the pony stalls, and the animals became greatly excited, causing us a lot of trouble. We worked till 3 A.M., landing pony fodder and general stores, and then knocked off and had some cocoa and a rest, intending to turn to at 6 A.M.

We had hardly started work again when a strong breeze sprung up with drifting snow. The ship began to bump heavily against the ice foot and twice dragged her anchors out, so, as there seemed no possibility of getting ahead with the landing of the stores under these conditions, we steamed out and tied up at the main ice face, about six miles to the south, close to where we had lain for the past few days. It blew fairly hard all day and right through the evening, but the wind went down on the afternoon of the 5th, and we returned to the bay that evening.

We lost no time in getting the ponies ashore. This was by no means an easy task, for some of the animals were very restive, and it required care to avoid accident to themselves or to us. Some time before we had thought of walking them down over a gangplank on to the ice, but afterward decided to build a rough horse box, get them into this, and then sling it over the side by means of the main gaff. We covered the decks with ashes and protected all sharp projections with bags and bales of fodder. The first pony went in fairly quietly, and in another moment or two had the honor of being the pioneer horse on the Antarctic ice. One after another the ponies were led out of the stalls into the horse box and were slung over on to the ice. They all seemed to feel themselves at home, for they immediately commenced pawing at the snow as they are wont to do in their own faraway Manchurian home, where, in the winter, they scrape away the snow to get out the rough tussocky grass that lies underneath. It was 3:30 A.M. on the morning of the 6th before we got all the ponies off the ship, and they were at once led up on to the land. The poor beasts were naturally stiff after the constant buffeting they had experienced in their narrow stalls on the rolling ship for over a month, and they walked very stiffly ashore.

They negotiated the tide crack all right, the fissure being narrow, and were soon picketed out on some bare earth at the entrance to a valley which lay about fifty

yards from the site of our hut. We thought that this
would be a good place, but the selection was to cost us
dearly in the future. The tide crack played an important
part in connection with the landing of the stores. In the
polar regions, both north and south, when the sea is
frozen over, there always appears between the fast ice,
which is the ice attached to the land, and the sea ice, a
crack which is due to the sea ice moving up and down
with the rise and fall of the tide. When the bottom of
the sea slopes gradually from the land, sometimes two
or three tide cracks appear running parallel to each
other. When no more tide cracks are to be seen land-
wards, the snow or ice foot has always been considered
as being a permanent adjunct to the land, and in our
case this opinion was further strengthened by the fact
that our soundings in the tide crack showed that the ice
foot on the landward side of it must be aground. I have
explained this fully, for it was after taking into consideration these points that I, for convenience sake, landed
the bulk of the stores below the bare rocks on what I
considered to be the permanent snow slope.

About 9 A.M. on the morning of February 6 we started
work with sledges, hauling provisions and pieces of the
hut to the shore. The previous night the foundation posts
of the hut had been sunk and frozen into the ground
with a cement composed of volcanic earth and water.
The digging of the foundation holes, on which job Dunlop, Adams, Joyce, Brocklehurst, and Marshall were engaged, proved hard work, for in some cases where the
hole had to be dug the bedrock was found a few inches
below the coating of the earth, and this had to be broken
through or drilled with chisel and hammer. Now that the
ponies were ashore it was necessary to have a party living ashore also, for the animals would require looking
after if the ship were forced to leave the ice foot at any
time, and, of course, the building of the hut could go on
during the absence of the ship. The first shore party
consisted of Adams, Marston, Brocklehurst, Mackay,
and Murray, and two tents were set up close to the hut,
with the usual sledging requisites, sleeping bags, cookers,
etc. A canvas cover was rigged on some oars to serve as

a cooking tent, and this, later on, was enlarged into a more commodious house, built out of bales of fodder.

The first things landed this day were bales of fodder for the ponies, and sufficient petroleum and provisions for the shore party in the event of the ship having to put to sea suddenly owing to bad weather. For facility in landing the stores, the whole party was divided into two gangs. Some of the crew of the ship hoisted the stores out of the hold and slid them down a wide plank on to the ice, others of the ship's crew loaded the stores on to the sledges, and these were hauled to land by the shore party, each sledge having three men harnessed to it. The road to the shore consisted of hard, rough ice, alternating with very soft snow, and as the distance from where the ship was lying at first to the tide crack was nearly a quarter of a mile, it was strenuous toil, especially when the tide crack was reached and the sledges had to be pulled up the slope. After the first few sledge loads had been hauled right up on to the land, I decided to let the stores remain on the snow slope beyond the tide crack, where they could be taken away at leisure. The work was so heavy that we tried to substitute mechanical haulage in place of man haulage, but had to revert to our original plan, and all that morning we did the work by man haulage. During the lunch hour we shifted the ship about a hundred yards nearer the shore alongside the ice face, from which a piece had broken out during the morning, leaving a level edge where the ship could be moored easily.

Just as we were going to commence work at 2 P.M. a fresh breeze sprang up from the southeast, and the ship began to bump against the ice foot, her movement throwing the water over the ice. We were then lying in a rather awkward position in the apex of an angle in the bay ice, and as the breeze threatened to become stronger, I sent the shore party on to the ice, and, with some difficulty, we got clear of the ice foot. The breeze freshening we stood out to the fast ice in the strait about six miles to the south and anchored there. It blew a fresh breeze with drift from the southeast all that afternoon and night, and did not ease up till the following afternoon. Thus, unfortunately two valuable working days were lost.

When I went ashore I found that the little party left behind had not only managed to get up to the site of the hut all the heavy timber that had been landed, but had also stacked on the bare land the various cases of provisions which had been lying on the snow slope by the tide crack. We worked till 2 A.M. on the morning of the 9th, and then knocked off till 9 A.M. Then we commenced again, and put in one of the hardest day's work one can imagine, pulling the sledges to the tide crack and then hauling them bodily over. Hour after hour all hands toiled on the work, the crossing of the tide crack becoming more difficult with each succeeding sledge load, for the ice in the bay was loosening, and it was over floating, rocking pieces of floe with gaps several feet wide between them that we hauled the sledges. In the afternoon the ponies were brought into action, as they had had some rest, and their arrival facilitated the discharge, though it did not lighten the labors of the perspiring staff. None of our party were in very good condition, having been cooped up in the ship, and the heavy cases became double heavy to our arms and shoulders by midnight.

Next day the work continued, the ice still holding in, but threatening every minute to go out. If there had been sufficient water for the ship to lie right alongside the shore we would have been pleased to see the ice go out, but at the place where we were landing the stores there was only twelve feet of water, and the Nimrod, at this time, drew fourteen. We tried to anchor one of the smaller loose pieces of bay ice to the ice foot, and this answered whilst the tide was setting in. As a result of the tidal movement, the influx of heavy pack in the bay where we were lying caused some anxiety, and more than once we had to shift the ship away from the landing place because of the heavy floes and hummocky ice which pressed up against the bay ice. One large berg sailed in from the north and grounded about a mile to the south of Cape Royds, and later another about the same height, not less than one hundred fifty feet, did the same, and these two bergs were frozen in where they grounded and remained in that position through the winter. The hummocky pack that came in and out with the tide was over fifteen feet in height, and, being of much greater depth below water, had ample power and force to damage the ship if a breeze should spring up.

When we turned to after lunch, and before the first sledge load reached the main landing place, we found that it would be impossible to continue working there any longer, for the small floe which we had anchored to the ice had dragged out the anchor and was being carried to sea by the ebbing tide. Some three hundred fifty yards further along the shore of the bay was a much steeper ice foot at the foot of the cliffs, and a snow slope narrower than the one on which we had been landing the provisions. This was the nearest available spot at which to continue discharging. We hoped that when the ship had left we could hoist the stores up over the cliff; they would then be within a hundred yards of the hut, and, after being carried for a short distance, they could be rolled down the steep snow slope at the head of the valley where it was being built. All this time the hut party were working day and night, and the building was rapidly assuming an appearance of solidity. The uprights were in, and the brace ties were fastened together, so that if it came on to blow there was no fear of the structure being destroyed.

The stores had now to be dragged a distance of nearly three hundred yards from the ship to the landing place, but this work was greatly facilitated by our being able to use four of the ponies, working two of them for an hour, and then giving these a spell whilst two others took their place. The snow was very deep, and the ponies sank in well above the knees; it was heavy going for the men who were leading them. A large amount of stores was landed in this way, but a new and serious situation arose through the breaking away of the main ice foot.

On the previous day an ominous-looking crack had been observed to be developing at the end of the ice foot nearest to Flagstaff Point, and it became apparent that if this crack continued to widen, it would cut right across the center of our stores, with the result that, unless removed, they would be irretrievably lost in the sea. Next day (the 10th) there was no further opening of the crack, but at seven o'clock that night another crack formed on the ice foot inside of Derrick Point where we were now landing stores. There was no immediate danger to be apprehended at this place, for the bay ice would have to go out before the ice foot could fall into the sea. Prudence suggested that it would be better to shift the stores already landed to a safer place before discharging any more from the ship, so at 8 P.M. on the 10th we commenced getting the remainder of the wood for the hut and the bales of cork for the lining up on to the bare land. This took till about midnight, when we knocked off for cocoa and a sleep.

We turned to at six o'clock next morning, and I decided to get the stores up the cliff face at Derrick Point before dealing with those at Front Door Bay, the first landing place, for the former ice foot seemed in the greater peril of collapse than did the latter. Adams, Joyce, and Wild soon rigged up a boom and tackle from the top of the cliff, making the heel of the boom fast by placing great blocks of volcanic rocks on it. A party remained below on the ice foot to shift and hook on the cases, whilst another party on top, fifty feet above, hauled away when the word was given from below, and on reaching the top of the cliff, the cases were hauled in by means of a guy rope. The men were hauling on the thin rope of the tackle from eight o'clock in the morning till one o'clock the following morning with barely a spell for a bit to eat.

We now had to find another and safer place on which to land the rest of the coal and stores. Further round the bay from where the ship was lying was a smaller bight where a gentle slope led on to bare rocks, and Back Door Bay, as we named this place, became our new depot. The ponies were led down the hill, and from Back Door Bay to the ship. This was a still longer journey than from Derrick Point, but there was no help for it, and we started landing the coal, after laying a tarpaulin on the rocks to keep the coal from becoming mixed with the earth. By this time there were several ugly looking cracks in the bay ice, and these kept opening and closing, having a play of seven or eight inches between the floes. We improvised bridges out of the bottom and sides of the motorcar case so that the ponies could cross the cracks, and by eleven o'clock were well under way with the work. Mackay had just taken ashore a load with a pony, Armytage was about to hook on another pony to a loaded sledge at the ship, and a third pony was standing tied to our stern anchor rope waiting its turn for sledging, when suddenly, without the slightest warning, the greater part of the bay ice opened out into floes, and the whole mass that had opened started to drift slowly out to sea. The ponies on the ice were now in a perilous position. The sailors rushed to loosen the one tied to the stern rope, and got it over the first crack, and Armytage also got the pony he was looking after off the floe nearest the ship on to the next floe. Just at that moment Mackay appeared around the corner from Back Door Bay with a third pony attached to an empty sledge, on his way back to the ship to load up. Orders were shouted to him not to come any further, but he did not at first grasp the situation, for he continued advancing over the ice, which was now breaking away more rapidly. The party working on the top of Derrick Point, by shouting and waving, made him realize what had occurred. He accordingly left his sledge and pony and rushed over toward where the other two ponies were adrift on the ice, and, by jumping the widening cracks, he reached the moving floe on which they were standing. This piece of ice gradually drew closer to a larger piece, from which the animals would be able to gain a place of safety. Mackay started to try and get the pony Chinaman across the crack when it was only about six inches wide, but the animal suddenly took fright, reared up on his hind legs, and backing toward the edge of the floe, which had at that moment opened to a width of a few feet, fell bodily into the ice cold water. It looked as if it was all over with poor Chinaman, but Mackay hung on to the head rope, and Davis, Mawson, Michell and one of the sailors who were on the ice close by rushed to his assistance. The pony managed to get his fore feet on to the edge of the ice floe. After great difficulty a rope sling was passed underneath him, and then by tremendous exertion he was lifted up far enough to enable him to scramble on to the ice. There he stood, wet and trembling in every limb. A few seconds later the floe closed up against the other one. It was providential that it had not done so during the time that the pony was in the water, for in that case the animal would inevitably have been squeezed to death between the two huge masses of ice. A bottle of brandy was thrown on to the ice from the ship, and half its contents were poured down Chinaman's throat. The ship was now turning around with the object of going bow on to the floe, in order to push it ashore, so that the ponies might cross on to the fast ice, and presently, with the engine at full speed, the floe was slowly but surely moved back against the fast ice. Directly the floe was hard up against the unbroken ice, the ponies were rushed across and taken straight ashore, and the men who were on the different floes took advantage of the temporary closing of the crack to get themselves and the stores into safety. I decided, after this narrow escape, not to risk the ponies on the sea ice again. The ship was now backed out, and the loose floes began to drift away to the west.

By 1 P.M. most of the ice had cleared out, and the ship came in to the edge of the fast ice, which was now abreast of Back Door Bay. Hardly were the ice anchors made fast before new cracks appeared, and within a quarter of an hour the ship was adrift again. As it was impossible to discharge under these conditions, the *Nimrod* stood off. We had now practically the whole of the wintering party ashore, so when lunch was over, the main party went on with the work at Derrick Point, refreshed by the hot tea and meat, which they had hastily swallowed.

I organized that afternoon a small party to shift the main stores into safety. We had not been long at work before I saw that it would need the utmost dispatch and our most strenuous endeavors to save the valuable cases; for the crack previously observed opened more each hour. Perspiration poured down our faces and bodies as we toiled in the hot sun. After two hours' work we had shifted into a place of safety all our cases of scientific instruments, and a large quantity of fodder, and hardly were they secured than, with a sharp crack, the very place where they had been lying fell with a crash into the sea. Had we lost these cases the result would have been very serious, for a great part of our scientific work could not have been carried out, and if the fodder had been lost, it would have meant the loss of the ponies also. The breaking of this part of the ice made us redouble our efforts to save the rest of the stores, for we could not tell when the next piece of ice might break off, though no crack was yet visible. The breaking up of the bay ice that morning turned out to be after all for the best, for I would not otherwise have gone on so early with this work. I ran up the hill to the top of Flagstaff Point to call the ship in, in order to obtain additional help from the crew; she had been dodging about outside of the point since one o'clock, but she was beyond hailing distance, and it was not till about seven o'clock that I saw her coming close in again. I at once hailed England and told him to send every available man ashore immediately. In a few minutes a boat came off with half a dozen men, and I sent a message back by the officer in charge for more members of the ship's crew to be landed at once, and only enough men left on board to steer the ship and work the engines. I had previously knocked off the party working on the hut, and with the extra assistance we "smacked things about" in a lively fashion. The ice kept breaking off in chunks, but we had the satisfaction of seeing every single package safe on the rocks by midnight.

Our party then proceeded to sledge the heavier cases and the tins of oil at the foot of Derrick Point around the narrow causeway of ice between the perpendicular rocks and the sea to the depot at Back Door Bay. I was astonished and delighted on arriving at the derrick to find the immense amount of stores that had been placed in safety by the efforts of the Derrick Point party, and by 1 A.M. on February 13 all the stores landed were in safety. About a ton of flour in cases remained to be hauled up, but as we already had enough ashore to last us for a year, and knowing that at Hut Point there were large quantities of biscuit left by the last expedition, which would be available if needed, we just rolled the cases on the ice foot into a hollow at the foot of the cliff, where they were in comparative safety, as the ice there would not be likely to break away immediately. We retrieved these after the ship left.

When making arrangements for the necessary equipment of the expedition, I tried to get the bulk of the stores into cases of uniform size and weight, averaging fifty to sixty pounds gross, and thus allow of more easy handling than would have been the case if the stores were packed in the usual way. The goods packed in Venesta cases could withstand the roughest treatment without breakage or damage to the contents. These Venesta cases are made of three thin layers of wood, fastened together by a patent process; the material is much tougher than ordinary wood, weighs much less than a case of the same size made of the usual deal, and being thinner, takes up much less room, a consideration of great moment to a Polar expedition. The wood could not be broken by the direct blow of a heavy hammer, and the empty cases could be used for the making of the hundred and one odds and ends that have to be contrived to meet requirements in such an expedition as this.

At 1 P.M. on the morning of February 13 I signaled the ship to come in and take off the crew, and a boat was sent ashore. There was a slight breeze blowing, and it took them some time to pull off to the *Nimrod,* which lay a long way out. We on shore turned in, and we were so tired that it was noon before we woke up. A glance out to sea showed that we had lost nothing by our sleep, for there was a heavy swell running into the bay and it would have been quite impossible to have landed any stores at all. In the afternoon the ship came in fairly close, but I signaled England that it was useless to send the boat. This northerly swell, which we could hear thundering on the ice foot, would have been welcome a fortnight before, for it would have broken up a large amount of fast ice to the south, and I could not help imagining that probably at this date there was open water up to Hut Point. Now, however, it was the worst thing possible for us, as the precious time was slipping by, and the still more valuable coal was being used up by the continual

working of the ship's engines. Next day the swell still
continued, so at 4 P.M. I signaled England to proceed to
Glacier Tongue and land a depot there. Glacier Tongue
is a remarkable formation of ice which stretches out into
the sea from the southwest slopes of Mount Erebus.
About five miles in length, running east and west, taper-
ing almost to a point at its seaward end, and having a
width of about a mile where it descends from the land,
cracked and crevassed all over and floating in deep
water, it is a phenomenon which still remains a mystery.
It lies about eight miles to the northward of Hut Point,
and about thirteen to the southward of Cape Royds, and
I thought this would be a good place at which to land a
quantity of sledging stores, as by doing so we would be
saved haulage at least thirteen miles, the distance between the spot on the southern route and Cape Royds.
The ship arrived there in the early evening, and landed
the depot on the north side of the Tongue. The Professor took bearings so that there might be no difficulty in
finding the depot when the sledging season commenced.
The sounding at this spot gave a depth of 157 fathoms.
From the seaward end of the glacier it was observed that
the ice had broken away only a couple of miles further
south, so the northerly swell had not been as far reaching in its effect as I had imagined. The ship moored at
the Tongue for the night.

During this day we, ashore at Cape Royds, were vari-
ously employed; one party continued the building of the
hut, whilst the rest of us made a more elaborate temporary dwelling and cook house than we had had up to
that time. The walls were constructed of bales of fodder,
which lent themselves admirably for this purpose, the
cook tent tarpaulin was stretched over these for a roof
and was supported on planks, and the outer walls were
stayed with uprights from the pony stalls. As the roof
was rather low and people could not stand upright, a
trench was dug at one end, where the cook could move
about without bending his back the whole time. In this
corner were concocted the most delicious dishes that
ever a hungry man could wish for. Wild acted as cook
till Roberts came ashore permanently, and it was a sight
to see us in the dim light that penetrated through the

door of the fodder hut as we sat in a row on cases, each
armed with a spoon manufactured out of tin and wood
by the ever inventive Day, awaiting with eagerness our
bowl of steaming hoosh or rich dark-colored penguin
breast, followed by biscuit, butter and jam; tea and
smokes ended up the meal, and, as we lazily stretched
ourselves out for the smoke, regardless of a temperature
of 16 or 18 degrees of frost, we felt that things were not
so bad.

The same day that we built the fodder hut we placed
inside it some cases of bottled fruit, hoping to save them
from being cracked by the severe frost outside. The bulk
of the cases containing liquid we kept on board the ship
till the last moment so that they could be put into the
main hut when the fire was lighted. We turned in about
midnight, and got up at seven next morning. The ship
had just come straight in, and I went off on board. Marshall also came off to attend to Mackintosh, whose
wound was rapidly healing. He was now up and about.
He was very anxious to stay with us, but Marshall did
not think it advisable for him to risk it. During the whole
of this day and the next, the 15th, the swell was too
great to admit of any stores being landed, but early on
the morning of the 16th we found it possible to get
ashore at a small ice foot to the north of Flagstaff Point,
and here, in spite of the swell, we managed to land six
boatloads of fruit, some oil, and twenty-four bags of
coal. The crew of the boat, whilst the stores were being
taken out, had to keep to their oars, and whenever the
swell rolled on the shelving beach, they had to back with
all their might to keep the bow of the boat from running
under the overhanging ice foot and being crushed under
the ice by the lifting wave. Davis, the chief officer of the
Nimrod, worked like a Titan. A tall, red-headed Irish-
man, typical of his country, he was always working and
always cheerful, having no time limit for his work. He
and Harbord, the second officer, a quiet, self-reliant
man, were great acquisitions to the expedition. These
two officers were ably supported by the efforts of the
crew. They had nothing but hard work and discomfort
from the beginning of the voyage, and yet they were
always cheerful, and worked splendidly. Dunlop, the

chief engineer, not only kept his department going smoothly on board but was the principal constructor of the hut. A great deal of the credit for the work being so cheerfully performed was due to the example of Cheetham, who was an old hand in the Antarctic, having been boatswain of the *Morning* on both the voyages she made for the relief of the *Discovery*. He was third mate and boatswain on this expedition.

When I had gone on board the previous day I found that England was still poorly and that he was feeling the strain of the situation. He was naturally very anxious to get the ship away and concerned about the shrinkage of the coal supply. I also would have been glad to have seen the *Nimrod* on her way north, but it was impossible to let her leave until the wintering party had received their coal from her. In view of the voyage home, the ship's main topmast was struck to lessen her rolling in bad weather. It was impossible to ballast the ship with rock, as the time needed for this operation would involve the consumption of much valuable coal, and I was sure that the heavy iron bark and oak hull, and the weight of the engine and boiler filled with water, would be sufficient to ensure the ship's safety.

We found it impossible to continue working at Cliff Point later on in the day, so the ship stood off whilst those on shore went on with the building of the hut. Some of the shore party had come off in the last boat to finish writing their final letters home, and during the night we lay to waiting for the swell to decrease. The weather was quite fine, and if it had not been for the swell we could have got through a great deal of work. February is by no means a fine month in the latitude we were in, and up till now we had been extremely fortunate, as we had not experienced a real blizzard.

The following morning, Monday, February 17, the sea was breaking heavily on the ice foot at the bottom of Cliff Point. The stores that had been landed the previous day had been hoisted up the overhanging cliff and now formed the fourth of our scattered depots of coal and stores. The swell did not seem so heavy in Front Door Bay, so we commenced landing the stores in the whale boat at the place where the ice foot had broken away,

a party on shore hauling the bags of coal and the cases
up the ice face, which was about fourteen feet high. The
penguins were still around us in large numbers. We had
not had any time to make observations on them, being
so busily employed discharging the ship, but just at this
particular time our attention was called to a couple of
these birds which suddenly made a spring from the water
and landed on their feet on the ice edge, having cleared
a vertical height of twelve feet. It seemed a marvelous
jump for these small creatures to have made, and shows
the rapidity with which they must move through the
water to gain the impetus that enables them to clear a
distance in vertical height four times greater than their
own, and also how unerring must be their judgment in
estimation of the distance and height when performing
this feat. The work of landing stores at this spot was
greatly hampered by the fact that the bay was more or
less filled with broken floes, through which the boat had
to be forced. It was impossible to use the oars in the
usual way, so, on arriving at the broken ice, they were
employed as poles. The bow of the boat was entered
into a likely looking channel, and then the crew, standing
up, pushed the boat forward by means of the oars, the
ice generally giving way on each side, but sometimes
closing up and nipping the boat, which, if it had been
less strongly built, would assuredly have been crushed.
The Professor, Mawson, Cotton, Michell and a couple
of seamen formed the boat's crew, and with Davis or
Harbord in the stern, they dodged the ice very well,
considering the fact that the swell was rather heavy at
the outside edge of the floes. When alongside the ice
foot one of the crew hung on to a rope in the bow, and
another did the same in the stern, hauling in the slack
as the boat rose on top of the swell, and easing out as
the water swirled downward from the ice foot. There
was a sharp pointed rock, which, when the swell receded,
was almost above water, and the greatest difficulty was
experienced in preventing the boat from crashing down
on the top of this. The rest of the staff in the boat and
on shore hauled up the cases and bags of coal at every
available opportunity. The coal was weighed at the top
of the ice foot, and the bags emptied on to a heap which

formed the main supply for the winter months. We had now three depots of coal in different places around the winter quarters. In the afternoon the floating ice at this place became impassable, but fortunately it had worked its way out of Back Door Bay, where, in spite of the heavy swell running against the ice foot, we were able to continue adding to the heap of coal until nearly eight tons had been landed. It was a dull and weary job except when unpleasantly enlivened by the imminent danger of the boat being caught between heavy pieces of floating ice and the solid ice foot. These masses of ice rose and fell on the swell, the water swirling around them as they became submerged, and pouring off their tops and sides as they rose to the surface. It required all Harbord's watchfulness and speediness of action to prevent damage to the boat. It is almost needless to observe that all hands were as grimy as coal heavers, especially the boat's crew, who were working in the half frozen slushy coal dust and sea spray. The Professor, Mawson, Cotton, and Michell still formed part of the crew. They had, by midnight, been over twelve hours in the boat, excepting for about ten minutes' spell for lunch, and after discharging each time had a long pull back to the ship. When each boat load was landed, the coal and stores had to be hauled up on a sledge over a very steep gradient to a place of safety, and after this was accomplished, there was a long wait for the next consignment.

Work was continued all night, though every one was nearly dropping with fatigue; but I decided that the boat returning to the ship at 5 A.M. (the 18th) should take a message to England that the men were to knock off for breakfast and turn to at 7 A.M. Meanwhile Roberts had brewed some hot coffee in the hut, where we now had the stove going, and, after a drink of this, our weary people threw themselves down on the sleeping bags in order to snatch a short rest before again taking up the work. At 7 A.M. I went to the top of Flagstaff Point, but instead of seeing the ship close in, I spied her hull down on the horizon, and could see no sign of her approaching the winter quarters to resume discharging. After watching her for about half an hour, I returned to the hut, woke up those of the staff who from utter weariness had dropped asleep, and told them to turn into their bags and have a proper rest. I could not imagine why the ship was not at hand, but at a quarter to eleven Harbord came ashore and said that England wanted to see me on board; so, leaving the others to sleep, I went off to the *Nimrod*. On asking England why the ship was not in at seven to continue discharging, he told me that all hands were so dead tired that he thought it best to let them have a sleep. The men were certainly worn out. Davis's head had dropped on the wardroom table, and he had gone sound asleep with his spoon in his mouth, to which he had just conveyed some of his breakfast. Cotton had fallen asleep on the platform of the engine room steps, whilst Mawson, whose lair was a little store-room in the engine room, was asleep on the floor. His long legs, protruding through the doorway, had found a resting place on the cross head of the engine, and his dreams were mingled with a curious rhythmical motion which was fully accounted for when he woke up, for the ship having got under way, the up-and-down motion of the piston had moved his limbs with every stroke. The sailors also were fast asleep; so, in the face of this evidence of absolute exhaustion, I decided not to start work again till after one o'clock, and told England definitely that when the ship had been reduced in coal to ninety-two tons as a minimum I would send her north. According to our experiences on the last expedition, the latest date to which it would be safe to keep the *Nimrod* would be the end of February, for the young ice forming about that time on the sound would seriously hamper her getting clear of the Ross Sea. Later observations of the ice conditions of McMurdo Sound at our winter quarters showed us that a powerfully engined ship could have gone north later in the year, perhaps even in the winter, for we had open water close to us all the time.

About 2 P.M. the *Nimrod* came close in to Flagstaff Point to start discharging again. I decided that it was time to land the more delicate instruments, such as watches, chronometers, and all personal gear. The members of the staff who were on board hauled their things out of Oyster Alley, and, laden with its valuable freight, we took the whale boat into Front Door Bay. Those who had been ashore now went on board to collect their goods and finish their correspondence. During the afternoon we continued boating coal to Front Door Bay, which was again free of ice, and devoted our attention almost entirely to this work.

About five o'clock on the afternoon of February 18, snow began to fall, with a light wind from the north, and as at times the boat could hardly be seen from the ship, instructions were given to the boat's crew that whenever the *Nimrod* was not clearly visible they were to wait alongside the shore until the snow squall had passed and she appeared in sight again. At six o'clock, just as the boat had come alongside for another load, the wind suddenly shifted to the southeast and freshened immediately. The whaler was hoisted at once, and the *Nimrod* stood off from the shore, passing between some heavy ice floes, against one of which her propeller struck, but fortunately without sustaining any damage. Within half an hour it was blowing a furious blizzard, and every sign of land, both east and west, was obscured in the scudding drift. I was aboard the vessel at the time. We were then making for the fast ice to the south, but the *Nimrod* was gaining but little headway against the terrific wind and short rising sea; so to save coal I decided to keep the engines just going slow and maintain our position in the sound as far as we could judge, though it was inevitable that we should drift northward to a certain extent. All night the gale raged with great fury. The speed of the gusts at times must have approached a force of a hundred miles an hour. The tops of the seas were cut off by the wind, and flung over the decks, mast, and rigging of the ship, congealing at once into hard ice, and the sides of the vessel were thick with the frozen sea water. "The masts were gray with the frozen spray, and the bows were a coat of mail." Very soon the cases and sledges lying on deck were hard and fast in a sheet of solid ice, and the temperature had dropped below zero. Harbord, who was the officer on watch, on whistling to call the crew aft, found that the metal whistle stuck to his lips, a painful intimation of the low temperature. I spent most of the night on the bridge, and hoped that the violence of the gale would be of but short duration.

This hope was not realized, for next morning, February 19, at 8 A.M., it was blowing harder than ever. During the early hours of the day the temperature was minus 16° F, and consistently kept below minus 12° F. The motion of the ship was sharp and jerky, yet, considering the nature of the sea and the trim of the vessel, she was remarkably steady. To a certain extent this was due to the fact that the main topmast had been lowered. We had constantly to have two men at the wheel, for the rudder, being so far out of the water, received the blows of the sea as they struck the quarter and stern; and the steersman having once been flung right over the steering chains against the side of the ship, it was necessary to have two always holding on to the kicking wheel. At times there would be a slight lull, the seas striking less frequently against the rudder, and the result would be that the rudder well soon got filled with ice, and it was found impossible to move the wheel at all. To overcome this dangerous state of things the steersmen had to keep moving the wheel alternately to port and starboard, after the ice had been broken away from the well. In spite of this precaution, the rudder well occasionally became choked, and one of the crew, armed with a long iron bar, had to stand by continually to break the frozen sea water off the rudder. In the blinding drift it was impossible to see more than a few yards from the ship, and once a large iceberg suddenly loomed out of the drift close to the weather bow of the *Nimrod;* fortunately the rudder had just been cleared, and the ship answered her helm, thus avoiding a collision.

All day on the 20th, through the night, and throughout the day and night of the 21st, the gale raged. Occasionally the drift ceased, and we saw dimly bare rocks, sometimes to the east and sometimes to the west, but the upper parts of them being enveloped in snow clouds, it was impossible to ascertain exactly what our position was. At these times we were forced to wear ship; that is, to turn the ship around, bringing the wind first astern and then on to the other side, so that we could head in the opposite direction. It was impossible in face of the storm to tack, *i.e.* to turn the ship's head into the wind, and around, so as to bring the wind on the other side.

About midnight on the 21st, whilst carrying out this evolution of wearing ship, during which the *Nimrod* always rolled heavily in the trough of the waves, she shipped a heavy sea, and, all the release water ports and scupper holes being blocked with ice, the water had no means of exit, and began to freeze on deck, where, already, there was a layer of ice over a foot in thickness. Any more weight like this would have made the ship unmanageable. The ropes, already covered with ice, would have been frozen into a solid mass, so we were forced to take the drastic step of breaking holes in the bulwarks to allow the water to escape. This had been done already in the forward end of the ship by the gales we experienced on our passage down to the ice, but as the greater part of the weight in the holds was aft, the water collected toward the middle and stern, and the job of breaking through the bulwarks was a tougher one than we had imagined; it was only by dint of great exertions that Davis and Harbord accomplished it. It was a sight to see Harbord, held by his legs hanging over the starboard side of the *Nimrod,* and wielding a heavy axe, whilst Davis, whose length of limb enabled him to lean over without being held, did the same on the other side. The temperature at this time was several degrees below zero. Occasionally on this night, as we approached the eastern shore, the coast of Ross Island, we noticed the sea covered with a thick yellowish-brown scum. This was due to the immense masses of snow blown off the mountain sides out to sea, and this scum, to a certain extent, prevented the tops of the waves from breaking. Had it not been for this unexpected protection we would certainly have lost our starboard boat, which had been unshipped in a sea and was hanging in a precarious position for the time being. It was hard to realize that so high and so dangerous a sea could possibly have risen in the comparatively narrow waters of McMurdo Sound. The wind was as strong as that we experienced in the gales that assailed us after we first left New Zealand, but the waves were not so huge as those which had the whole run of the Southern Ocean in which to gather strength before they met us. At 2 A.M. the weather suddenly cleared, and though the wind still blew strongly and gustily, it was apparent that the force of the gale had been expended. We could now see our position clearly. The wind and current, in spite of our efforts to keep our position, had driven us over thirty miles to the north, and at this time we were abeam of Cape Bird. The sea was rapidly decreasing in height, and we were able to steam for Cape Royds.

We arrived there in the early morning, and I went ashore at Back Door Bay; after pushing the whale boat through pancake ice and slush, the result of the gale. Hurrying over to the hut I was glad to see that it was intact, and then I received full details of the occurrences of the last three days on shore. The report was not very reassuring as regards the warmth of the hut, for the inmates stated that, in spite of the stove being alight the whole time, no warmth was given off. Of course the building was really not at all complete. It had not been lined, and there were only makeshift protections for the windows, but what seemed a grave matter was the behavior of the stove, for on the efficiency of this depended not only our comfort but our very existence. The shore party had experienced a very heavy gale indeed. The hut had trembled and shaken the whole time, and if the situation had not been so admirable I doubt whether there would have been a hut at all after the gale. A minor accident had occurred, for our fodder hut had failed to withstand the gale, and one of the walls had collapsed, killing one of Possum's pups. The roof had been demolished at the same time.

On going down to our main landing place, the full effect of the blizzard became apparent. There was hardly a sign to be seen of the greater part of our stores. At first it appeared that the drifting snow had covered the cases and bales and the coal, but a closer inspection showed that the real disappearance of our stores from view was due to the sea. Such was the force of the wind blowing straight on to the shore from the south that the spray had been flung in sheets over everything and had been carried by the wind for nearly a quarter of a mile inland, and consequently in places our precious stores lay buried to a depth of five or six feet in a mass of frozen sea water. The angles taken up by the huddled

masses of cases and bales had made the surface of this
mass of ice assume a most peculiar shape. We feared
that it would take weeks of work to get the stores clear
of the ice. It was probable also that the salt water would
have damaged the fodder, and worked its way into cases
that were not tin lined or made of Venesta wood, and
that some of the things would never be seen again. No
one would have recognized the landing place as the spot
on which we had been working during the past fortnight,
so great was the change wrought by the furious storm.
Our heap of coal had a sheet of frozen salt water over
it, but this was a blessing in disguise, for it saved the
smaller pieces of coal from being blown away.

There was no time then to do anything about releasing
the stores from the ice; the main thing was to get the
remainder of the coal ashore and send the ship north.
We immediately started landing coal at the extreme edge
of Front Door Bay. The rate of work was necessarily
very slow, for the whole place was both rough and slippery from the newly formed ice that covered everything.
Before 10 P.M. on February 22, the final boatload of coal
arrived. We calculated that we had in all only about
eighteen tons, so that the strictest economy would be
required to make this amount spin out until the sledging
commenced in the following spring. I should certainly
have liked more coal, but the delays that had occurred
in finding winter quarters, and the difficulties encountered in landing the stores, had caused the *Nimrod* to
be kept longer than I had intended already. We gave
our final letters and messages to the crew of the last
boat, and said goodbye. Cotton, who had come south
just for the trip, was among them, and never had we a
more willing worker. At 10 P.M. the *Nimrod*'s bows were
pointed to the north, and she was moving rapidly away
from the winter quarters with a fair wind. Within a
month I hoped she would be safe in New Zealand, and
her crew enjoying a well earned rest. We were all de-
voutly thankful that the landing of the stores had been
finished at last, and that the state of the sea would no
longer be a factor in our work, but it was with something
of a pang that we severed our last connection with the
world of men. We could hope for no word of news from

civilization until the *Nimrod* came south again in the following summer, and before that we had a good deal of difficult work to do, and some risks to face.

There was scant time for reflection, even if we had been moved that way. We turned in for a good night's rest as soon as possible after the departure of the ship, and the following morning we started digging the stores out of the ice, and transporting everything to the vicinity of the hut. It was necessary that the stores should be close by the building, partly in order that there might be no difficulty in getting what goods we wanted during the winter, and partly because we would require all the protection that we could get from the cold, and the cases, when piled around our little dwelling, would serve to keep off the wind. We hoped, as soon as the stores had all been placed in position, to make a start with the scientific observations that were to be an important part of the work of the expedition.

CHAPTER VII

Winter Quarters at Cape Royds
Outside and Inside

THE next four or five days were spent in using pick and
shovel and iron crowbars on the envelope of ice that
covered our cases, corners of which only peeped out
from the mass. The whole had the appearance of a piece
of the sweet known as almond rock, and there was as
much difficulty in getting the cases clear of the ice as
would be experienced if one tried to separate almonds
from that sticky conglomerate without injury. Occasionally the breaking out of a case would disclose another
which could be easily extracted, but more often each
case required the pick or crowbars. A couple of earnest
miners might be seen delving and hewing the ice off a
case, of which only the corner could be seen, and after
ten minutes' hard work it would be hauled up, and the
stenciled mark of its contents exposed to view. Brocklehurst took great interest in the recovery of the chocolate,
and during this work took charge of one particular case
which had been covered by the ice. He carried it himself
up to the hut so as to be sure of its safety, and he was
greeted with joy by the Professor, who recognized in the
load some of his scientific instruments which were playing the part of the cuckoo in an old chocolate box. Needless to say Brocklehurst's joy was not as heartfelt as
the Professor's.

After about four days' hard work at the Front Door
Bay landing place, the bulk of the stores was recovered,
and I think we may say that there was not much lost
permanently, though, as time went on, and one or two
cases that were required did not turn up, we used to

wonder whether they had been left on board the ship, or lay buried under the ice. We do know for certain that our only case of beer lies to this day under the ice, and it was not until a few days before our final departure that one of the scientists of the expedition dug out some volumes of the Challenger reports, which had been intended to provide us with useful reading matter during the winter nights. A question often debated during the long, dark days was which of these stray sheep, the Challenger reports or the case of beer, any particular individual would dig for if the time and opportunity were available. In moving up the recovered stores, as soon as a load arrived within fifteen yards of the hut, where, at this time of the year, the snow ended, and the bare earth lay uncovered, the sledges were unpacked, and one party carried the stuff up to the south side of the hut, whilst the sledges returned to the landing place for more. We were now utilizing the ponies every day, and they proved of great assistance in moving things to and fro. The stores on the top of the hill at Derrick Point were fortunately quite clear of snow, so we did not trouble to transport them, contenting ourselves with getting down things that were of immediate importance. Day by day we continued collecting our scattered goods, and within ten days after the departure of the ship we had practically everything handy to the hut, excepting the coal. The labor had been both heavy and fertile in minor accidents. Most of us at one time or another had wounds and bruises to be attended to by Marshall, who was kept busy part of every day dressing the injuries. Adams was severely cut in handling some iron-bound cases, and I managed to jam my fingers in the motorcar. The annoying feature about these simple wounds was the length of time it took for them to heal in our special circumstances. The irritation seemed to be more pronounced if any of the earth got into the wound, so we always took care, after our first experiences, to go at once to Marshall for treatment, when the skin was broken. The day after the ship left we laid in a supply of fresh meat for the winter, killing about a hundred penguins and burying them in a snow drift close to the hut. By February 28 we were practically in a position to feel contented with ourselves, and to look further afield and explore the neighborhood of our winter quarters.

From the door of our hut, which faced the northwest, we commanded a splendid view of the sound and the western mountains. Right in front of us, at our door, lay a small lake, which came to be known as Pony Lake; to the left of that was another sheet of ice that became snow covered in the autumn, and it was here in the dark months that we exercised the ponies, and also ourselves. Six times up and down the "Green Park," as it was generally called, made a mile, and it was here that we played hockey and soccer. To the left of Green Park was a gentle slope leading down between two cliffs to the sea, and ending in a little bay known as Dead Horse Bay. On either side of this valley lay the penguin rookery, the slopes being covered with guano, and during the fairly high temperatures that held sway up to April, the smell from these deserted quarters of the penguins was extremely unpleasant. On coming out of the hut one had only to go around the corner of the building in order to catch a glimpse of Mount Erebus, which lay directly behind us. Its summit was about fifteen miles from our winter quarters, but its slopes and foothills commenced within three-quarters of a mile of the hut. Our view was cut off in all directions from the east to the southwest by the ridge at the head of the valley where the hut stood. On ascending this ridge, one looked over the bay to the southeast, where lay Cape Barne. To the right was Flagstaff Point, and to the left lay, at the head of the Bay, the slopes of Erebus. There were many localities which became favorite places for walks. Sandy Beach, about a mile away to the northwest of the hut, was generally the goal of anyone taking exercise, when the uncertainty of the weather warned us against venturing further afield, and while the dwindling light still permitted us to go so far. It was here that we sometimes exercised the ponies, and they much enjoyed rolling in the soft sand. The beach was formed of black volcanic sand, blown from the surrounding hills, and later on the pressed up ice, which had been driven ashore by the southward movement of the pack, also became covered with the wind-borne dust and sand. The coastline from Flagstaff Point right round to Horse Shoe Bay, on the north side of Cape Royds, was jagged and broken up. At some points ice cliffs, in others bare rocks, jutted out into the sea, and here and there small beaches composed of volcanic sand were interposed. Our local scenery, though not on a grand scale, loomed large in the light of the moon as the winter nights lengthened. Fantastic shadows made the heights appear greater and the valleys deeper, casting a spell of unreality around the place, which never seemed to touch it by day. The greatest height of any of the numerous sharp pointed spurs of volcanic rock was not more than three hundred feet, but we were infinitely better off as regards the interest and the scenery of our winter quarters than the expedition which wintered in McMurdo Sound between 1901 and 1904. Our walks amongst the hills and across the frozen lakes were a great source of health and enjoyment, and as a field of work for geologists and biologists, Cape Royds far surpassed Hut Point. The largest lake, which lay about half a mile to the northeast, was named Blue Lake, from the intensely vivid blue of the ice. This lake was peculiarly interesting to Mawson, who made the study of ice part of his work. Beyond Blue Lake, to the northward, lay Clear Lake, the deepest inland body of water in our vicinity. To the left as one looked north, close to the coast, was a circular basin which we called Coast Lake, where, when we first arrived, hundreds of skua gulls were bathing and flying about. Following the coast from this point back toward winter quarters was another body of water called Green Lake. In all these various lakes something of interest to science was discovered, and though they were quite small, they were very important to our work and in our eyes, and were a source of continuous interest to us during our stay in the vicinity. Beyond Blue Lake, to the east, rose the lower slopes of Mount Erebus, covered with ice and snow. After passing one or two ridges of volcanic rocks, there stretched a long snow plain, across which sledges could travel without having their runners torn by gravel. The slope down to Blue Lake was picked out for skiing, and it was here, in the early days, when work was over, that some of our party used to slide from the top of the slope for about two hundred feet, arriving at the bottom in a few seconds, and shooting out across the frozen surface of the lake, until brought up by the rising slope on the other side. To the north of Clear Lake the usual hills of volcanic rock separated by valleys filled more or less with snow drifts, stretched for a distance of about a mile. Beyond this lay the coast, to the right of which, looking north, was Horse Shoe Bay, about four miles from our winter quarters; further to the right of the northern end of Cape Royds the slopes of Erebus were reached again. From the northern coast a good view could be obtained of Cape Bird, and from the height we could see Castle Rock to the south, distant about eighteen miles from the winter quarters. The walk from Hut Point to Castle Rock was familiar to us on the last expedition. It seemed much nearer than it really was, for in the Antarctic the distances are most deceptive, curiously different effects being produced by the variations of light and the distortion of mirage.

As time went on we felt more and more satisfied with our location, for there was work of interest for every one. The Professor and Priestley saw open before them a new chapter of geological history of great interest, for Cape Royds was a happier hunting-ground for the geologist than was Hut Point. Hundreds of erratic boulders lay scattered on the slopes of the adjacent hills, and from these the geologists hoped to learn something of the past conditions of Ross Island. For Murray, the lakes were a fruitful field for new research. The gradually deepening bay was full of marine animal life, the species varying with the depth, and here also an inexhaustible treasure ground stretched before the biologist. Adams, the meteorologist, could not complain, for Mount Erebus was in full view of the meteorological station, and this fortunate proximity to Erebus and its smoke cloud led, in a large measure, to important results in this branch. For the physicist the structure of the ice, varying on various lakes, the different salts in the earth, and the magnetic conditions of the rocks claimed investigation, though, indeed, the magnetic nature of the rocks proved a disadvantage in carrying out magnetic observations, for the delicate instruments were often affected by the local attraction. From every point of view I must say that we were extremely fortunate in the winter quarters to which we had been led by the state of the sea ice, for no other spot could have afforded more scope for work and exercise.

Before we had been ten days ashore the hut was practically completed, though it was over a month before it had been worked up from the state of an empty shell to attain the fully furnished appearance it assumed after every one had settled down and arranged his belongings. It was not a very spacious dwelling for the accommodation of fifteen persons, but our narrow quarters were warmer than if the hut had been larger. The coldest part of the house when we first lived in it was undoubtedly the floor, which was formed of inch tongue-and-groove boarding, but was not double lined. There was a space of about four feet under the hut at the northwest end, the other end resting practically on the ground, and it was obvious to us that as long as this space remained we would suffer from the cold, so we decided to make an airlock of the area under the hut. To this end we decided to build a wall round the southeast and southerly sides, which were to windward, with the bulk of the provision cases. To make certain that no air would penetrate from these sides we built the first two or three tiers of cases a little distance out from the walls of the hut, pouring in volcanic earth until no gaps could be seen, and the earth was level with the cases; then the rest of the stores were piled up to a height of six.or seven feet. This accounted for one side and one end. On either side of the porch two other buildings were gradually erected. One, built out of biscuit cases, the roof covered with felt and canvas, was a storeroom for Wild, who looked after the issue of all food stuffs. The building on the other side of the porch was a much more ambitious affair, and was built by Mawson, to serve as a chemical and physical laboratory. It was destined, however, to be used solely as a storeroom, for the temperature within its walls was practically the same as that of the outside air, and the warm, moist atmosphere rushing out from the hut covered everything inside this storeroom with fantastic ice crystals.

The lee side of the hut ultimately became the wall of

the stables, for we decided to keep the ponies sheltered during the winter. During the blizzard we experienced on February 18, and for the three following days, the animals suffered somewhat, mainly owing to the knocking about they had received whilst on the way south in the ship. We found that a shelter, not necessarily warmed to a high temperature, would keep the ponies in better condition than if they were allowed to stand in the open, and by February 9 the stable building was complete. A double row of cases of maize, built at one end to a height of five feet eight inches, made one end, and then the longer side of the shelter was composed of bales of fodder. A wide plank at the other end was cemented into the ground, and a doorway left. Over all this was stretched the canvas tarpaulin which we had previously used in the fodder hut, and with planks and battens on both sides to make it windproof, the stable was complete. A wire rope was stretched from one end to the other on the side nearest to the hut, and the ponies' head ropes were made fast to this. The first night that they were placed in the stable there was little rest for any of us, and during the night some of the animals broke loose and returned to their valley. Shortly afterwards Grisi, one of the most high-spirited of the lot, pushed his head through a window, so the lower halves of the hut windows had to be boarded up. The first strong breeze we had shook the roof of the stable so much that we expected every moment it would blow away, so after the gale all the sledges except those which were in use were laid on the top of the stable, and a stout rope passed from one end to the other. The next snowfall covered the sledges and made a splendid roof, upon which no subsequent wind had any effect. Later, another addition was made to the dwellings outside the hut in the shape of a series of doghouses for those animals about to pup, and as that was not an uncommon thing down there, the houses were constantly occupied.

On the southeast side of the hut a storeroom was built, constructed entirely of cases, and roofed with hammocks sewn together. Here we kept the tool chest, shoemaker's outfit, which was in constant requisition, and any general stores that had to be issued at stated times.

The first heavy blizzard found this place out, and after the roof had been blown off, the wall fell down, and we had to organize a party, when the weather got fine, to search for anything that might be lost, such as mufflers, woolen helmets, and so on. Some things were blown more than a mile away. I found a Russian felt boot, weighing five pounds, lying three-quarters of a mile from the crate in which it had been stowed, and it must have had a clear run in the air for the whole of this distance, for there was not a scratch on the leather; if it had been blown along the rocks, which lay in the way, the leather would certainly have been scratched all over. The chimney, which was an iron pipe, projecting two or three feet above the roof of the hut, and capped by a cowl, was let through the roof at the southeast end, and secured by numerous rope stays supporting it at every point from which the wind could blow.

We were quite free from the trouble of down drafts or choking with snow, such as had been of common occurrence in the large hut on the *Discovery* expedition. Certainly the revolving cowl blew off during the first blizzard, and this happened again in the second, so we took the hint and left it off for good, without detriment, as it happened, to the efficiency of the stove.

The dog kennels were placed close to the porch of the hut, but only three of the dogs were kept constantly chained up. The meteorological station was on the weather side of the hut on the top of a small ridge, about twenty feet above the hut and forty feet above sea level, and a natural path led to it. Adams laid it out, and the regular readings of the instruments began on March 22. The foundation of the thermometer screen consisted of a heavy wooden case resting on rocks. The case was three-quarters filled with rock, and around the outside were piled more blocks of kenyte; the crevices between them were filled with volcanic earth on to which water was poured, the result being a structure as rigid as the ground itself. On each side of the box a heavy upright was secured by the rocks inside the case and by bolts at the sides, and to these uprights the actual meteorological screen, one of the Stevenson pattern and of standard size, was bolted. As readings of the instruments were to be taken day and night at intervals of two hours, and as it was quite possible that the weather might be so thick that a person might be lost in making his way between the screen and the hut, a line was rigged up on posts, which were cemented into the ground by ice, so that in the thickest weather the observer could be sure of finding his way by following this very substantial clue.

The inside of the hut was not long in being fully furnished, and a great change it was from the bare shell of our first days of occupancy. The first thing done was to peg out a space for each individual, and we saw that the best plan would be to have the space allotted in sections, allowing two persons to share one cubicle. This space for two men amounted to six feet six inches in length and seven feet in depth from the wall of the hut toward the center. There were seven of these cubicles, and a space for the leader of the expedition; thus providing for the fifteen who made up the shore party. The accompanying photographs will give an idea of the hut as finished. One of the most important parts of the interior construction was the darkroom for the photographers. We were very short of wood, so cases of bottled fruit, which had to be kept inside the hut to prevent them freezing, were utilized for building the walls. The darkroom was constructed in the left-hand corner of the hut as one entered, and the fruit cases were turned with their lids facing out, so that the contents could be removed without demolishing the walls of the building. These cases, as they were emptied, were turned into lockers, where we stowed our spare gear and so obtained more room in the little cubicles. The interior of the darkroom was fitted up by Mawson and the Professor. The sides and roof were lined with the felt left over after the hut was completed. Mawson made the fittings complete in every detail, with shelves, tanks, etc., and the result was as good as any one could desire in the circumstances.

On the other side of the doorway, opposite the darkroom, was my room, six feet long, seven feet deep, built of boards and roofed, the roof being seven feet above the floor. I lined the walls inside with canvas, and the bed place was constructed of fruit boxes, which, when emptied, served, like those outside, for lockers. My room contained the bulk of our library, the chronometers, the chronometer watches, barograph, and the electric recording thermometer; there was ample room for a table, and the whole made a most comfortable cabin. On the roof we stowed those of our scientific instruments which were not in use, such as theodolites, spare thermometers, dip circles, etc. The gradual accumulation of weight produced a distinct sag in the roof, which sometimes seemed to threaten collapse as I sat inside, but no notice was taken, and nothing happened. On the roof of the darkroom we stowed all our photographic gear and our few cases of wine, which were only drawn upon on special occasions, such as Midwinter Day. The acetylene gas plant was set up on a platform between my room and the darkroom. We had tried to work it from the porch, but the temperature was so low there that the water froze and the gas would not come, so we shifted it inside the hut, and had no further trouble. Four burners, including a portable standard light in my room, gave ample illumination. The simplicity and portability of the apparatus and the high efficiency of the light represented the height of luxury under polar conditions and did much to render our sojourn more tolerable than would have been possible in earlier days. The particular form that we used was supplied by Mr. Morrison, who had been chief engineer on the *Morning* on her voyage to the relief of the *Discovery*. The only objectionable feature, due to having the generating plant in our living room was the unpleasant smell given off when the carbide tanks were being recharged, but we soon got used to this, though the daily changing always drew down strong remarks on the unlucky head of Day—who had the acetylene plant especially under his charge. He did not have a hitch with it all the time. Flexible steel tubes were carried from the tank, and after being wound around the beams of the roof, served to suspend the lights at the required positions.

A long ridge of rope wire was stretched from one end of the hut to the other on each side, seven feet out from the wall; then at intervals of six feet another wire was brought out from the wall of the hut, and made fast to the fore and aft wire. These lines marked the boundaries of the cubicles, and sheets of duck sewn together hung

from them, making a good division. Blankets were
served out to hang in the front of the cubicle, in case
the inhabitants wanted at any time to "sport their oak."
As each of the cubicles had distinctive features in the
furnishing and general design, especially as regards beds,
it is worthwhile to describe them fully. This is not so
trivial a matter as it may appear to some readers, for
during the winter months the inside of the hut was the
whole inhabited world to us. The wall of Adams and
Marshall's cubicle, which was next to my room, was fitted with shelves made out of Venesta cases, and there
was so much neatness and order about this apartment
that it was known by the address, "No. 1 Park Lane."
In front of the shelves hung little gauze curtains, tied up
with blue ribbon, and the literary tastes of the occupants
could be seen at a glance from the bookshelves. In
Adams' quarter the period of the French Revolution and
the Napoleonic era filled most of his bookshelves,
though a complete edition of Dickens came in a good
second. Marshall's shelves were stocked with bottles of
medicine, medical works, and some general literature.
The dividing curtain of duck was adorned by Marston
with life-sized colored drawings of Napoleon and Joan
of Arc. Adams and Marshall did Sandow exercises daily,
and their example was followed by other men later on,
when the darkness and bad weather made open air work
difficult. The beds of this particular cubicle were the
most comfortable in the hut, but took a little longer to
rig up at night than most of the others. This disadvantage was more than compensated for by the free space
gained during the day, and by permission of the owners
it was used as consulting room, dispensary, and op-
erating theater. The beds consisted of bamboos lashed
together for extra strength, to which strips of canvas
were attached, so that each bed looked like a stretcher.
The wall end rested on stout cleats screwed on to the
side of the hut, the other ends on chairs, and so supported, the occupants slept soundly and comfortably.

The next cubicle on the same side was occupied by
Marston and Day, and as the former was the artist and
the latter the general handy man of the expedition, one
naturally found an ambitious scheme of decoration. The

shelves were provided with beading, and the Venesta boxes were stained brown. This idea was copied from "No. 1 Park Lane," where they had stained all their walls with Condy's Fluid. Marston and Day's cubicle was known as "The Gables," presumably from the gabled appearance of the shelves. Solid wooden beds, made out of old packing cases and upholstered with wood shavings covered with blankets, made very comfortable couches, one of which could be pushed during meal times out of the way of the chairs. The artist's curtain was painted to represent a fireplace and mantelpiece in civilization; a cheerful fire burned in the grate, and a bunch of flowers stood on the mantelpiece. The dividing curtain between it and No. 1 Park Lane, on the other side of the cubicle, did not require to be decorated, for the color of Joan of Arc, and also portions of Napoleon, had oozed through the canvas. In "The Gables" was set up the lithographic press, which was used for producing pictures for the book which was printed at our winter quarters.

The next cubicle on the same side belonged to Armytage and Brocklehurst. Here everything in the way of shelves and fittings was very primitive. I lived in Brocklehurst's portion of the cubicle for two months, as he was laid up in my room, and before I left it I constructed a bed of empty petrol cases. The smell from these for the first couple of nights after rigging them up was decidedly unpleasant, but it disappeared after a while. Next to Brocklehurst's and Armytage's quarters came the pantry. The division between the cubicle and the pantry consisted of a tier of cases, making a substantial wall between the food and the heads of the sleepers. The pantry, bakery, and storeroom, all combined, measured six feet by three, not very spacious, certainly, but sufficient to work in. The far end of the hut constituted the other wall of the pantry, and was lined with shelves up to the slope of the roof. These shelves were continued along the wall behind the stove, which stood about four feet out from the end of the house, and an erection of wooden battens and burlap or sacking concealed the biological laboratory. The space taken up by this important department was four feet by four, but lack of ground area was made up for by the shelves, which con-

tained dozens of bottles soon to be filled with Murray's
biological captures.

Beyond the stove, facing the pantry, was Mackay and
Roberts' cubicle, the main feature of which was a ponderous shelf, on which rested mostly socks and other
light articles, the only thing of weight being our gramophone and records. The bunks were somewhat feeble
imitations of those belonging to No. 1 Park Lane, and
the troubles that the owners went through before finally
getting them into working order afforded the rest of the
community a good deal of amusement. I can see before
me now the triumphant face of Mackay, as he called all
hands around to see his design. The inhabitants of No.
1 Park Lane pointed out that the bamboo was not a rigid
piece of wood, and that when Mackay's weight came on
it the middle would bend and the ends would jump off
the supports unless secured. Mackay undressed before a
critical audience, and he got into his bag and expatiated
on the comfort and luxury he was experiencing, so different to the hard boards he had been lying on for months.
Roberts was anxious to try his couch, which was constructed on the same principle, and the audience were
turning away disappointed at not witnessing a catastro-
phe, when suddenly a crash was heard, followed by a
strong expletive. Mackay's bed was half on the ground,
one end of it resting at a most uncomfortable angle.
Laughter and pointed remarks as to his capacity for
making a bed were nothing to him; he tried three times
that night to fix it up, but at last had to give it up for a
bad job. In due time he arranged fastenings, and after
that he slept in comfort.

Between this cubicle and the next there was no division, neither party troubling about the matter. The result
was that the four men were constantly at war regarding
alleged encroachments on their ground. Priestley, who
was long-suffering, and who occupied the cubicle with
Murray, said he did not mind a chair or a volume of the
Encyclopedia Britannica being occasionally deposited on
him while he was asleep, but that he thought it was a
little too strong to drop wet boots, newly arrived from
the stables, on top of his belongings. Priestley and Murray had no floor space at all in their cubicle, as their

beds were built of empty dog biscuit boxes. A division of boxes separated the two sleeping places, and the whole cubicle was garnished on Priestley's side with bits of rock, ice axes, hammers and chisels, and on Murray's with biological requisites.

Next came one of the first cubicles that had been built. Joyce and Wild occupied the "Rogues' Retreat," a painting of two very tough characters drinking beer out of pint mugs, with the inscription *The Rogues' Retreat* painted underneath, adorning the entrance to the den. The couches in this house were the first to be built, and those of the opposite dwelling, The Gables, were copied from their design. The first bed had been built in Wild's storeroom for secrecy's sake; it was to burst upon the view of everyone, and to create mingled feelings of admiration and envy, admiration for the splendid design, envy of the unparalleled luxury provided by it. However, in building it, the designer forgot the size of the doorway he had to take it through, and it had ignominiously to be sawn in half before it could be passed out of the storeroom into the hut. The printing press and type case for the polar paper occupied one corner of this cubicle.

The next and last compartment was the dwelling place of the Professor and Mawson. It would be difficult to do justice to the picturesque confusion of this compartment; one hardly likes to call it untidy, for the things that covered the bunks by daytime could be placed nowhere else conveniently. A miscellaneous assortment of cameras, spectroscopes, thermometers, microscopes, electrometers, and the like lay in profusion on the blankets. Mawson's bed consisted of his two boxes, in which he had stowed his scientific apparatus on the way down, and the Professor's bed was made out of kerosene cases. Everything in the way of tin cans or plug-topped, with straw wrappers belonging to the fruit bottles, was collected by these two scientific men. Mawson, as a rule, put his possessions in his storeroom outside, but the Professor, not having any retreat like that, made a pile of glittering tins and colored wrappers at one end of his bunk, and the heap looked like the nest of the Australian bower bird. The straw and the tins were generally cleared away when the Professor and Priestley went in for a day's packing of geological specimens; the straw wrappers were utilized for wrapping around the rocks and the tins were filled with paper wrapped around the more delicate geological specimens. The name given, though not by the owners, to this cubicle was "The Pawn Shop," for not only was there always a heterogeneous mass of things on the bunks, but the wall of the darkroom and the wall of the hut at this spot could not be seen for the multitude of cases ranged as shelves and filled with a varied assortment of notebooks and instruments.

In order to give as much free space as possible in the center of the hut we had the table so arranged that it could be hoisted up over our heads after meals were over. This gave ample room for the various carpentering and engineering efforts that were constantly going on. Murray built the table out of the lids of packing cases, and though often scrubbed, the stenciling on the cases never came out. We had no tablecloth, but this was an advantage, for a well scrubbed table had a cleaner appearance than would be obtained with such washing as could be done in an Antarctic laundry. The legs of the table were détachable, being after the fashion of trestles, and the whole affair, when meals were over, was slung by a rope at each end about eight feet from the floor. At first we used to put the boxes containing knives, forks, plates, and bowls on top of the table before hauling it up, but after these had fallen on the unfortunate head of the person trying to get them down, we were content to keep them on the floor.

I had been very anxious as regards the stove, the most important part of the hut equipment, when I heard that, after the blizzard that kept me on board the *Nimrod,* the temperature of the hut was below zero, and that socks put to dry in the baking ovens came out as damp as ever the following morning. My anxiety was dispelled after the stove had been taken to pieces again, for it was found that eight important pieces of its structure had not been put in. As soon as this omission was rectified the stove acted splendidly, and the makers deserve our thanks for the particular apparatus they picked out as suitable for us. The stove was put to a severe test, for it was kept going day and night for over nine months without once being out for more than ten minutes, when occasion required it to be cleaned. It supplied us with sufficient heat to keep the temperature of the hut sixty to seventy degrees above the outside air. Enough bread could be baked to satisfy our whole hungry party of fifteen every day; three hot meals a day were also cooked, and water melted from ice at a temperature of perhaps twenty degrees below zero in sufficient quantity to afford as much as we required for ourselves, and to water the ponies twice a day, and all this work was done on a consumption not exceeding five hundredweight of coal per week. After testing the stove by running it on an accurately measured amount of coal for a month, we were reassured about our coal supply being sufficient to carry us through the winter right on to sledging time.

As the winter came on and the light grew faint outside, the hut became more and more like a workshop, and it seems strange to me now, looking back to those distant days, to remember the amount of trouble and care that was taken to furnish and beautify what was only to be a temporary home. One of our many kind friends had sent us a number of pictures, which were divided between the various cubicles, and these brightened up the place wonderfully. During our first severe blizzard, the hut shook and trembled so that every moment we expected the whole thing to carry away, and there is not the slightest shadow of a doubt that if we had been located in the open, the hut and everything in it would have been torn up and blown away. Even with our sheltered position I had to lash the chronometers to the shelf in my room, for they were apt to be shaken off when the walls trembled in the gale. When the storm was over we put a stout wire cable over the hut, burying the ends in the ground and freezing them in, so as to afford additional security in case heavier weather was in store for us in the future.

Divine service was held in the hut on Sundays during the winter months.

Sledging Equipment

I WILL now give some details of the sledging outfits used by the various expeditions that left our winter quarters. The first, and one of the most important of the items was, of course, the sledge, though, indeed, everything taken on a sledge journey is absolutely essential; one does not load up odds and ends on the chance of their proving useful, for the utmost reduction of weight compatible with efficiency is the first and last thing for the polar explorer to aim at.

The sledge which we used is the outcome of the experience of many former explorers, but it is chiefly due to Nansen that it has become the very useful vehicle that it is at the present day. On the *Discovery* expedition we had sledges of various lengths, seven feet, nine feet, eleven feet and twelve feet. Our experience on that occasion showed that the eleven-foot sledge was the best for all round use, but I had taken with me a certain number of twelve-foot sledges as being possibly more suitable for pony traction. A good sledge for Antarctic or Arctic traveling must be rigid in its upright and cross bars, and yet give to uneven surfaces, so that in traveling over sastrugi the strain will not come on the whole of the sledge. A well-constructed sledge, traveling over an uneven surface, appears to have an undulating, snake-like movement, and the attainment of this suppleness without interfering with the strength of the structure as a whole is the main point to be aimed at; in our case there was nothing wanting in this respect. The wooden runners were about four inches wide and made of hickory, split from the tree with the grain of the wood and not sawn. Many pieces were inspected and rejected and only those passed as perfect were used. This method of preparing the runners, it can easily be seen, allows much greater scope for bending than would be the case if the wood were sawn regardless of the run of the grain. In pulling the sledge the direction of the grain on the snow surface has to be observed, and it is wonderful what a difference it makes whether one is pulling with or against the grain of the runner. The second point to consider is the height of the framework of the sledge above the surface of the snow. Naturally, with a low framework there is less chance of the sledgeload capsizing when passing over rough ground, and the aim of the explorer is therefore to keep the load as low as possible on the sledge. It has been found that a clearance of six inches is ample in all ordinary circumstances, so the uprights of our sledges were only about six inches high. These uprights were fastened at intervals into holes on the upper side of the runners, and instead of being fastened on the underside of the latter, other holes were bored in the ridge of the upper side and raw hide lashings passed through them and through the upright. Cross-pieces were fastened by a sort of dovetailing process, supplemented by marlin lashings, and the angle made by the vertical upright and horizontal cross-piece was crossed by a short iron stay. This junction of cross-piece and upright was the only absolutely rigid part of the whole sledge. Every other portion of a good sledge gives somewhat as it takes up the various strains, and it entirely depends on good workmanship and sailorlike lashings whether, on the strain being removed, the sledge returns to its normal shape or is permanently distorted. Two long runners or bearers, about an inch square, rested on the uprights, and cross-pieces projecting the whole length of the sledge and fastened by extra strong marlin lashings, covered with leather to protect them from the chafing of the equipment stowed on top, formed a sort of platform on which the stores were placed. The fore end of the sledge had a bow of wood, forming practically a semicircle, the two ends being fastened to the slightly upturned ends of the runners. The upper bearers were pressed down, and also lashed to this bow. This upturning at the forward end of the sledge allowed for the meeting of unequal surfaces, and the shape of the bow was intended to prevent the ends of the sledge being driven into snow or ice obstructions. The rear end of the sledge was also slightly turned up, and the top bearers bent down and lashed to the bare ends. Of course, a bow was not necessary at that end. At each end of the sledge, made fast round the first two uprights and the last two on both sides, were two pieces of alpine rope, which combines strength with lightness. The bight of this rope was formed into a becket, and by this means a toggle attached to the sledge harness could readily be put in. When sledges are running in line, one behind the other, particular care has to be taken with these ropes, so that the tracks of the second sledge coincide with the first. By doing this the amount of friction on the runners of the second sledge is greatly reduced, for the forward sledge does practically all the work of breaking the trail, and the following ones run lightly over the made track. An eleven-foot sledge, fully loaded, is at its best working weight with about 650 lb. on it, but this by no means represents its actual strength capacity, for we tested ours most rigorously during the unloading of the ship, often placing over a thousand pounds' weight on a sledge without it sustaining the slightest damage. After our experience on the Barrier surface during the *Discovery* expedition, I had decided to dispense with metal runners, so only a few sets of detachable steel under runners were provided, to be used for work on ground bare of snow or on rough glacier ice. In order to fasten the stores on the sledge we riveted straps on to the bearers, and thus formed a handy and trustworthy means of fastening things with the least possible loss of time.

Another vitally important article of equipment for the polar explorer is the cooker and cooking stove. Here again we were indebted to the practical genius of Nansen, who designed the form of cooker that is now invariably used in polar work. The stove was the ordinary "primus," burning kerosene, vaporized in the usual way. This stove is highly efficient, and, with strict economy, one gallon of oil will last three men for ten days, allowing three hot meals per day. This economy is due, in a large measure, to the qualities of the cooker. The form we used consisted of an outer cover of aluminum drawn out of one piece, inside which was a ring-shaped vessel so designed that the heated air could circulate around it. Inside this vessel was the center cooking pot, and these pots were all mounted on a concave plate of aluminum which fitted over the top of the primus lamp. The middle cooker was first filled with snow or ice, pressed tightly down, the lid was put on and this vessel placed inside the outer, ring-shaped cooker, which was also filled with snow; over all this apparatus the aluminum outside cover was placed, inverted. The heated gases from the stove, after heating the bottom of the center cooker, mounted into the space between the two vessels, and were then forced down the outside of the ring-shaped cooker by the cover, finally escaping at the lower edge. Experiments showed that about 92 percent of the heat generated by the lamp was used in the cooker, a most satisfactory result, for economy in fuel is of great importance when the oil has to be carried on sledges. I did not have draw off taps on the cookers, but they were so arranged that the boiling pot in the center lifted in and out easily. Such was the efficiency of the cooker and stove that, in a temperature of forty or fifty degrees below zero, the snow or ice, which would be at this temperature, could be melted and a hot meal prepared within half an hour from the time the cooker was first placed on the primus. The whole apparatus, including the primus, did not weigh more than fifteen pounds. When the cooker was empty after meals, our feeding utensils were placed inside. They consisted of pannikins and spoons only. The former were made of aluminum in pairs, and fitted one into another. The outer pannikin, for holding the hot tea or cocoa, was provided with handles, and the other fitted over the top of this and was used for the more solid food. There was no "washing up" on the march, for spoons were licked clean and pannikins scraped assiduously when sledging appetites had been developed.

The next important item was the tent. The usual unit for sledging consists of three men, and our tents were designed to contain that number. The tent cloth was thin Willesden duck, with a "snow cloth" of thicker material round the lower edge. This snow cloth was spread out on the ground and snow or ice piled on it so that the form of the tent was like that of an inverted convolvulus. Instead of a single tent pole we used five male bamboo rods, eight feet six inches in length, fastened together at one end in a cap, over which the apex of the tent fitted. The bamboos were stretched out, and the tent was slung over the top, with the door, which took the form of a sort of spout of Burberry material, on the lee side. This Burberry spout was loose and could be tied up by being gathered together when the occupants were inside the tent, or could be left open when desired. Inside the tent was placed on the snow a circle of thick Willesden waterproof canvas to protect the sleeping bags from actual contact with the ground. The material of which the tents were constructed appeared flimsy and the bamboos were light, but one could trust them with absolute confidence to encounter successfully the fiercest blizzards of this exceptionally stormy part of the world. There was no instance of damage to a tent owing to bad weather during the expedition.

The next important item of our equipment was the sleeping bag. It has been generally assumed by polar explorers, despite our experience with the *Discovery* expedition, that it is absolutely necessary for sledge travelers to wrap themselves up in furs. We have found this to be quite unnecessary, and I think that I am justified, from my experience during two expeditions in what is, undoubtedly, a more rigorous climate than exists in the north polar regions, in stating that, except for the hands and feet, in the way of personal clothing, and the sleeping bags for camping, furs are entirely unnecessary. Our sleeping bags were made of hides of young reindeer (fur inside). The term "bag" literally describes this portion of the sledging gear. It is a long bag, with closely sewn seams, and is entered by means of a slit at the upper end. A large sleeping bag will hold three men. We were well supplied with one man bags.

Having considered various parts of the equipment of a sledge party, we now come to the important item of food. The appetite of a man who has just come to camp after a five hours' march in a low temperature is something that the ordinary individual at home would scarcely understand, and, indeed, the sledger himself has moments of surprise when, after finishing his ration, he feels just about as hungry as when he started.

In selecting our supplies I had based my plans on previous experience; and, for the sledging journeys I had tried to provide the maximum amount of heat giving and flesh forming materials, and to avoid as far as possible foods containing a large amount of moisture, which means so much dead weight to be carried. Our cuisine was not very varied, but a voracious appetite has no nice discernment and requires no sauce to make the meal palatable; indeed, all one wants is more, and this is just what cannot be allowed if a party is to achieve anything in the way of distance whilst confined to a man haulage. It is hard for a hungry man to rest content with the knowledge that the particular food he is eating contains so much nourishment and is sufficient for his needs, if at the same time he does not feel full and satisfied after the meal and if, within an hour or so, the aching void again makes itself felt, and he has to wait another five hours before he can again temporarily satisfy the craving. One of the main items of our food supply was pemmican, which consisted of the finest beef powdered with 60 percent of fat added. This is one of the staple foods in polar work, and the fat has properties specially tending to promote heat. Our pemmican for use on the long sledge journeys was obtained from Messrs. Beauvais, of Copenhagen, and was similar to the pemmican we had on the *Discovery* expedition. Biscuits are a standard food also, and in this matter I had made a departure from the example of the previous expedition. We found then that the thin wholemeal biscuits which we used in sledging work were apt to break, and it was difficult to make out the exact allowance for each day, the result being that sometimes we used up our supply for the week too early. I secured thicker biscuits, but the principal change was in the composition itself. The Plasmon Company supplied a ton of the best wholemeal biscuit, containing 25 percent of plasmon; the plasmon tended to harden the biscuit, and, as is well known, it is an excellent food. These biscuits were specially baked, and, with an allowance of one pound for each man per day, were a distinct advance on the farinaceous food of the previous expedition. This allowance, I may mention, was reduced very considerably when food began to run short on the southern and northern journeys, but we had no fault to find with the quality of the biscuits. The addition of the plasmon certainly increased their food value. Tea and cocoa were selected as our beverages for use on the march. We used tea for breakfast and lunch, and cocoa, which tends to produce sleepiness, for dinner at night. Sugar is a very valuable heat forming substance, and our allowance of this amounted to about a third of a pound for each man for a day. We also took chocolate, cheese, and oatmeal, so that, though there was not very much variety, we felt we were getting the most nutritious food possible. We had a much more varied selection of foods at the winter quarters, and the supplies taken on the sledging journeys would be varied to some extent according to the necessities of the occasion.

The following firms presented us with food stuffs, all of which proved entirely satisfactory: Messrs. J. and J. Colman, Ltd., of Norwich: 9 tons wheat flour, ½ ton self-raising flour, ½ ton wheatmeal, 100 lb. corn flour, 84 lb. best mustard, 1¾ gross mixed mustard; Messrs. Rowntree and Co., Ltd., York: 1700 lb. Elect cocoa (28 percent of fat), 200 lb. Queen's chocolate; Messrs. Alfred Bird and Sons, Ltd., Birmingham: 120 doz. custard, baking, egg, crystal jelly, and blancmange powders; Liebig's Extract of Meat Co., Ltd., London: "Oxo," "Service oxo emergency food," "Lemco," and Fray Bentos ox tongues; Evans, Sons, Lescher and Webb, Ltd., London: 27 cases Montserrat lime juice; Messrs. Lipton, Ltd.: 350 lb. Ceylon tea.

The clothing usually worn for sledging work consisted of thick Jaeger underclothing, heavy blue pilot cloth trousers, a Jaeger pajama jacket for coat, and over this as our main protection against cold and wind, the Burberry blouse and trousers.

On the hands we wore woolen gloves and then fur mits, and on the feet several pairs of heavy woolen socks and then finnesko. Any one feeling the texture and lightness of the Burberry material would hardly believe that it answers so well in keeping out the cold and wind and affords a complete protection, during a blizzard, against the fine drifting snow that permeates almost everything.

The head gear was a matter on which there were marked differences of opinion, but the most general method of keeping head and ears warm was to wrap a woolen muffler twice around the chin and head, thus forming protection for the ears, which are the first parts of the body to show signs of frostbite; the muffler was then brought round the neck, and over the muffler was pulled a fleecy traveling cap, a woolen helmet, something like an old-time helmet without the visor. If a blizzard were blowing, the muffler was discarded, the helmet put on, and over this the Burberry helmet, which has a stiff flap in front that can be buttoned into a funnel shape. The sledge traveler thus equipped could be assured that his features and body would be exempt from frostbite under all ordinary circumstances. In very low temperatures, or with a moderately low temperature and a breeze, it was necessary, occasionally, to inspect each others' faces for the sign of frostbite; if the white patch denoting this was visible, it had to be attended to at once.

In considering the various methods of haulage in the Antarctic the experience of the National Antarctic Expedition proved of very great value. The equipment, as far as the sledges and harness, etc., were concerned, was excellent—but this expedition was dependent on dogs for haulage purposes, and the use of these animals on the Barrier was not at all successful. Only twenty dogs were taken with the *Discovery*, and the trouble they gave and their eventual collapse and failure are matters of common knowledge amongst those interested in Antarctic exploration. The knowledge I gained of the Barrier surface on that occasion suggested to me the feasibility of using ponies for traction purposes, for I had heard that in Siberia and Northern Manchuria ponies of a peculiarly hardy and sturdy stock did excellent work in hauling sledges and carrying packs over snow and ice at very low temperatures and under very severe weather conditions.

It seems to be generally assumed that a Manchurian pony can drag a sledge over a broken trail at the rate of twenty to thirty miles a day, pulling not less than twelve hundred pounds. It was a risk to take ponies from the far north through the tropics and then across two thousand miles of stormy sea on a very small ship, but I felt that if it could be done it would be well worth the trouble, for, compared with the dog, the pony is a far more efficient animal, one pony doing the work of at least ten dogs on the food allowance for ten dogs, and traveling a longer distance in a day.

We established ourselves at the winter quarters with eight ponies, but unfortunately we lost four of them within a month of our arrival. The loss was due, in the case of three of the four, to the fact that they were picketed when they first landed on sandy ground, and it was not noticed that they were eating the sand. I had neglected to see that the animals had a supply of salt given to them, and as they found a saline flavor in the volcanic sand under their feet, due to the fact that the blizzards had sprayed all the land near the shore with sea water, they ate it at odd moments. All the ponies seem to have done this, but some were more addicted to the habit than the others. Several of them became ill, and we were quite at a loss to account for the trouble until Sandy died. Then a postmortem examination revealed the fact that his stomach contained many pounds of sand, and the cause of the illness of the other ponies became apparent. We shifted them at once from the place where they were picketed, so that they could get no more sand, and gave them what remedial treatment lay in our power, but two more died in spite of all our efforts. The loss of the fourth pony was due to poisoning. The Manchurian ponies will eat anything at all that can be chewed, and this particular animal seems to have secured some shavings in which chemicals had been packed. The postmortem examination showed that there were distinct signs of corrosive poisoning. The losses were a matter of deep concern to us.

We were left with four ponies, Quan, Socks, Grisi, and Chinaman, and it is a rather curious fact that the survivors were the white or light colored animals, while disaster had befallen all the dark animals. The four ponies were very precious in our eyes, and they were watched and guarded with keen attention.

During the winter months those of us who generally took the ponies out for exercise got to learn the different traits and character of each individual animal. Every one of them seemed to possess more cunning and sense than the ordinary broken-in horse at home, and this cunning, when put into practice to gain any end of their own, was a constant source of petty annoyance to us. Quan was the worst offender, his particular delight being to bite through his head rope and attack the bales of fodder stacked behind him; then, when we put a chain on to prevent this, he deliberately rattled it against the side of the hut, which kept us awake. He had at first suffered from eating sand, and we had to use great care to prevent him getting at it again, he being greatly addicted to the practice; if he were given the smallest opportunity down would go his head and he would be crunching a mouthful of the loose volcanic material.

Grisi was our best looking pony, with a very pretty action and in color a dapple grey; his conduct in the stables, however, was not friendly to the other ponies and we had to build him a separate stall in the far corner, as on the slightest provocation he would lash out with his hind feet. Socks was a pretty little pony, shaped something like a miniature Clydesdale, very willing to work and always very fiery. The last of our remaining ponies, Chinaman, was a strong beast, sulky in appearance, but in reality one of the best of the horses; he also had a penchant for biting through his lead rope, but a chain stopped this. When we first landed we had an idea of not building a stable, as information from people in Siberia suggested that the ponies were able to resist cold unsheltered, but after the first blizzard it was quite obvious that if they were to keep any sort of condition it would be necessary to stable them. A little army of pups used to sleep in the stables during the cold weather, and if by any means a pony got adrift, they at once surrounded him, barking furiously, and the noise conveyed to the night watchman that the outside watchers had observed something wrong. I remember one night that Grisi got free and dashed out of the stables, followed by the whole party of pups, who rounded him up on the Green Park, and after a struggle Mackay secured the truant and brought him back, the dogs following with an air of pride as though conscious of having done their duty.

We had been able to obtain only nine dogs,* five bitches and four dogs, but so prolific were they that before midwinter we had a young family of nine pups, five of these being born on the *Nimrod*. There were many more births, but most of the puppies came to an untimely end, there being a marked difference between the mothers as regards maternal instincts. Gwendoline, known as the "mad bitch," took no care at all of her pups, whilst Daisy not only mothered her own but also a surviving puppy belonging to Gwen, which was taken from her when the culpable carelessness she had exhibited in the rearing of her offspring had resulted in the death of the remainder. The younger pups born at winter quarters did not attain the same size when grown up as did Possum's pups, born on the *Nimrod*. This may be due either to the very cold world they were born into or to the fact that their mothers were much smaller than Possum. The old dogs that we brought were kept tied up except when out for exercise or training in a sledge, for not only did they chase and kill penguins when we had these birds with us, and hunt placid, stupid Weddell seals, but two of the best dogs had a violent antipathy toward each other, and more than once fierce fights took place in consequence. Tripp, one of our dogs, was pure white in color, and was a fine upstanding beast of a very affectionate disposition. Adams looked after Tripp, taking him for his sledge-training, whilst Marshall fancied Scamp, who was an older dog, more set in his bones and with a black-and-white coat. It was between these two that the battles raged, and I think there was little to

*We were agreeably surprised with these dogs, for it must be remembered that their forebears had not lived under polar conditions since 1899, and that none of the animals had experienced antarctic weather, nor had they been trained for the work they had to perform on the ice.

choose between them as far as strength and courage were concerned.

The presence of the dogs around winter quarters and on our walks was very cheerful, and gave a homelike feeling to the place, and our interest in the pups was always fresh, for as they gradually grew up each one developed characteristics and peculiarities of its own. Names were given to them regardless of their sex. Roland, for example, did not belong to the sterner sex, and was in her earlier days a very general favorite. She had a habit of watching for the door to be opened, and then launching herself, a white furry ball, into the midst of the party in the hut. Ambrose, a great big sleepy dog, was so named by Adams, perhaps owing to his portly proportions, which might bear resemblance to the well favored condition of a monk.

All the pups were white, or would have been white if some of them had not elected to sleep in the dustbin where the warm ashes were thrown at night time; indeed, the resting places these little creatures found were varied and remarkable. In cold weather they always gravitated to the light and heat of the stables, but if the temperature was not much below zero, they slept outside, three or four bundled together inside a cork bale, another squeezed into an empty tin, another in the dustbin, and so on. Most of them learned by sad experience the truth of the ancient words!

> Such are the perils that environ
> The man who meddles with cold iron,

for sometimes an agonizing wail would proceed from a puppy and the poor little beast would be found with its tongue frozen fast to a tin in which it had been searching for some succulent remains. I have mentioned the puppies' usefulness in keeping watch on the ponies. They did the same service as regards the older dogs, which were tied up, for if by chance one of these dogs got adrift, he was immediately pursued by a howling mob of puppies; when the larger puppies were eventually chained up, the smaller ones watched them, too, with jealous eye. After enjoying some months of freedom, it seemed to be a terrible thing to the young dogs when first a collar was put on and their freedom was taken from them, and even less did they enjoy the experience of being taken to the sledge and there taught to pull.

Our experience on the *Discovery* expedition, specially during the long southern journey when we had so much trouble with our mixed crowd of dogs, rather prejudiced me against these animals as a means of traction, and we only took them as a standby in the event of the ponies breaking down. Since we were reduced to four ponies, it became necessary to consider the dogs as a possible factor in our work, and so their training was important. Peary's account of his expeditions shows that in the Arctic regions dogs have been able to traverse long distances very quickly. In one instance over ninety miles were accomplished in twenty-three hours, but this evidently had been done on smooth sea ice or on the smooth glaciated surface of the land: such a feat would be impossible on the Antarctic Barrier surface.

CHAPTER IX

The Conquest of Mount Erebus

March 5: Party starts from Winter Quarters to ascend Mount
Erebus: Camp 2750 ft. above Sea level: March 6, altitude
5630 ft. and Depot made: March 7, Fierce Blizzard,
Brocklehurst badly frostbitten: March 8, Camp 11,400 ft.:
March 9, Highest Point reached 13,370 ft.:
Descent safely accomplished

THE arrangement of all the details relating to settling in
our winter quarters, the final touches to the hut, the
building of the pony stables and the meteorological
screen, and the collection of stores, engaged our attention up to March 3. Then we began to seek some outlet
for our energies that would be useful in advancing the
cause of science, and the work of the expedition. I was
very anxious to make a depot to the south for the fur-
therance of our southern journey in the following summer, but the sheet of open water that intervened
between us and Hut Point forbade all progress in that
direction, neither was it possible for us to make a journey toward the western mountains, where the geology
might have been studied with the probability of most
interesting results.

There was one journey possible, a somewhat difficult
undertaking certainly, yet gaining an interest and excitement from that very reason, and this was an attempt to
reach the summit of Mount Erebus. For many reasons
the accomplishment of this work seemed to be desirable.
In the first place the observations of temperature and
wind currents at the summit of this great mountain
would have an important bearing on the movements of
the upper air, a meteorological problem as yet but im-
perfectly understood. From a geological point of view
the mountain ought to reveal some interesting facts, and
apart from scientific considerations, the ascent of a
mountain over 13,000 ft. in height, situated so far south,
would be a matter of pleasurable excitement both to

those who were selected as climbers and to the rest of us who wished for our companions' success. After consideration I decided that Professor David, Mawson, and Mackay should constitute the party that was to try to reach the summit, and they were to be provisioned for ten days. A supporting party, consisting of Adams, Marshall, and Brocklehurst, was to assist the main party as far as feasible. The whole expedition was to be under Adams' charge until he decided that it was time for his party to return, and the Professor was then to be in charge of the advance party. In my written instructions to Adams, he was given the option of going on to the summit if he thought it feasible for his party to push on; and, he actually did so, though the supporting party was not so well equipped for the mountain work as the advance party, and was provisioned for six days only. Instructions were given that the supporting party was not to hamper the main party, especially as regarded the division of provisions, but, as a matter of fact, instead of hampering, the three men became of great assistance to the advance division, and lived entirely on their own stores and equipment during the whole trip. No sooner was it decided to make the ascent, which was arranged for, finally, on March 4, than the winter quarters became busy with the bustle of preparation. There were crampons to be made, food bags to be prepared and filled, sleeping bags to be overhauled, ice axes to be got out and a hundred and one things to be seen to; yet such was the energy thrown into this work that the men were ready for the road and made a start at 8:30 A.M. on the 5th.

In a previous chapter I have described the nature and extent of equipment necessary for a sledging trip, so that it is not necessary now to go into details regarding the preparations for this particular journey, the only variation from the usual standard arrangement being in the matter of quantity of food. In the ascent of a mountain such as Erebus it was obvious that a limit would soon be reached beyond which it would be impossible to use a sledge. To meet these circumstances the advance party had made an arrangement of straps by which their single sleeping bags could be slung in the form of a knapsack upon their backs, and inside the bags the remainder of their equipment could be packed. The men of the supporting party, in case they should journey beyond ice over which they could drag the sledge, had made the same preparations for transferring their load to their shoulders. When they started I must confess that I saw but little prospect of the whole party reaching the top, yet when, from the hut, on the third day out, we saw through Armytage's powerful telescope six tiny black spots slowly crawling up the immense deep snowfield to the base of the rugged rocky spurs that descended to the edge of the field, and when I saw next day out on the skyline the same small figures, I realized that the supporting party were going the whole way. On the return of this expedition Adams and the Professor made a full report, with the help of which I will follow the progress of the party, the members of which were winning their spurs not only on their first Antarctic campaign, but in their first attempt at serious mountaineering.

Mount Erebus bears a name that has loomed large in the history of polar exploration both north and south. Sir James Clark Ross, on January 28, 1841, named the great volcano at whose base our winter quarters were placed after the leading ship of his expedition. The final fate of that ship is linked with the fate of Sir John Franklin and one of the most tragic stories of Arctic exploration, but though both the *Erebus* and *Terror* have sunk far from the scenes of their first exploration, that brilliant period of Antarctic discovery will ever be remembered by the mountains which took their names from those stout ships. Standing as a sentinel at the gate of the Great Ice Barrier, Erebus forms a magnificent picture. The great mountain rises from sea level to an altitude of over 13,000 ft., looking out across the Barrier, with its enormous snow clad bulk towering above the white slopes that run up from the coast. At the top of the mountain an immense depression marks the site of the old crater, and from the side of this rises the active cone, generally marked by steam or smoke. The ascent of such a mountain would be a matter of difficulty in any part of the world, hardly to be attempted without experienced guides, but the difficulties were accentuated by the latitude of Erebus, and the party started off with the full expectation of encountering very low temperatures. The men all recognized, however, the scientific value of the achievement at which they were aiming, and they were determined to do their utmost to reach the crater itself. How they fared and what they found will be told best by extracts from the report which was made to me.

On March 5, after the busy day and night of preparation, the start was made. Breakfast was served at 6 A.M., and one of the eleven foot sledges was packed and lashed, the total weight of the load and sledge being 560 lb. I took a photograph of the party as they started off. They got under way from the hut at a quarter to nine, all hands accompanying them across the rocky ridge at the back of the hut, lifting the sledge and load bodily over this, and then helping the party to pull along the slopes of Back Door Bay across Blue Lake up the eastern slope to the first level. There we said farewell to the mountain party. They first steered straight up a snow slope and skirted closely some rocky ridges and moraines in order to avoid crevassed glaciers. About a mile out and four hundred feet above sea level a glacial moraine barred their path, and they had to portage the sledge over it by slipping ice axes under the load between the runners and bearers of the sledge and lifting it over the obstruction. On the further side of the moraine was a sloping surface of ice and névé on which the sledge capsized for the first time. Light snow was falling, and there was a slight wind. The report supplied to me by Professor David and Adams depicts in a graphic manner these first experiences of this party in sledging.

Pulling the sledge proved fairly heavy work in places; at one spot, on the steep slope of a small glacier, the party had a hard struggle, mostly on their hands and knees, in their efforts to drag the sledge up the surface of smooth blue ice thinly coated with loose snow. This difficulty surmounted, they encountered some sastrugi, which impeded their progress somewhat. "Sastrugi" means wind furrow, and is the name given to those annoying obstacles to sledging, due to the action of the wind on the snow. A blizzard has the effect of scooping out hollows in the snow, and this is especially the case when local currents are set up owing to some rock or point of land interrupting the free run of the wind. These sastrugi vary in depth from two or three inches to three or four feet, according to the position of any rock masses that may be near and to the force of the wind forming them. The raised masses of snow between the hollows are difficult to negotiate with a sledge, especially when they run more or less parallel to the course of the traveler. Though they have many disadvantages, still there are times when their presence is welcome; especially is this the case when the sky is overcast and the low stratus cloud obliterates all landmarks. At these times a dull grey light is over everything, and it is impossible to see the way to steer unless one takes the line of sastrugi and notes the angle it makes with the compass course, the compass for the moment being placed on the snow to obtain the direction. In this way one can steer a fairly accurate course, occasionally verifying it by calling a halt and laying off the course again with the compass, a precaution that is very necessary, for at times the sastrugi alter in direction.

The sledgers, at this particular juncture, had much trouble in keeping their feet, and the usual equanimity of some of the men was disturbed, their remarks upon the subject of sastrugi being audible above the soft pad of the finnesko, the scrunch of the ski boots, and the gentle sawing sound of the sledge runners on the soft snow. About 6 P.M. the party camped at a small nunatak of black rock, about 2750 ft. above sea level and a distance of seven miles from winter quarters. After a good hot dinner they turned into their sleeping bags in the tents and were soon sound asleep. The following morning, when the men got up for breakfast, the temperature was 10° below zero Fahrenheit, whilst at our winter quarters at the same time it was zero. They found, on starting, that the gradient was becoming much steeper, being 1 in 5, and sastrugi, running obliquely to their course, caused the sledge to capsize frequently. The temperature was 8° below zero Fahrenheit, but the pulling was heavy work and kept the travelers warm. They camped that night, March 6, at an altitude of 5630 ft., having traveled only three miles during the whole day, but they had ascended over 2800 ft. above their previous camp. The temperature that night was 28° below zero Fahrenheit. The second camp was in a line with the oldest crater of Erebus, and from the nature of the volcanic fragments lying around, the Professor was of the opinion that Erebus had been producing a little lava within its crater quite recently.

On the following morning Adams decided that the supporting party should make the attempt with the forward party to reach the summit. I had left the decision in this matter to his discretion, but I myself had not considered there would be much chance of the three men of the supporting party gaining the summit, and had not arranged their equipment with that object in view. They were thus handicapped by having a three man sleeping bag, which bulky article one man had to carry; they also were not so well equipped for carrying packs, bits of rope having to act as substitutes for the broad straps provided for the original advance party. The supporting party had no crampons, and so found it more difficult, in places, to get a grip with their feet on the slippery surface of the snow slopes. However, the Professor, who had put bars of leather on his ski boots, found that these answered as well as crampons, and lent the latter to Marshall. Both Adams and the Professor wore ski boots during the whole of the ascent. Skis could not be used for such rough climbing, and had not been taken. All the men were equipped with both finnesko and ski boots and with the necessaries for camping, and individual tastes had been given some latitude in the matter of the clothing worn and carried.

The six men made a depot of the sledge, some of the provisions and part of the cooking utensils at the second camp, and then resumed the climb again. They started off with tent poles amongst other equipment, but after going for half a mile they realized it would be impossible to climb the mountain with these articles, which were taken back to the depot. Each man carried a weight of about 40 lb., the party's gear consisting chiefly of sleeping bags, two tents, cooking apparatus, and provisions for three days. The snow slopes became steeper, and at

one time Mackay, who was cutting steps on the hard
snow with his ice axe, slipped and glissaded with his load
for about a hundred feet, but his further downward career was checked by a projecting ledge of snow, and he
was soon up again. On the third evening, March 7, the
party camped about 8750 ft. above sea level, the temperature at that time being 20° below zero Fahrenheit.

Between 9 and 10 P.M. that night a strong wind sprang
up, and when the men awoke the following morning they
found a fierce blizzard blowing from the southeast. It
increased in fury as the day wore on, and swept with
terrific force down the rocky ravine where they were
camped. The whirling snow was so dense and the roaring
wind so loud that, although the two sections were only
about ten yards apart, they could neither see nor hear
each other. Being without tent poles, the tents were just
doubled over the top ends of the sleeping bags so as to
protect the openings from the drifting snow, but, in spite
of this precaution, a great deal of snow found its way
into the bags. In the afternoon Brocklehurst emerged
from the three man sleeping bag, and instantly a fierce
gust whirled away one of his wolfskin mits; he dashed
after it, and the force of the wind swept him some way
down the ravine. Adams, who had left the bag at the
same time as Brocklehurst, saw the latter vanish suddenly, and in endeavoring to return to the bag to fetch
Marshall to assist in finding Brocklehurst he also was
blown down by the wind. Meanwhile, Marshall, the only
remaining occupant of the bag, had much ado to keep
himself from being blown, sleeping bag and all, down
the ravine. Adams had just succeeded in reaching the
sleeping bag on his hands and knees when Brocklehurst
appeared, also on his hands and knees, having, by desperate efforts, pulled himself back over the rocks. It was
a close call for he was all but completely gone, so biting
was the cold, before he reached the haven of the sleeping bag. He and Adams crawled in, and then, as the bag
had been much twisted up and drifted with snow while
Marshall had been holding it down, Adams and Marshall
got out to try and straighten it out. The attempt was not
very successful, as they were numb with cold and the
bag, with only one person inside, blew about, so they got

into it again. Shortly afterwards Adams made another attempt, and whilst he was working at it the wind got inside the bag, blowing it open right way up. Adams promptly got in again, and the adventure thus ended satisfactorily. The men could do nothing now but lie low whilst the blizzard lasted. At times they munched a plasmon biscuit or some chocolate. They had nothing to drink all that day, March 8, and during the following night, as it would have been impossible to have kept a lamp alight to thaw out the snow. They got some sleep during the night in spite of the storm. On awaking at 4 A.M. the following day, the travelers found that the blizzard was over, so, after breakfast, they started away again at about 5:30 A.M.

The angle of ascent was now steeper than ever, being thirty-four degrees, that is, a rise of 1 in 1½. As the hard snow slopes were much too steep to climb without cutting steps with an ice axe, they kept as much as possible to the bare rocks. Occasionally the arête would terminate upward in a large snow slope, and when this was the case they cut steps across the slope to any other bare rocks which seemed to persist for some distance in an upward direction. Brocklehurst, who was wearing ski boots, began to feel the cold attacking his feet, but did not think it was serious enough to change into finnesko. At noon they found a fair camping ground, and made some tea. They were, at this time, some 800 ft. below the rim of the old crater and were feeling the effects of the high altitude and the extreme cold. Below them was a magnificent panorama of clouds, coast and Barrier snow, but they could not afford to spend much time admiring it. After a hasty meal they tackled the ascent again. When they were a little distance from the top of the rim of the main crater, Mackay elected to work his way alone with his ice axe up a long and very steep névé slope instead of following the less difficult and safer route by the rocks where the rest of the party were proceeding. He passed out of sight, and then the others heard him call out that he was getting weak and did not think he could carry on much longer. They made haste to the top of the ridge, and Marshall and the Professor dropped to the point where he was likely to be found.

Happily, they met him coming toward them, and Marshall took his load, for he looked much done up. It appeared that Mackay had found the work of cutting steps with his heavy load more difficult than he had anticipated, and he only just managed to reach safety when he fell and fainted. No doubt this was due, in part, to mountain sickness, which, under the severe conditions and at the high altitude the party had attained, also affected Brocklehurst.

Having found a camping place, they dropped their loads, and the members of the party were at leisure to observe the nature of their surroundings. They had imagined an even plain of névé or glacier ice filling the extinct crater to the brim and sloping up gradually to the active cone at its southern end, but instead of this they found themselves on the very brink of a precipice of black rock, forming the inner edge of the old crater. This wall of dark lava was mostly vertical, while, in some places, it overhung, and was from eighty to a hundred feet in height. The base of the cliff was separated from the snow plain beyond by a deep ditch like a huge dry moat, which was evidently due to the action of blizzards. These winds, striking fiercely from the southeast against the great inner wall of the old crater, had given rise to a powerful back eddy at the edge of the cliff, and it was this eddy which had scooped out the deep trench in the hard snow. The trench was from thirty to forty feet deep, and was bounded by more or less vertical sides. Around our winter quarters any isolated rock or cliff face that faced the southeast blizzard wind exhibited a similar phenomenon, though, of course, on a much smaller scale. Beyond the wall and trench was an extensive snow field with the active cone and crater at its southern end, the latter emitting great volumes of steam, but what surprised the travelers most were the extraordinary structures which rose here and there above the surface of the snow field. They were in the form of mounds and pinnacles of the most varied and fantastic appearance. Some resembled beehives, others were like huge ventilating cowls, others like isolated turrets, and others again resembled various animals in shape. The men were unable at first sight to understand the origin of these remarkable structures, and as it was time for food, they left the closer investigation for later in the day.

As they walked along the rampart of the old crater wall to find a camping ground, their figures were thrown up against the skyline, and down at our winter quarters they were seen by us, having been sighted by Armytage with his telescope. He had followed the party for the first two days with the glasses, but they were lost to view when they began to work through the rocky ground, and it was just on the crater edge that they were picked up again by the telescope.

The camp chosen for the meal was in a little rocky gully on the northwest slope of the main cone, and about fifty feet below the rim of the old crater. Whilst some cooked the meal, Marshall examined Brocklehurst's feet, as the latter stated that for some time past he had lost all feeling in them. When his ski boots and socks had been taken off, it was found that both his big toes were black, and that four more toes, though less severely affected, were also frostbitten. From their appearance it was evident that some hours must have elapsed since this had occurred. Marshall and Mackay set at work at once to restore circulation in the feet by warming and chafing them. Their efforts were, under the circumstances, fairly successful, but it was clear that ultimate recovery from so severe a frostbite would be both slow and tedious. Brocklehurst's feet, having been thoroughly warmed, were put into dry socks and finnesko stuffed with sennegrass, and then all hands went to lunch at 3:30 P.M. It must have required great pluck and determination on his part to have climbed almost continuously for nine hours up the steep and difficult track they had followed with his feet so badly frostbitten. After lunch Brocklehurst was left safely tucked up in the three-man sleeping bag, and the remaining five members of the party started off to explore the floor of the old crater. Ascending to the crater rim, they climbed along it until they came to a spot where there was a practicable breach in the crater wall and where a narrow tongue of snow bridged the névé trench at its base.

They all roped up directly they arrived on the hard snow in the crater and advanced cautiously over the

snow plain, keeping a sharp lookout for crevasses. They
steered for some of the remarkable mounds already
mentioned, and when the nearest was reached and examined, they noticed some curious hollows, like partly
roofed-in drains, running toward the mound. Pushing on
slowly, they reached eventually a small parasitic cone,
about 1000 ft. above the level of their camp, and over a
mile distant from it. Sticking out from under the snow
were lumps of lava, large feldspar crystals, from one to
three inches in length, and fragments of pumice; both
feldspar and pumice were in many cases coated with
sulphur. Having made as complete an examination as
time permitted, they started to return to camp, no longer
roped together, as they had not met any definite crevasses on their way out. They directed their steps toward
one of the ice mounds, which bore a whimsical resemblance to a lion couchant, and from which smoke appeared to be issuing. To the Professor the origin of these
peculiar structures was now no longer a mystery, for he
recognized that they were the outward and visible signs
of fumaroles. In ordinary climates, a fumarole, or volcanic vapor well, may be detected by the thin cloud of
steam above it, and usually one can at once feel the
warmth by passing one's hand into the vapor column,
but in the rigor of the Antarctic climate the fumaroles
of Erebus have their vapor turned into ice as soon as it
reaches the surface of the snow plain. Thus ice mounds,
somewhat similar in shape to the sinter mounds formed
by the geysers of New Zealand, of Iceland and of Yel-
lowstone Park, are built up round the orifices of the
fumaroles of Erebus. Whilst exploring one of these fumaroles, Mackay fell suddenly up to his thighs into one
of its concealed conduits, and only saved himself from
falling in deeper still by means of his ice axe. Marshall
had a similar experience at about the same time.

The party arrived at camp shortly after 6 P.M., and
found Brocklehurst progressing as well as could be expected. They sat on the rocks after tea admiring the
glorious view to the west. Below them was a vast rolling
sea of cumulus cloud, and far away the western mountains glowed in the setting sun. Next morning, when they
got up at 4 A.M., they had a splendid view of the shadow

of Erebus projected on the field of cumulus cloud below them by the rising sun. Every detail of the profile of the mountain as outlined on the clouds could readily be recognized. After breakfast, while Marshall was attending to Brocklehurst's feet, the hypsometer, which had become frozen on the way up, was thawed out and a determination of the boiling-point made. This, when reduced and combined with the mean of the aneroid levels, made the altitude of the old crater rim, just above the camp, 11,400 ft. At 6 A.M. the party left the camp and made all speed to reach the summit of the present crater. On their way across the old crater, Mawson photographed the fumarole that resembled the lion and also took a view of the active crater about one and a half miles distant, though there was considerable difficulty in taking photographs owing to the focal plane shutter having become jammed by frost. Near the furthest point reached by the travelers on the preceding afternoon they observed several patches of yellow ice and found on examination that the color was due to sulphur. They next ascended several rather steep slopes formed of alternating beds of hard snow and vast quantities of large and perfect feldspar crystals, mixed with pumice. A little farther on they reached the base of the volcano's active cone. Their progress was now painfully slow, as the altitude and cold combined to make respiration difficult. The cone of Erebus is built up chiefly of blocks of pumice, from a few inches to a few feet in diameter. Externally these were gray or often yellow owing to incrustations of sulphur, but when broken they were of a resinous brown color. At last, a little after 10 A.M., on March 10, the edge of the active crater was reached, and the little party stood on the summit of Erebus, the first men to conquer perhaps the most remarkable summit in the world. They had traveled about two and a half miles from the last camp, and had ascended just 2000 ft., and this journey had taken them over four hours, The report describes most vividly the magnificent and awe-inspiring scene before them.

"We stood on the verge of a vast abyss, and at first could see neither to the bottom nor across it on account of the huge mass of steam filling the crater and soaring aloft in a column 500 to 1000 ft. high. After a continuous loud hissing sound, lasting for some minutes, there would come from below a big dull boom, and immediately great globular masses of steam would rush upwards to swell the volume of the snow-white cloud which ever sways over the crater. This phenomenon recurred at intervals during the whole of our stay at the crater. Meanwhile, the air around us was extremely redolent of burning sulphur. Presently a pleasant northerly breeze fanned away the steam cloud, and at once the whole crater stood revealed to us in all its vast extent and depth. Mawson's angular measurement made the depth 900 ft. and the greatest width about half a mile. There were at least three well defined openings at the bottom of the cauldron, and it was from these that the steam explosions proceeded. Near the southwest portion of the crater there was an immense rift in the rim, perhaps 300 to 400 ft. deep. The crater wall opposite the one at the top of which we were standing presented features of special interest. Beds of dark pumiceous lava or pumice alternated with white zones of snow. There was no direct evidence that the snow was bedded with the lava, though it was possible that such may have been the case. From the top of one of the thickest of the lava or pumice beds, just where it touched the belt of snow, there rose scores of small steam jets all in a row. They were too numerous and too close together to have been each an independent fumarole; the appearance was rather suggestive of the snow being converted into steam by the heat of the layer of rock immediately below it."

While at the crater's edge the party made a boiling point determination by the hypsometer, but the result was not so satisfactory as that made earlier in the morning at the camp. As the result of averaging aneroid levels, together with the hypsometer determination at the top of the old crater, Erebus may be calculated to rise to a height of 13,370 ft. above sea level. As soon as the measurements had been made and some photographs had been taken by Mawson, the party returned to the camp, as it had been decided to descend to the base of the main cone that day, a drop of 8000 ft.

On the way back a traverse was made of the main

crater and levels taken for constructing a geological section. Numerous specimens of the unique feldspar crystals and of the pumice and sulphur were collected. On arriving in camp the travelers made a hasty meal, packed up, shouldered their burdens once more and started down the steep mountain slope. Brocklehurst insisted on carrying his own heavy load in spite of his frostbitten feet. They followed a course a little to the west of the one they took when ascending. The rock was rubbly and kept slipping under their feet, so that falls were frequent. After descending a few hundred feet they found that the rubbly spur of rock down which they were floundering ended abruptly in a long and steep névé slope. Three courses were now open to them: they could retrace their steps to the point above them where the rocky spur had deviated from the main arête; cut steps across the névé slope; or glissade down some five or six hundred feet to a rocky ledge below. In their tired state preference was given to the path of least resistance, which was offered by the glissade, and they therefore rearranged their loads so that they would roll down easily. They were now very thirsty, but they found that if they gathered a little snow, squeezed it into a ball and placed it on the surface of a piece of rock, it melted at once almost on account of the heat of the sun and thus they obtained a makeshift drink. They launched their loads down the slope and watched them as they bumped and bounded over the wavy ridges of névé. Brocklehurst's load, which contained the cooking utensils, made the noisiest descent, and the aluminum cookers were much battered when they finally fetched up against the rocks below. Then the members of the party, grasping their ice axes firmly, followed their gear. As they gathered speed on the downward course and the chisel edge of the ice axe bit deeper into the hard névé, their necks and faces were sprayed with a shower of ice. All reached the bottom of the slope safely, and they repeated this glissade down each succeeding snow slope toward the foot of the main cone. Here and there they bumped heavily on hard sastrugi and both clothes and equipment suffered in the rapid descent; unfortunately also, one of the aneroids was lost and one of the hypsometer thermometers bro-

ken. At last the slope flattened out to the gently inclined
terrace where the depot lay, and they reached it by walking. Altogether they had dropped down 5000 ft. between
three in the afternoon and seven in the evening.

Adams and Marshall were the first to reach the depot,
the rest of the party, with the exception of Brocklehurst,
having made a detour to the left in consequence of having to pursue some lost luggage in that direction. At the
depot they found that the blizzard of the 8th had played
havoc with their gear, for the sledge had been overturned and some of the load scattered to a distance and
partly covered with drift snow. After dumping their
packs, Adams and Marshall went to meet Brocklehurst,
for they noticed that a slight blizzard was springing up.
Fortunately, the wind soon died down, the weather
cleared, and the three were able to regain the camp. Tea
was got ready, and the remainder of the party arrived
about 10 P.M. They camped that night at the depot and
at 3 A.M. next day got up to breakfast. After breakfast
a hunt was made for some articles that were still missing,
and then the sledge was packed and the march homeward commenced at 5:30 A.M. They now found that the
sastrugi caused by the late blizzard were very trouble-
some, as the ridges were from four to five feet above
the hollows and lay at an oblique angle to the course.
Rope brakes were put on the sledge runners, and two
men went in front to pull when necessary, while two
steadied the sledge, and two were stationed behind
to pull back when required. It was more than trying to
carry on at this juncture, for the sledge either refused to
move or suddenly it took charge and overran those who
were dragging it, and capsizes occurred every few minutes. Owing to the slippery nature of the ground some
members of the party who had not crampons or barred
ski boots were badly shaken up, for they sustained numerous sudden falls. One has to experience a surface
like this to realize how severe a jar a fall entails. The
only civilized experience that is akin to it is when one
steps unknowingly on a slide which some small street
boy has made on the pavement. Marshall devised the
best means of assisting the progress of the sledge. When
it took charge he jumped on behind and steered it with

his legs as it bumped and jolted over the sastrugi, but
he found sometimes that his thirteen stone weight did
not prevent him from being bucked right over the sledge
and flung on the névé on the other side.

They reached the nunatak where they had made their
first camp on the way up, six miles distant from Cape
Royds, at about 7:30 A.M. By this time there was every
symptom of the approach of a blizzard, and the snow
was beginning to drift before a gusty southeasterly wind.
This threatened soon to cut them off from all view of
the winter quarters. They were beginning to feel very
tired, one of the tents had a large hole burned in it, the
oil supply was almost done, and one of the primus stoves
had been put out of action as the result of the glissade;
so, in the circumstances, they decided to make a dash
for Cape Royds, leaving their sledge and equipment to
be picked up later. In the gray uncertain light the sastrugi did not show up in relief, and every few feet some
member of the party stumbled and fell, sprawling over
the snow. At last their eyes were gladdened by the shining surface of the Blue Lake only half a mile distant
from winter quarters. Now that the haven was at hand,
and the stress and strain over, their legs grew heavy and
leaden, and that last half mile seemed one of the hardest
they had covered. It was fortunate that the weather did
not become worse.

Meanwhile, at winter quarters, we had been very busy
opening cases and getting things shipshape outside, with
the result that the cubicles of the absentees were more
or less filled with a general accumulation of stores. When
Armytage reported that he saw the party on their way
down the day before they arrived at the hut, we decided
to make the cubicles tidy for the travelers. We had just
begun on the Professor's cubicle when, about 11 A.M. I
left the hut for a moment and was astonished to see
within thirty yards of me, coming over the brow of the
ridge by the hut, six slowly moving figures. I ran toward
them shouting: "Did you get to the top?" There was no
answer, and I asked again. Adams pointed with his hand
upward, but this did not satisfy me, so I repeated my
question. Then Adams said: "Yes," and I ran back to the
hut and shouted to the others, who all came streaming

out to cheer the successful venturers. We shook hands all around and opened some champagne, which tasted like nectar to the wayworn people. Marshall prescribed a dose to us stay-at-home ones, so that we might be able to listen quietly to the tale the party had to tell.

Except to Joyce, Wild, and myself, who had seen similar things on the former expedition, the eating and drinking capacity of the returned party was a matter of astonishment. In a few minutes Roberts had produced a great saucepan of Quaker oats and milk, the contents of which disappeared in a moment, to be followed by the greater part of a fresh cut ham and homemade bread, with New Zealand fresh butter. The six had evidently found on the slopes of Erebus six fully developed, polar sledging appetites. The meal at last ended, came more talk, smokes and then bed for the weary travelers.

After some days' delay on account of unfavorable weather, a party consisting of Adams, the Professor, Armytage, Joyce, Wild and Marshall, equipped with a seven-foot sledge, tent, and provisions, as a precaution against possible bad weather, started out to fetch in the eleven-foot sledge with the explorers' equipment. After a heavy pull over the soft, new-fallen snow, in cloudy weather, with the temperature at midday 29° below zero Fahrenheit, and with a stiff wind blowing from the southeast, they sighted the nunatak, recovered the abandoned sledge and placing the smaller one on top, pulled them both back as far as Blue Lake. I went out to meet the party, and we left the sledge at Blue Lake until the following day, when two of the Manchurian ponies were harnessed to the sledges and the gear was brought into winter quarters.

Professor David gave me a short summary of the scientific results of the ascent, from which I have made the following extracts:

"Among the scientific results may be mentioned the calculation of the height of the mountain. Sir Jas. C. Ross in 1841 estimated the height to be 12,367 ft. The National Antarctic Expedition, 1901, determined its height at first to be 13,120 ft., but this was subsequently altered to 12,922 ft., the height now given on the Admiralty Chart of this region. Our observations for altitude were made partly with aneroids and partly with a hypsometer. All the aneroid levels and hypsometer observations have been calculated by means of simultaneous readings of the barometer taken at our winter quarters, Cape Royds. These observations show that the rim of the second or main crater of Erebus is about 11,350 ft. above sea level and that the summit of the active crater is about 13,350 ft. above sea level. The fact may be emphasized that in both the methods adopted by us for estimating the altitude of the mountain, atmospheric pressure was the sole factor on which we relied. The determination arrived at by the *Discovery* was based on measurements made with a theodolite from sea level. It is, of course, quite possible that Ross' original estimate may have been correct, as this native volcano may have increased in height by about a thousand feet during the sixty-seven years which have elapsed since his expedition.

"As regards the geological structure of Erebus, there is evidence of the existence of four superimposed craters. The oldest and lowest, and at the same time the largest, of these attained an altitude of between 6000 and 7000 ft. above sea level, and was fully six miles in diameter: the second rises to 11,350 ft. and has a diameter of over two miles: the third crater rises to a height of fully 12,200 ft.; and its former outline has now been almost obliterated by the material of the modern active cone and crater. The latter, which rises about 800 ft. above the former, is composed chiefly of fragments of pumice. These vary in size from an inch or so to a yard in diameter. Quantities of feldspar crystals are interspersed with them, and both are encrusted with sulphur.

"The active crater measures about half a mile by one-third of a mile in diameter, and is about 900 ft. in depth. The active crater of Erebus is about three times as deep as that of Vesuvius. The fresh volcanic bombs picked up by us at spots four miles distant from the crater and lying on the surface of comparatively new snow are evidences that Erebus has recently been projecting lava to great heights.

"Two features in the geology of Erebus which are specially distinctive are: the vast quantities of large and perfect feldspar crystals, and the ice fumaroles. The crystals are from two or three inches in length; many of them have had their angles and edges slightly rounded by attrition, but numbers of them are beautifully perfect.

"Its remarkable crystals, rare lavas and unique fumaroles are some of its most interesting geological features: it served as a gigantic tide gauge to record the flood level of the greatest recent glaciation of Antarctica, when the whole of Ross Island was but a nunatak in a gigantic field of ice.

"Its situation between the belt of polar calms and the South Pole; its isolation from the disturbing influence of large land masses; its great height, which enables it to penetrate the whole system of atmospheric circulation, and the constant steam cloud at its summit, swinging to and fro like a huge wind vane, combine to make Erebus one of the most interesting places on earth to the meteorologist."

CHAPTER X

Winter Quarters During Polar Night 1908
Notes on Spring Sledging Journeys

Meteorological Observations: The Anemometer: Night
Watchman's Duties: Fierce Blizzard on March 13:
Preliminary Journey on the Barrier Surface starts August 12:
Hut Point reached August 14: Party starts for Hut Point
on September 1, to leave there some Gear and Provisions in
readiness for the Southern Journey

AFTER the journey to the summit of Erebus we began
to settle down and prepare for the long winter months
that were rapidly approaching. Already the nights were
lengthening and stars becoming familiar objects in the
sky. Our main work was to secure the hut firmly against
possible damage from the southeast blizzards. After everything had been made safe as far as it lay in our
power, we felt that if anything untoward happened it
would not be our fault, so we turned our attention to
the scientific studies that lay to our hand. As we were
only a small party, it was impossible for all of us to carry
on scientific work and, at the same time, attend to what
I might call the household duties. It was the most important for the geologists of the expedition to get as far
afield as practicable before the winter night closed in on
us, so every day both the Professor and Priestley were
out early and late, with their collecting bags and geological hammers, finding on every successive trip they made
within a radius of three or four miles of the winter quarters new and interesting geological specimens, the examination of which would give them plenty of work in the
winter months. Scattered around Cape Royds were large
numbers of granite boulders of every size and color, deposited there by the great receding ice sheet that once
filled McMurdo Sound and covered the lower slopes of
Erebus. The geologists were full of delight that circumstances should have placed our winter quarters at a spot

133

so fruitful for their labors. Murray was equally pleased
at the prospect of the biological work which lay before
him, for hardly a day passed without someone bringing
in a report of the existence of another lake or tarn, and
soon we realized that around us lay more than a dozen
of these lakelets which might possibly prove a fruitful
field for biological study. To Mawson the many varied
forms of ice and snow, both in the lakes and on the
surrounding hills, gave promise of encouraging results
in that branch of physics in which he was particularly
interested. The lengthening nights also gave us indications that the mysterious Aurora Australis would soon
be waving its curtains and beams over our winter quarters, and as information on this phenomenon was greatly
needed, Mawson made preparations for recording the
displays.

The meteorological screen had been set up and observations begun before the Erebus party left. Now that all
hands were back at the hut, a regular system of recording the observations was arranged. Adams, who was
the meteorologist of the expedition, took all the observations from 8 A.M. to 8 P.M. The night watchman took
them from 10 P.M. to 6 A.M. These observations were
taken every two hours, and it may interest the reader to
learn what was done in this way, though I do not wish
to enter here into a lengthy dissertation on meteorology.
The observations on air temperature, wind, and direction
of cloud have an important bearing on similar observations taken in more temperate climes, and in a place like
the Antarctic, where up till now our knowledge has been
so meager, it was most essential that every bit of information bearing on meteorological phenomena should be
noted. We were in a peculiarly favorable position for observing not only the changes that took place in the lower
atmosphere but also those which took place in the higher
strata of the atmosphere. Erebus, with steam and smoke
always hanging above it, indicated by the direction assumed by the cloud what the upper air currents were doing,
and thus we were in touch with an excellent high level
observatory.

The instruments under Adams' care were as complete
as financial considerations had permitted. The meteoro-

logical screen contained a maximum thermometer, that is, a thermometer which indicates the highest temperature reached during the period elapsing between two observations. It is so constructed that when the mercury rises in the tube it remains at its highest point, though the temperature might fall greatly shortly afterward. After reading the recorded height, the thermometer is shaken, and this operation causes the mercury to drop to the actual temperature obtaining at the moment of observation; the thermometer is then put back into the screen and is all ready for the next reading taken two hours later. A minimum thermometer registered the lowest temperature that occurred between the two hourly readings, but this thermometer was not a mercury one, as mercury freezes at a temperature of about 39° below zero, and we therefore used spirit thermometers. When the temperature drops the surface of the column of spirit draws down a little black indicator immersed in it, and if the temperature rises and the spirit advances in consequence, the spirit flows past the indicator, which remains at the lowest point, and on the observations being taken its position is read on the graduated scale. By these instruments we were always able to ascertain what the highest temperature and what the lowest temperature had been throughout the two hours during which the observation screen had not been visited. In addition to the maximum and minimum thermometers, there were the wet and dry bulb thermometers. The dry bulb records the actual temperature of the air at the moment, and we used a spirit thermometer for this purpose. The wet bulb consisted of an ordinary thermometer, around the bulb of which was tied a little piece of muslin that had been dipped in water and of course froze at once on exposure to the air. The effect of the evaporation from the ice which covered the bulb was to cause the temperature recorded to be lower than that recorded by the dry bulb thermometer in proportion to the amount of water present in the atmosphere at the time. To ensure accuracy the wet bulb thermometers were changed every two hours, the thermometer which was read being brought back to the hut and returned to the screen later freshly sheathed in ice. It was, of course, impossible to wet the exposed thermometer with a brush dipped in water, as is the practice in temperate climates, for water could not be carried from the hut to the screen without freezing into solid ice. To check the thermometers there was also kept in the screen a self-recording thermometer, or thermograph. This is a delicate instrument fitted with metal discs, which expand or contract readily with every fluctuation of the temperature. Attached to these discs is a delicately poised lever carrying a pen charged with ink, and the point of this pen rests against a graduated roll of paper fastened to a drum, which is revolved by clockwork once in every seven days. The pen thus draws a line on the paper, rising and falling in sympathy with the changes in the temperature of the air.

All these instruments were contained inside the meteorological screen, which was so constructed that while there was free access of air, the wind could not strike through it with any violence, neither could the sun throw its direct beams on the sensitive thermometers inside. On the flat top of the screen were nailed two pieces of wood in the form of a cross, the long axis of which lay in the true meridian, that is, one end pointing due south, the other end due north. On a small rod attached to the fore end of the screen was a vane that floated out in the opposite direction to that from which the wind was blowing, and by reference to the vane and the cross the direction of the wind was ascertained and noted when the other observations were taken. To record the force of the wind and the number of miles it traveled between each observation, there was an instrument called an anemometer, which rested on one of the uprights supporting the meteorological screen; the type of anemometer used by the expedition is known as the "Robinson." It consists of four cups or hemispheres revolving on a pivot which communicates by a series of cogs with a dial having two hands like the hands of a watch. The long hand makes one revolution and records five miles, and the smaller hand records up to five hundred miles. At a glance we could thus tell the number of miles the wind had blown during the time elapsing between successive observations. In ordinary climates the work of reading these instruments was a matter of little difficulty and only took a few minutes, but in the Antarctic, especially when a blizzard was blowing, the difficulty was much increased and the strong wind often blew out the hurricane lamp which was used to read the instruments in the darkness. On these occasions the unfortunate observer had to return to the hut, relight the lamp and again struggle up the windy ridge to the screen.

In addition to the meteorological screen, there was another erection built on the top of the highest ridge by Mawson, who placed there an anemometer of his own construction to register the strength of the heaviest gusts of wind during a blizzard. We found that the squalls frequently blew with a force of over a hundred miles an hour. There remained still one more outdoor instrument connected with weather observation, that was the snow gauge. The Professor, by utilizing some spare lengths of stove chimney, erected a snow gauge into which was collected the falling snow whenever a blizzard blew. The snow was afterward taken into the hut in the vessel into which it had been deposited, and when it was melted down we were able to calculate fairly accurately the amount of the snowfall. This observation was an important one, for much depends on the amount of precipitation in the Antarctic regions. It is on the precipitation in the form of snow, and on the rate of evaporation, the calculations regarding the formation of the huge snow fields and glaciers depend. We secured our information regarding the rate of evaporation by suspending measured cubes of ice and snow from rods projecting at the side of the hut, where they were free from the influence of the interior warmth. Inside the hut was kept a standard mercurial barometer, which was also read every two hours, and in addition to this there was a barograph which registered the varying pressure of the atmosphere in a curve for a week at a time. Every Monday morning Adams changed the paper on both thermograph and barograph, and every day recorded the observations in the meteorological log. It will be seen that the meteorologist had plenty to occupy his time, and generally when the men came in from a walk they had some information to record.

As soon as the ice was strong enough to bear in the

bay, Murray commenced his operations there. His object
was the collection of the different marine creatures that
rest on the bottom of the sea or creep about there, and
he made extensive preparations for their capture. A hole
was dug through the ice, and a trap let down to the
bottom; this trap was baited with a piece of penguin or
seal, and the shellfish, crustacea and other marine animals found their way in through the opening in the top,
and the trap was usually left down for a couple of days.
When it was hauled up, the contents were transferred to
a tin containing water, and then taken to the hut and
thawed out, for the contents always froze during the
quarter of a mile walk homeward. As soon as the animals thawed out they were sorted into bottles and then
killed by various chemicals, put into spirits and bottled
up for examination when they reached England. Later
on Murray found that the trap business was not fruitful
enough, so whenever a crack opened in the bay ice, a
line was let down, one end being made fast at one end
of the crack, and the length of the line allowed to sink
in the water horizontally for a distance of sixty yards. A
hole was dug at each end of the line and a small dredge
was let down and pulled along the bottom, being hauled
up through the hole at the far end. By this means much
richer collections were made, and rarely did the dredge
come up without some interesting specimens. When the
crack froze over again, the work could still be continued
so long as the ice was broken at each end of the line,
and Priestley for a long time acted as Murray's assistant,
helping him to open the holes and pull the dredge.

When we took our walks abroad, every one kept his
eyes open for any interesting specimen of rock or any
signs of plant life, and Murray was greatly pleased one
day when we brought back some moss. This was found
in a fairly sheltered spot beyond Back Door Bay and
was the only specimen that we obtained in the neighborhood of the winter quarters before the departure of the
sun. Occasionally we came across a small lichen and
some curious algae growing in the volcanic earth, but
these measured the extent of the terrestrial vegetation
in this latitude. In the north polar regions, in a corresponding latitude, there are eighteen different kinds of

flowering plants, and there even exists a small stunted tree, a species of willow.

Although terrestrial vegetation is so scanty in the Antarctic, the same cannot be said of the subaqueous plant life. When we first arrived and some of us walked across the north shore of Cape Royds, we saw a great deal of open water in the lakes, and a little later, when all these lakes were frozen over, we walked across them, and looking down through the clear ice, could see masses of brilliantly colored algae and fungi. The investigation of the plant life in the lakes was one of the principal things undertaken by Murray, Priestley, and the Professor during the winter months.

After the Erebus party returned, a regular winter routine was arranged for the camp. Brocklehurst took no part in the duties at this time, for his frostbitten foot prevented his moving about, and shortly after his return Marshall saw that it would be necessary to amputate at least part of the big toe. The rest of the party all had a certain amount of work for the common weal, apart from their own scientific duties. From the time we arrived we always had a night watchman, and we now took turns to carry out this important duty. Roberts was exempt from night watchman's duties, as he was busy with the cooking all day, so for the greater part of the winter every thirteenth night each member took the night watch. The ten o'clock observations was the night watchman's first duty, and from that hour till nine o'clock next morning he was responsible for the well being and care of the hut, ponies, and dogs. His most important duties were the two hourly meteorological observations, the upkeep of the fire and the care of the acetylene gas plant. The fire was kept going all through the night, and hot water was ready for making the breakfast when Roberts was called at 7:30 in the morning. The night watch was by no means an unpleasant duty, and gave each of us an opportunity, when his turn came around of washing clothes, darning socks, writing and doing little odd jobs which could not receive much attention during the day. The night watchman generally took his bath either once a fortnight or once a month, as his inclination prompted him.

Some individuals had a regular program which they adhered to strictly. For instance, one member, directly the rest of the staff had gone to bed, cleared the small table in front of the stove, spread a rug on it and settled down to a complicated game of patience, having first armed himself with a supply of coffee against the wiles of the drowsy god. After the regulation number of games had been played, the despatch box was opened, and letters, private papers and odds and ends were carefully inspected and replaced in their proper order, after which the journal was written up. These important matters over, a ponderous book on historical subjects received its share of attention.

Socks were the only articles of clothing that had constantly to be repaired, and various were the expedients used to replace the heels, which, owing to the hard footgear, were always showing gaping holes. These holes had to be constantly covered, for we were not possessed of an unlimited number of any sort of clothes, and many and varied were the patches. Some men used thin leather, others canvas, and others again a sort of coarse flannel to sew on instead of darning the heels of the socks. Toward the end of the winter, the wardrobes of the various members of the expedition were in a very patched condition.

During the earlier months the night watchman was kept pretty busy, for the ponies took a long time to get used to the stable and often tried to break loose and upset things out there generally. These sudden noises took the watchman out frequently during the night, and it was a comfort to us when the animals at least learned to keep fairly quiet in their stable. The individual was fortunate who obtained a good bag of coal for his night watch, with plenty of lumps in it, for there was then no difficulty in keeping the temperature of the hut up to 40° Fahrenheit, but a great deal of our coal was very fine and caused much trouble during the night. To meet this difficulty we had recourse to lumps of seal blubber, the watchman generally laying in a stock for himself before his turn came for night duty. When placed on top of the hot coal the blubber burned fiercely, and it was a comfort to know that with the large supply of seals that could easily be obtained in these latitudes, no expedition need fear the lack of emergency fuel. There was no perceptible smell from the blubber in burning, though fumes came from the bit of hairy hide generally attached to it. The thickness of the blubber varied from two to four inches. Some watchmen during the night felt disinclined to do anything but read and take the observations, and I was amongst this number, for though I often made plans and resolutions as to washing and other necessary jobs, when the time came, these plans fell through, with the exception of the bath.

Toward the middle of winter some of our party stayed up later than during the time when there was more work outside, and there gradually grew into existence an institution know as eleven o'clock tea. The Professor was greatly attached to his cup of tea and generally undertook the work of making it for men who were still out of bed. Some of us preferred a cup of hot fresh milk, which was easily made from the excellent dried milk of which we had a large quantity. By one o'clock in the morning, however, nearly all the occupants of the hut were wrapped in deep and more or less noisy slumber. Some had a habit of talking in their sleep, and their fitful phrases were carefully treasured up by the night watchman for retailing at the breakfast table next morning; sometimes also the dreams of the night before were told by the dreamer to his own great enjoyment, if not to that of his audience. About five o'clock in the morning came the most trying time for the watchman. Then one's eyes grew heavy and leaden, and it took a deal of effort to prevent oneself from falling fast asleep. Some of us went in for cooking more or less elaborate meals. Marshall, who had been to a school of cookery before we left England, turned out some quite respectable bread and cakes. Though people jeered at the latter when placed on the table, one noticed that next day there were never any left. At 7:30 A.M. Roberts was called, and the watchman's night was nearly over. At this hour also Armytage or Mackay was called to look after the feeding of the ponies, but before midwinter day Armytage had taken over the entire responsibility of the stables and ponies, and he was the only one to get up.

At 8:30 A.M. all hands were called, special attention being paid to turning out the messman for the day, and after some minutes of luxurious half wakefulness, people began to get up, expressing their opinions forcibly if the temperature of the hut was below freezing point, and informing the night watchman of his affinity to Jonah if his report was that it was a windy morning. Dressing was for some of the men a very simple affair, consisting merely in putting on their boots and giving themselves a shake; others, who undressed entirely, got out of their pajamas into their cold underclothing. At a quarter to nine the call came to let down the table from its position near the roof, and the messman then bundled the knives, forks and spoons on to the board, and at nine o'clock sharp every one sat down to breakfast.

The night watchman's duties were over for a fortnight, and the messman took on his work. The duties of the messman were more onerous than those of the night watchman. He began, as I have stated, by laying the table—a simple operation owing to the primitive conditions under which we lived. He then garnished this with three or four sorts of hot sauces to tickle the tough palates of some of our party. At nine o'clock, when we sat down, the messman passed up the bowls of porridge and the big jug of hot milk, which was the standing dish every day. Little was heard in the way of conversation until this first course had been disposed of. Then came the order from the messman, "Up bowls," and reserving our spoons for future use, the bowls were passed along. If it were a "fruit day," that is, a day when the second course consisted of bottled fruit, the bowls were retained for this popular dish.

At twenty-five minutes to ten breakfast was over and we had had our smokes. All dishes were passed up, the table hoisted out of the way, and the messman started to wash up the breakfast things, assisted by his cubicle companion and by one or two volunteers who would help him to dry up. Another of the party swept out the hut; and this operation was performed three times a day, so as to keep the building in a tidy state. After finishing the breakfast things, the duty of the man in the house was to replenish the melting pots with ice, empty the ashes and tins into the dust box outside, and get in a bag of coal. By half past ten the morning work was accomplished and the messman was free until twenty minutes to one, when he put the water on for the midday tea. At one o'clock tea was served and we had a sort of counter lunch. This was a movable feast, for scientific and other duties often made some of our party late, and after it was over there was nothing for the messman to do in the afternoon except to have sufficient water ready to provide tea at four o'clock. At a quarter past six the table was brought down again and dinner, the longest meal of the day, was served sharp at 6:30. One often heard the messman anxiously inquiring what the dinner dishes were going to consist of, the most popular from his point of view being those which resulted in the least amount of grease on the plates. Dinner was over soon after seven o'clock and then tea was served. Tobacco and conversation kept us at table until 7:30, after which the same routine of washing up and sweeping out the hut was gone through. By 8:30 the messman had finished his duties for the day, and his turn did not come around again for another thirteen days. The state of the weather made the duties lighter or heavier, for if the day happened to be windy, the emptying of dishwater and ashes and the getting in of fresh ice was an unpleasant job. In a blizzard it was necessary to put on one's Burberries even to walk the few yards to the ice box and back.

In addition to the standing jobs of night watchman and messman there were also special duties for various members of the expedition who had particular departments to look after. Adams every morning, directly after breakfast, wound up the chronometers and the chronometer watches, and rated the instruments. He then attended to the meteorological work and took out his pony for exercise. If he were going far afield he delegated the readings to some members of the scientific staff who were generally in the vicinity of winter quarters. Marshall, as surgeon, attended to any wounds, and issued necessary pills, and then took out one of the ponies for exercise. Wild, who was storekeeper, was responsible for the issuing of all stores to Roberts, and had to open the cases of tinned food and dig out of the snowdrifts in

which it was buried the meat required for the day, either
penguin, seal, or mutton. Joyce fed the dogs after breakfast, the puppies getting a dish of scraps over from our
meals after breakfast and after dinner. When daylight
returned after our long night, he worked at training the
dogs to pull a sledge every morning. The Professor generally went off to "geologize" or Priestley and Murray
worked on the floe dredging or else took the temperati-
tures of the ice in shafts which the former had energeti-
cally sunk in the various lakes around us. Mawson was
occupied with his physical work, which included auroral
observations and the study of the structure of the ice,
the determination of atmospheric electricity and many
other things. In fact, we were all busy, and there was
little cause for us to find the time hang heavy on our
hands; the winter months sped by and this without our
having to sleep through them, as has often been done
before by polar expeditions. This was due to the fact
that we were only a small party and that our household
duties, added to our scientific work, fully occupied our
time.

It would only be repetition to chronicle our doings
from day to day during the months that elapsed from
the disappearance of the sun until the time arrived when
the welcome daylight come back to us. We lived under
conditions of steady routine, affected only by short spells
of bad weather, and found amply sufficient to occupy
ourselves in our daily work, so that the specter known
as "polar ennui" never made its appearance. Midwinter's
day and birthdays were the occasions of festivals, when
our teetotal regime was broken through and a sort of
mild spree indulged in. Before the sun finally went
hockey and soccer were the outdoor games, while in-
doors at night some of us played bridge, poker, and
dominoes. Joyce, Wild, Marston, and Day during the
winter months spent much time in the production of the
"Aurora Australis," the first book every written, printed,
illustrated, and bound in the Antarctic. Through the generosity of Messrs. Joseph Causton and Sons, Limited, we
had been provided with a complete printing outfit and
the necessary paper for the book, and Joyce and Wild
had been given instruction in the art of typesetting and

printing, Marston being taught etching and lithography. They had hardly become skilled craftsmen, but they had gained a good working knowledge of the branches of the business. When we had settled down in the winter quarters, Joyce and Wild set up the little hand press and sorted out the type, these preliminary operations taking up all their spare time for some days, and then they started to set and print the various contributions that were sent in by members of the expedition. The early days of the printing department were not exactly happy, for the two amateur typesetters found themselves making many mistakes, and when they had at last "set up" a page, made all the necessary corrections, and printed off the required number of copies, they had to undertake the laborious work of "dissing," that is, of distributing the type again. They plodded ahead steadily, however, and soon became more skilful, until at the end of a fortnight or three weeks they could print two pages in a day. A lamp had to be placed under the type rack to keep it warm, and a lighted candle was put under the inking plate, so that the ink would keep reasonably thin in consistency. The great trouble experienced by the printers at first was in securing the right pressure on the printing plate and even inking of the page, but experience showed them were they had been at fault. Day meanwhile prepared the binding by cleaning, planing, and polishing wood taken from the Venesta cases in which our provisions were packed. Marston reproduced the illustrations by algraphy, or printing from aluminum plates. He had not got a proper lithographic press, so had to use an ordinary etching press, and he was handicapped by the fact that all our water had a trace of salt in it. This mineral acted on the sensitive plates, but Marston managed to produce what we all regarded as creditable pictures. In its final form the book had about one hundred and twenty pages, and it had at least assisted materially to guard us from the danger of lack of occupation during the polar night.

On March 13 we experienced a very fierce blizzard. The hut shook and rocked in spite of our sheltered position, and articles that we had left lying loose outside were scattered far and wide. Even cases weighing from

fifty to eighty pounds were shifted from where they had
been resting, showing the enormous velocity of the wind.
When the gale was over we put everything that was
likely to blow away into positions of greater safety. It
was on this day also that Murray found living microscop-
ical animals on some fungus that had been thawed out
from a lump of ice taken from the bottom of one of the
lakes. This was one of the most interesting biological
discoveries that had been made in the Antarctic, for the
study of these minute creatures occupied our biologist
for a great part of his stay in the south, and threw a new
light on the capability of life to exist under conditions
of extreme cold and in the face of great variations of
temperature. We all became vastly interested in the rotifers during our stay, and the work of the biologist in this
respect was watched with keen attention. From our point
of view there was an element of humor in the endeavors
of Murray to slay the little animals he had found. He
used to thaw them out from a block of ice, freeze them
up again, and repeat this process several times without
producing any result as far as the rotifers were concerned. Then he tested them in brine so strongly saline
that it would not freeze at a temperature above minus
7°F, and still the animals lived. A good proportion of
them survived a temperature of 200°F. It became a con-
test between rotifers and scientist, and generally the rotifers seemed to triumph.

At the end of March there was still open water in the
bay and we observed a killer whale chasing a seal. About
this time we commenced digging a trench in Clear Lake
and obtained, when we came to water, samples of the
bottom mud and fungus, which was simply swarming
with living organisms. The sunsets at the beginning of
April were wonderful; arches of prismatic colors, crimson and golden tinged clouds, hung in the heavens nearly
all day, for time was going on and soon the sun would
have deserted us. The days grew shorter and shorter,
and the twilight longer. During these sunsets the western
mountains stood out gloriously and the summit of Erebus was wrapped in crimson when the lower slopes had
faded into gray. To Erebus and the western mountains
our eyes turned when the end of the long night grew

near in the month of August, for the mighty peaks are the first to catch up and tell the tale of the coming glory and the last to drop the crimson mantle from their high shoulders as night draws on. Tongue and pencil would sadly fail in attempting to describe the magic of the coloring in the days when the sun was leaving us. The very clouds at this time were iridescent with rainbow hues. The sunsets were poems. The change from twilight into night, sometimes lit by a crescent moon, was extraordinarily beautiful, for the white cliffs gave no part of their color away, and the rocks beside them did not part with their blackness, so the effect of deepening night over these contrasts was singularly weird. In my diary I noted that throughout April hardly a day passed without an auroral display. On more than one occasion the auroral showed distinct lines of color, merging from a deep red at the base of the line of light into a greenish hue on top. About the beginning of April the temperature began to drop considerably, and for some days in calm, still weather the thermometer often registered 40° below zero.

On April 6, Marshall decided that it was necessary to amputate Brocklehurst's big toe, as there was no sign of it recovering like the other toes from the frostbite he had received on the Erebus journey. The patient was put under chloroform and the operation was witnessed by an interested and sympathetic audience. After the bone had been removed, the sufferer was shifted into my room, where he remained till just before Midwinter's Day, when he was able to get out and move about again. We had about April 8 one of the peculiar southerly blizzards so common during our last expedition, the temperature varying rapidly from minus 23° to plus 4°F. This blizzard continued till the evening of the 11th, and when it had abated we found the bay and sound clear of ice again. I began to feel rather worried about this and wished for it to freeze over, for across the ice lay our road to the south. We observed occasionally about this time that peculiar phenomenon of McMurdo Sound called "earth shadows." Long dark bars, projected up into the sky from the western mountains, made their appearance at sunrise. These lines are due to the shadow of the giant Erebus being cast across the western mountains. Our days were now getting very short and the amount of daylight was a negligible quantity. We boarded up the remainder of the windows, and depended entirely upon the artificial light in the winter quarters. The light given by the acetylene gas was brilliant, the four burners lighting the whole of the hut.

When daylight returned and sledging began about the middle of August, on one of our excursions on the Cape Royds peninsula, we found growing under volcanic earth a large quantity of fungus. This was of great interest to Murray, as plant life of any sort is extremely rare in the Antarctic. Shortly after this a strong blizzard cast up a quantity of seaweed on our ice foot; this was another piece of good fortune, for on the last expedition we obtained very little seaweed.

When Midwinter's Day had passed and the twilight, that presaged the return of the sun began to be more marked day by day, I set on foot the arrangements for the sledging work in the forthcoming spring. It was desirable that, at as early a date as possible, we should place a depot of stores at a point to the south, in preparation for the departure of the Southern Party, which was to march toward the Pole. I hoped to make this depot at least one hundred miles from the winter quarters. Then it was desirable that we should secure some definite information regarding the condition of the snow surface on the Barrier, and I was also anxious to afford the various members of the expedition some practice in sledging before the serious work commenced. Some of us had been in the Antarctic before, but the majority of the men had not yet had any experience of marching and camping on snow and ice, in low temperatures.

The ponies had been kept in good training by means of regular exercise and constant attention during the winter, but although they were thoroughly fit, and, indeed, apparently anxious for an opportunity to work off some of their superfluous energy, I did not propose to take them on the preliminary sledging journeys. It seemed to be unwise to take any unnecessary risk of further loss now that we had only four ponies left, few enough for the southern journey later in the season. For this reason, manhauling was the order for the first journeys.

During the winter I had given a great deal of earnest consideration to the question of the date at which the party that was to march toward the Pole should start from the hut. The goal that we hoped to attain lay over 880 statute miles to the south, and the brief summer was all too short a time in which to march so far into the unknown and return to winter quarters. The ship would have to leave for the north about the end of February, for the ice would then be closing in, and, moreover, we could not hope to carry on our sledges much more than a three months' supply of provisions, on anything like full rations. I finally decided that the Southern Party should leave the winter quarters about October 28, for if we started earlier it was probable that the ponies would suffer from the severe cold at nights, and we would gain no advantage from getting away early in the season, if, as a result, the ponies were incapacitated before we had made much progress.

The date for the departure of the Southern Party having been fixed, it became necessary to arrange for the laying of the depot during the early spring, and I thought that the first step toward this should be a preliminary journey on the Barrier surface, in order to gain an idea of the conditions that would be met with, and to ascertain whether the motor car would be of service, at any rate for the early portion of the journey. The sun had not yet returned and the temperature was very low indeed, but we had proved in the course of the *Discovery* expedition that it is quite possible to travel under these conditions. I therefore started on this preliminary journey on August 12, taking with me Professor David, who was to lead the Northern Party toward the South Magnetic Pole, and Bertram Armytage, who was to take charge of the party that was to make a journey into the mountains of the west later in the year. The reader can imagine that it was not with feelings of unalloyed pleasure that we turned our backs on the warm, well found hut and faced our little journey out into the semi-darkness and intense cold, but we did get a certain amount of satisfaction from the thought that at last we were actually beginning the work we had come south to undertake.

We were equipped for a fortnight with provisions and camp gear, packed on one sledge, and had three gallons of petroleum in case we should decide to stay out longer. A gallon of oil will last a party of three men for about ten days under ordinary conditions, and we could get more food at Hut Point if we required it. We took three one-man sleeping bags, believing that they would be sufficiently warm in spite of the low temperature. The larger bags, holding two or three men, certainly give greater warmth, for the occupants warm one another, but, on the other hand, one's rest is very likely to be disturbed by the movements of a companion. We were heavily clothed for this trip, because the sun would not rise above the horizon until another ten days had passed.

Our comrades turned out to see us off, and the pony Quan pulled the sledge with our camp gear over the sea ice until we got close to the glacier south of Cape Barne, about five miles from the winter quarters. Then he was sent back, for the weather was growing thick, and, as already explained, I did not want to run any risk of losing another pony from our sadly diminished team. We proceeded close in by the skuary, and a little further on pitched camp for lunch. Professor David, whose thirst for knowledge could not be quenched, immediately went off to investigate the geology of the neighborhood. After lunch we started to pull our sledge around the coast toward Hut Point, but the weather became worse, making progress difficult, and at 6 P.M. we camped close to the tide crack at the south side of Turk's Head. We slept well and soundly, although the temperature was about forty degrees below zero, and the experience made me more than ever convinced of the superiority of one-man sleeping bags.

On the following morning, August 13, we marched across to Glacier Tongue, having to cross a wide crack that had been ridged up by ice pressure between Tent Island and the Tongue. As soon as we had crossed we saw the depot standing up clear against the skyline on the Tongue. This was the depot that had been made by the ship soon after our first arrival in the sound. We found no difficulty in getting on to the Tongue, for a fairly gentle slope led up from the sea ice to the glacier surface. The snow had blown over from the south during the winter and made a good way. We found the depot intact though the cases, lying on the ice, had been bleached to a light yellow color by the wind and sun. We had lunch on the south side of the Tongue, and found there another good way down to the sea ice. There is a very awkward crack on the south side, but this can hardly be called a tide crack. I think it is due to the fact that the tide has more effect on the sea ice than on the heavy mass of the Tongue, though there is no doubt this also is afloat; the rise and fall of the two sections of ice are not coincident, and a crack is produced. The unaccustomed pulling made us tired, and we decided to pitch a camp about four miles off Hut Point, before reaching Castle Rock. Castle Rock is distant three miles and a half from Hut Point, and we had always noticed that after we got abeam of the rock the final march on to the hut seemed very long, for we were always weary by that time.

We reached the old *Discovery* winter quarters at Hut Point on the morning of August 14, and after a good breakfast I took the Professor and Armytage over all the familiar ground. It was very interesting to me to revisit the old scenes. There was the place where, years before, when the *Discovery* was lying fast in the ice close to the shore, we used to dig for the ice that was required for the supply of fresh water. The marks of the picks and shovels were still to be seen. I noticed an old case bedded in the ice, and remembered the day when it had been thrown away. Around the hut was collected a very large amount of debris. The only lake, or rather pool, that lay near these winter quarters was quite a tiny sheet of water in comparison with the large lakes at Cape Royds, and I realized more fully the special advantages we had at our winter quarters as far as biological and zoological work were concerned. Through the Gap we saw the Barrier stretched out before us—the long white road that we were shortly to tread. The fascination of the unknown was strong upon me, and I longed to be away toward the south on the journey that I hoped would lay bare the mysteries of the place of the pole.

We climbed to the top of Crater Hill with a collecting bag and the Professor's camera, and here we took some photographs and made an examination of the cone. Professor David expressed the opinion that the ice sheet had certainly passed over this hill, which is about 1100 ft. high, for there was distinct evidence of glaciation. We climbed along the ridge to Castle Rock, about four miles to the north, and made an examination of the formation there. Then we returned to the hut to have a square meal and get ready for our journey across the Barrier.

The old hut had never been a very cheerful place, even when we were camped alongside it in the *Discovery,* and it looked doubly inhospitable now, after having stood empty and neglected for six years. One side was filled with cases of biscuit and tinned meat, and the snow that had found its way in was lying in great piles around the walls. There was no stove, for this had been taken away with the *Discovery,* and coal was scattered about the floor with other debris and rubbish. Besides the biscuits and the tinned beef and mutton there was some tea and coffee stored in the hut. We cleared a spot on which to sleep, and decided that we would use the cases of biscuit and meat to build another hut inside the main one, so that the quarters would be a little more cozy. I proposed to use this hut as a stores depot in connection with the southern journey, for if the ice broke out in the Sound unexpectedly early, it would be difficult to convey provisions from Cape Royds to the Barrier, and, moreover, Hut Point was twenty miles further south than our winter quarters. We spent that night on the floor of the hut, and slept fairly comfortably, though not as well as on the previous night in the tent, because we were not so close to one another.

On the morning of the following day (August 15) we started away about 9 A.M., crossed the smooth ice to Winter Harbor, and passed close around Cape Armitage. We there found cracks and pressed up ice, showing that there had been Barrier movement, and about three miles further on we crossed the spot at which the sea ice joins the Barrier, ascending a slope about eight feet high. Di-

rectly we got on to the Barrier ice we noticed undulations on the surface. We pushed along and got to a
distance of about twelve miles from Hut Point in eight
hours. The surface generally was hard, but there were
very marked sastrugi, and at times patches of soft snow.
The conditions did not seem favorable for the use of the
motor car because we had already found that the machine could not go through soft snow for more than a
few yards, and I foresaw that if we brought it out on to
the Barrier it would not be able to do much in the soft
surface that would have to be traversed. The condition
of the surface varied from mile to mile, and it would be
impracticable to keep changing the wheels of the car in
order to meet the requirements of each new surface.

The temperature was very low, although the weather
was fine. At 6 P.M. the thermometer showed fifty-six degrees below zero, and the petroleum used for the lamp
had become milky in color and of a creamy consistency.
That night the temperature fell lower still, and the moisture in our sleeping bags, from our breath and Burberries, made us very uncomfortable when the bags had
thawed out with the warmth of our bodies. Everything
we touched was appallingly cold, and we got no sleep
at all. The next morning (August 16) the weather was
threatening, and there were indications of the approach
of a blizzard, and I therefore decided to march back to
Hut Point, for there was no good purpose to be served
by taking unnecessary risks at that stage of the expedition. We had some warm food, of which we stood sorely
in need after the severe night, and then started at 8 A.M.
to return to Hut Point. By hard marching, which had
the additional advantage of warming us up, we reached
the old hut again at three o'clock that afternoon, and
we were highly delighted to get into its shelter. The sun
had not yet returned, and though there was a strong
light in the sky during the day, the Barrier was not
friendly under winter conditions.

We reached the hut none too soon, for a blizzard
sprang up, and for some days we had to remain in shelter. We utilized the time by clearing up the portion of
the hut that we proposed to use, even sweeping it with
an old broom we found, and building a shelter of the

packing cases, piling them right up to the roof around a space about twenty feet by ten; and thus we made comparatively cozy quarters. We rigged a table for the cooking gear, and put everything neatly in order. My two companions were, at this time, having their first experience of polar life under marching conditions as far as equipment was concerned, and they were gaining knowledge that proved very useful to them on the later journeys.

On the morning of August 22, the day on which the sun once more appeared above the horizon, we started back for the winter quarters, leaving Hut Point at 5 A.M. in the face of a bitterly cold wind from the northeast, with low drift. We marched without a stop for nine miles, until we reached Glacier Tongue and then had an early lunch. An afternoon march of fourteen miles took us to the winter quarters at Cape Royds, where we arrived at 5 P.M. We were not expected at the hut, for the weather was thick and windy, but our comrades were delighted to see us, and we had a hearty dinner and enjoyed the luxury of a good bath.

The chief result of this journey was to convince me that we could not place much reliance on the motor car for the southern journey. Professor David and Armytage had received a good baptism of frost, and as it was very desirable that all the members of the expedition should have personal experience of traveling over the ice and snow in low temperatures before the real work began, I arranged to despatch a small party every week to sledge stores and equipment south to Hut Point. These journeys were much alike in general character, though they all gave rise to incidents that were afterward related in the winter quarters.

On September 1, Wild, Day, and Priestley started for Hut Point via Glacier Tongue with 450 lb. of gear and provisions, their instructions being to leave 230 lb. of provisions at the *Discovery* hut in readiness for the southern journey. They made a start at 10:20 A.M., being accompanied by Brocklehurst with a pony for the first five miles. The weather was fine, but a very low barometer gave an indication that bad weather was coming. I did not hesitate to let these parties face bad weather, because the road they were to travel was well known, and a rough experience would be very useful to the men later in the expedition's work. The party camped in the snow close to the south side of Glacier Tongue.

Next morning (September 2) the weather was still bad, and they were not able to make a start until after noon. At 1:20 P.M. they ran out of the northerly wind into light southerly airs with intervals of calm, and they noticed that at the meeting of the two winds the clouds of drift were formed into whirling columns, some of them over forty feet high. They reached the *Discovery* hut at 4:30 P.M., and soon turned in, the temperature being forty degrees below zero. When they dressed at 5:30 A.M. (September 3) they found that a southerly wind with heavy drift rendered a start on the return journey inadvisable. After breakfast they walked over to Observation Hill, where they examined a set of stakes which Ferrar and Wild had placed in the Gap glacier in 1902. The stakes showed that the movement of the glacier during the six years since the stakes had been put into position had amounted to a few inches only. The middle stake had advanced eight inches and those next it on either side about six inches. At noon the wind dropped, and although the drift was still thick, the party started back, steering by the sastrugi till the Tongue was reached. They camped for the night in the lee of the glacier, with a blizzard blowing over them and the temperature rising, the result being that everything was uncomfortably wet. They managed to sleep, however, and when they awoke the next morning the weather was clear, and they had an easy march in, being met beyond Cape Barne by Joyce, Brocklehurst, and the dogs. They had been absent four days.

Each party came back with adventures to relate, experiences to compare, and its own views on various matters of detail connected with sledge traveling. Curiously enough, every one of the parties encountered bad weather, but there were no accidents, and all the men seemed to enjoy the work.

Early in September a party consisting of Adams, Marshall, and myself started for Hut Point, and we decided to make one march of the twenty-three miles, and not

camp on the way. We started at 8 A.M., and when we
were nearly at the end of the journey, and were struggling slowly through bad snow toward the hut, close to
the end of Hut Point, a strong blizzard came up. Fortunately I knew the bearings of the hut, and how to get
over the ice foot. We abandoned the extra weights we
were pulling for the depot, and managed to get to the
hut at 10 P.M. in a sorely frostbitten condition, almost
too tired to move. We were able to get ourselves some
hot food, however, and were soon all right again. I mention the incident merely to show how constantly one has
to be on guard against the onslaughts of the elements in
the inhospitable regions of the south.

CHAPTER XI

The Southern Journey

BY the middle of September a good supply of provisions,
oil, and gear had been stored at Hut Point. All the supplies required for the southern journey had been taken
there, in order that the start might be made from the
most southern base available. During this period, while
the men were gaining experience and getting into training, the ponies were being exercised regularly along the
sea ice from winter quarters across to Cape Barne, and
I was more than satisfied with the way in which they did
their work. I felt that the little animals were going to
justify the confidence I had reposed in them when I had
brought them all the way from Manchuria to the bleak
Antarctic. I tried the ponies with loads of varying
weights in order to ascertain as closely as possible how
much they could haul with maximum efficiency, and
after watching the results of the experiments very carefully came to the conclusion that a load of 650 lb. per
pony should be the maximum. It was obvious that if the
animals were overloaded their speed would be reduced,
so that there would be no gain to us, and if we were to
accomplish a good journey to the south it was important
that they should not be tired out in the early stages of
the march over the Barrier surface. The weight I have
mentioned was to include that of the sledge itself, which
was about 60 lb.

When the question of weight came to be considered I
could realize the seriousness of the loss of the four ponies, during the winter. It was evident that we would be
unable to take with us toward the Pole as much food as
I would have liked.

I decided to place a depot one hundred geographical
miles south of the *Discovery* winter quarters, the depot
to consist of pony maize. The party, consisting of Adams,

Marshall, Wild, Marston, Joyce and myself, left Cape
Royds on September 22 with a load of about 170 lb.
per man, and the motor car towed the sledges as far as
Inaccessible Island, at the rate of about six miles an
hour. We took two tents and two three-man sleeping
bags, for we expected to meet very low temperatures. I
had decided to take neither ponies nor dogs, so we took
the sledges on ourselves, traveling over a fairly good
surface as far as the *Discovery* hut, where we passed
the first night. The journey was a severe one, for the
temperature, at times, got down to 59° below zero F.
We reached the main depot in latitude 79° 36' South,
longitude 168° East, on October 6. This we called
"Depot A." It was marked with an upturned sledge and
a black flag on a bamboo rod. We deposited a gallon tin
of oil and 167 lb. of pony maize so that our load would
be considerably reduced for the first portion of the journey when we started south. The weather was very severe
on the return journey and we did not reach the old *Discovery* winter quarters until October 13. We had been
twenty-one days out, but had been able to march only
on fourteen and a half days. The next day we started
for Cape Royds and had the good fortune to meet the
motor car a mile and a half south of Cape Barne. The
sledges were soon hitched on, and we drove trium-
phantly to winter quarters—having traveled 320 statute
miles since September 22.

During our absence the Northern Party consisting of
Professor David, Mawson, and Mackay, had started on
the journey that was to result in the attainment of the
South Magnetic Pole. I had said good-bye to Professor
David and his two companions on September 22 and
we did not meet again until March 1, 1909. In chapter
xxii the Professor tells the story of the Northern
journey.

The Southern Party was to leave winter quarters on
October 29; so on the return of the party from Depot
A we commenced final preparations for the attempt to
reach the South Pole. I decided that four men should go
south, I myself to be one of them, and that we should
take provisions for ninety-one days: this amount of food

with the other equipment would bring the load per pony up to the weight fixed as the maximum safe load. Early in 1907 I had proposed that one party should travel to the east across the Barrier surface toward King Edward VII Land but the accidents that had left us with only four ponies caused me to abandon this project. The ponies would have to go south, the motor car would not travel on the Barrier, and the dogs were required for the southern depot journey. I deemed it best to confine the efforts of the sledging parties to the two Poles, Geographical and Magnetic, and to send a third party into the western mountains with the object of studying geological conditions and, in particular, of searching for fossils.

The men selected to go with me were Adams, Marshall, and Wild. A supporting party was to accompany us for a certain distance in order that we might start fairly fresh from a point beyond the rough ice off Minna Bluff, and we would take the four ponies and four sledges.

Arrangements were made for sending out a party early in December to lay a depot for the Northern Party. When this had been done, the same party would proceed to the western mountains. On January 15, 1909, a depot party, under the command of Joyce, was to lay a depot near Minna Bluff containing sufficient stores for the return of the Southern Party from that point. This same party was to return to Hut Point, reload its sledge and march out to the depot a second time, there to await the arrival of the Southern Party until February 10, 1909. If the Southern Party had not arrived by that date Joyce and his companions were to go back to Hut Point and thence to the ship.

Before my departure from winter quarters on the southern journey, I left instructions which provided for the conclusion of the work of the Expedition in its various branches, and for the relief of the men left in the Antarctic, in the event of the nonreturn of the Southern Party. I gave Murray command of the Expedition in my absence and full instructions. The trials of the motor car in the neighborhood of the winter quarters had proved that it could not travel over a soft snow surface, and the depot journey had shown me that the surface of the Barrier was covered with soft snow, much softer and heavier than it had been in 1902, at the time of the *Discovery* expedition. In fact I was satisfied that, with the Barrier in its then condition, no wheeled vehicle could travel over it. The wheels would simply sink in until the body of the car rested on the snowy surface. We had made alterations in the wheels and we had reduced the weight of the car to an absolute minimum by the removal of every unnecessary part, but still it could do little on a soft surface, and it would certainly be quite useless with any weight behind, for the driving wheels would simply scoop holes for themselves. The use of sledge runners under the front wheel, with broad, spiked driving wheels, might have enabled us to get the car over some of the soft surfaces, but this equipment would not have been satisfactory on hard, rough ice, and constant changes would occupy too much time. I had confidence in the ponies, and I thought it best not to attempt to take the car south from the winter quarters.

The provisioning of the Southern Party was a matter that received long and anxious consideration. Marshall went very carefully into the question of the relative food values of the various supplies, and we were able to derive much useful information from the experience of previous expeditions. We decided on a daily ration of 34 oz. per man; the total weight of food to be carried, on the basis of supplies for ninety-one days, would therefore be 773½ lb. The staple items were to be biscuits and pemmican. The biscuits, as I have stated, were of wheatmeal with 25 percent of plasmon added, and analysis showed that they did not contain more than 3 percent of water. The pemmican had been supplied by Beauvais, of Copenhagen, and consisted of the finest beef, dried and powdered, with 60 percent of beef fat added. It contained only a small percentage of water. The effort of the polar explorer is to get his foods as free from water as possible, for the moisture represents so much useless weight to be carried.

The daily allowance of food for each man on the journey, as long as full rations were given, was to be as follows:

	Oz.
Pemmican	7.5
Emergency ration	1.5
Biscuit	16.0
Cheese or chocolate	2.0
Cocoa	.7
Plasmon	1.0
Sugar	4.3
Quaker Oats	1.0
	34.0

Tea, salt, and pepper were extras not weighed in with the daily allowance. We used about two ounces of tea per day for the four men. The salt and pepper were carried in small bags, each bag to last one week. Some of the biscuit had been broken up and 1 lb. per week for each man was intended to be used for thickening the hoosh, the amount so used to be deducted from the ordinary allowance of biscuit.

Everything was ready for the start on the journey toward the Pole as the end of October approached, and we looked forward with keen anticipation to the venture. The supporting party was to consist of Joyce, Marston, Priestley, Armytage, and Brocklehurst, and was to accompany us for ten days. Day was to have been a member of this party, but he damaged his foot while tobogganing down a slope at the winter quarters, and had to stay behind. The weather was not very good during our last days at the hut, but there were signs that summer was approaching. The ponies were in good condition. We spent the last few days overhauling the sledges and equipment, and making sure that everything was sound and in its right place. In the evenings we wrote letters for those at home, to be delivered in the event of our not returning from the unknown regions into which we hoped to penetrate.

Events of the southern journey were recorded day by day in the diary I wrote during the long march. I read this diary when we had got back to civilization, and arrived at the conclusion that to rewrite it would be to take away the special flavor which it possesses. It was written under conditions of much difficulty, and often of great stress, and these conditions I believe it reflects. I am therefore publishing the diary with only such minor amendments in the phraseology as are necessary in order to make it easily understood. The reader will understand that when one is writing in a sleeping bag, with the temperature very low and food rather short, a good proportion of the "ofs," "ands" and "thes" get left out. The story will probably seem bald, but it is at any rate a faithful record of what occurred. I will deal more fully with some aspects of the journey in a later chapter. The altitudes given in the diary were calculated at the time, and were not always accurate. The corrected altitudes are given on the map and in a table at the end of the book. The distances were calculated by means of a sledge meter, checked by observations of the sun, and are approximately accurate.

October 29, 1908. A glorious day for our start; brilliant sunshine and a cloudless sky, a fair wind from the north, in fact, everything that could conduce to an auspicious beginning. We had breakfast at 7 A.M., and at 8:30 the sledges that the motor was to haul to Glacier Tongue were taken down by the penguin rookery and over to the rough ice. At 9:30 A.M. the supporting party started and was soon out of sight, as the motor was running well. At 10 A.M. we four of the Southern Party followed. As we left the hut where we had spent so many months in comfort, we had a feeling of real regret that never again would we all be together there. It was dark inside, the acetylene was feeble in comparison with the sun outside, and it was small compared to an ordinary dwelling, yet we were sad at leaving it. Last night as we were sitting at dinner the evening sun entered through the ventilator and a circle of light shone on the picture of the Queen. Slowly it moved across and lit up the photograph of his Majesty the King. This seemed an omen of good luck, for only on that day and at that particular time could this have happened, and today we started to strive to plant the Queen's flag on the last spot of the world. At 10 A.M. we met Murray and Roberts, and said good-bye, then went on our way. Both of these, who were to be left, had done for me all that men could do in their own particular line of work to try and make our little expedition a success. A clasp of the hands means more than many words, and as we turned to acknowledge their cheer and saw them standing on the ice by the familiar cliffs, I felt that we must try to do well for the sake of everyone concerned in the expedition.

Hardly had we been going for an hour when Socks went dead lame. This was a bad shock, for Quan had for a full week been the same. We had thought that our troubles in this direction were over. Socks must have hurt himself on some of the sharp ice. We had to go on, and I trust that in a few days he will be all right. I shall not start from our depot at Hut Point until he is better or until I know actually what is going to happen. The lameness of a pony in our present situation is a serious thing. If we had eight, or even six, we could adjust matters more easily, but when we are working to the bare ounce it is very serious.

At 1 P.M. we halted and fed the ponies. As we sat close to them on the sledge Grisi suddenly lashed out, and striking the sledge with his hoof, struck Adams just below the knee. Three inches higher and the blow would have shattered his knee cap and ended his chance of going on. As it was the bone was almost exposed, and he was in great pain, but said little about it. We went on and at 2:30 P.M. arrived at the sledges which had gone on by motor yesterday, just as the car came along after having dragged the other sledges within a quarter of a mile of the Tongue. I took on one sledge, and Day started in rather soft snow with the other sledges, the car being helped by the supporting party in the worst places. Pressure ridges and drift just off the Tongue prevented the car going further, so I gave the sledge Quan was dragging to Adams, who was leading Chinaman, and went back for the other. We said goodbye to Day, and he went back, with Priestley and Brocklehurst helping him, for his foot was still very weak.

We got to the south side of Glacier Tongue at 4 P.M., and after a cup of tea started to grind up the maize in the depot. It was hard work, but we each took turns at the crusher, and by 8 P.M. had ground sufficient maize for the journey. It is now 11 P.M., and a high warm sun is shining down, the day calm and clear. We had hoosh at 9 P.M. Adams' leg is very stiff and sore. The horses are fairly quiet, but Quan has begun his old tricks and is biting his tether. I must send for wire rope if this goes on.

At last we are out on the long trail, after four years' thought and work. I pray that we may be successful, for my heart has been so much in this.

There are numbers of seals lying close to our camp. They are nearly all females, and will soon have young. Erebus is emitting three distinct columns of steam today, and the fumaroles on the old crater can be seen plainly. It is a mercy that Adams is better tonight. I cannot imagine what he would have done if he had been knocked out for the southern journey, his interest in the expedition has been so intense. Temperatures plus 2°F, distance for the day, 14½ miles.

October 30. At Hut Point. Another gloriously fine day. We started away for Hut Point at 10:30 A.M., leaving the supporting party to finish grinding the maize. The ponies were in good fettle and went away well, Socks walking without a sledge, while Grisi had 500 lb., Quan 430 lb., and Chinaman 340 lb. Socks seems better today. It is a wonderful change to get up in the morning and put on ski boots without any difficulty, and to handle cooking vessels without "burning" one's fingers on the frozen metal. I was glad to see all the ponies so well, for there had been both wind and drift during the night. Quan seems to take a delight in biting his tether when anyone is looking, for I put my head out of the tent occasionally during the night to see if they were all right, and directly I did so Quan started to bite his rope. At other times they were all quiet.

We crossed one crack that gave us a little trouble, and at 1:30 P.M. reached Castle Rock, traveling at one mile and three-quarters per hour. There I changed my sledge, taking on Marshall's sledge with Quan, for Grisi was making hard work of it, the surface being very soft in places. Quan pulled 500 lb. just as easily and at 3 P.M. we reached Hut Point, tethered the ponies, and had tea. There was a slight north wind. At 5 P.M. the supporting party came up. We have decided to sleep in the hut, but the supporting party are sleeping in the tent at the very spot where the *Discovery* wintered six years ago. Tomorrow I am going back to the Tongue for the rest of the fodder. The supporting party elected to sleep out because it is warmer, but we of the southern party will not have a solid roof over our heads for some months to come, so will make the most of it. We swept the debris out. Wild killed a seal for fresh meat and washed the liver at the seal hole, so tomorrow we will have a good feed. Half a tin of jam is a small thing for one man to eat when he has a sledging appetite, and we are doing our share, as when we start there will be no more of these luxuries. Adams' leg is better, but stiff. Our march was nine and a half miles today. It is now 10 P.M.

October 31. This day started with a dull snowy appearance, which soon developed into a snowstorm, but a mild one with little drift. I wanted to cross to Glacier Tongue with Quan, Grisi, and Chinaman.

During the morning we readjusted our provision weights and unpacked the bags. In the afternoon it cleared, and at 3:30 P.M. we got under way, Quan pulling our sleeping equipment. We covered the eight miles and a half to Glacier Tongue in three hours, and as I found no message from the hut, nor the gear I had asked to be sent down, I concluded it was blowing there also, and so decided to walk on after dinner. I covered the twelve miles in three hours, arriving at Cape Royds at 11:30, and had covered the twenty-three miles between Hut Point and Cape Royds in six hours, marching time. They were surprised to see me, and were glad to hear that Adams and Socks were better. I turned in at 2 A.M. for a few hours' sleep. It had been blowing hard with thick drift, so the motor had not been able to start for Glacier Tongue. On my way to Cape Royds I noticed several seals with young ones, evidently just born. Murray tells me that the temperature has been plus 22°F.

November 1. Had breakfast at 6 A.M., and Murray came on the car with me, Day driving. There was a fresh easterly wind. We left Cape Royds at 8 A.M., and arrived off Inaccessible Island at twenty minutes past eight, having covered a distance of eight miles. The car was running very well. Then off Tent Island we left the car, and hauled the sledge, with the wire rope, etc., around to our camp off Glacier Tongue. Got under way at 10 A.M., and reached Hut Point at 2 P.M., the ponies pulling 500 and 550 lb. each. Grisi bolted with his sledge, but soon stopped. The ponies pulled very well, with a bad light and a bad surface. We arranged the packing of the sledges in the afternoon, but we are held up because of Socks. His foot is seriously out of order, It is almost a disaster, for we want every pound of hauling power. This evening it is snowing hard, with no wind. Adams' leg is much better. Wild noticed a seal giving birth to a pup. The baby measured 3 ft. 10 in. in length, and weighed 50 lb. I turned in early tonight, for I had done thirty-nine miles in the last twenty-four hours.

November 2. Dull and snowy during the early hours of today. When we awoke we found that Quan had bitten through his tether and played havoc with the maize and other fodder. Directly he saw me coming down the ice foot, he started off, dashing from one sledge to another, tearing the bags to pieces and trampling the food out. It was ten minutes before we caught him. Luckily one sledge of fodder was untouched. He pranced around, kicked up his heels, and showed that it was a deliberate piece of destructiveness on his part, for he had eaten his fill. His distended appearance was obviously the result of many pounds of maize.

In the afternoon three of the ponies hauled the sledges with their full weights across the junction of the sea and the Barrier ice, and in spite of the soft snow they pulled splendidly. We are now all ready for a start the first thing tomorrow. Socks seems much better, and not at all lame. The sun is now (9 P.M.) shining gloriously, and the wind has dropped, all auguring for a fine day tomorrow. The performance of the ponies was most satisfactory, and if they will only continue so for a month, it will mean a lot to us. Adams' leg is nearly all right.

November 3. Started at 9:30 from Hut Point, Quan pulling 660 lb., Grisi 615 lb., Socks 600 lb., and Chinaman 600 lb. Five men hauled 660 lb., 153 lb. of this being pony feed for our party. It was a beautifully fine day, but we were not long under way when we found that the surface was terribly soft, the ponies at times sinking in up to their bellies and always over their hocks.

We picked up the other sledges at the Barrier junction, and Brocklehurst photographed us all, with our sledge flags flying and the Queen's Union Jack. At 10:50 we left the sea ice, and instead of finding the Barrier surface better, discovered that the snow was even softer than earlier in the day. The ponies pulled magnificently, and the supporting party toiled on painfully in their wake. Every hour the pony leaders changed places with the sledge haulers. At 1 P.M. the advance party with the ponies pitched camp and tethered out the ponies, and soon lunch was under way, consisting of tea with plasmon, plasmon biscuits, and cheese. At 2:30 we struck camp, the supporting party with the man sledge going on in advance, while the others with the ponies did the camp work. By 4 P.M. the surface had improved in places, so that the men did not break through the crust so often, but it was just as hard work as ever for the ponies. The weather kept beautifully fine, with a slight southeast wind. The weather sides of the ponies were quite dry, but their lee sides were frosted with congealed sweat. Whenever it came to our turn to pull, we perspired freely. As the supporting party are not traveling as fast as the ponies, we have decided to take them on only for two more days, and then we of the Southern Party will carry the remainder of the pony feed from their sledge on our backs. So tomorrow morning we will depot nearly 100 lb. of oil and provisions, which will lighten the load on the supporting party's sledge a good deal.

We camped at 6 P.M., and, after feeding the ponies, had our dinner, consisting of pemmican, emergency ration, plasmon biscuits and plasmon cocoa, followed by a smoke, the most ideal smoke a man could wish for after a day's sledging. As there is now plenty of biscuit to spare, we gave the gallant little ponies a good feed of them after dinner. They are now comfortably standing in the sun, with the temperature plus 14°F, and occasionally pawing the snow. Grisi has dug a large hole already in the soft surface. We have been steering a southeast course all day, keeping well to the north of

White Island to avoid the crevasses. Our distance for the day is 12 miles (statute) 300 yards.

November 4. Started at 8:30 this morning; fine weather, but bad light. Temperature plus 9°F. We wore goggles, as already we are feeling the trying light. The supporting party started first, and with an improved surface during the morning they kept ahead of the ponies, who constantly broke through the crust. As soon as we passed the end of White Island, the surface became softer, and it was trying work for both men and ponies. However, we did 9 miles 500 yards (statute) up to 1 P.M., the supporting party going the whole time without being relieved. Their weights had been reduced by nearly 100 lb., as we depoted that amount of oil and provision last night. In the afternoon the surface was still softer, and when we came to camp at 6 P.M. the ponies were plainly tired. The march for the day was 16 miles, 500 yards (statute), over fourteen miles geographical, with a bad surface, so we have every reason to be pleased with the ponies. The supporting party pulled hard. The cloud rolled away from Erebus this evening, and it is now warm, clear, and bright to the north, but dark to the south. I am steering about east southeast to avoid the crevasses off White Island, but tomorrow we go southeast. We fixed our position tonight from bearings, and find that we are thirty-four miles south of Cape Royds. Every one is fit and well.

November 5. On turning out this morning, we found the weather overcast, with slight snow falling and only a few landmarks visible to the north, nothing to the south. We got under way at 8:15 A.M., steering by compass. The light was so bad that the sastrugi could not be seen, though of the latter there was not much, for there was a thick coating of fallen snow. The surface was very bad for ponies and men. The ponies struggled gamely on through the tiring morning, and we camped for lunch at 1 P.M., having done 8 miles 1200 yards. After lunch we started at 2:15 P.M. in driving snow, but our steering was very wild. We had been making a southeast course all the morning, but in the afternoon the course was a devious one. Suddenly Marshall, who was leading Grisi, got his legs into a crevasse, and Grisi also; they recovered themselves, and Marshall shouted out to me. I stopped my horse and went to his assistance in getting the sledge off the snow bridge covering the chasm. The crevasse was about 3 ft. wide, with the sides widening out below. No bottom could be seen. The line of direction was northwest by southeast. I at once altered the course to east, but in about a quarter of an hour Wild, Adams, and Marshall got into a narrow crevasse, so I stopped and pitched camp, to wait until the weather cleared and we could get some idea of our actual position. This was at 3 P.M., the sledge meter recording 9 miles 1200 yards (statute) for the day. At 4 P.M. it commenced to drift and blow, and it is blowing hard and gustily now. It is very unfortunate to be held up like this, but I trust that it will blow itself out tonight and be fine tomorrow. The ponies will be none the worse for the rest. We wore goggles today, as the light was so bad and some of us got a touch of snow blindness.

November 6. Lying in our sleeping bags all day except when out feeding the ponies, for it has been blowing a blizzard, with thick drift, from south by west. It is very hard to be held up like this, for each day means the consumption of 40 lb. of pony feed alone. We only had a couple of biscuits each for lunch, for I can see that we must retrench at every setback if we are going to have enough food to carry us through. We started with ninety-one days' food, but with careful management we can make it spin out to 110 days. If we have not done the job in that time it is God's will. Some of the supporting party did not turn out for any meal during the last twenty-four hours. Quan and Chinaman have taken their feeds constantly, but Socks and Grisi not so well. They all like Maujee ration and eat that up before touching the maize. They have been very quiet, standing tails to the blizzard, which has been so thick that at times we could not see them from the peepholes of our tents. There are great drifts all around the tents, and some of the sledges are buried. This evening about 5:30 the weather cleared a bit and the wind dropped. When getting out the feed boxes at 6 P.M. I could see White Island and the Bluff, so I hope that tomorrow will be fine. The barometer has been steady all day at 28.60 in., with the temperature up to 18°F, so it is quite warm, and in our one-man sleeping bags each of us has a little home, where he can read and write and look at the penates and lares brought with him. I read *Much Ado About Nothing* during the morning. The surface of the Barrier is better, for the wind has blown away a great deal of the soft snow, and we will, I trust, be able to see any crevasses before we are on to them. This is our fourth day out from Hut Point, and we are only twenty miles south. We must do better than this if we are to make much use of the ponies. I would not mind the blizzard so much if we had only to consider ourselves, for we can save on the food, whereas the ponies must be fed full.

November 7. Another disappointing day. We got up at 5 A.M. to breakfast, so as to be in time to start at 8 A.M. We cleared all the drift off our sledges, and, unstowing them, examined the runners, finding them to be in splendid condition. This work, with the assistance of the supporting party, took us till 8:30 A.M. Shortly afterward we got under way, saying good-bye to the supporting party, who are to return today. As we drew away, the ponies pulling hard, our comrades gave us three cheers. The weather was thick and overcast, with no wind. Part of White Island could be seen, and Observation Hill, astern, but before us lay a dead white wall, with nothing, even in the shape of a cloud, to guide our steering. Almost immediately after we left we crossed a crevasse, and before we had gone half a mile we found ourselves in a maze of them, only detecting their presence by the ponies breaking through the crust and saving themselves, or the man leading a pony putting his foot through. The first one Marshall crossed with Grisi was 6 ft. wide, and when I looked down there was nothing to be seen but a black yawning void. Just after this, I halted Quan on the side of one, as I thought in the uncertain light, but I found that we were standing on the crust in the center, so I very gingerly unharnessed him from the sledge and got him across. Then the sledge, with our three months' provisions, was pulled out of danger. Following this, Adams crossed another crevasse, and Chinaman got his forefoot into the hole at the side. I, following with Quan, also got into difficulties, and so I decided that it was too risky to proceed, and we camped between two large crevasses. We picketed the ponies out and pitched one tent, to wait till the light became better, for we were courting disaster by proceeding in that weather. Thus ended our day's march of under a mile, for about 1 P.M. it commenced to snow, and the wind sprang up from the southwest with drift. We pitched our second tent and had lunch, consisting of a pot of tea, some chocolate and two biscuits each. The temperature was plus 12°F at noon.

It blew a little in the afternoon, and I hope to find it clear away this pall of dead white stratus that stops us. The ponies were in splendid trim for pulling this morning, but, alas! we had to stop. Grisi and Socks did not eat up their food well at lunch or dinner. The temperature this evening is plus 9°F, and the ponies feel chilly. Truly this work is one demanding the greatest exercise of patience, for it is more than trying to have to sit here and watch the time going by, knowing that each day lessens our stock of food. The supporting party got under way about 9:30 A.M., and we could see them dwindling to a speck in the north. They will, no doubt, be at Hut Point in a couple of days. We are now at last quite on our own resources, and as regards comfort in the tents are very well off, for with only two men in each tent, there is ample room. Adams is sharing one with me, whilst Marshall and Wild have the other. Wild is cook this week, so they keep the cooker and the primus lamp in their tent, and we go across to meals, after first feeding the ponies. Next week Adams will be cook, so the cooking will be done in the tent I am in. We will also shift about so that we will take turns with each other as tent mates. On the days on which we are held up by weather we read, and I can only trust that these days may not be many. I am just finishing reading *The Taming of the Shrew*. I have Shakespeare's Comedies, Marshall has Borrow's, "The Bible in Spain," Adams has Arthur Young's "Travels in France," and Wild has "Sketches by Boz." When we have finished we will change around. Our allowance of tobacco is very limited, and on days like these it disappears rapidly, for our anxious minds are relieved somewhat by a smoke. In order to economize my cigarettes, which are my luxury, I whittled out a holder from a bit of bamboo today, and so get a longer smoke, and also avoid the paper sticking to my lips, which have begun to crack already from the hot metal pot and the cold air.

NOTE. The difficulties of traveling over snow and ice in a bad light are very great. When the light is diffused by clouds or mist, it casts no shadows on the dead white surface, which consequently appears to the eye to be uniformly level. Often as we marched, the sledges would be brought up all standing by a sastrugus, or snow mound, caused by the wind, and we would be lucky if we were not tripped up ourselves. Small depressions would escape the eye altogether, and when we thought that we were marching along on a level surface, we would suddenly step down two or three feet. The strain on the eyes under these conditions is very great, and it is when the sun is covered and the weather is thickish that snow blindness is produced. Snow blindness, with which we all became acquainted during the southern journey, is a very painful complaint. The first sign of the approach of the trouble is running at the nose; then the sufferer begins to see double, and his vision gradually becomes blurred. The more painful symptoms appear very soon. The blood vessels of the eyes swell, making one feel as though sand had got in under the lids, and then the eyes begin to water freely and gradually close up. The best method of relief is to drop some cocaine into the eye, and then apply a powerful astringent, such as sulphate of zinc, in order to reduce the distended blood vessels. The only way to guard against an attack is to wear goggles the whole time, so that the eyes may not be exposed to the strain caused by the reflection of the light from all quarters. These goggles are made so that the violet rays are cut off, these rays being the most dangerous, but in warm weather, when one is perspiring on account of exertion with the sledges, the glasses fog, and it becomes necessary to take them off frequently in order to wipe them. The goggles we used combined red and green glasses, and so gave a yellow tint to everything and greatly subdued the light. When we removed them, the glare from the surrounding whiteness was intense, and the only relief was to get inside one of the tents which were made of green material, very restful to the eyes. We noticed that during the spring journey, when the temperature was very low and the sun was glaring on us, we did not suffer from snow blindness. The glare of the light reflected from the snow on bright days places a very severe strain on the eyes, and the rays of the sun are flashed back from millions of crystals. The worst days, as far as snow blindness was concerned, were when the sun was obscured, so that the light came equally from every direction, and the temperature was comparatively high.

November 8. Drawn blank again! In our bags all day while outside the snow is drifting hard and blowing freshly at times. The temperature was plus 8°F at noon. The wind has not been really strong; if it had been I believe that the weather would have been over sooner. It is a sore trial to one's hopes and patience to lie and watch the drift on the tent side and to know that our valuable pony food is going, and this without benefiting the animals themselves. Indeed, Socks and Grisi have not been eating well, and the hard maize does not agree with them. At lunch we had only a couple of biscuits and some chocolate, and used our oil to boil some Maujee ration for the horses, so that they had a hot hoosh. They all ate it readily which is a comfort. This standing for four days in drift with 24° of frost is not good for them, and we are anxiously looking for finer weather. Tonight it is clearer, and we could see the horizon and some of the crevasses. We seem to be in a regular nest of them. The occupants of the other tent have discovered that it is pitched on the edge of a previously unseen one. We had a hot hoosh tonight, consisting of pemmican, with emergency ration and the cocoa. This warmed us up, for to lie from breakfast time at 6 A.M. for twelve or thirteen hours without hot food in this temperature is chilly work. If only we could get under way and put some good marches in, we would feel more happy. It is 750 miles as the crow flies from our winter quarters to the Pole, and we have done only fifty-one miles as yet. But still the worst will turn to the best, I doubt not. That a polar explorer needs a large stock of patience in his equipment there was no denying. The sun is showing thin and pale through the drift this evening, and the wind is more gusty, so we may have it really fine tomorrow. I read some of Shakespeare's comedies today.

November 9. A different story today. When we woke up at 4:30 A.M. it was fine, calm, and clear, such a change from the last four days. We got breakfast at 5 A.M., and then dug the sledges out of the drift. After this we four walked out to find a track amongst the crevasses, but unfortunately they could only be detected by probing with our ice axes, and these disclosed all sorts, from narrow cracks to great ugly chasms with no bottom visible. A lump of snow thrown down one would make no noise, so the bottom must have been very far below. The general direction was southeast and northwest, but some curved around to the south and some to the east. There was nothing for it but to trust to Providence, for we had to cross them somewhere. At 8:30 A.M. we got under way, the ponies not pulling very well, for they have lost condition in the blizzard and were stiff. We got over the first few crevasses without difficulty, then all of a sudden Chinaman went down a crack which ran parallel to our course. Adams tried to pull him out and he struggled gamely, and when Wild and I, who were next, left our sledges and hauled along Chinaman's sledge, it gave him more scope, and he managed to get on to the firm ice, only just in time, for three feet more and it would have been all up with the southern journey. The three-foot crack opened out into a great fathomless chasm, and down that would have gone the horse, all our cooking gear and biscuits and half the oil, and probably Adams as well. But when things seem the worst they turn to the best, for that was the last crevasse we encountered, and with a gradually improving surface, though very soft at times, we made fair headway. We camped for lunch at 12:40 P.M., and the ponies ate fairly well. Quan is pulling 660 lb., and had over 700 lb. till lunch; Grisi has 590 lb., Chinaman 570 lb., and Socks 600 lb. In the afternoon the surface further improved, and at 6 P.M. we camped,

having done 14 miles 600 yards, statute. The Bluff is
showing clear, and also Castle Rock miraged up astern
of us. White Island is also clear, but a stratus cloud over-
hangs Erebus, Terror, and Discovery. At 6:20 P.M. we
suddenly heard a deep rumble, lasting about five seconds, that made the air and the ice vibrate. It seemed
to come from the eastward, and resembled the sound
and had the effect of heavy guns firing. We conjecture
that it was due to some large mass of the Barrier breaking away, and the distance must be at least fifty miles
from where we are. It was startling, to say the least of
it. Tonight we boiled some Maujee ration for the ponies,
and they took this feed well. It has a delicious smell,
and we ourselves would have enjoyed it. Quan is now
engaged in the pleasing occupation of gnawing his tether
rope. I tethered him up by the hind leg to prevent him
attacking this particular thong, but he has found out that
by lifting his hind leg he can reach the rope, so I must
get out and put a nose bag on him. The temperature is
now plus 5°F, but it feels much warmer, for there is a
dead calm and the sun is shining.

CHAPTER XII

Beyond All Former Footsteps
November 10 to December 4

Steady Progress: The Sighting of New Land

November 10. Got up to breakfast at 6 A.M., and under way at 8:15 A.M. During the night we had to get out to the ponies. Quan had eaten away the straps on his rug, and Grisi and Socks were fighting over it. Quan had also chewed Chinaman's tether, and the latter was busy at one of the sledges, chewing rope. Happily he has not the same mischievous propensities as Quan, so the food bags were not torn about. All these things mean work for us when the day's march is over, repairing the damage done. The ponies started away well, with a good hard surface to travel on, but a bad light, so we, being in finnesko, had frequent falls over the sastrugi. I at last took my goggles off, and am paying the penalty tonight, having a touch of snow blindness. During the morning the land to the west became more distinct, and the going still better, so that when we camped for lunch, we had covered nine and a half statute miles. All the ponies, except Quan, showed the result of the Maujee ration, and are quite loose. Directly we started after lunch, we came across the track of an Adelie penguin. It was most surprising, and one wonders how the bird came out here. It had evidently only passed a short time before, as its tracks were quite fresh. It had been traveling on its stomach a good way, and its course was due east toward the sea, but where it had come from was a mystery, for the nearest water in the direction from which it came was over fifty miles away, and it had at least another fifty miles to do before it could reach food and water. The surface in the afternoon became appallingly soft, the ponies sinking in up to their hocks, but there was hard snow underneath. At 6 P.M. we camped, with a march for the day of 15 miles 1550 yards statute. The sun came out in the afternoon, so we turned our sleeping bags inside out and dried them. Today's temperature ranged

from plus 3°F in the morning to plus 12°F. at noon. At
8 P.M. it was plus 5°F. There is now a light north wind,
and I expect Erebus will be clear soon; bearings and
angles put us sixty miles from our depot, where lies 167
lb. of pony food.

November 11. It was 8:40 before we got under way
this morning, for during the night the temperature
dropped well below zero, and it was minus 12° when we
got up and found our finnesko and all our gear frozen
hard, just like spring sledging times. We had to unpack
the sledges and scrape the runners, for the sun had
melted the snow on the upper surfaces, and the water
had run down and frozen hard during the night on the
under sides. The surface was again terribly soft, but
there were patches of hard sastrugi beneath, and on one
of these Quan must have stepped, for to our great anxiety he suddenly went lame about 11 A.M. I thought it
was just the balling of the snow on his feet, but on
scraping this off he still was lame. Fortunately, however,
he improved greatly and was practically all right after
lunch. During the night, the snow always balls on the
ponies' feet, and it is one of our regular jobs to scrape
it off, before we harness up in the morning. The snow
was not so thick on the surface in the afternoon, only
about 5 in., and we got on fairly well. The Bluff is now
sixteen miles to the northwest of us, and all the well
known land is clear, Erebus sending out a huge volume
of steam, that streams away to the southwest right past
Mount Discovery, fifty miles from its crater. Again this
afternoon we passed an Adelie penguin track. The bird
was making the same course as the one we had passed
before. At 6:30 P.M. we camped, having done fifteen statute miles. After dinner we got bearings which put us
forty-seven miles from our depot. I do trust that the
weather will hold up till we reach it. It is cold tonight
· writing, the temperature being minus 9°F. The land to
the south southwest is beautifully clear.

November 13. No diary yesterday, for I had a bad
attack of snow blindness, and am only a bit better tonight. We did a good march yesterday of over fifteen
miles over fair surface, and again today did fifteen miles,
but the going was softer. The ponies have been a trouble

again. I found Quan and Chinaman enjoying the former's rug. They have eaten all the lining. The weather has been beautifully fine, but the temperature down to 12° below zero. The others' eyes are all right. Wild, who has been suffering, has been better today. Snow blindness is a particularly unpleasant thing. One begins by seeing double, then the eyes feel full of grit; this makes them water and eventually one cannot see at all. All yesterday afternoon, though I was wearing goggles, the water kept running out of my eyes, and, owing to the low temperature, it froze on my beard. However, the weather is beautiful, and we are as happy as can be, with good appetites, too good in fact for the amount of food we are allowing ourselves. We are on short rations, but we will have horse meat in addition when the ponies go under. We have saved enough food to last us from our first depot into the Bluff, where, on the way back, we will pick up another depot that is to be laid out by Joyce during January next. I trust we will pick up the depot tomorrow night and it will be a relief, for it is a tiny speck in this snowy plain, and is nearly sixty miles from the nearest land. It is much the same as picking up a buoy in the North Sea with only distant mountains for bearings. We are now clear of the pressure round the Bluff, and the traveling should be good until we reach the depot. On the spring journey we got into the crevasses off the Bluff, these crevasses being due to the movement of the ice-sheet impinging against the long arm of the Bluff reaching out to the eastward. Close in the pressure is much more marked, the whole surface of the Barrier rising into hillocks and splitting into chasms. When the summer sun plays on these and the wind sweeps away the loose snow, a very slippery surface is presented, and the greatest care has to be exercised to prevent the sledges skidding into the pits, often over 100 ft. deep. As one gets further away from the area of disturbance the ridges flatten out, the pits disappear, and the crevasses become cracks. We are now on to level going, clear of any dangers.

November 14. Another beautiful day, but with a low temperature (minus 7°F at 6 P.M.). During the morning there was a wind from the west southwest, bitterly cold on our faces and burst lips, but the sun was warm on our backs. The ponies pulled well, and in spite of somewhat deep snow they got on very well. We stopped at noon for bearings, and to get the sun's altitude for latitude, and at lunch worked out our position. We expected to see the depot tonight or tomorrow morning, but during the afternoon, when we halted for a spell, we found that our "ready use" tin of kerosene had dropped off a sledge, so Adams ran back three miles and found it. This caused a delay, and we camped at 6 P.M. We were just putting the position on the chart after dinner when Wild, who was outside looking through the Goertz glasses, shouted out that he could see the depot, and we rushed out. There were the flag and sledge plainly to be seen through the glasses. It is an immense relief to us, for there is stored at the depot four days' pony feed and a gallon of oil. We will sleep happily tonight. The Barrier surface now is covered with huge sastrugi, rounded off and running west southwest and east northeast, with soft snow between. We have never seen the surface alike for two consecutive days. The Barrier is as wayward and as changeful as the sea.

November 15. Another beautiful day. We broke camp at 8 A.M., and reached our depot at 9:20 A.M. We found everything intact, the flag waving merrily in the breeze, the direction of which was about west southwest. We camped there and at once proceeded to redistribute weights and to parcel our provisions to be left there. We found that we had saved enough food to allow for three days' rations, which ought to take us into the Bluff on our return, so we made up a bag of provisions and added a little oil to the tin we had been using from, leaving half a gallon to take us the fifty odd miles to the Bluff on the way back. We then depoted our spare gear and finnesko, and our tin of sardines and pot of black currant jam. We had intended these provisions for Christmas Day, but the weight is too much; every ounce is of importance. We took on the maize, and the ponies are now pulling 449 lb. each. Quan was pulling 469 lb. before the depot was reached, so he had nothing added to his load. All this arranging took time, and it was nearly noon before we had finished. We took an observation for latitude and variation, and found the latitude to be 79° 36' South, and the variation 155° East. Had lunch at noon and started due south at 1:15 P.M., the ponies pulling well. As the afternoon went on the surface of the Barrier altered to thick, crusty snow, with long rounded sastrugi about 4 ft. high, almost looking like small undulations, running southwest to northwest, with small sastrugi on top running west and east. Camped at 6 P.M., having done 12 miles 1500 yards (statute) today. There are some high, stratified, light clouds in the sky, the first clouds we have had for nearly a week. The sun now, at 9 P.M., is beautifully warm, though the air temperature is minus 2°F. It is dead calm. We are going to build a snow mound at each camp as a guide to our homeward track, and as our camps will only be seven miles apart, these marks ought to help us. The mystery of the Barrier grips us, and we long to know what lies in the unknown to the south. This we may do with good fortune in another fortnight.

NOTE. I wrote that the provisions left at the depot would suffice for three days, but as a matter of fact there was not more than a two days' supply. We felt that we ought to take on every ounce of food that we could, and that if we got back to the depot we would be able to manage as far as the Bluff all right. During the winter we had thought over the possibility of making the mounds as a guide for the return march, and had concluded that though they would entail extra work, we might be well repaid if we picked up only one or two of them at critical times. We had with us two shovels, and ten minutes' work was sufficient to raise a mound 6 or 7 ft. high. We wondered whether the mounds would disappear under the influence of wind and sun, and our tracks remain, whether the tracks would disappear and the mounds remain, whether both tracks and mounds would disappear, or whether both would remain. As we were not keeping in towards the land, but were making a bee-line for the south, it was advisable to neglect no precaution, and as events turned out, the mounds were most useful. They remained after the sledge tracks had

disappeared, and they were a very great comfort to us
during the journey back from our farthest south point.

November 16. We started again this morning in gloriously fine weather, the temperature minus 15°F (down
to minus 25°F during the night). The ponies pulled
splendidly. All the western mountains stood up, miraged
into the forms of castles. Even the Bluff could be seen
in the far distance, changed into the semblance of a giant
keep. Before starting, which we did at 7:40 A.M., we
made a mound of snow, 6 ft. high, as a guide to us on
our homeward way, and as it was built on a large sastrugi, we saw it for two and a half statute miles after
starting. At twenty minutes to twelve, we halted for latitude observations, and found that we had reached 78°
50' South. After lunch the surface changed somewhat,
but the going was fairly good, in fact we covered 17
miles 200 yards (statute), a record day for us. This evening it is cloudy, high cumulus going from southeast to
northwest. The temperature tonight is minus 5°F, but it
being dead calm we feel quite warm. A hot sun during
the day dried our reindeer skin sleeping bags, the water,
or rather ice, all drying out of them, so we sleep in dry
bags again. It has been a wonderful and successful week,
so different to this time six years ago, when I was toiling
along five miles a day over the same ground. Tonight
one can see the huge mountain range to the south of
Barne Inlet. In order to further economize food we are
saving three lumps of sugar each every day, so in time
we will have a fair stock. The great thing is to advance
our food supply as far south as possible before the ponies give out. Every one is in splendid health, eyes all
right again, and only minor troubles, such as split lips,
which do not allow us to laugh. Wild steered all day,
and at every hourly halt I put the compass down to
make the course we are going straight as a die to the
south. Chinaman, or "The Vampire," as Adams calls
him, is not so fit; he is stiff in the knees and has to be
hauled along. Quan, *alias* "Blossom," is A1, but one
cannot leave him for a moment, otherwise he would
have his harness chewed up. Within the last week he has
had the greater part of a horse cloth, about a fathom of

rope, several pieces of leather, and odds and ends such as a nose-bag buckle, but his digestion is marvelous, and he seems to thrive on his strange diet. He would rather eat a yard of creosoted rope than his maize and Maujee, indeed he often, in sheer wantonness, throws his food all over the snow.

November 17. A dull day when we started at 9:50 A.M., but the mountains abeam were in sight till noon. The weather then became completely overcast, and the light most difficult to steer in; a dead white wall was what we seemed to be marching to, and there was no direct light to cast even the faintest shadow on the sastrugi. I steered from noon to 1 P.M., and from lunch till 6 P.M., but the course was most erratic, and we had to stop every now and then to put the compass down to verify our course and alter it if necessary. Our march for the day was 16 miles 200 yard (statute) through a bad surface, the ponies sinking in up to their hocks. This soft surface is similar to that we experienced last trip south, for the snow had a crust easily broken through and about 6 in. down an airspace, then similar crusts and airspaces in layers. It was trying work for the ponies, but they all did splendidly in their own particular way. Old "Blossom" plods stolidly through it; Chinaman flounders rather painfully, for he is old and stiff nowadays; Grisi and Socks take the soft places with a rush; but all get through the day's work and feed up at night, though Quan evinces disgust at not having more Maujee ration and flings his maize out of his nose-bag. One wonders each night what trouble they will get into. This morning, on turning out, we found Grisi lying down unable to get up. He had got to the end of his tether, and could not draw back his leg. He was shivering with cold, though the temperature was only minus 5°. Today we had a plus temperature, for the first time since leaving—plus 9°F at noon, and plus 5°F at 6 P.M. The pall of cloud no doubt acts as a blanket, and so we were warm, too warm in fact for marching.

November 18. Started at 8 A.M. in clearer weather, and the sun remained visible all day, though during the morning it was snowing from the south, and made the steering very difficult. The surface has been simply awful. We seem to have arrived at a latitude where there is no wind and the snow remains where it falls, for we were sinking in well over our ankles, and the poor ponies are having a most trying time. They break through the crust on the surface and flounder up to their hocks, and at each step they have to pull their feet out through the brittle crust. It is telling more on Chinaman than on the others, and he is going slowly. The chafing of the snow crust on his fetlocks has galled them, so we will have to shoot him at the next depot in about three days' time. The ponies are curious animals. We give them full meals, and yet they prefer to gnaw at any odd bits of rope. Quan got my jacket in his teeth this morning as I was scraping the snow off his hind feet, and I had to get out last night to stop Socks biting and swallowing lumps out of Quan's tail. If we had thought that they would have been up to these games, we would have had a longer wire to tether them, so as to keep them apart. It is possible that we have reached the windless area around the Pole, for the Barrier is a dead, smooth, white plain, weird beyond description, and having no land in sight, we feel such tiny specks in the immensity around us. Overhead this afternoon, when the weather cleared, were wonderful lines of clouds, radiating from the southwest, traveling very fast to the northeast. It seems as though we were in some other world, and yet the things that concern us most for the moment are trivial, such as split lips and big appetites. Already the daily meals seem all too short, and we wonder what it will be like later on, when we were really hungry. I have had that experience once, and my companions will soon have it again with me. All the time we are moving south to our wished-for goal, and each day we feel that another gain has been made. We did 15 miles 500 yards today.

November 19. Started at 8:15 this morning with a fresh southerly breeze and drift. The temperature was plus 2°F, and this was the temperature all day, making it cold traveling, but good for the ponies, who, poor beasts, had to plough through a truly awful surface, sinking in 8 or 10 in. at every step. This does not seem very deep, but when one goes on hour after hour it is a strain on man and horse, for we have to hold the ponies up as they stumble along. In spite of the surface and the wind and drift, we cover 15 miles 200 yards (statute) by 6 P.M. and were glad to camp, for our beards and faces were coated in ice, and our helmets had frozen stiff on to our faces. We got sights for latitude at noon, and found that we were in latitude 80° 32' South. On the last journey I was not in that latitude till December 16, though we left Hut Point on November 2, a day earlier than we did this time. The ponies have truly done well. I wrote yesterday that we seemed to be in a windless area, but today alters that opinion. The sastrugi are all pointing clearly due south, and if we have the wind on our way back it will be a great help. The same radiant points in the clouds southeast to northwest were visible again today, and at times when it cleared somewhat a regular nimbus cloud, similar to the rain clouds in the "doldrums," could be seen. At the base of the converging point of the southeast part of cloud there seemed to rise other clouds to meet the main body. The former trended directly from the horizon at an angle of 30° to meet the main body, and did not seem to be more than a few miles off. The drift on the Barrier surface was piled up into heaps of very fine snow, with the smallest grains, and on encountering these the sledges ran heavily. The crust that has formed, when broken through, discloses loose grained snow, and the harder crust, about 8 in. down, is almost even. I suppose that the top 8 in. represents the year's snowfall.

November 20. Started at 8:55 A.M. in dull, overcast weather again, but the sun broke through during the morning, so we had something to steer by. The surface has been the worst we have encountered so far, terribly soft, but we did 15 miles 800 yards (statute) for the day. The latter part of the afternoon was better. It seems to savor of repetition to write each day of the heavy going and the soft surface, but these factors play a most important part in our daily work, and it causes us a great deal of speculation as to what we will eventually find as we get further south. The whole place and conditions seem so strange and so unlike anything else in the world in our experience, that one cannot describe them in fitting words. At one moment one thinks of Coleridge's "An-

cient Mariner": "Alone, alone; all, all alone, alone on a
wide, wide sea," and then when the mazy clouds spring
silently from either hand and drift quickly across our
zenith, not followed by any wind, it seems uncanny.
There comes a puff of wind from the north, another
from the south, and anon one from the east or west,
seeming to obey no law, acting on erratic impulses. It is
as though we were truly at the world's end, and were
bursting in on the birthplace of the clouds and the nesting home of the four winds, and one has a feeling that
we mortals are being watched with a jealous eye by the
forces of nature. To add to these weird impressions that
seem to grow on one in the apparently limitless waste,
the sun tonight was surrounded by mock suns and in the
zenith was a bow, turning away from the great vertical
circle around the sun. These circles and bows were the
color of the rainbow. We are all fairly tired tonight, and
Wild is not feeling very fit, but a night's rest will do him
good. The ponies are all fit except poor old Chinaman,
and he must go tomorrow. He cannot keep up with the
others, and the bad surface has played him out. The
temperature is zero F.

November 21. Started at 7:30 A.M. as we had to come
to camp early tonight, and we wanted to get a good
latitude observation at noon. Although we got away
early, however, all morning we were steering through
thick weather with driving ice crystals, and at noon there
was no chance of getting the sun for latitude. We came
to camp at 12:30 P.M., just as the weather cleared a little,
and we could see land on our right hand, but only the
base of the mountains, so could not identify them. Chinaman came up at last, struggling painfully along, so
when we made our depot this evening he was shot. We
will use the meat to keep us out longer, and will save
on our dried stores. The temperature at noon was only
plus 8°F, and the little wind that there was has been
extremely cold. The wind veers round and round the
compass, and the clouds move in every direction. The
surface of the Barrier was better today, but still the ponies sank in 8 in. at least. The sastrugi point toward the
southeast, this being the direction of the most usual wind
here. This evening it cleared, and we could see land al-

most ahead, and the great mass of land abaft the beam
to the north of Barne Inlet. Our day's march was 15
miles 450 yards. We are now south of the 81st parallel,
and feel that we are well on the road to our wished-for
goal. This is now our second depot, and we intend to
leave about 80 lb. of pony meat, one tin of biscuits (27
lb.), some sugar, and one tin of oil, to see us back to
Depot A. It is late now, for all arrangements for the
depot took time. There was a lot of work in the arranging of the sledges for the remaining three ponies, packing stores, skinning Chinaman, and cutting him up, all
in a low temperature.

NOTE. The killing of the ponies was not pleasant work,
but we had the satisfaction of knowing that the animals
had been well fed and well treated up to the last, and
that they suffered no pain. When we had to kill a pony,
we threw up a snow mound to leeward of the camp, so
that no smell of blood could come down wind, and took
the animal behind this, out of sight of the others. As a
matter of fact, the survivors never displayed any interest
at all in the proceedings, even the report of the revolver
used in the killing failing to attract their attention. The
sound did not travel far on the wide open plain. The
revolver was held about 3 in. from the forehead of the
victim and one shot was sufficient to cause instant death.
The throat of the animal was cut immediately and the
blood allowed to run away. Then Marshall and Wild
would skin the carcass, and we took the meat off the
legs, shoulders, and back. In the case of Chinaman the
carcass was opened and the liver and undercut secured,
but the job was such a lengthy one that we did not repeat it in the case of the other animals. Within a very
short time after killing the carcass would be frozen solid,
and we always tried to cut the meat up into as small
pieces as possible before this occurred, for the cutting
became very much more difficult after the process of
freezing was complete. On the following days, whenever
there was time to spare, we would proceed with the cutting until we had got all the meat ready for cooking. It
was some time before we found out that it was better
merely to warm the meat through when we wanted to

eat it, and not attempt to cook it properly. It was fairly
tender when only warmed, but if it were boiled it became very tough, and we would not spare enough oil to
stew it in order to soften it thoroughly. Our supply of
oil had been cut down very fine in order to save weight.
The only meat that we cooked thoroughly was that from
Grisi, because we found, at a later stage of the journey,
that this meat was not good, and we thought that cooking might make it less liable to cause attacks of dysentery. We used the harness from the dead pony to make
stays for the sledge which would be left at the depot.
The sledge was reared on to its end, about 3 ft. being
sunk into the snow, and a bamboo with a black flag
stuck on the top, so that we might be able to find the
little "cache" of food on the return journey. Stays were
required lest a blizzard should blow down the whole
erection.

November 22. A beautiful morning. We left our depot
with its black flag flying on the bamboo lashed to a discarded sledge, stuck upright in the snow, at 8:20 A.M.
We have now three ponies dragging 500 lb. each, and
they did splendidly through the soft snow. The going, I
am thankful to say, is getting better, and here and there
patches of harder surface are to be met with. The outstanding feature of today's march is that we have seen
new land to the south—land never seen by human eyes
before. The land consists of great snow-clad heights rising beyond Mount Longstaff, and also far inland to the
north of Mounts Markham. These heights we did not
see on our journey south on the last expedition, for we
were too close to the land or, rather, foothills, but now
at the great distance we are out they can be seen plainly.
It has been a beautifully clear day, and all the well-
known mountains are clearly visible. The coast trends
about south by east, so that we are safe for a good long
way south. We camped at noon and got a good meridian
altitude and azimuth. We found our latitude to be 81°
8' South. In the afternoon we steered a little to the east
of south, and camped at 6 P.M. with 15 miles 250 yards
(statute) to the credit of the day. This is good, for the
ponies have a heavy load, but they are well fed. We

were rather long at lunch camp, for we tried to pull out Adams' tooth, which has given him great pain, so much that he has not slept at night at all. But the tooth broke, and he has a bad time now. We were not equipped on this trip for tooth-pulling. Wild is better today, but fatty food is not to his taste just now, so he had a good feed of horse flesh. We all liked it, for it filled us well, in spite of being somewhat tough. The flavor was good and it means a great saving of our other food. The temperature has risen to plus 7°F, and the surface of the Barrier is good for sledge-hauling.

November 23. Our record march today, the distance being 17 miles 1650 yards statute. It has been a splendid day for marching, with a cool breeze from the south and the sun slightly hidden. The horses did very well indeed, and the surface has improved, there being fairly hard sastrugi from the south. We are gradually rising the splendid peaks of Longstaff and Markham. The former, from our present bearing, has several sharp peaks, and the land fades away in the far distance to the south, with numbers of peaks showing, quite new to human eyes. All the old familiar mountains, toward which I toiled so painfully last time I was here, are visible, and what a difference it is now! Tonight there is a fresh wind from what appears at this distance to be a strait between Longstaff and Markham, and a low drift is flying along. Wild is better tonight, but he was tired after the long march. We made him a cup of our emergency Oxo for lunch, and that bucked him up for the afternoon. He has not eaten much lately, but says that he feels decidedly better tonight. Marshall has just succeeded in pulling out Adams' tooth so now the latter will be able to enjoy horse meat. This evening we had it fried, and so saved all our other food except biscuits and cocoa. It is my week as cook now, and Wild is my tent companion.

November 24. Started this morning at 7:55, and made a good march of 10 miles 600 yards (statute) up to 1 P.M., when we camped for lunch. We marched from 2:30 to 6 P.M., and camped then for the night. When we started there was a searching breeze in our faces, which gradually increased during the day with low drift, and it was blowing a summer blizzard when we camped this evening, the temperature up to plus 17°F, and the drift melting in the tent and on all our gear. The ponies did splendidly again, in spite of soft surface, our day's run being 17 miles 680 yards statute. The Barrier surface is still as level as a billiard table, with no sign of any undulation or rise; but if the Barrier shows no sign of change it is otherwise with the mountains. Each mile shows us new land, and most of it consists of lofty mountains, whose heights at present we cannot estimate. They are well over 10,000 ft. The great advantage of being out from the coast is now obvious, for we can see a long range of sharp peaked mountains running to the westward from Mounts Markham, and forming the south side of Shackleton Inlet on the east side of Mounts Markham, and other peaks and one table-topped mountain standing away to the south between Longstaff and Markham. There appears to be a wide strait or inlet between Longstaff and the new land east of Markham. Then trending about southeast from Longstaff is a lofty range of mountains which we will see more closely as we move south. I trust that the blizzard will blow itself out tonight, so that we may have easy going tomorrow. Wild is much better today, and took his ordinary food. We had fried pony for dinner tonight, and raw pony frozen on the march. The going is very good, but we can only afford a little oil to cook up the meat for meals.

November 25. Started at 8 A.M. this morning in fairly good weather. The wind has gone during the night, leaving our tents drifted up with fine snow. The land was obscured nearly all day, but toward the evening it cleared and we could see the details of the coast. There appears to be a series of inlets and capes opening at all angles, and with no fixed coastline, though the lofty range of mountains continues to the south with a very slight trend to the eastward. The surface of the Barrier was very trying today, for the snow had no consistency and slipped away as one trod on it. It was not so trying for the ponies, and they did 17 miles 1600 yards. We had frozen raw pony meat to eat on the march, and a good hoosh of pony meat and pemmican for dinner. Wild is practically all right, and Adams finds a wisdom tooth growing in place of the one he lost. Our eyes are not too comfortable just now. It is a wonderful place we are in, all new to the world, and yet I feel that I cannot describe it. There is an impression of limitless solitude about it all that makes us feel so small as we trudge along, a few dark specks on the snowy plain, and watch the new land appear.

November 26. A day to remember, for we have passed the "farthest South" previously reached by man. Tonight we are in latitude 82° 18½' South, longitude 168° East, and this latitude we have been able to reach in much less time than on the last long march with Captain Scott, when we made latitude 82° 16½' our "farthest South." We started in lovely weather this morning, with the temperature plus 19°F, and it has been up to plus 20°F during the day, giving us a chance to dry our sleeping bags. We were rather anxious at starting about Quan, who had a sharp attack of colic, the result no doubt of his morbid craving for bits of rope and other odds and ends in preference to his proper food. He soon got well enough to pull, and we got away at 7:40 A.M., the surface still very soft. There are abundant signs that the wind blows strongly from the south southeast during the winter, for the sastrugi are very marked in that direction. There are extremely large circular crystals of snow on the Barrier surface, and they seem hard and brittle. They catch the light from the sun, each one forming a reflector that dazzles the eyes as one glances at the million points of light. As each hour went on today, we found new interest to the west, where the land lies, for we opened out Shackleton Inlet, and up the inlet lies a great chain of mountains, and far into the west appear more peaks; to the west of Cape Wilson appears another chain of sharp peaks about 10,000 ft. high, stretching away to the north beyond the Snow Cape, and continuing the land on which Mount A. Markham lies. To the south southeast ever appear new mountains. I trust that no land will block our path. We celebrated the breaking of the "farthest South" record with a four-ounce bottle of Curacao, sent us by a friend at home. After this had been shared out into two tablespoonfuls each, we had a smoke and a talk before turning in. One wonders what the next month will bring forth. We ought by that time to be near our goal, all being well.

NOTE. It falls to the lot of few men to view land not previously seen by human eyes, and it was with feelings of keen curiosity, not unmingled with awe, that we watched the new mountains rise from the great unknown that lay ahead of us. Mighty peaks they were, the eternal snows at their bases, and their rough-hewn forms rising high toward the sky. No man of us could tell what we would discover in our march south, what wonders might not be revealed to us, and our imaginations would take wings until a stumble in the snow, the sharp pangs of hunger, or the dull ache of physical weariness brought back our attention to the needs of the immediate present. As the days wore on, and mountain after mountain came into view, grimly majestic, the consciousness of our insignificance seemed to grow upon us. We were but tiny black specks crawling slowly and painfully across the white plain, and bending our puny strength to the task of wresting from nature secrets preserved inviolate through all the ages. Our anxiety to learn what lay beyond was nonetheless keen, however, and the long days of marching over the Barrier surface were saved from monotony by the continued appearance of new land to the southeast.

November 27. Started at 8 A.M., the ponies pulling well over a bad surface of very soft snow. The weather is fine and clear save for a strong mirage, which throws all the land up much higher than it really is. All day we have seen new mountains arise, and it is causing us some anxiety to note that they trend more and more to the eastward, for that means an alteration of our course from nearly due south. Still they are a long way off, and when we get up to them we may find some strait that will enable us to go right through them and on south. One speculates greatly as we march along, but patience is what is needed. I think that the ponies are feeling the day in, day out drudgery of pulling on this plain. Poor beasts, they cannot understand, of course, what it is all for, and the wonder of the great mountains is nought to them, though one notices them at times looking at the distant land. At lunch time I took a photograph of our camp, with Mount Longstaff in the background. We had our sledge flags up to celebrate the breaking of the southern record. The long snow cape marked on the chart as being attached to Mount Longstaff is not really so. It is attached to a lower bluff mountain to the north of Mount Longstaff. The most northerly peak of Mount Longstaff goes sheer down into the Barrier, and all along this range of mountains are very steep glaciers, greatly crevassed. As we pass along the mountains the capes disappear, but there are several well marked ones of which we have taken angles. Still more mountains appeared above the horizon during the afternoon, and when we camped tonight some were quite clearly defined, many, many miles away. The temperature has been up to plus 22°F today, and we took the opportunity of drying our sleeping bags, which we turned inside out and laid on the sledges. Tonight the temperature is plus 13°F. We find that raw frozen pony meat cools one on the march, and during the ten minutes' spell after an hour's march we all cut up meat for lunch or dinner; in the hot sun it thaws well. This fresh meat ought to keep away scurvy from us. Quan seems much better today, but Grisi does not appear fit at all. He seems to be snow blind. Our distance today was 16 miles 1200 yards.

November 28. Started at 7:50 A.M. in beautiful weather, but with a truly awful surface, the ponies sinking in very deeply. The sledges ran easily, as the temperature was high, plus 17° to plus 20°F, the hot sun making the snow surface almost melt. We halted at noon for a latitude observation, and found our latitude to be 82° 38' South. The land now appears more to the east, bearing southeast by south, and some very high mountains a long way off with lower foothills, can be seen in front, quite different to the land abeam of us, which consists of huge sharp pointed mountains with crevassed glaciers moving down gullies in their sides. Marshall is making a careful survey of all the principal heights. All day we have been traveling up and down long undulations, the width from crest to crest being about one and a half miles, and the rise about 1 in 100. We can easily see the line by our tracks sometimes being cut off sharp when we are on the down gradient and appearing again a long way astern as we rise. The first indication of the undulation was the fact of the mound we had made in the morning disappearing before we had traveled a quarter of a mile. During the afternoon the weather was very hot. A cool breeze had helped us in the forenoon, but it died away later. Marshall has a touch of snow blindness, and both Grisi and Socks were also affected during the day. When we camped tonight Grisi was shot. He had fallen off during the last few days, and the snow blindness was bad for him, putting him off his feed. He was the one chosen to go at the depot we made this evening. This is Depot C, and we are leaving one week's provisions and oil, with horse meat, to carry us back to Depot B. We will go on tomorrow with 1200 lb. weight (nine weeks' provisions), and we four will pull with the ponies, two on each sledge. It is late now, 11 P.M., and we have just turned in. We get up at 5:30 every morning. Our march for the day was 15 miles 1500 yards statute.

November 29. Started at 8:45 A.M. with adjusted loads of 630 lb. on each sledge. We harnessed up ourselves, but found that the ponies would not pull when we did, and as the loads came away lightly, we untoggled our harness. The surface was very soft, but during the morning there were occasional patches of hard sastrugi, all pointing south southeast. This is the course we are now steering, as the land is trending about southeast by east. During the day still more great mountains appeared to the southeast, and to the west we opened up several huge peaks, 10,000 to 15,000 ft. in height. The whole country seems to be made up of range after range of mountains, one behind the other. The worst feature of today's march was the terribly soft snow in the hollows of the great undulations we were passing. During the afternoon one place was so bad that the ponies sank in right up to their bellies, and we had to pull with might and main to get the sledges along at all. When we began to ascend the rise on the southern side of the undulation it got better. The ponies were played out by 5:45 P.M., especially old Quan, who nearly collapsed, not from the weight of the sledge, but from the effort of lifting his feet and limbs through the soft snow. The weather is calm and clear, but very hot, and it is trying to man and beast. We are on a short allowance of food, for we must save all we can, so as to help the advance as far as possible. Marshall has taken the angles of the new land today. He does this regularly. The hypsometer readings at 1 P.M. are very high now if there is no correction, and it is not due to weather. We must be at about sea level. The undulations run about east by south, and west by west, and are at the moment a puzzle to us. I cannot think that the feeding of the glaciers from the adjacent mountains has anything to do with their existence. There are several glaciers, but their size is inconsiderable compared to the vast extent of Barrier affected. The glaciers are greatly crevassed. There are enormous granite cliffs at the foot of the range we are passing, and they stand vertically about 4000 to 5000 ft. without a vestige of snow upon them. The main bare rocks appear to be like the schists of the western mountains opposite our winter quarters, but we are too far away, of course, to be able to tell with any certainty. Down to the south are mountains entirely clear of snow, for their sides are vertical, and they must be not less than 8000 to 9000 ft. in height. Altogether it is a weird and wonderful country. The only familiar thing is the broad expanse of Barrier to the east, where as yet no land appears. We did 14 miles 900 yards (statute) today, and are tired. The snow came well above our ankles, and each step became a labor. Still we are making our way south, and each mile gained reduces the unknown. We have now done over 300 miles due south in less than a month.

November 30. We started at 8 A.M. this morning. Quan very shaky and seemingly on his last legs, poor beast. Both he and Socks are snow blind, so we have improvised shades for their eyes, which we trust will help them a little. We took turns of an hour each hauling at Quan's sledge, one at each side, to help him. Socks, being faster, always gets ahead and then has a short spell, which eases him considerably. We advanced very slowly today, for the surface was as bad as ever till the afternoon, and the total distance covered was 12 miles 150 yards. Quan was quite played out, so we camped at 5:45 P.M. We give the ponies ample food, but they do not eat it all, though Quan whinnies for his every meal time. He is particularly fond of the Maujee ration, and neglects his maize for it. Again today we saw new land to the south, and unfortunately for our quick progress in that direction, we find the trend of the coast more to the eastward. A time is coming, I can see, when we will have to ascend the mountains, for the land runs round more and more in an easterly direction. Still after all we must not expect to find things cut and dried and all suited to us in such a place. We will be thankful if we can keep the ponies as far as our next depot which will be in latitude 84° South. They are at the present moment lying down in the warm sun. It is a beautifully calm clear evening; indeed as regards weather we have been wonderfully fortunate, and it has given Marshall the chance to take all the necessary angles for the survey of these new mountains and coastline. Wild is cook this week, and my week is over so I am now living in the other tent. We are all fit and well, but our appetites are increasing at an alarming rate. We noticed this tonight after the heavy pulling today. A great deal of the land we are passing seems to consist of granite in huge masses, and here and there are much crevassed glaciers pouring down between the mountains, perhaps from some inland ice sheet similar to that in the north of Victoria Land. The mountains show great similarity in outline, and there is no sign of any volcanic action at all so far. The temperature for the day has ranged between plus 16° and plus 12°F, but the hot sun has made things appear much warmer.

December 1. Started at 8 A.M. today. Quan has been growing weaker each hour, and we practically pulled the sledge. We passed over three undulations, and camped at 1 P.M. In the afternoon we only did four miles, Quan being led by Wild. He also led Socks with one sledge, whilst Adams, Marshall, and I hauled 200 lb. each on the other sledge, over a terribly soft surface. Poor old Quan was quite finished when we came to camp at 6 P.M., having done 12 miles 200 yards, so he was shot. We all felt losing him, I particularly, for he was my special horse ever since he was ill last March. I had looked after him, and in spite of all his annoying tricks he was a general favorite. He seemed so intelligent. Still it was best for him to go, and like the others he was well fed to the last. We have now only one pony left, and are in latitude 83° 16' South. Ahead of us we can see the land stretching away to the east, with a long white line in front of it that looks like a giant Barrier, and nearer a very crusted-up appearance, as though there were great pressure ridges in front of us. It seems as though the Barrier end had come, and that there is now going to be a change in some gigantic way in keeping with the vastness of the whole place. We fervently trust that we will not be delayed in our march south. We are living mainly on horsemeat now, and on the march, to cool our throats when pulling in the hot sun, we chew some raw frozen meat. There was a slight breeze for a time today, and we felt chilly, as we were pulling stripped to our shirts. We wear our goggles all the time, for the glare from the snow surface is intense and the sky is cloudless. A few wisps of fleecy cloud settle on the tops of the loftiest mountains, but that is all. The surface of the Barrier still sparkles with the million frozen crystals which stand apart from the ordinary surface snow. One or two new peaks came in sight today, so we are ever adding to the chain of wonderful mountains that we have found. At one moment our thoughts are on the grandeur of the scene, the next of what we would have to eat if only we were let loose in a good restaurant. We are very hungry these days, and we know that we are likely to be for another three months. One of the granite cliffs we are nearing is over 6000 ft. sheer, and much bare rock is showing, which must have running water on it as the hot sun plays down. The moon was visible in the sky all day and it was something familiar, yet far removed from these days of hot sunshine and wide white pathways. The temperature is now plus 16°F, and it is quite warm in the tent.

December 2. Started at 8 A.M., all four of us hauling one sledge, and Socks following behind with the other. He soon got into our regular pace, and did very well indeed. The surface during the morning was extremely bad and it was heavy work for us. The sun beat down on our heads and we perspired freely, though we were

BEYOND ALL FORMER FOOTSTEPS   197

working only in shirts and pajama trousers, whilst our
feet were cold in the snow. We halted for lunch at 1
P.M., and had some of Quan cooked, but he was very
tough meat, poor old beast. Socks, the only pony left
now, is lonely. He whinnied all night for his lost companion. At 1 P.M. today we had got close enough to the
disturbance ahead of us to see that it consisted of enormous pressure ridges, heavily crevassed and running a
long way east, with not the slightest chance of our being
able to get southing that way any longer on the Barrier.
So after lunch we struck due south in toward the land,
which is now running in a southeast direction, and at 6
P.M. we were close to the ridges off the coast. There is
a red hill about 3000 ft. in height, which we hope to
ascend tomorrow, so as to gain view of the surrounding
country. Then we will make our way if possible, with
the pony up a glacier ahead of us on to the huge ice,
and on to the Pole if all goes well. It is an anxious time
for us, for time is precious and food more so; we will
be greatly relieved if we find a good route through the
mountains. Now that we are close to the land we can see
more clearly the nature of the mountains. From Mount
Longstaff in a southeast direction, the land appears to
be far more glaciated than further north, and since the
valleys are very steep, the glaciers that they contain are
heavily crevassed. These glaciers bear out in a northeast
direction into the Barrier. Immediately opposite our
camp the snow seems to have been blown off the steep
mountain sides. The mountain ahead of us, which we
are going to climb tomorrow, is undoubtedly granite, but
very mildly weathered. In the distance it looked like volcanic rock, but now there can be no doubt that it consists
of granite. Evidently the great ice sheet has passed over
this part of the land, for the rounded forms could not
have been caused by ordinary weathering. Enormous
pressure ridges that run out from the south of the mountain ahead must be due to a glacier far greater in extent
than any we have yet met. The glacier that comes out
of Shackleton Inlet makes a disturbance in the Barrier
ice, but not nearly as great as the disturbance in our
immediate neighborhood at the present time. The glacier
at Shackleton Inlet is quite a short one. We have now

closed in to the land, but before we did so we could
see the rounded tops of great mountains extending in a
southeasterly direction. If we are fortunate enough to
reach the summit of the mountain tomorrow, we should
be able to see more clearly the line of these mountains
to the southeast. It would be very interesting to follow
along the Barrier to the southeast, and see the trend of
the mountains but that does not enter into our program.
Our way lies to the south. How one wishes for time and
unlimited provisions. Then indeed we could penetrate
the secrets of this great lonely continent. Regrets are
vain, however, and we wonder what is in store for us
beyond the mountains if we are able to get there. The
closer observation of these mountains ought to give geological results of importance. We may have the good
fortune to discover fossils, or at any rate to bring back
specimens that will determine the geological history of
the country and prove a connection between the granite
boulders lying on the slopes of Erebus and Terror and
the land lying to the far south. Our position tonight is
latitude 83° 28' South, longitude 171° 30' East. If we can
get on the mountain tomorrow, it will be the pioneer
landing in the far south. We traveled 11 miles 1450 yards
(statute) today, which was not bad, seeing that we were
pulling 180 lb. per man on a bad surface. We got a photograph of the wonderful red granite peaks close to us,
for now we are only eight miles or so off the land. The
temperature is plus 20°, with a high barometer. The
same fine weather continues, but the wind is cold in the
early morning, when we turn out at 5:30 A.M. for
breakfast.

December 4. Unable to write yesterday owing to bad
attack of snow blindness, and not much better tonight,
but I must record the events of the two most remarkable
days that we have experienced since leaving the winter
quarters. After breakfast at 5:30 A.M. yesterday, we
started off from camp, leaving all camp gear standing
and a good feed by Socks to last him the whole day. We
got under way at 9 A.M., taking four biscuits, four lumps
of sugar, and two ounces of chocolate each for lunch.
We hoped to get water at the first of the rocks when we
landed. Hardly had we gone one hundred yards when

we came to a crevasse, which we did not see very distinctly, for the light was bad, and the sun obscured by clouds. We roped up and went on in single file, each with his ice-pick handy. I found it very difficult to see clearly with my goggles, and so took them off, and the present attack of snow blindness is the result, for the sun came out gloriously later on. We crossed several crevasses filled with snow except at the sides, the gaps being about 2 ft. wide, and the whole crevasses from 10 to 20 ft. across. Then we were brought up all standing by an enormous chasm of about 80 ft. wide and 300 ft. deep which lay right across our route. This chasm was similar to, only larger than, the one we encountered in latitude 80° 30' South when on the southern journey with Captain Scott during the *Discovery* expedition. By making a detour to the right we found that it gradually pinched out and became filled with snow, and so we were able to cross and resume our line to the land, which very deceptively appeared quite close but was really some miles away.

Crossing several ridges of ice pressure and many more crevasses, we eventually at 12:30 P.M. reached an area of smooth blue ice in which were embedded several granite boulders, and here we obtained a drink of delicious water formed by the sun playing on the rock face and heating the ice at the base. After traveling for half a mile, we reached the base of the mountain which we hoped to climb in order to gain a view of the surrounding country. This hill is composed of granite, the red appearance being no doubt due to iron. At 1 P.M. we had a couple of biscuits and some water, and then started to make our way up the precipitous rock face. This was the most difficult part of the whole climb, for the granite was weathered and split in every direction, and some of the larger pieces seemed to be just nicely balanced on smaller pieces, so that one could almost push them over by a touch. With great difficulty we clambered up this rock face, and then ascended a gentle snow slope to another rocky bit, but not so difficult to climb. From the top of this ridge there burst upon our view an open road to the south, for there stretched before us a great glacier running almost south and north between two huge mountain ranges. As far as we could see, except toward the mouth, the glacier appeared to be smooth, yet this was not a certainty, for the distance was so great. Eagerly we clambered up the remaining ridges and over a snow slope, and found ourselves at the top of the mountain, the height being 3350 ft. according to aneroid and hypsometer. From the summit we could see the glacier stretching away south inland till at last it seemed to merge in high inland ice. Where the glacier fell into the Barrier about northeast bearing, the pressure waves were enormous, and for miles the surface of the Barrier was broken up. This was what we had seen ahead of us the last few days, and we now understood the reason of the commotion on the Barrier surface. To the southeast we could see the lofty range of mountains we had been following still stretching away in the same direction, and we can safely say that the Barrier is bounded by a chain of mountains extending in a southeasterly direction as far as the 86th parallel South. The mountains to the west appear to be more heavily glaciated than the ones to the eastward. There are some huge granite faces on the southern sides of the mountains, and these faces are joined up by cliffs of a very dark hue. To the south southeast, toward what is apparently the head of the glacier, there are several sharp cones of very black rock, eight or nine in all. Beyond these are red granite faces, with sharp, needlelike spurs, similar in appearance to the "cathedral" rocks described by Armitage in connection with the *Discovery* expedition to the western mountains. Further on to the south the mountains have a bluff appearance, with long lines of stratification running almost horizontally. This bluff mountain range seems to break about sixty miles away, and beyond can be seen dimly other mountains. Turning to the west, the mountains on that side appeared to be rounded and covered with huge masses of ice, and glaciers showing the lines of crevasses. In the far distance there is what looked like an active volcano. There is a big mountain with a cloud on the top, bearing all the appearance of steam from an active cone. It would be very interesting to find an active volcano so far south. After taking bearings of the trend of the mountains, Barrier and gla-

cier, we ate our frugal lunch and wished for more, and
then descended. Adams had boiled the hypsometer and
taken the temperature on the top, whilst Marshall, who
had carried the camera on his back all the way up, took
a couple of photographs. How we wished we had more
plates to spare to get a record of the wonderful country
we were passing through. At 4 P.M. we began to descend,
and at 5 P.M. we were on the Barrier again. We were
rather tired and very hungry when, at 7 P.M., we reached
our camp. After a good dinner, and a cupful of Maujee
ration in the hoosh as an extra, we turned in.

Today, December 4, we got under way at 8 A.M. and
steered into the land, for we could see that there was
no question as to the way we should go now. Though
on the glacier, we might encounter crevasses and difficulties not to be met with on the Barrier, yet on the
latter we could get no further than 86° South, and then
would have to turn in toward the land and get over the
mountains to reach the Pole. We felt that our main difficulty on the glacier route would be with the pony
Socks, and we could not expect to drag the full load
ourselves as yet without relay work. Adams, Marshall,
and I pulled one sledge with 680 lb. weight, and Wild
followed with Socks directly in our wake, so that if we
came to a crevasse he would have warning. Everything
went on well except that when we were close in to land,
Marshall went through the snow covering of a crevasse.
He managed to hold himself up by his arms. We could
see no bottom to this crevasse. At 1 P.M. we were close
to the snow slope up which we hoped to reach the interior of the land and thence get on to the glacier. We
had lunch and then proceeded, finding, instead of a
steep, short slope, a long, fairly steep gradient. All the
afternoon we toiled at the sledge, Socks pulling his load
easily enough, and eventually, at 5 P.M., reached the
head of the pass, 2000 ft. above sea level. From that
point there was a gentle descent toward the glacier, and
at 6 P.M. we camped close to some blue ice with granite
boulders embedded in it, around which were pools of
water. This water saves a certain amount of our oil, for
we have not to melt snow or ice. We turned in at 8 P.M.,
well satisfied with the day's work. The weather now is

wonderfully fine, with not a breath of wind, and a warm sun beating down on us. The temperature was up to plus 22°F at noon, and is now plus 18°F. The pass through which we have come is flanked by great granite pillars at least 2000 ft. in height and making a magnificent entrance to the "Highway to the South." It is all so interesting and everything is on such a vast scale that one cannot describe it well. We four are seeing these great designs and the play of nature in her grandest moods for the first time, and possibly they may never be seen by man again. Poor Marshall had another four miles' walk this evening, for he found that he had lost his Jaeger jacket off the sledge. He had therefore to tramp back uphill for it, and found it two miles away on the trail. Socks is not feeding well. He seems lonely without his companions. We gave him a drink of thaw water this evening, but he did not seem to appreciate it, preferring the snow at his feet.

CHAPTER XIII

On the Great Glacier
December 5 to 17

Appearance of a Bird in 83° 40' South Latitude: Our last
Pony engulfed, December 7: Dangerous Traveling in a
Maze of Crevasses: Discovery of Coal at an
altitude of 6100 ft.

December 5. Broke camp sharp at 8 A.M. and proceeded
south down an icy slope to the main glacier. The ice was
too slippery for the pony, so Wild took him by a circuitous route to the bottom on snow. At the end of our
ice slope, down which the sledge skidded rapidly, though
we had put on rope brakes and hung on to it as well as
we could, there was a patch of soft snow running parallel
with the glacier, which here trended about southwest by
south. Close ahead of us were the massed up, fantasti-
cally shaped and split masses of pressure across which it
would have been impossible for us to have gone, but,
fortunately, it was not necessary even to try, for close
into the land was a snow slope free from all crevasses,
and along this gentle rise we made our way. After a time
this snow slope gave place to blue ice, with numberless
cracks and small crevasses across which it was quite impossible for the pony to drag the sledge without a serious
risk of a broken leg in one of the many holes, the depth
of which we could not ascertain. We therefore unharnessed Socks, and Wild took him over this bit of ground
very carefully, whilst we others first hauled our sledge
and then the pony sledge across to a patch of snow
under some gigantic granite pillars over 2000 ft. in
height, and here, close to some thaw water, we made
our lunch camp. I was still badly snow blind, so stayed
in camp whilst Marshall and Adams went on to spy out
a good route to follow after lunch was over. When they
returned they informed me that there was more cracked-
up blue ice ahead, and that the main pressure of the
glacier came in very close to the pillar of granite that
stood before us, but that beyond that there appeared to

be a snow slope and good going. The most remarkable thing they reported was that as they were walking along a bird, brown in color with a white line under each wing, flew just over their heads and disappeared to the south. It is, indeed, strange to hear of such an incident in latitude 83° 40' South. They were sure it was not a skua gull, which is the only bird I could think of that would venture down here, and the gull might have been attracted by the last dead pony, for when in latitude 80° 30' South, on my last southern trip, a skua gull arrived shortly after we had killed a dog.

After lunch we started again, and by dint of great exertions managed, at 6 P.M., to camp after getting both sledges and then the pony over another couple of miles of crevassed blue ice. We then went on and had a look ahead, and saw that we are going to have a tough time tomorrow to get along at all. I can see that it will, at least, mean relaying three or four times across nearly half a mile of terribly crevassed ice, covered in places with treacherous snow, and razor edged in other places, all of it sloping down toward the rock debris-strewn shore on the cliff side. We are camped under a wonderful pillar of granite that has been arounded by the winds into a perfectly symmetrical shape, and is banded by lines of gneiss. There is just one little patch of snow for our tents, and even that bridges some crevasses. Providence will look over us tonight, for we can do nothing more. One feels that at any moment some great piece of rock may come hurtling down, for all around us are pieces of granite, ranging from the size of a hazelnut to great boulders twenty to forty tons in weight, and on one snow slope is the fresh track of a fallen rock. Still we can do no better, for it is impossible to spread a tent on the blue ice, and we cannot get any further tonight. We are leaving a depot here. My eyes are my only trouble, for their condition makes it impossible for me to pick out the route or do much more than pull. The distance covered today was 9 miles with 4 miles relay.

December 6. Started at 8 A.M. today in fine weather to get our loads over the half mile of crevassed ice that lay between us and the snow slope to the south southwest. We divided up the load and managed to get the whole lot over in three journeys, but it was an awful job, for every step was a venture, and I, with one eye entirely blocked up because of snow blindness, felt it particularly uncomfortable work. However, by 1 P.M. all our gear was safely over, and the other three went back for Socks. Wild led him, and by 2 P.M. we were all camped on the snow again. Providence has indeed looked after us. At 3 P.M. we started south southwest up a long slope to the right of the main glacier pressure. It was very heavy going, and we camped at 5 P.M. close to a huge crevasse, the snow bridge of which we crossed. There is a wonderful view of the mountains, with new peaks and ranges to the southeast, south and southwest. There is a dark rock running in conjunction with the granite on several of the mountains. We are now over 1700 ft. up on the glacier, and can see down on to the Barrier. The cloud still hangs on the mountain ahead of us; it certainly looks as though it were a volcano cloud, but it may be due to condensation. The lower current clouds are traveling very fast from south southeast to north northwest. The weather is fine and clear, and the temperature plus 17°F.

December 7. Started at 8 A.M., Adams, Marshall and self pulling one sledge. Wild leading Socks behind. We traveled up and down slopes with very deep snow, into which Socks sank up to his belly, and we plunged in and out continuously, making it very trying work. Passed several crevasses on our right hand and could see more to the left. The light became bad at 1 P.M., when we camped for lunch, and it was hard to see the crevasses, as most were more or less snow covered. After lunch the light was better, and as we marched along we were congratulating ourselves upon it when suddenly we heard a shout of "help" from Wild. We stopped at once and rushed to his assistance, and saw the pony sledge with the forward end down a crevasse and Wild reaching out from the side of the gulf grasping the sledge. No sign of the pony. We soon got up to Wild, and he scrambled out of the dangerous position, but poor Socks had gone. Wild had a miraculous escape. He was following up our tracks, and we had passed over a crevasse which was entirely covered with snow, but the weight of the pony broke through the snow crust and in a second all was over. Wild says he just felt a sort of rushing wind, the leading rope was snatched from his hand, and he put out his arms and just caught the further edge of the chasm. Fortunately for Wild and us, Socks' weight snapped the swingle-tree of the sledge, so it was saved, though the upper bearer is broken. We lay down on our stomachs and looked over into the gulf, but no sound or sign came to us; a black bottomless pit it seemed to be. We hitched the pony sledge to ourselves and started off again, now with a weight of 1000 lb. for the four of us. Camped at 6:20 P.M., very tired, having to retreat from a maze of crevasses and rotten ice on to a patch where we could pitch our tents. We are indeed thankful for Wild's escape. When I think over the events of the day I realize what the loss of the sledge would have meant to us. We would have had left only two sleeping bags for the four of us, and I doubt whether we could have got back to winter quarters with the short equipment. Our chance of reaching the Pole would have been gone. We take on the maize to eat ourselves. There is one ray of light in this bad day, and that is that, anyhow we could not have taken Socks on much further. We would have had to shoot him tonight, so that although his loss is a serious matter to us, for we had counted on the meat, still we know that for traction purposes he would have been of little further use. When we tried to camp tonight we stuck our ice axes into the snow to see whether there were any more hidden crevasses, and everywhere the axes went through. It would have been folly to have pitched our camp in that place, as we might easily have dropped through during the night. We had to retreat a quarter of a mile to pitch the tent. It was very unpleasant to turn back, even for this short distance, but on this job one must expect reverses.

December 8. Started at 8 A.M. and immediately began dodging crevasses and pits of unknown depth. Wild and I were leading, for, thank heaven, my eyes are fit and well again. We slowly toiled up a long crevassed slope, and by lunch time were about 1900 ft. up the glacier. We had covered 6 miles 150 yards of an uphill drag, with about 250 lb. per man to haul. After lunch we still traveled up, but came on to blue glacier ice almost free from crevasses, so did much better, the sledges running easily. We camped at 6 P.M., the day's journey having been 12 miles 150 yards. The slope we went up in the morning, was not as bad as we had anticipated, but quite bad enough for us to be thankful that we are out, at any rate for a time, from the region of hidden crevasses. The hypsometer tonight gave our height as 2300 ft. above sea level. It is beautifully fine still. We have been wonderfully fortunate in this, especially in view of the situation we are in.

December 9. Another splendid day as far as the weather is concerned, and much we needed it, for we have had one of our hardest day's work and certainly the most dangerous so far. We started at 7:45 A.M. over the blue ice, and in less than an hour were in a perfect maze of crevasses, some thinly bridged with snow and others with a thicker and therefore more deceptive covering. Marshall went through one and was only saved by his harness. He had quite disappeared down below the level of the ice, and it was one of those crevasses that open out from the top, with no bottom to be seen, and I daresay there was a drop of at least 1000 ft. Soon after, Adams went through, then I did. The situation became momentarily more dangerous and uncertain. The sledges, skidding about, came up against the sheer, knife-like edges of some of the crevasses, and thus the bow of the second sledge, which had been strained when Socks fell, gave way. We decided to relay our gear over this portion of a glacier until we got on to safer ground, and it was well past eleven o'clock before we had got both sledges on to better ice. We camped at 11:45 A.M. to get the sun's meridian altitude, and, to save time while watching the sun's rise and fall, decided to lunch at noon. The latitude we found to be 84° 2' South, which is not so bad considering that we have been hauling our heavy load of 250 lb. per man uphill for the last two days. At noon we were nearly 2500 ft. above sea level. In the afternoon we had another heavy pull, and now are camped between two huge crevasses, but on a patch of hard snow. We pitched camp at 6 P.M., very tired and extremely hungry after dragging uphill all the afternoon for over five hours. It is 8 P.M. now, and we are nearly

3000 ft. above sea level. Low cumulus clouds are hanging to the south of us, as they have done for many days past, obscuring any view in that direction. We are anxiously hoping to find soon a level and inland ice sheet so that we can put on more speed. The distance today was 11 miles 1450 yards plus two miles relay. The talk now is mainly about food and the things we would like to eat, and at meal times our hoosh disappears with far too great speed. We are all looking forward to Christmas Day, for then, come what may, we are going to be full of food.

December 10. Falls, bruises, cut shins, crevasses, razor edged ice, and a heavy upward pull have made up the sum of the day's trials, but there has been a measure of compensation in the wonderful scenery, the marvelous rocks and the covering of a distance of 11 miles 860 yards toward our goal. We started at 7:30 A.M. amongst crevasses, but soon got out of them and pulled up a long slope of snow. Our altitude at noon was 3250 ft. above sea level. Then we slid down a blue ice slope, after crossing crevasses. Marshall and I each went down one. We lunched at 1 P.M. and started at 2 P.M. up a long ridge by the side moraine of the glacier. It was heavy work, as the ice was split and presented knife-like edges between the cracks, and there were also some crevasses. Adams got into one. The going was terribly heavy, as the sledges brought up against the ice edges every now and then, and then there was a struggle to get them started again. We changed our foot gear, substituting ski boots for the finnesko, but nevertheless had many painful falls on the treacherous blue ice, cutting our hands and shins. We are all much bruised. We camped on a patch of snow by the land at 6 P.M. The rocks of the moraine are remarkable, being of every hue and description. I cannot describe them, but we will carry specimens back for the geologists to deal with. The main rocks of the "Cloud Maker," the mountain under which we are camped, appear to be slates, reef quartz and a very hard, dark brown rock, the name of which I do not know. The erratics of marble, conglomerate, and breccia are beautiful, showing a great mass of wonderful colors, but these rocks we cannot take away. We can only take with us small specimens of the main rocks, as weight is of importance to us, and from these small specimens the geologists must determine the character of the land. This mountain is the one we thought might be an active volcano when we saw it from the mountain at the foot of the glacier, but the cloud has blown away from its head today, and we can see definitely that it is not a volcano. It is a remarkable sight as it towers above us with the snow clinging to its sides. Tonight there is a cold north wind. I climbed about 600 ft. up the mountain and got specimens of the main rocks in situ. The glacier is evidently moving very slowly, and not filling as much of the valley as it did at some previous date, for the old moraines lie higher up in terraces. Low cumulus clouds to the south are hiding some of the new land in that direction. We are all very hungry and tired tonight after the day's fight with glacier. Whilst I went up the mountain to spy out the land the others ground up the balance of the maize, brought for pony feed, between flat stones, in order that we may use it ourselves to eke out our supply of food. The method of preparation was primitive, but it represented the only way of getting it fit to cook without the necessity of using more oil than we can spare for lengthy boiling. The temperature was plus 12°F at noon today, and is plus 14° now at 8 P.M. We are getting south, and we hope to reach the inland ice in a couple of days; then our marching will be faster. The weather is still fine.

December 11. A heavy day. We started away at 7:40 A.M. and tried to keep alongside the land, but the ice of the glacier sloped so much that we had to go on to the ridge, where the sledges could run without side slipping. This slipping cuts the runners very badly. We crossed the medial moraine, and found rock there with what looked like plant impressions. We collected some specimens.

In the afternoon we found the surface better, as the cracks were nearly all filled up with water turned to ice. We camped for lunch on rubbly ice. After lunch we rounded some pressure ridges fairly easily, and then pulled up a long ice slope with many sharp points. All the afternoon we were passing over ice in which the

cracks had been closed up, and we began to have great
hopes that the end of the glacier was in sight, and that
we would soon be able to put in some good marches on
the plateau. At 5 P.M. we found more cracks and a mass
of pressure ice ahead and land appeared as the clouds
ahead lifted. I cannot tell what it means, but the position
makes us anxious. The sledges will not stand much more
of this ice work, and we are still 340 geographical miles
away from the Pole. Thank God the weather is fine still.
We camped at 6 P.M. on hard ice between two crevasses.
There was no snow to pack round the tents, so we had
to put the sledges and the provision bags on the snow
cloths. We made the floor level inside by chipping away
the points of ice with our ice axes. We were very hungry
after hoosh tonight. Awkward features about the glacier
are the little pits filled with mud, of which I collected a
small sample.* It seems to be ground down rock material, but what the action has been I cannot tell. The hot
sun, beating down on this mud, makes it gradually sink
into the body of the glacier, leaving a rotten ice covering
through which we often break. It is like walking over a
cucumber frame, and sometimes the boulders that have
sunk down through the ice can be seen 3 to 4 ft. below
the surface. The ice that has formed above the sunken
rocks is more clear than the ordinary glacier ice. We are
3700 ft. up, and made 8 miles 900 yards to the good
today. We have the satisfaction of feeling that we are
getting south, and perhaps tomorrow may see the end
of all our difficulties. Difficulties are just things to overcome after all. Every one is very fit.

December 12. Our distance—three miles for the day—
expresses more readily than I can write it the nature of
the day's work. We started at 7:40 A.M. on the worst
surface possible, sharp edged blue ice full of chasms and
crevasses, rising to hills and descending into gullies; in
fact, a surface that could not be equaled in any polar
work for difficulty in traveling. Our sledges are suffering
greatly, and it is a constant strain on us both to save the
sledges from breaking or going down crevasses, and to
save ourselves as well. We are a mass of bruises where

*These pits are known as cryoconite holes.

we have fallen on the sharp ice, but, thank God, no one has even a sprain. It has been relay work today, for we could only take on one sledge at a time, two of us taking turns at pulling the sledge whilst the others steadied and held the sledge to keep it straight. Thus we would advance one mile, and then return over the crevasses and haul up the other sledge. By repeating this today for three miles we marched nine miles over a surface where many times a slip meant death. Still we have advanced three miles to the south, and tonight we are camped on a patch of névé. By using our ice axes we made a place for the tent. The weather is still splendidly fine, though low clouds obscure our horizon to the south. We are anxiously hoping to cross the main pressure tomorrow, and trust that we will then have better traveling. Given good traveling, we will not be long in reaching our goal. Marshall is putting in the bearings and angles of the new mountains. They still keep appearing to the west and east. Distance 3 miles 500 yards, with relays 9 miles 1500 yards.

December 13. We made a start at 8 A.M. and once again went up hill and down dale, over crevasses and blue, ribbed ice, relaying the sledges. We had covered about a mile when we came to a place where it seemed almost impossible to proceed. However, to our right, bearing about southwest by south, there seemed to be better surface and we decided to make a detour in that direction in order, if possible, to get round the pressure. While returning for one of the sledges I fell on the ice and hurt my left knee, which was a serious matter, or rather might have been. I have had a bandage on all the afternoon while pulling, and the knee feels better now, but one realizes what it would mean if any member of our party were to be damaged under these conditions and in this place. This afternoon we came on to a better surface, and were able to pull both sledges instead of relaying. We are still gradually rising, and tonight our hypsometer gives 203.7, or 4370 ft. up. There is a cool southerly wind; indeed, more than we have had before, and as we have only a patch of névé on the glacier for our tents, we had to take the provision bags and gear off the sledges to keep the tent cloths down. The temperature is plus 19°F. New mountains are still appearing to the west southwest as we rise. We seem now to be going up a long yellow track, for the ice is not so blue, and we are evidently traveling over an old moraine, where the stones have sunk through the ice when its onward movement has been retarded. I am sure that the bulk of the glacier is growing less, but the onward movement still continues, though at a much slower pace than at some previous period. The gain for the day was five miles, and in addition we did four miles relay work.

December 14. This has been one of our hardest day's work so far. We have been steering all day about south southwest up the glacier, mainly in the bed of an ancient moraine, which is full of holes through which the stones and boulders have melted down long years ago. It has been snowing all day with a high temperature, and this has made everything very wet. We have ascended over 1000 ft. today, our altitude at 6 P.M. being 5600 ft. above sea level, so the mountains to the west must be from 10,000 to 15,000 ft. in height, judging from their comparative elevation. My knee is better today. We have had a heavy pull and many falls on the slippery ice. Just before camping, Adams went through some snow, but held up over an awful chasm. Our sledges are much the worse for wear, and the one with the broken bow constantly strikes against the hard, sharp ice, pulling us up with a jerk and often flinging us down. At this high altitude the heavy pulling is very trying, especially as we slip on the snow covering the blue ice. There has evidently been an enormous glaciation here, and now it is dwindling away. Even the mountains show signs of this. Tonight our hopes are high that we are nearly at the end of the rise and that soon we will reach our longed for plateau. Then southward indeed! Food is the determining factor with us. We did 7½ miles today.

December 15. Started at 7:40 A.M. in clear weather. It was heavy going uphill on the blue ice, but gradually we rose the land ahead, and it seemed as though at last we were going to have a change, and that we would see something new. At lunchtime we were on a better surface, with patches of snow, and we could see stretching out in front of us what was apparently a long, wide plain.

It looked as though now really we were coming to the level ground for which we have longed, especially as the hypsometer gave us an altitude of 7230 ft., but this altitude at night came down to 5830 ft., so the apparent height may be due to barometric pressure and change of weather, for in the afternoon a stiff breeze from the southwest sprang up. The temperature was plus 18°F at noon, and when the wind came up it felt cold, as we were pulling in our pajama trousers, with nothing underneath. We have been going steadily uphill all the afternoon, but on a vastly improved surface, consisting of hard névé instead of blue ice and no cracks, only covered in crevasses, which are easily seen. Ahead of us really lies the plateau. We can also see ahead of us detached mountains, piercing through the inland ice, which is the road to the south for us. Huge mountains stretch out to the east and west. After last week's toil and anxiety the change is delightful. The distance covered today was 13 miles 200 yards.

December 16. We started at 7 A.M., having had breakfast at 5:30 A.M. It was snowing slightly for the first few hours, and then the weather cleared. The surface was hard and the going good. We camped at noon and took sights for latitude, and ascertained that our position was 84° 50' South. Ahead of us we could see a long slope, icy and crevassed, but we did 13 miles 1650 yards for the day. We camped at 5:30 P.M., and got ready our depot gear. We have decided to travel as lightly as possible, taking only the clothes we are wearing, and we will leave four days' food, which I calculate should get us back to the last depot on short ration. We have now traversed nearly one hundred miles of crevassed ice, and risen 6000 ft. on the largest glacier in the world. One more crevassed slope, and we will be on the plateau, please God. We are all fit and well. The temperature tonight is plus 15°F, and the wind is blowing freshly from the southwest. There are splendid ranges of mountains to the west southwest, and we have an extended view of glacier and mountains. Ahead of us lie three sharp peaks, connected up and forming an island in what is apparently inland ice or the head of the glacier. The peaks lie due south of us. To the eastward and westward of this island the ice bears down from the inland ice sheet, and joins the head of the glacier proper. To the westward the mountains along the side of the glacier are all of the bluff type, and the lines of stratification can be seen plainly. Still further to the westward, behind the frontal range, lie sharper peaks, some of them almost perfect cones. The trend of the land from the "Cloudmaker" is about south southwest. We are traveling up the west side of the glacier. On the other side, to the east, there is a break in the bluff mountains, and the land beyond runs away more to the southeast. The valley is filled with pressure ice, which seems to have come from the inland ice sheet. The mountains to the southeast also show lines of stratification. I hope that the photographs will be clear enough to give an idea of the character of this land. These mountains are not beautiful in the ordinary acceptance of the term, but they are magnificent in their stern and rugged grandeur. No foot has ever trod on their mighty sides, and until we reached this frozen land no human eyes had seen their forms.

December 17. We made a start at 7:20 A.M. and had an uphill pull all the morning over blue ice with patches of snow, which impeded our progress until we learned that the best way was to rush the sledges over them, for it was very difficult to keep one's footing on the smooth ice, and haul the sledges astern over the snow. By 1 P.M. we had done eight miles of this uphill work, and in the afternoon we did four more. We had worked from 7:23 A.M. until 6:40 P.M. with one hour's rest for lunch only and it seems as though twelve miles was not much, but the last two hours' going was very stiff. We had to take on one sledge at a time up the icy slope, and even then we had to cut steps with our ice axes as we went along. The work was made more difficult by the fact that a strong southerly wind was dead in our faces. The second sledge we hauled up the rise by means of the alpine rope. We made it fast to the sledge, went on with the first sledge till the rope was stretched out to its full length, then cut a place to stand on, and by our united efforts hauled the sledge up to where we stood. We repeated this until we had managed to reach a fairly level spot with both the sledges, and we pitched our tents on

a small patch of snow. There was not enough of the
snow to make fast the snow cloths of the tents, and we
had to take the gear off the sledges and pile that round
to supplement the snow. We have burned our boats behind us now as regards warm clothing, for this afternoon
we made a depot in by the rocks of the island we are
passing, and there left everything except the barest necessaries. After dinner tonight Wild went up the hillside
in order to have a look at the plateau. He came down
with the news that the plateau is in sight at last, and that
tomorrow should see us at the end of our difficulties.
He also brought down with him some very interesting
geological specimens, some of which certainly look like
coal. The quality may be poor, but I have little doubt
that the stuff is coal. If that proves to be the case, the
discovery will be most interesting to the scientific world.
Wild tells me that there are about six seams of this dark
stuff, mingled with sandstone, and that the seams are
from 4 in. to 7 or 8 ft. in thickness. There are vast quantities of it lying on the hillside. We took a photograph
of the sandstone, and I wish very much that we could
spare time to examine the rocks more thoroughly. We
may be able to do this on the way back. We have but
little time for geological work, for our way is south and
time is short, but we found that the main rock is sandstone and on our way back we will collect some. I expect
that this will be the most southerly rock that we shall
obtain, for we ought to reach the plateau tomorrow, and
then there will be no more land close to us. It is gusty
tonight, but beautifully clear. The altitude, according to
the hypsometer, is 6100 ft.

NOTE. When I showed the specimens to Professor
David after our return to the *Nimrod,* he stated definitely that some of them were coal and others "mother
of coal."

CHAPTER XIV

On the Plateau to the Farthest South
December 18, 1908 to January 8, 1909

December 21, Midsummer Day, with 28° of Frost: Christmas
Day at an Altitude of 9500 ft. in Latitude 85° 55' South:
Christmas Fare: Last Depot on January 4: Blinding Blizzard
for two Days, January 7, 8: Altitude 11,600 ft.

December 18. Almost up: The altitude tonight is 7400 ft.
above sea level. This has been one of our hardest days,
but worth it, for we are just on the plateau at last. We
started at 7:30 A.M., relaying the sledges, and did 6 miles
600 yards, which means nearly 19 miles for the day of
actual traveling. All the morning we worked up loose,
slippery ice, hauling the sledges up one at a time by
means of the alpine rope, then pulling in harness on the
less stiff rises. We camped for lunch at 12:45 P.M. on the
crest of a rise close to the pressure and in the midst of
crevasses, into one of which I managed to fall, also
Adams. Whilst lunch was preparing I got some rock
from the land, quite different to the sandstone of yesterday. The mountains are all different just here. The land
on our left shows beautifully clear stratified lines, and
on the west side sandstone stands out, greatly weathered.
All the afternoon we relayed up a long snow slope, and
we were hungry and tired when we reached camp. We
have been saving food to make it spin out, and that
increases our hunger; each night we all dream of foods.
We save two biscuits per man per day, also pemmican
and sugar, eking out our food with pony maize, which
we soak in water to make it less hard. All this means
that we have now five weeks' food, while we are about
300 geographical miles from the Pole, with the same distance back to the last depot we left yesterday, so we
must march on short food to reach our goal. The temperature is plus 16°F tonight, but a cold wind all the morning cut our faces and broken lips. We keep crevasses
with us still, but I think that tomorrow will see the end
of this. When we passed the main slope today, more

mountains appeared to the west of south, some with sheer cliffs and others rounded off, ending in long snow slopes. I judge the southern limit of the mountains to the west to be about latitude 86° South.

December 19. Not on the plateau level yet, though we are tonight 7888 ft. up, and still there is another rise ahead of us. We got breakfast at 5 A.M. and started at 7 A.M. sharp, taking on one sledge. Soon we got to the top of a ridge, and went back for the second sledge, then hauled both together all the rest of the day. The weight was about 200 lb. per man, and we kept going until 6 P.M., with a stop of one hour for lunch. We got a meridian altitude at noon, and found that our latitude was 85° 5' South. We seem unable to get rid of the crevasses, and we have been falling into them and steering through them all day in the face of a cold southerly wind, with a temperature varying from plus 15° to plus 9°F. The work was very heavy, for we were going uphill all day, and our sledge runners, which have been suffering from the sharp ice and rough traveling, are in a bad way. Soft snow in places greatly retarded our progress, but we have covered our ten miles, and now are camped on good snow between two crevasses. I really think that tomorrow will see us on the plateau proper. This glacier must be one of the largest, if not the largest, in the world. The sastrugi seem to point mainly to the south, so we may expect head winds all the way to the Pole. Marshall has a cold job tonight, taking the angles of the new mountains to the west, some of which appeared today. After dinner we examined the sledge runners and turned one sledge end for end, for it had been badly torn while we were coming up the glacier, and in the soft snow it clogged greatly. We are still favored with splendid weather, and that is a great comfort to us, for it would be almost impossible under other conditions to travel amongst these crevasses, which are caused by the congestion of the ice between the headlands when it was flowing from the plateau down between the mountains. Now there is comparatively little movement, and many of the crevasses have become snow-filled. Tonight we are 290 geographical miles from the Pole. We are thinking of our Christmas dinner. We will be full that day, anyhow.

December 20. Not yet up, but nearly so. We got away from camp at 7 A.M., with a strong head wind from the south, and this wind continued all day, with a temperature ranging from plus 7° to plus 5°. Our beards coated with ice. It was an uphill pull all day around pressure ice, and we reached an altitude of over 8000 ft. above sea level. The weather was clear, but there were various clouds, which were noted by Adams. Marshall took bearings and angles at noon, and we got the sun's meridian altitude, showing that we were in latitude 85° 17' South. We hope all the time that each ridge we come to will be the last, but each time another rises ahead, split up by pressure, and we begin the same toil again. It is trying work and as we have now reduced our food at breakfast to one pannikin of hoosh and one biscuit, by the time the lunch hour has arrived, after five hours' hauling in the cold wind up the slope, we are very hungry. At lunch we have a little chocolate, tea with plasmon, a pannikin of cocoa, and three biscuits. Today we did 11 miles, 950 yards (statute), having to relay the sledges over the last bit, for the ridge we were on was so steep that we could not get the two sledges up together. Still, we are getting on; we have only 279 more miles to go, and then we will have reached the southeast Pole. The land appears to run away to the southeast now, and soon we will be just a speck on this great inland waste of snow and ice. It is cold tonight. I am cook for the week, and started tonight. Every one is fit and well.

December 21. Midsummer Day, with 28° of frost! We have frostbitten fingers and ears, and a strong blizzard wind has been blowing from the south all day, all due to the fact that we have climbed to an altitude of over 8000 ft. above sea level. From early morning we have been striving to the south, but six miles is the total distance gained, for from noon, or rather from lunch at 1 P.M., we have been hauling the sledges up, one after the other, by standing pulls across crevasses and over great pressure ridges. When we had advanced one sledge some distance, we put up a flag on a bamboo to mark its position, and then roped up and returned for the other.

The wind, no doubt, has a great deal to do with the low temperature, and we feel the cold, as we are going on short commons. The altitude adds to the difficulties, but we are getting south all the time. We started away from camp at 6:45 A.M. today, and except for an hour's halt at lunch, worked on until 6 P.M. Now we are camped in a filled-up crevasse, the only place where snow to put around the tents can be obtained, for all the rest of the ground we are on is either névé or hard ice. We little thought that this particular pressure ridge was going to be such an obstacle; it looked quite ordinary, even a short way off, but we have now decided to trust nothing to eyesight, for the distances are so deceptive up here. It is a wonderful sight to look down over the glacier from the great altitude we are at, and to see the mountains stretching away east and west, some of them over 15,000 ft. in height. We are very hungry now, and it seems as cold almost as the spring sledging. Our beards are masses of ice all day long. Thank God we are fit and well and have had no accident, which is a mercy, seeing that we have covered over 130 miles of crevassed ice.

December 22. As I write of today's events, I can easily imagine I am on a spring sledging journey, for the temperature is minus 5°F and a chilly southeasterly wind is blowing and finds its way through the walls of our tent, which are getting worn. All day long, from 7 A.M., except for the hour when we stopped for lunch, we have been relaying the sledges over the pressure mounds and across crevasses. Our total distance to the good for the whole day was only four miles southward, but this evening our prospects look brighter, for we must now have come to the end of the great glacier. It is flattening out, and except for crevasses there will not be much trouble in hauling the sledges tomorrow. One sledge today, when coming down with a run over a pressure ridge, turned a complete somersault, but nothing was damaged, in spite of the total weight being over 400 lb. We are now dragging 400 lb. at a time up the steep slopes and across the ridges, working with the alpine rope all day, and roping ourselves together when we go back for the second sledge, for the ground is so treacherous that many times during the day we are saved only by the rope from falling into fathomless pits. Wild describes the sensation of walking over this surface, half ice and half snow, as like walking over the glass roof of a station. The usual query when one of us falls into a crevasse is! "Have you found it?" One gets somewhat callous as regards the immediate danger, though we are always glad to meet crevasses with their coats off, that is, not hidden by the snow covering. Tonight we are camped in a filled-in crevasse. Away to the north down the glacier a thick cumulus cloud is lying, but some of the largest mountains are standing out clearly. Immediately behind us lies a broken sea of pressure ice. Please God, ahead of us there is a clear road to the Pole.

December 23. Eight thousand eight hundred and twenty feet up, and still steering upward amid great waves of pressure and ice falls, for our plateau, after a good morning's march, began to rise in higher ridges, so that it really was not the plateau after all. Today's crevasses have been far more dangerous than any others we have crossed, as the soft snow hides all trace of them until we fall through. Constantly today one or another of the party has had to be hauled out from a chasm by means of his harness, which had alone saved him from death in the icy vault below. We started at 6:40 A.M. and worked on steadily until 6 P.M., with the usual lunch hour in the middle of the day. The pony maize does not swell in the water now, as the temperature is very low and the water freezes. The result is that it swells inside after we have eaten it. We are very hungry indeed, and talk a great deal of what we would like to eat. In spite of the crevasses, we have done thirteen miles today to the south, and we are now in latitude 85° 41' South. The temperature at noon was plus 6°F and at 6 P.M. it was minus 1°F, but it is much lower at night. There was a strong southeast to south southeast wind blowing all day, and it was cutting to our noses and burst lips. Wild was frostbitten. I do trust that tomorrow will see the end of this bad traveling, so that we can stretch out our legs for the Pole.

December 24. A much better day for us; indeed, the brightest we have had since entering our Southern Gateway. We started off at 7 A.M. across waves and undulations of ice, with some one or other of our little party falling through the thin crust of snow every now and then. At 10:30 A.M. I decided to steer more to the west, and we soon got on to a better surface, and covered 5 miles 250 yards in the forenoon. After lunch, as the surface was distinctly improving, we discarded the second sledge, and started our afternoon's march with one sledge. It has been blowing freshly from the south and drifting all day, and this, with over 40° of frost, has coated our faces with ice. We get superficial frost bites every now and then. During the afternoon the surface improved greatly, and the cracks and crevasses disappeared, but we are still going uphill, and from the summit of one ridge saw some new land, which runs south southeast down to latitude 86° South. We camped at 6 P.M., very tired and with cold feet. We have only the clothes we stand up in now, as we depoted everything else, and this continued rise means lower temperatures than I had anticipated. Tonight we are 9095 ft. above sea level, and the way before us is still rising. I trust that it will soon level out, for it is hard work pulling at this altitude. So far there is no sign of the very hard surface that Captain Scott speaks of in connection with his journey on the Northern Plateau. There seem to be just here regular layers of snow, not much wind swept, but we will see better the surface conditions in a few days. Tomorrow will be Christmas Day, and our thoughts turn to home and all the attendant joys of the time. One longs to hear "the hansoms slurring through the London mud." Instead of that, we are lying in a little tent, isolated high on the roof of the end of the world, far, indeed, from the ways trodden of men. Still, our thoughts can fly across the wastes of ice and snow and across the oceans to those whom we are striving for and who are thinking of us now. And, thank God, we are nearing our goal. The distance covered today was 11 miles 250 yards.

December 25. Christmas Day. There has been from 45° to 48° of frost, drifting snow and a strong biting south wind, and such has been the order of the day's march from 7 A.M. to 6 P.M. up one of the steepest rises we have yet done, crevassed in places. Now, as I write, we are 9500 ft. above sea level, and our latitude at 6

P.M. was 85° 55' South. We started away after a good breakfast, and soon came to soft snow, through which our worn and torn sledge-runners dragged heavily. All morning we hauled along, and at noon had done 5 miles 250 yards. Sights gave us latitude 85° 51' South. We had lunch then, and I took a photograph of the camp with the Queen's flag flying and also our tent flags, my companions being in the picture. It was very cold, the temperature being minus 16°F, and the wind went through us. All the afternoon we worked steadily uphill, and we could see at 6 P.M. the new land plainly trending to the southeast. This land is very much glaciated. It is comparatively bare of snow, and there are well-defined glaciers on the side of the range, which seems to end up in the southeast with a large mountain like a keep. We have called it "The Castle." Behind these the mountains have more gentle slopes and are more rounded. They seem to fall away to the southeast, so that, as we are going south, the angle opens and we will soon miss them. When we camped at 6 P.M. the wind was decreasing. It is hard to understand this soft snow with such a persistent wind, and I can only suppose that we have not yet reached the actual plateau level, and that the snow we are traveling over just now is on the slopes, blown down by the south and southeast wind. We had a splendid dinner. First came hoosh, consisting of pony ration boiled up with pemmican and some of our emergency Oxo and biscuit. Then in the cocoa water I boiled our little plum pudding, which a friend of Wild's had given him. This, with a drop of medical brandy, was a luxury which Lucullus himself might have envied; then came cocoa, and lastly cigars and a spoonful of *creme de menthe* sent us by a friend in Scotland. We are full tonight, and this is the last time we will be for many a long day. After dinner we discussed the situation, and we have decided to still further reduce our food. We have now nearly 500 miles, geographical, to do if we are to get to the Pole and back to the spot where we are at the present moment. We have one month's food, but only three weeks' biscuit, so we are going to make each week's food last ten days. We will have one biscuit in the morning, three at mid-day, and two at night. It is the only thing to do. Tomorrow we will throw away everything except the most absolute necessities. Already we are, as regards clothes, down to the limit, but we must trust to the old sledge runners and dump the spare ones. One must risk this. We are very far away from all the world, and home thoughts have been much with us today, thoughts interrupted by pitching forward into a hidden crevasse more than once. Ah, well, we shall see all our own people when the work here is done. Marshall took our temperatures tonight. We are all two degrees subnormal, but as fit as can be. It is a fine open air life and we are getting south.

December 26. Got away at 7 A.M sharp, after dumping a lot of gear. We marched steadily all day except for lunch, and we have done 14 miles 480 yards on an uphill march, with soft snow at times and a bad wind. Ridge after ridge we met, and though the surface is better and harder in places, we feel very tired at the end of ten hours' pulling. Our height tonight is 9590 ft. above sea level according to the hypsometer. The ridges we meet with are almost similar in appearance. We see the sun shining on them in the distance, and then the rise begins very gradually. The snow gets soft, and the weight of the sledge becomes more marked. As we near the top the soft snow gives place to a hard surface, and on the summit of the ridge we find small crevasses. Every time we reach the top of a ridge we say to ourselves: "Perhaps this is the last," but it never is the last; always there appears away ahead of us another ridge. I do not think that the land lies very far below the ice sheet, for the crevasses on the summits of the ridges suggest that the sheet is moving over land at no great depth. It would seem that the descent toward the glacier proper from the plateau is by a series of terraces. We lost sight of the land today, having left it all behind us, and now we have the waste of snow all around. Two more days and our maize will be finished. Then our hooshes will be more woefully thin than ever. This shortness of food is unpleasant, but if we allow ourselves what, under ordinary circumstances, would be a reasonable amount, we would have to abandon all idea of getting far south.

December 27. If a great snow plain, rising every seven

miles in a steep ridge, can be called a plateau, then we are on it at last, with an altitude above the sea of 9820 ft. We started at 7 A.M. and marched till noon, encountering at 11 A.M. a steep snow ridge which pretty well cooked us, but we got the sledge up by noon and camped. We are pulling 150 lb. per man. In the afternoon we had good going till 5 P.M. and then another ridge as difficult as the previous one, so that our backs and legs were in a bad way when we reached the top at 6 P.M., having done 14 miles 930 yards for the day. Thank heaven it has been a fine day, with little wind. The temperature is minus 9°F. This surface is most peculiar, showing layers of snow with little sastrugi all pointing south southeast. Short food make us think of plum puddings, and hard half-cooked maize gives us indigestion, but we are getting south. The latitude is 86° 19' South tonight. Our thoughts are with the people at home a great deal.

December 28. If the Barrier is a changing sea, the plateau is a changing sky. During the morning march we continued to go up hill steadily, but the surface was constantly changing. First there was soft snow in layers, then soft snow so deep that we were well over our ankles, and the temperature being well below zero, our feet were cold through sinking in. No one can say what we are going to find next, but we can go steadily ahead. We started at 6:55 A.M., and had done 7 miles 200 yards by noon, the pulling being very hard. Some of the snow is blown into hard sastrugi, some that look perfectly smooth and hard have only a thin crust through which we break when pulling; all of it is a trouble. Yesterday we passed our last crevasse, though there are a few cracks or ridges fringed with crystals shining like diamonds, warning us that the cracks are open. We are now 10,199 ft. above sea level, and the plateau is gradually flattening out, but it was heavy work pulling this afternoon. The high altitude and a temperature of 48° of frost made breathing and work difficult. We are getting south—latitude 86° 31' South tonight. The last sixty miles we hope to rush, leaving everything possible, taking one tent only and using the poles of the other as marks every ten miles, for we will leave all our food

sixty miles off the Pole except enough to carry us there
and back. I hope with good weather to reach the Pole
on January 12, and then we will try and rush it to get
to Hut Point by February 28. We are so tired after each
hour's pulling that we throw ourselves on our backs for
a three minute spell. It took us over ten hours to do 14
miles 450 yards today, but we did it all right. It is a
wonderful thing to be over 10,000 ft. up, almost at the
end of the world. The short food is trying, but when we
have done the work we will be happy. Adams had a bad
headache all yesterday, and today I had the same trouble, but it is better now. Otherwise we are all fit and
well. I think the country is flattening out more and more,
and hope tomorrow to make fifteen miles, at least.

December 29. Yesterday I wrote that we hoped to do
fifteen miles today, but such is the variable character of
this surface that one cannot prophesy with any certainty
an hour ahead. A strong southerly wind, with from 44°
to 49° of frost, combined with the effect of short rations,
made our distance 12 miles 600 yards instead. We have
reached an altitude of 10,310 ft., and an uphill gradient
gave us one of the most severe pulls for ten hours that
would be possible. It looks serious, for we must increase
the food if we are to get on at all, and we must risk a
depot at seventy miles off the Pole and dash for it then.
Our sledge is badly strained, and on the abominably bad
surface of soft snow is dreadfully hard to move. I have
been suffering from a bad headache all day, and Adams
also was worried by the cold. I think that these head-
aches are a form of mountain sickness, due to our high
altitude. The others have bled from the nose, and that
must relieve them. Physical effort is always trying at a
high altitude, and we are straining at the harness all day,
sometimes slipping in the soft snow that overlies the
hard sastrugi. My head is very bad. The sensation is as
though the nerves were being twisted up with a corkscrew and then pulled out. Marshall took our temperatures tonight, and we are all at about 94°, but in spite
of this we are getting south. We are only 198 miles off
our goal now. If the rise would stop the cold would not
matter, but it is hard to know what is man's limit. We
have only 150 lb. per man to pull, but it is more severe

work than the 250 lb. per man up the glacier was. The Pole is hard to get.

December 30. We only did 4 miles 100 yard today. We started at 7 A.M., but had to camp at 11 A.M., a blizzard springing up from the south. It is more than annoying. I cannot express my feelings. We were pulling at last on a level surface, but very soft snow, when at about 10 A.M. the south wind and drift commenced to increase, and at 11 A.M. it was so bad that we had to camp. And here all day we have been lying in our sleeping bags trying to keep warm and listening to the threshing drift on the tent side. I am in the cooking tent, and the wind comes through, it is so thin. Our precious food is going and the time also, and it is so important to us to get on. We lie here and think of how to make things better, but we cannot reduce food now, and the only thing will be to rush all possible at the end. We will do and are doing all humanly possible. It is with Providence to help us.

December 31. The last day of the old year, and the hardest day we have had almost, pushing through soft snow uphill with a strong head wind and drift all day. The temperature is minus 7°F, and our altitude is 10,477 ft. above sea level. The altitude is trying. My head has been very bad all day, and we are all feeling the short food, but still we are getting south. We are in latitude 86° 54' South tonight, but we have only three weeks' food and two weeks' biscuit to do nearly 500 geographical miles. We can only do our best. Too tired to write more tonight. We all get iced up about our faces, and are on the verge of frostbite all the time. Please God the weather will be fine during the next fourteen days. Then all will be well. The distance today was eleven miles.

NOTE. If we had only known that we were going to get such cold weather as we were at this time experiencing, we would have kept a pair of scissors to trim our beards. The moisture from the condensation of one's breath accumulated on the beard and trickled down on to the Burberry blouse. Then it froze into a sheet of ice inside, and it became very painful to pull the Burberry off in camp. Little troubles of this sort would have seemed less serious to us if we had been able to get a decent feed at the end of the day's work, but we were very hungry. We thought of food most of the time. The chocolate certainly seemed better than the cheese, because the two spoonfuls of cheese per man allowed under our scale of diet would not last as long as the two sticks of chocolate. We did not have both at the same meal. We had the bad luck at this time to strike a tin in which the biscuits were thin and overbaked. Under ordinary circumstances they would probably have tasted rather better than the other biscuits, but we wanted bulk. We soaked them in our tea so that they would swell up and appear larger, but if one soaked a biscuit too much, the sensation of biting something was lost, and the food seemed to disappear much too easily.

January 1, 1909. Head too bad to write much. We did 11 miles 900 yards (statute) today, and the latitude at 6 P.M. was 87° 6½' South, so we have beaten North and South records. Struggling uphill all day in very soft snow. Every one done up and weak from want of food. When we camped at 6 P.M. fine warm weather, thank God. Only 172½ miles from the Pole. The height above sea level, now 10,755 ft., makes all work difficult. Surface seems to be better ahead. I do trust it will be so tomorrow.

January 2. Terribly hard work today. We started at 6:45 A.M. with a fairly good surface, which soon became very soft. We were sinking in over our ankles, and our broken sledge, by running sideways, added to the drag. We have been going uphill all day, and tonight are 11,034 ft. above sea level. It has taken us all day to do 10 miles 450 yards, though the weights are fairly light. A cold wind, with a temperature of minus 14°F, goes right through us now, as we are weakening from want of food, and the high altitude makes every movement an effort, especially if we stumble on the march. My head is giving me trouble all the time. Wild seems the most fit of us. God knows we are doing all we can, but the outlook is serious if this surface continues and the plateau gets higher, for we are not traveling fast enough to make our food spin out and get back to our depot in time. I cannot think of failure yet. I must look at the matter sensibly and consider the lives of those who are with me. I feel that if we go on too far it will be impossible to get back over this surface, and then all the results will be lost to the world. We can now definitely locate the South Pole on the highest plateau in the world, and our geological work and meteorology will be of the greatest use to science; but all this is not the Pole. Man can only do his best, and we have arrayed against us the strongest forces of nature. This cutting south wind with drift plays the mischief with us, and after ten hours of struggling against it one pannikin of food with two biscuits and a cup of cocoa does not warm one up much. I must think over the situation carefully tomorrow, for time is going on and food is going also.

January 3. Started at 6:55 A.M., cloudy but fairly warm. The temperature was minus 8°F at noon. We had a terrible surface all the morning, and did only 5 miles 100 yards. A meridian altitude gave us latitude 87° 22' South at noon. The surface was better in the afternoon, and we did six geographical miles. The temperature at 6 P.M. was minus 11°F. It was an uphill pull toward the evening, and we camped at 6:20 P.M., the altitude being 11,220 ft. above the sea. Tomorrow we must risk making a depot on the plateau, and make a dash for it, but even then, if this surface continues, we will be two weeks in carrying in through.

January 4. The end is in sight. We can only go for three more days at the most, for we are weakening rapidly. Short food and a blizzard wind from the south, with driving drift, at a temperature of 47° of frost, have plainly told us today that we are reaching our limit, for we were so done up at noon with cold that the clinical thermometer failed to register the temperature of three of us at 94°. We started at 7:40 A.M., leaving a depot on this great wide plateau, a risk that only this case justified, and one that my comrades agreed to, as they have to every one so far, with the same cheerfulness and regardlessness of self that have been the means of our getting as far as we have done so far. Pathetically small looked the bamboo, one of the tent poles, with a bit of bag sewn on as a flag, to mark our stock of provisions, which has to take us back to our depot, one hundred and fifty miles north. We lost sight of it in half an hour, and are now trusting to our footprints in the snow to guide us back to each bamboo until we pick up the depot again. I trust that the weather will keep clear. Today we have done 12½ geographical miles, and with only 70 lb. per man to pull it is as hard, even harder, work than the 100 odd lb. was yesterday, and far harder than the 250 lb. were three weeks ago, when we were climbing the glacier. This, I consider, is a clear indication of our failing strength. The main thing against us is the altitude of 11,200 ft. and the biting wind. Our faces are cut, and our feet and hands are always on the verge of frostbite. Our fingers, indeed, often go, but we get them around more or less. I have great trouble with two fingers on my left hand. They had been badly jammed when we were getting the motor up over the ice face at winter quarters, and the circulation is not good. Our boots now are pretty well worn out, and we have to halt at times to pick the snow out of the soles. Our stock of sennegrass is nearly exhausted, so we have to use the same frozen stuff day after day. Another trouble is that the lamp wick with which we tie the finnesko is chafed through, and we have to tie knots in it. These knots catch the snow under our feet, making a lump that has to be cleared every now and then. I am of the opinion that to sledge even in the height of summer on this plateau, we should have at least forty ounces of food a day per man, and we are on short rations of the ordinary allowance of thirty-two ounces. We depoted our extra underclothing to save weight about three weeks ago, and are now in the same clothes night and day. One suit of underclothing, shirt and guernsey, and our thin Burberries, now all patched. When we get up in the morning, out of the wet bag, our Burberries become like a coat of mail at once, and our heads and beards get iced-up with the moisture when breathing on the march. There is half a gale blowing dead in our teeth all the time. We hope to reach within 100 geographical miles of the Pole; I am confident that the Pole lies on the great plateau we have discovered, miles and miles from any outstanding land. The temperature tonight is minus 24°F.

January 5. Today headwind and drift again, with 50°
of frost, and a terrible surface. We have been marching
through 8 in. of snow, covering sharp sastrugi, which
plays havoc with our feet, but we have done 13⅓ geographical miles, for we increased our food, seeing that
it was absolutely necessary to do this to enable us to
accomplish anything. I realize that the food we have
been having has not been sufficient to keep up our
strength, let alone supply the wastage caused by exertion, and now we must try to keep warmth in us, though
our strength is being used up. Our temperatures at 5
A.M. were 94°F. We got away at 7 A.M. sharp and
marched till noon, then from 1 P.M. sharp till 6 P.M. All
being in one tent makes our camp work slower, for we
are so cramped for room, and we get up at 4:40 A.M. so
as to get away by 7 A.M. Two of us have to stand outside
the tent at night until things are squared up inside, and
we find it cold work. Hunger grips us hard, and the food
supply is very small. My head still gives me great trouble.
I began by wishing that my worst enemy had it instead
of myself, but now I don't wish even my worst enemy
to have such a headache; still, it is no use talking about
it. Self is a subject that most of us are fluent on. We
find the utmost difficulty in carrying through the day,
and we can only go for two or three more days. Never
once has the temperature been above zero since we got
on to the plateau, though this is the height of summer.
We have done our best, and we thank God for having
allowed us to get so far.

January 6. This must be our last outward march with
the sledge and camp equipment. Tomorrow we must
leave camp with some food, and push as far south as
possible, and then plant the flag. Today's story is 57° of
frost, with a strong blizzard and high drift; yet we
marched 13¼ geographical miles through soft snow,
being helped by extra food. This does not mean full
rations, but a bigger ration than we have been having
lately. The pony maize is all finished. The most trying
day we have yet spent, our fingers and faces being frostbitten continually. Tomorrow we will rush south with the
flag. We are at 88° 7' South tonight. It is our last outward
march. Blowing hard tonight. I would fail to explain my

feelings if I tried to write them down, now that the end
has come. There is only one thing that lightens the disappointment, and that is the feeling that we have done all
we could. It is the forces of nature that have prevented
us from going right through. I cannot write more.

January 7. A blinding, shrieking blizzard all day, with
the temperature ranging from 60° to 70° of frost. It has
been impossible to leave the tent, which is snowed up
on the lee side. We have been lying in our bags all day,
only warm at food time, with fine snow making through
the walls of the worn tent and covering our bags. We
are greatly cramped. Adams is suffering from cramp
every now and then. We are eating our valuable food
without marching. The wind has been blowing eighty to
ninety miles an hour. We can hardly sleep. Tomorrow I
trust this will be over. Directly the wind drops we march
as far south as possible, then plant the flag, and turn
homeward. Our chief anxiety is lest our tracks may drift
up, for to them we must trust mainly to find our depot;
we have no land bearings in this great plain of snow. It
is a serious risk that we have taken, but we had to play
the game to the utmost, and Providence will look after
us.

January 8. Again all day in our bags, suffering considerably physically from cold hands and feet, and from
hunger, but more mentally, for we cannot get on south,
and we simply lie here shivering. Every now and then
one of our party's feet go, and the unfortunate beggar
has to take his leg out of the sleeping bag and have his
frozen foot nursed into life again by placing it inside the
shirt, against the skin of his almost equally unfortunate
neighbor. We must do something more to the south,
even though the food is going, and we weaken lying in
the cold, for with 72° of frost the wind cuts through our
thin tent, and even the drift is finding its way in and on
to our bags, which are wet enough as it is. Cramp is not
uncommon every now and then, and the drift all round
the tent has made it so small that there is hardly room
for us at all. The wind has been blowing hard all day;
some of the gusts must be over seventy or eighty miles
an hour. This evening it seems as though it were going
to ease down, and directly it does we shall be up and

away south for a rush. I feel that this march must be our limit. We are so short of food, and at this high altitude, 11,600 ft., it is hard to keep any warmth in our bodies between the scanty meals. We have nothing to read now, having depoted our little books to save weight, and it is dreary work lying in the tent with nothing to read, and too cold to write much in the diary.

CHAPTER XV

Farthest South
January 9, 1909

The Union Jack planted in 88° 23' South,
Longitude 162° East

January 9. Our last day outwards. We have shot our bolt, and the tale is latitude 88° 23' South, longitude 162° East. The wind eased down at 1 A.M., and at 2 A.M. we were up and had breakfast. At 4 A.M. started south, with the Queen's Union Jack, a brass cylinder containing stamps and documents to place at the furthest south point, camera, glasses, and compass. At 9 A.M. we were in 88° 23' South, half running and half walking over a surface much hardened by the recent blizzard. It was strange for us to go along without the nightmare of a sledge dragging behind us. We hoisted Her Majesty's flag and the other Union Jack afterwards, and took possession of the plateau in the name of His Majesty. While the Union Jack blew out stiffly in the icy gale that cut us to the bone, we looked south with our powerful glasses, but could see nothing but the dead white snow plain. There was no break in the plateau as it extended toward the Pole, and we feel sure that the goal we have failed to reach lies on this plain. We stayed only a few minutes, and then, taking the Queen's flag and eating our scanty meal as we went, we hurried back and reached our camp about 3 P.M. We were so dead tired that we only did two hours' march in the afternoon and camped at 5:30 P.M. The temperature was minus 19°F. Fortunately for us, our tracks were not obliterated by the blizzard; indeed, they stood up, making a trail easily followed. Homeward bound at last. Whatever regrets may be, we have done our best.

CHAPTER XVI

The Return March
January 10 to February 22

January 10. We started at 7:30 A.M. with a fair wind, and
marched all day, with a stop of one hour for lunch, doing
over 18½ geographical miles to the north. It has, indeed,
been fortunate for us that we have been able to follow
our outward track for the force of the gale had torn the
flags from the staffs. We will be all right when we pick
up our depot. It has been a big risk leaving our food on
the great white plain, with only our sledge tracks to
guide us back. Tonight we are all tired out, but we have
put a good march behind us. The temperature is minus
9°F.

January 11. A good day. We have done nearly 17 geographical miles. We have picked up our depot and now
are following the sledge tracks to the north. The temperature has been minus 15°F. There has been tremendous
wind here and the sastrugi are enormous.

January 12. We did 14 miles 100 yards today with little
wind to help us. The surface was very heavy and we
found enormous sastrugi. The wind is getting up tonight.
I hope for a good breeze behind us tomorrow.

January 13. It was heavy pulling all day, but we did a
good distance in spite of it, getting 15 miles 1650 yards
to the north. We have the sail up continually, but I cannot say that it has been very much help today. The temperature, minus 18°F nearly all the time, makes things
very cold, and we ourselves slept badly last night. I did
not sleep at all, for both my heels are frostbitten and
have cracked open, and also have cracks under some of
my toes; but we can march all right, and are moving
over the ground very fast. We must continue to do so,
for we have only about 20 lb. of biscuit to last us over
140 miles, and I expect there will be little in the locker

by the time we strike our glacier head depot. The surface
has been very severe today.

January 14. A strong following blizzard all day gave
us our best day's run of the whole trip, 20 miles 1600
yards in ten hours. We decided to cut down the rations
by another biscuit, as we have only six days' biscuit left
on short ration, and 120 miles to go before we reach the
depot, so we feel very hungry, and with the temperature
minus 18°F to minus 21°F, all day in the wind, one easily
gets frostbitten.

January 15. Started in a strong blizzard at 7:30 A.M.
with a temperature of minus 23°F, and march steadily
till noon, doing 9½ miles; then marched from 1:30 P.M.
till 6 P.M., making a total distance for the day of 20 miles,
statute. It has been thick, with a pale sun only shining
through, but we are still able to follow our old sledge
tracks, though at times they are very faint. Unfortunately, when we halted at 3:30 P.M. for a spell, we found
that the sledge meter had disappeared, and discovered
that it had broken off short at the brass fitting. This is
a serious loss to us, for all our Barrier distances between
depots are calculated on it, and although we have another depoted at the foot of the glacier we do not know
the slip. We must now judge distance till we get a sight
of land.

January 16. With a strong following blizzard, we did
18½ miles to the north today. My burst heels gave me
great pain all day. Marshall dressed them tonight. We
saw land again today after being out of sight of it for
nearly three weeks.

January 17. Started sharp at 7 A.M., in a fresh blizzard
wind, with a temperature of minus 23°F, we did our best
march, for it was mainly downhill and we covered 22½
miles. At 10 A.M. we came up to our Christmas camp,
and there took on a bamboo we had left, and which now
comes in useful for our sail. This sail is now our great
help. We dropped over 500 ft. today, and in three days
ought to reach our depot at this rate.

January 18. Our best day, 26½ miles downhill, with a
strong following wind. We have nearly got to the end of
the main icefall. The temperature has risen sensibly, it
being minus 14°F tonight, and the hypsometer, 196.5°,

shows a good rise. With luck we may reach our depot tomorrow night. With food now in hand, we had a decent feed tonight. I have been very unlucky today, falling into many crevasses and hurting my shoulder badly. I have also had many falls, besides the trouble with the bad heels on the hard stuff.

January 19. Another record day, for we have done about twenty-nine miles to the north, rushing under sail down ice falls and through crevasses, till, at 6 P.M., we picked up our sledge tracks of December 18 outwards. We camped, dead beat, at 6:30 P.M., and had a good hoosh. We have descended to 7500 ft., and the temperature tonight is minus 14°F. We are now only 8½ miles from our depot, which we will reach tomorrow morning, all being well. This strong blizzard wind has been an immense help this way, though not outwards for us.

January 20. Although we have not covered so much ground today, we have had an infinitely harder time. We started at 7 A.M. on our tracks of December 19, and at 7:30 passed the camp of the evening of the 18th. For two hours we were descending a snow slope, with heavy sastrugi, and then struck a patch of badly crevassed névé, about half a mile across. After that we got on to blue slippery ice, where our finnesko had no hold. A gale was blowing, and often fierce gusts came along, sweeping the sledge sideways, and knocking us off our feet. We all had many falls, and I had two specially heavy ones which shook me up severely. When we reached the steep slopes where we had roped the sledges up on our outward journey, we lowered the sledge down by means of the alpine rope, using an ice axe as a bollard to lower by. On several occasions one or more of us lost our footing, and were swept by the wind down the ice slope, with great difficulty getting back to our sledge and companions. We arrived at our depot at 12:30 P.M. with sore and aching bodies. The afternoon was rather better, as, after the first hour, we got off the blue ice on to snow. However, bad as the day has been, we have said farewell to that awful plateau, and are well on our way down the glacier.

January 21. Started at 7:45 A.M. with a fresh southerly breeze, so we still have valuable assistance from our sail. The heavy falls I had yesterday have so shaken me that

I have been very ill today. I harnessed up for a while, but soon had to give up pulling and walk by the sledge; but, as the course has been downhill nearly all day and a fair wind has been assisting, the others have had no difficulty in getting along at a good pace, and we have covered seventeen miles. The weather is much warmer, the temperature tonight being about minus 1°F.

January 22. Started at 7:30 A.M. on a good surface that changed to crevassed ice slopes in the afternoon, down which we made fair progress. Am still too ill to harness up, but as the pull was not much it did not matter. Indeed, we had another man out of harness guiding the sledge. The distance today was 15½ miles.

January 23. Similar weather, surface and work. Fine and warm; temperature plus 8°F.

January 24. One of our hardest day's work, and certainly the longest, for we started at 6:45 A.M., went on till 12:50 P.M., had lunch, started at 2 P.M., went on till 6 P.M., had a cup of tea, and went on till 9 P.M. Then we had our single pot of hoosh and one biscuit, for we have only two days' food left and one day's biscuit on much reduced ration, and we have to cover forty miles of crevasses to reach our depot before we can get any more food. I am now all right again, though rather weak. We had a terribly hard time in the crevassed ice this morning, and now our sledge has not much more than half a runner on one side, and is in a very shaky state. However, I believe we are safe now. The distance today was sixteen miles, statute.

January 25. We started away from camp at 6:45 A.M., marched till noon, when we had a cup of tea, and then marched till 3 P.M., when we had lunch, consisting of a cup of tea, two biscuits, two spoonsful of cheese. Then we marched till 9 P.M. when we had one pot of hoosh and one biscuit. We did twenty-six miles; fine weather. The food is all finished but one meal. No biscuit, only cocoa, tea, salt, and pepper left, very little of these also. Must reach depot tomorrow. It was fairly good going today till the last two hours, and then we were falling into most dangerous crevasses and were saved only by our harness. Very tired indeed. Thank God warm and fine weather. We can see our depot rock in the distance, so hope to reach it tomorrow. Turning in now, 11 P.M.; breakfast as usual 5 A.M. The temperature is plus 12°F.

January 26 and 27. Two days written up as one, and they have been the hardest and most trying we have ever spent in our lives, and will ever stand in our memories. Tonight (the 27th) we have had our first solid food since the morning of the 26th. We came to the end of all our provisions except a little cocoa and tea, and from 7 A.M. on the 26th till 2 P.M. on the 27th we did sixteen miles over the worst surfaces and most dangerous crevasses we have ever encountered, only stopping for tea or cocoa till they were finished, and marching twenty hours at a stretch, through snow 10 to 18 in. thick as a rule, with sometimes 2½ ft. of it. We fell into hidden crevasses time after time, and were saved by each other and by our harness. In fact, only an all merciful Providence has guided our steps to tonight's safety at our depot. I cannot describe adequately the mental and physical strain of the last forty-eight hours. When we started at 7 A.M. yesterday, we immediately got into soft snow, an uphill pull with hidden crevasses. The biscuit was all finished, and with only one pannikin of hoosh, mostly pony maize, and one of tea, we marched till noon. Then we had one pannikin of tea and one ounce of chocolate, and marched till 4:45 P.M. We had one pannikin of tea. There was no more food. We marched till 10 P.M., then one small pannikin of cocoa. Marched till 2 A.M., when we were played out. We had one pannikin of cocoa, and slept till 8 A.M. Then a pannikin of cocoa, and we marched till 1 P.M. and camped, about half a mile from the depot. Marshall went on for food, and we got a meal at 2 P.M. We turned in and slept. Adams fell exhausted in his harness, but recovered and went on again. Wild did the same the night before.

January 28. Thank God we are on the Barrier again at last. We got up at 1 A.M. this morning, had breakfast, consisting of tea and one biscuit, and got under way at 3 A.M. We reached the depot in half an hour without any difficulty. The snow here was deep enough to carry us over the crevasses that had impeded our progress so much on the outward march. We had proper breakfast at 5 A.M. then dug out our depot. The alternate falls of snow and thaws had frozen solidly in a great deal of our gear, and our spare sledge meter was deeply buried. We marched along till we were close to the Gap, then had lunch. At 1 P.M. we were through the Gap and on to the crevassed and ridged Barrier surface. We are now safe, with six days' food and only fifty miles to the depot, but Wild has developed dysentery. We are at a loss to know what is the cause of it. It may possibly be due to the horse meat. The weather has been fairly fine all day, though clouding up from the south towards noon, and we were assisted by a fresh southerly breeze up the slope to the head of the Gap. Indeed, we needed it, for the heavy surface and our dilapidated sledge made the hauling extremely hard. Just before we left the glacier I broke through the soft snow, plunging into a hidden crevasse. My harness jerked up under my heart, and gave me rather a shakeup. It seemed as though the glacier were saying: "There is the last touch of you; don't you come up here again." It was with a feeling of intense relief that we left this great glacier, for the strain had been hard, and now we know that except for blizzards and thick weather, which two factors can alone prevent us from finding our depots in good time, we will be all right. The light became bad this evening when we were on the last hour before camping, and we cannot say for certain whether we are clear of the main chasm by the land or not, so must give its line of direction a wide berth. The temperature is well up, plus 26°F, and it is warm indeed after the minus temperatures which have been our lot for the last month or so.

January 29. We are having a most unfriendly greeting from the Barrier. We got up as usual and had breakfast at 5:30 A.M. the weather thick and overcast, but the land showing enough for us to steer by. We got away at 7:20 A.M., and soon after it began to snow, which in a temperature of plus 30°F melted on the sledge and all our gear, making everything into a miserably wet state. We had to put the compass down every now and then, for it became too thick to see any landmarks, and at 9:30 the wind suddenly sprang up from the east, cold and strong, freezing solid all our wet clothes, and the various things on the sledge. It was blowing a blizzard with snow and heavy drift in less than five minutes from the time the wind started, and with difficulty we managed to get up one tent and crawl into it, where we waited in the hope that the weather would clear. As there was no sign of an improvement at noon we pitched the other tent, had food, and lay in our bags patching our worn-out clothes. All day the blizzard has continued to blow hard, with extra violent gusts at times. Our tents get snowed up, and we have to clear them by kicking at the snow every now and then.

January 30. We made a start at 8:15 A.M., after spending three-quarters of an hour digging out our sledges and tents from the drift of the blizzard, which stopped at 1 A.M. It was clear over part of the land as we started, but soon snow began to fall again and the weather became very thick; yet, steering on a course, we came through the crevasses and drift without even touching one, though before, in good light, we have had to turn and twist to avoid them. The surface was heavy for pulling on, owing to the fine snow from the blizzard, but we did thirteen miles for the day, working a full ten hours till 7:50 P.M. The weather cleared right up in the afternoon, and we made a good course. Wild is seedy today, but we hope that as soon as he reaches Grisi depot he will be better. We have no variety of food, and only have four miserably thin biscuits a day to eke out the horse meat. The plasmon is all finished and so are we ourselves by the end of the day's march. The sledge also is in a terribly bad state, but as soon as we reach the depot all will be well. The surface in the afternoon improved, and is much better than we had hoped for. The temperature is plus 24°F, fine and warm. A heavy day's pull, but we were assisted by the wind in the afternoon. Wild is still seedy, just walking in harness. The surface is good, and we are rapidly nearing the depot. Short of food, down to twenty ounces a day. Very tired. Good weather.

January 31. Started at 7 A.M., Wild bad with dysentery. Picked up mound 4 P.M., and camped at 6 P.M. Very bad surface. Did 13½ miles.

February 1. Started 7 A.M.; awful surface at times.

Wild very bad. Picked up mound. Camped 6 P.M., having done nearly fourteen miles.

February 2. Started at 6:40 A.M. and camped 7 P.M. at depot. Wild and self dysentery; dead tired, bad surface, with undulations. Did 13½ miles. Ray's birthday, celebrated with two lumps of sugar, making five each in cocoa.

February 3. Started with new sledge and 150 lb. more weight at 8:40 A.M.; camped at 5:30 P.M. Only five miles; awfully soft snow surface. All acute dysentery due to meat. Trust that sleep will put us right. Could go no farther tonight. Wild very bad, self weaker, others assailed also. Bad light, short food, surface worse than ever. Snow one foot deep. Got up 4:30 A.M. after going to bed 11 P.M. No more tonight. Temperature plus 5°F. Dull.

February 4. Cannot write more. All down with acute dysentery; terrible day. No march possible; outlook serious. . . . Fine weather.

February 5. Eight miles today; dead tired. Dysentery better, but Adams not too right. Camped at 5:30 P.M. We are picking up the mounds well. Too weak on half rations to write much. Still hanging on to geological specimens. Please God we will get through all right. Great anxiety.

February 6. Did ten miles today. All better and a better surface. Terribly hungry. Six biscuits per day and one pannikin horse meat each meal. Picked up November 28 mound and made camp. I do trust this hunger will not weaken us too much. It has been great anxiety. Thank God the dysentery stopped and the surface better. We may do more tomorrow, as there are signs of wind from the southeast. Temperature plus 9°F.

February 7. Blowing hard blizzard. Kept going till 6 P.M. Adams and Marshall renewed dysentery. Dead tired. Short food; very weak.

February 8. Did twelve miles. We had fine weather after 10 A.M. Started from camp in blizzard. Adams and Marshall still dysentery; Wild and I all right. Feel starving for food. Talk of it all day. Anyhow, getting north, thank God. Sixty-nine miles to Chinaman depot.

February 9. Strong following blizzard, and did 14½

miles to north. Adams not fit yet. All thinking and talking of food.

February 10. Strong following wind. Did 20 miles 300 yards. Temperature plus 22°F. All thinking and talking of food.

February 11. We did 16½ miles today, and continued to pick up the mounds, which is a great comfort. The temperature is plus 20°F tonight. All our thoughts are of food. We ought to reach the depot in two days. Now we are down to half a pannikin of meat and five biscuits a day. Adams not all right yet, and Wild shaky tonight. Good surface and following wind. We were up at 4:45 A.M. and camped at 6 P.M.

February 12. Fine day, with no wind. We were up at 4:30 A.M., and marched till 6 P.M., doing 14½ miles. Adams sighted the depot flag at 6 P.M. The temperature has ranged from plus 5° to plus 20°F. Passed sastrugi running south southeast in the afternoon. Slight westerly wind. Very tired.

February 13. Breakfast at 4:40 A.M. We packed up, with a cold wind blowing, and reached the depot, with all our food finished, at 11:30 A.M. There we got Chinaman's liver, which we have had tonight. It tasted splendid. We looked round for any spare bits of meat, and while I was digging in the snow I came across some hard red stuff, Chinaman's blood frozen into a solid core. We dug it up, and found it a welcome addition to our food. It was like beef tea when boiled up. The distance today was twelve miles, with a light wind.

February 14. A good surface today, but no wind. The pulling was hard, and the temperature plus 10° to plus 18°F. We did 11¾ miles. We are still weak, but better, the horse blood helps. Burst lips are our greatest trouble.

February 15. My birthday today. I was given a present of a cigarette made out of pipe tobacco and some coarse paper we had with us. It was delicious. A hard pull today, and my head is very bad again. The distance was 12¼ miles, with a fairly good surface and fine weather. We are picking up our mounds with great regularity. The land can be seen faintly through the haze in the distance. We have found undulations even out here, but not very marked, running in the usual direction. Temperature minus 3°F, at noon.

February 16. A fair surface today, but no wind. The sastrugi are disappearing. We are appallingly hungry. We are down to about half a pannikin of half cooked horsemeat a meal and four biscuits a day. We covered thirteen miles today, with the temperature from zero to minus 7°F. There are appearances of wind from the south, long windy streamers of torn stratus. We are so weak now that even to lift our depleted provision bag is an effort. When we break camp in the morning we pull the tent off the poles and take it down before we move the things inside, for the effort of lifting the sleeping bags, etc., through the doorway is too great. At night when we have come to camp we sometimes have to lift our legs one, at a time with both hands in getting into the tent. It seems a severe strain to lift one's feet without aid after we have stiffened from the day's march. Our fingers are extremely painful. Some of us have big blisters that burst occasionally.

February 17. I thought we were in for it and was not wrong. Today we have been marching in a blinding blizzard, with 42° of frost, but, thank heaven, the wind was behind us and we have done nineteen miles, the sledge with the sail up often over running us, and then at other times getting into a patch of soft snow and bringing us up with a jerk. The harness round our weakened stomachs gives us a good deal of pain when we are brought up suddenly. We started at 6:40 A.M. and marched till 6 P.M., and today we had three pannikins of semi cooked horse meat and six biscuits on the strength of the good march. We all have tragic dreams of getting food to eat, but rarely have the satisfaction of dreaming that we are actually eating. Last night I did taste bread and butter. We look at each other as we eat our scanty meals and feel a distinct grievance if one man manages to make his hoosh last longer than the rest of us. Sometimes we do our best to save a bit of biscuit for the next meal, but it is a much debated question whether it is best to eat all the food at once or to save. I eat all my lunch biscuit, but keep a bit from dinner to eat in the bag so as to induce sleep. The smaller the quantity of biscuits grows the more delicious they taste.

February 18. The wind dropped during the night, and at 4:40 A.M. we got up, picked our buried sledge out of the drift, and were under way at 7 A.M. There was little wind, and the temperature was minus 20°F at noon. This afternoon we sighted old Discovery. What a homelike appearance it has. Its big bluff form showed out in the northwest, and we felt that the same mountain might at that very moment be drawing the eyes of our own people at winter quarters. It seemed to be a connecting link. Perhaps they will be wondering whether we are in sight of it.

February 19. A very cold south wind today, but we turned out at 4:40 A.M., with a temperature of minus 20° F. We have been hungry and cold all day, but did 14½ miles on a good surface. We sighted Mount Erebus in the morning. The old landmarks are so pleasant. Camped at 6 P.M., temperature minus 10° F. We ought to reach Depot A tomorrow. We have picked up the last mound except one. If we had food all would be well, but we are now at the end of our supplies again, except for some scraps of meat scraped off the bones of Grisi after they had been lying on the snow in the sun for all these months. We dare not risk it until the worst comes. Still in five days more we ought to be in the land of plenty.

February 20. Started to get up at 4:40 A.M. It is almost a farce to talk of getting up to "breakfast" now, and there is no call of "Come on, boys; good hoosh." No good hoosh is to be had. In less time than it has taken me to write this the food is finished, and then our hopes and thoughts lie wholly in the direction of the next feed, so called from force of habit. It was dull and overcast today, and we could see only a little way. Still we made progress, and at 4 P.M. we reached Depot A. The distance for the day was fourteen miles, with 52° of frost. We sighted the depot at 2:30·P.M., and now we have enough food to carry us to the Bluff Depot. We had run out of food when we reached the depot today, and we have had a good hoosh tonight. The unaccustomed pemmican fat made me feel quite queer, but I enjoyed the pudding we made out of biscuits and the tin of jam which we originally intended to have for Christmas Day, but which we left behind when on the way south in order to save weight. Our depoted tobacco and cigarettes were here, and it is difficult to describe the enjoyment and luxury of a good smoke. I am sure that the tobacco will make up for the shortage of food I do not doubt but that the Bluff Depot will have been laid all right by Joyce. Anyhow we must stake on it, for we have not enough food to carry us to the ship. Joyce knows his work well and we talk now of nothing but the feeds that we will have when we reach the Bluff. That depot has been the bright beacon ahead through these dark days of hunger. Each time we took in another hole in our belts we have said that it will be all right when we get to the Bluff Depot, and now we are getting toward it.

February 21. We got up at 4:40 A.M., just as it commenced to blow, and the wind continued all day, a blizzard with as low as 67° of frost. We could not get warm, but we did twenty miles. In ordinary polar work one would not think of traveling in such a severe blizzard, but our need is extreme, and we must keep going. It is neck or nothing with us now. Our food lies ahead, and death stalks us from behind. This is just the time of the year when the most bad weather may be expected. The sun now departs at night, and the darkness is palpable by the time we turn in, generally about 9:30 P.M. We are so thin that our bones ache as we lie on the hard snow in our sleeping bags, from which a great deal of the hair has gone. Tonight we stewed some of the scraps of Grisi meat, and the dish tasted delicious. Too cold to write more. Thank God, we are nearing the Bluff.

February 22. A splendid day. We did 20½ miles, and on the strength of the distance had a good feed. About 11 A.M. we suddenly came across the tracks of a party of four men, with dogs. Evidently the weather has been fine and they have been moving at a good pace toward the south. We could tell that the weather has been fine, for they were wearing ski boots instead of finnesko, and occasionally we saw the stump of a cigarette. The length of the steps showed that they were going fast. We are now camped on the tracks, which are fairly recent, and we will try to follow them to the Bluff, for they must have come from the depot. This assures us that the depot was laid all right. I cannot imagine who the fourth man can be, unless it was Buckley, who might be there now that the ship is in. We passed their noon camp, and I am certain that the ship is in, for there were tins lying around bearing brands different from those of the original stores. We found three small bits of chocolate and a little bit of biscuit at the camp after carefully searching the ground for such unconsidered trifles, and we "turned backs" for them. I was unlucky enough to get the bit of biscuit, and a curious unreasoning anger took possession of me for a moment at my bad luck. It shows how primitive we have become, and how much the question of even a morsel of food affects our judgment. We are near the end of our food, but as we have staked everything on the Bluff Depot, we had a good feed tonight. If we do not pick up the depot, there will be absolutely no hope for us.

CHAPTER XVII

The Final Stage
February 23 to March 4

Bluff Depot reached: Marshall's Condition worse on
February 25: Marshall and Adams remain in Camp while
Shackleton and Wild make a Forced March to Hut Point:
On board *Nimrod*: Relief Party start to bring in Marshall
and Adams: All Safe on Board Ship March 4, 1909

February 23. Started at 6:45 A.M. in splendid weather,
and at 11 A.M., while halting for a spell, Wild saw the
Bluff Depot miraged up. It seemed to be quite close,
and the flags were waving and dancing as though to say,
"Come, here I am, come and feed." It was the most
cheerful sight our eyes have ever seen, for we had only
a few biscuits left. These we at once devoured. The Grisi
meat had given Wild renewed dysentery. After a short
camp we pushed on. A flashing light appeared to be on
the depot, and when we reached it at 4 P.M., this turned
out to be a biscuit tin, which had been placed in the
snow so as to catch the light of the sun. It was like a
great cheerful eye twinkling at us. The depot had appeared much closer than it really was, because we were
accustomed to judging from the height of an ordinary
depot, whereas this one was built on a snow mound over
10 ft. high, with two bamboos lashed together on top,
and three flags. It was a splendid mark. Joyce and his
party have done their work well. Now we are safe as
regards food, and it only remains for us to reach the
ship. I climbed up on top of the depot, and shouted to
those below of the glorious feeds that awaited us. First
I rolled down three tins of biscuits, then cases containing
luxuries of every description, many of them sent by
friends. There were Carlsbad plums, eggs, cakes, plum
puddings, gingerbread and crystallized fruit, even fresh
boiled mutton from the ship. After months of want and
hunger, we suddenly found ourselves able to have meals
fit for the gods, and with appetites that the gods might
have envied. Apart from the luxuries there was an ample

247

supply of ordinary sledging rations. Tonight we improvised a second cooking stand out of a biscuit tin, and used our second primus to cook some of the courses. Our dream of food has come true, and yet after we had eaten biscuits and had two pannikins of pemmican, followed by cocoa, our contracted bodies would not stand the strain of more food, and reluctantly we had to stop. I cannot tell what a relief it has been to us. There is nothing much in the way of news from the ship, only just a letter saying that she had arrived on January 5, and that all was well. This letter, dated January 20, is signed by Evans, who evidently is the Evans who towed us down in the *Koonya.* We now only have to catch the ship, and I hope we will do that. Wild is better tonight. The temperature is plus 10°F, fine and warm. I am writing in my bag with biscuits beside me, and chocolate and jam.

February 24. We got up at 5 A.M., and at 7 A.M. had breakfast, consisting of eggs, dried milk, porridge, and pemmican, with plenty of biscuits. We marched until 1 P.M., had lunch and then marched until 8 P.M., covering a distance of fifteen miles for the day. The weather was fine. Though we have plenty of weight to haul now we do not feel it so much as we did the smaller weights when we were hungry. We have good food inside us, and every now and then on the march we eat a bit of chocolate or biscuit. Warned by the experience of Scott and Wilson on the previous southern journey, I have taken care not to overeat. Adams has a wonderful digestion, and can go on without any difficulty. Wild's dysentery is a bit better today. He is careful of his feeding and has only taken things that are suitable. It is a comfort to be able to pick and choose. I cannot understand a letter I received from Murray about Mackintosh getting adrift on the ice, but no doubt this will be cleared up on our return. Anyhow, every one seems to be all right. There was no news of the Northern Party or of the Western Party. We turned in full of food tonight.

February 25. We turned out at 4 A.M. for an early start, as we are in danger of being left if we do not push ahead rapidly and reach the ship. On going into the tent for breakfast I found Marshall suffering from paralysis of the stomach and renewed dysentery, and while we were eating a blizzard came up. We secured everything as the Bluff showed masses of ragged cloud, and I was of opinion that it was going to blow hard. I did not think Marshall fit to travel through the blizzard. During the afternoon, as we were lying in the bags, the weather cleared somewhat, though it still blew hard. If Marshall is not better tonight, I must leave him with Adams and push on, for time is going on, and the ship may leave on March 1, according to orders, if the Sound is not clear of ice. I went over through the blizzard to Marshall's tent. He is in a bad way still, but thinks that he could travel tomorrow.

February 27 (1 A.M.). The blizzard was over at midnight, and we got up at 1 A.M., had breakfast at 2, and made a start at 4. At 9:30 A.M. we had lunch, at 3 P.M. tea, at 7 P.M. hoosh, and then marched till 11 P.M. Had another hoosh, and turned in at 1 A.M. We did twenty-four miles. Marshall suffered greatly, but stuck to the march. He never complains.

March 5. Although we did not turn in until 1 A.M. on Feb. 27th, we were up again at 4 A.M. and after a good hoosh, we got under way at 6 A.M. and marched until 1 P.M. Marshall was unable to haul, his dysentery increasing, and he got worse in the afternoon, after lunch. At 4 P.M. I decided to pitch camp, leave Marshall under Adams' charge, and push ahead with Wild, taking one day's provisions and leaving the balance for the two men at the camp. I hoped to pick up a relief party at the ship. We dumped everything off the sledge except a prismatic compass, our sleeping bags and food for one day, and at 4:30 P.M. Wild and I started, and marched till 9 P.M. Then we had a hoosh, and marched until 2 A.M. of the 28th, over a very hard surface. We stopped for one hour and a half off the northeast end of White Island, getting no sleep, and marched till 11 A.M., by which time our food was finished. We kept flashing the heliograph in the hope of attracting attention from Observation Hill, where I thought that a party would be on the lookout, but there was no return flash. The only thing to do was to push ahead, although we were by this time very tired. At 2:30 P.M. we sighted open water ahead, the ice having evidently broken out four miles south of Cape Armitage, and an hour and a half later a blizzard wind started to blow, and the weather got very thick. We thought once that we saw a party coming over to meet us, and our sledge seemed to grow lighter for a few minutes, but the "party" turned out to be a group of penguins at the ice edge. The weather was so thick that we could not see any distance ahead, and we arrived at the ice edge suddenly. The ice was swaying up and down, and there was grave risk of our being carried out. I decided to abandon the sledge, as I felt sure that we would get assistance at once when we reached the hut, and time was becoming important. It was necessary that we should get food and shelter speedily. Wild's feet were giving him a great deal of trouble. In the thick weather we could not risk making Pram Point, and I decided to follow another route seven miles round by the other side of Castle Rock. We clambered over crevasses and snow slopes, and after what seemed an almost interminable struggle reached Castle Rock, from whence I could see that there was open water all around the north. It was indeed a different homecoming from what we had expected. Out on the Barrier and up on the plateau our thoughts had often turned to the day when we would get back to the comfort and plenty of the winter quarters, but we had never imagined fighting our way to the back door, so to speak, in such a cheerless fashion. We reached the top of Ski Slope at 7:45 P.M., and from there we could see the hut and the bay. There was no sign of the ship, and no smoke or other evidence of life at the hut. We hurried on to the hut, our minds busy with gloomy possibilities, and found not a man there. There was a letter stating that the Northern Party had reached the Magnetic Pole, and that all the parties had been picked up except ours. The letter added that the ship would be sheltering under Glacier Tongue until February 26. It was now February 28, and it was with very keen anxiety in our minds that we proceeded to search for food. If the ship was gone, our plight, and that of the two men left out on the Barrier, was a very serious one.

We improvised a cooking vessel, found oil and a Primus lamp, and had a good feed of biscuit, onions, and plum pudding, which were amongst the stores left at the hut. We were utterly weary but we had no sleeping gear, our bags having been left with the sledge, and the temperature was very low. We found a piece of roofing felt, which we wrapped around us, and then we sat up all night, the darkness being relieved only when we occasionally lighted the lamp in order to secure a little warmth. We tried to burn the magnetic hut in the hope of attracting attention from the ship, but we were not able to get it alight. We tried, too, to tie the Union Jack to Vince's cross, on the hill, but we were so played out that our cold fingers could not manage the knots. It was a bad night for us, and we were glad indeed when the light came again. Then we managed to get a little warmer, and at 9 A.M. we got the magnetic hut alight, and put up the flag. All our fears vanished when in the distance we saw the ship, miraged up. We signaled with the heliograph, and at 11 A.M. on March 1 we were on board the *Nimrod* and once more safe amongst friends. I will not attempt to describe our feelings. Everyone was glad to see us, and keen to know what we had done. They had given us up for lost, and a search party had been going to start that day in the hope of finding some trace of us. I found that every member of the expedition was well, that the plans had worked out satisfactorily, and that the work laid down had been carried out. The ship had brought nothing but good news from the outside world. It seemed as though a great load had been lifted from my shoulders.

The first thing was to bring in Adams and Marshall, and I ordered out a relief party at once. I had a good feed of bacon and fried bread, and started at 2:30 P.M. from the Barrier edge with Mackay, Mawson, and McGillan, leaving Wild on the *Nimrod*. We marched until 10 P.M., had dinner and turned in for a short sleep. We were up again at 2 A.M. the next morning (March 2), and traveled until 1 P.M., when we reached the camp where I had left the two men. Marshall was better, the rest having done him a lot of good, and he was able to march and pull. After lunch we started back again, and marched until 8 P.M. in fine weather. We were under way again at 4 A.M. the next morning, had lunch at noon, and reached the ice edge at 3 P.M. There was no sign of the ship, and the sea was freezing over. We waited until 5 P.M., and then found that it was possible to strike land at Pram Point. The weather was coming on bad, clouding up from the southeast, and Marshall was suffering from renewed dysentery, the result of the heavy marching. We therefore abandoned one tent and one sledge at the ice edge, taking on only the sleeping bags and the specimens. We climbed up by Crater Hill, leaving everything but the sleeping bags, for the weather was getting worse, and at 9:35 P.M. commenced to slide down toward Hut Point. We reached the winter quarters at 9:50, and Marshall was put to bed. Mackay and I lighted a carbide flare on the hill by Vince's cross, and after dinner all hands turned in except Mackay and myself. A short time after Mackay saw the ship appear. It was now blowing a hard blizzard, but Mackintosh had seen our flare from a distance of nine miles. Adams and I went on board the *Nimrod,* and Adams, after surviving all the dangers of the interior of the Antarctic continent, was nearly lost within sight of safety. He slipped at the ice edge, owing to the fact that he was wearing new finnesko, and he only just saved himself from going over. He managed to hang on until he was rescued by a party from the ship.

A boat went back for Marshall and the others, and we were all safe on board at 1 A.M. on March 4.

CHAPTER XVIII

Some Notes on the Southern Journey

"Turning Backs": Pony Soup: The "Wild Roll": Frostbite:
Glacier Surfaces: Painful Falls: Particular Duties assigned
to each Member of the Southern Party

WE brought back with us from the journey toward the
Pole vivid memories of how it feels to be intensely,
fiercely hungry. During the period from November 15,
1908, to February 23, 1909, we had but one full meal,
and that was on Christmas Day. Even then we did not
keep the sense of repletion for very long for within an
hour or two it seemed to us that we were as hungry as
ever. Our daily allowance of food would have been a
small one for a city worker in a temperate climate, and
in our case hunger was increased by the fact that we
were performing vigorous physical labor in a very low
temperature. We looked forward to each meal with keen
anticipation, but when the food was in our hands it
seemed to disappear without making us any the less rav-
enous. The evening meal at the end of ten hours' sledging used to take us a long time to prepare. The sledges
had to be unpacked and the camp pitched. Then the
cooker was filled with snow and the primus lamp lit,
often no easy matter with our cold, frostbitten fingers.
The materials for the thin hoosh would be placed in the
boiling pot, with the addition, perhaps, of some pony
maize, and the allowance of tea was placed in the outer
boiler. The tea was always put in a strainer, consisting
of a small tin in which we had punched a lot of holes,
and it was removed directly the water had come to the
boil. We used to sit around the cooker waiting for our
food, and at last the hoosh would be ready and would
be ladled into the pannikins by the cook of the week.
The scanty allowance of biscuit would be distributed and
we would commence the meal. In a couple of minutes
the hot food would be gone, and we would gnaw carefully around the sides of our biscuits, making them last

as long as possible. Marshall used sometimes to stand his pannikin of hoosh in the snow for a little while, because it got thicker as it cooled, but it was a debatable point whether this paid. One seemed to be getting more solid food, but there was a loss of warmth and in the minus temperatures on the plateau we found it advisable to take our hoosh very hot. We would make the biscuits last as long as possible, and sometimes we tried to save a bit to eat in the sleeping bag later on, but it was hard to do this. If one of us dropped a crumb, the others would point it out, and the owner would wet his finger in his mouth and pick up the morsel. Not the smallest fragment was allowed to escape.

We used to "turn backs" in order to ensure equitable division of the food. The cook would pour the hoosh into the pannikins and arrange the biscuits in four heaps. Perhaps some one would suggest that one pannikin had rather less in it than another, and if this view was endorsed by the others there would be a readjustment. Then when we were all satisfied that the food had been divided as fairly as possible, one man would turn his back, and another, pointing at one pannikin or group of biscuits would say, "Whose?" The man who had his back turned, and therefore could not see the food, would give a name, and so the distribution would proceed, each of us always feeling sure that the smallest share had fallen to his lot. At lunch time there would be chocolate or cheese to distribute on alternate days, and we much preferred the chocolate days to the cheese days. The chocolate seemed more satisfying, and it was more easily divided. The cheese broke up into very small fragments on the march, and the allowance, which amounted to two spoonfuls per man, had to be divided up as nearly as possible into four equal heaps. The chocolate could be easily separated into sticks of equal size. It can be imagined that the cook for the week had no easy task. His work became more difficult still when we were using pony meat, for the meat and blood, when boiled up, made a delightful broth, while the fragments of meat sunk to the bottom of the pot. The liquor was much the better part of the dish, and no one had much relish for the little dice of tough and stringy meat, so the cook had to be very careful indeed. Poor old Chinaman was a particularly tough and stringy horse.

We found that the meat from the neck and rump was the best, the most stringy portions coming from the ribs and legs. We took all the meat we could, tough or tender, and as we went south in the days when the horse meat was fairly plentiful, we used to suck frozen, raw fragments as we marched along. Later we could not afford to use the meat except on a definite allowance. The meat to be used during the day was generally cut up when we took a spell in the morning, and the bag containing the fragments was hung on the back of the sledge in order that the meat might be softened by the sun. It cut more easily when frozen than when partially thawed, but our knives gradually got blunt, and on the glacier we secured a rock on which to sharpen them. During the journey back, when every ounce of weight was of great importance, we used one of our geological specimens, a piece of sandstone, as a knife-sharpener. The meat used to bulk large in the pot, but as fresh meat contains about 60 percent of moisture, it used to shrink considerably in the process of cooking, and we did not have to use very much snow in the pot.

We used the meat immediately we had started to kill the ponies in order to save the other food, for we knew that the meat contained a very large percentage of water, so that we would be carrying useless weight with it. The pemmican and biscuits, on the other hand, contained very little moisture, and it was more profitable to keep them for the march further south, when we were likely to want to reduce the loads as far as possible. We left meat at each depot, to provide for the march back to the coast, but always took on as much as possible of the prepared foods. The reader will understand that the loss of Socks, which represented so many pounds of meat, was a very severe blow to us, for we had after that to use sledging stores at the depots to make up for the lost meat. If we had been able to use Socks for food, I have no doubt that we would have been able to get further south, perhaps even to the Pole itself, though in that case we could hardly have got back in time to catch the ship before she was forced to leave by the approach of winter.

When we were living on meat our desire for cereals and farinaceous foods became stronger; indeed any particular sort of food of which we were deprived seemed to us to be the food for which nature craved. When we were short of sugar we would dream of sweet stuffs, and when biscuits were in short supply our thoughts were concerned with crisp loaves and all the other good things displayed in the windows of the bakers' shops. During the last weeks of the journey outwards, and the long march back, when our allowance of food had been reduced to twenty ounces per man a day, we really thought of little but food. The glory of the great mountains that towered high on either side, the majesty of the enormous glacier up which we traveled so painfully, did not appeal to our emotions to any great extent. Man becomes very primitive when he is hungry and short of food, and we learned to know what it is to be desperately hungry. I used to wonder sometimes whether the people who suffer from hunger in the big cities of civilization felt as we were feeling, and I arrived at the conclusion that they did not, for no barrier of law and order would have been allowed to stand between us and any food that had been available. The man who starves in a city is weakened, hopeless, spiritless, and we were vigorous and keen. Until January 9 the desire for food was made the more intense by our knowledge of the fact that we were steadily marching away from the stores of plenty.

We could not joke about food, in the way that is possible for the man who is hungry in the ordinary sense. We thought about it most of the time, and on the way back we used to talk about it, but always in the most serious manner possible. We used to plan out the enormous meals that we proposed to have when we got back to the ship and, later, to civilization. On the outward march we did not experience really severe hunger until we got on the great glacier, and then we were too much occupied with the heavy and dangerous climbing over the rough ice and crevasses to be able to talk much. We had to keep some distance apart in case one man fell into a crevasse. Then on the plateau our faces were generally coated with ice, and the blizzard wind blowing from the south made unnecessary conversation out of the question. Those were silent days, and our remarks to one another were brief and infrequent. It was on the march back that we talked freely of food, after we had got down the glacier and were marching over the barrier surface. The wind was behind us, so that the pulling was not very heavy, and as there were no crevasses to fear we were able to keep close together. We would get up at 5 A.M. in order to make a start at 7 A.M., and after we had eaten our scanty breakfast, that seemed only to accentuate hunger, and had begun the day's march, we could take turns in describing the things we would eat in the good days to come. We were each going to give a dinner to the others in turn, and there was to be an anniversary dinner every year, at which we would be able to eat and eat and eat. No French chef ever devoted more thought to the invention of new dishes than we did.

It is with strange feelings that I look back over our notes, and see the wonderful meals that we were going to have. We used to tell each other, with perfect seriousness, about the new dishes that we had thought of, and if the dish met with general approval there would be a chorus of, "Ah! That's good." Sometimes there would be an argument as to whether a suggested dish was really an original invention, or whether it did not too nearly resemble something that we had already tasted in happier days. The "Wild roll" was admitted to be the high water mark of gastronomic luxury. Wild proposed that the cook should take a supply of well-seasoned minced meat, wrap it in rashers of fat bacon, and place around the whole an outer covering of rich pastry so that it would take the form of a big sausage-roll. Then this roll would be fried with plenty of fat. My best dish, which I must admit I put forward with a good deal of pride as we marched over the snow, was a sardine pastry, made by placing well fried sardines inside pastry. At least ten tins of sardines were to be emptied on to a bed of pastry, and the whole then rolled up and cooked, preparatory to its division into four equal portions. I remember one day Marshall came forward

with a proposal for a thick roll of suet pudding with
plenty of jam all over it, and there arose quite a heated
argument as to whether he could fairly claim this dish
to be an invention, or whether it was not the jam roll
already known to the housewives of civilization. There
was one point on which we were all agreed, and that
was that we did not want any jellies or things of that
sort at our future meals. The idea of eating such elusive
stuff as jelly had no appeal to us at all.

On a typical day during this backward march we
would leave camp at about 6:40 A.M., and half an hour
later would have recovered our frost bitten fingers, while
the moisture on our clothes, melted in the sleeping bags,
would have begun to ablate, after having first frozen
hard. We would be beginning to march with some degree of comfort, and one of us would remark, "Well,
boys, what are we going to have for breakfast today?"
We had just finished our breakfast as a matter of fact,
consisting of half a pannikin of tea, but the meal had
not taken the keenness from our appetites. We used to
try to persuade ourselves that our half biscuit was not
quite a half, and sometimes we managed to get a little
bit more that way. The question would receive our most
serious and careful consideration at once, and we would
proceed to weave from our hungry imaginations a tale
of a day spent in eating. "Now we are on board ship,"
one man would say. "We wake up in a bunk, and the
first thing we do is to stretch out our hands to the side
of the bunk and get some chocolate, some Garibaldi
biscuits and some apples. We eat those in the bunk, and
then we get up for breakfast. Breakfast will be at eight
o'clock, and we will have porridge, fish, bacon and eggs,
cold ham, plum pudding, sweets, fresh roll and butter,
marmalade and coffee. At eleven o'clock we will have
hot cocoa, open jam tarts, fried cods' roe and slices of
heavy plum cake. That will be all until lunch at one
o'clock. For lunch we will have Wild roll, shepherd's pie,
fresh soda bread, hot milk, treacle pudding, nuts, raisins,
and cake. After that we will turn in for a sleep, and we
will be called at 3:45, when we will reach out again from
the bunks and have doughnuts and sweets. We will get
up then and have big cups of hot tea and fresh cake and

chocolate creams. Dinner will be at six, and we will have thick soup, roast beef and Yorkshire pudding, cauliflower, peas, asparagus, plum pudding, fruit, apple pie with thick cream, scones and butter, port wine, nuts, and almonds and raisins. Then at midnight we will have a really big meal, just before we go to bed. There will be melon, grilled trout and butter sauce, roast chicken with plenty of livers, a proper salad with eggs and very thick dressing, green peas and new potatoes, a saddle of mutton, fried suet pudding, peach Melba, egg curry, plum pudding and sauce, Welsh rarebit, Queen's pudding, angels on horseback, cream cheese and celery, fruit, nuts, port wine, milk, and cocoa. Then we will go to bed and sleep till breakfast time. We will have chocolate and biscuits under our pillows, and if we want anything to eat in the night we will just have to get it." Three of us would listen to this program and perhaps suggest amendments and improvements generally in the direction of additional dishes, and then another one of us would take up the running and sketch another glorious day of feeding and sleeping.

I daresay that all this sounds very greedy and uncivilized to the reader who has never been on the verge of starvation, but as I have said before, hunger makes a man primitive. We did not smile at ourselves or at each other as we planned wonderful feats of overeating. We were perfectly serious about the matter, and we noted down in the back pages of our diaries details of the meals that we had decided to have as soon as we got back to the places where food was plentiful. All the morning we would allow our imaginations to run riot in this fashion. Then would come one o'clock, and I would look at my watch and say "Camp!" We would drop the harness from our tired bodies and pitch the tent on the smoothest place available, and three of us would get inside to wait for the thin and scanty meal, while the other man filled the cooker with snow and fragments of frozen meat. An hour later we would be on the march again, once more thinking and talking of food, and this would go on until the camp in the evening. We would have another scanty meal, and turn into the sleeping bags, to dream wildly of food that somehow we could never manage to eat.

The dysentery from which we suffered during the latter part of the journey back to the coast was certainly due to the meat from the pony Grisi. This animal was shot one night when in a greatly exhausted condition, and I believe that his flesh was made poisonous by the presence of the toxin of exhaustion, as is the case with animals that have been hunted. Wild was the first to suffer, at the time when we started to use Grisi meat with the other meat, and he must have been unfortunate enough to get the greater part of the bad meat on that occasion. The other meat we were using then came from Chinaman, and seemed to be quite wholesome. A few days later we were all eating Grisi meat, and we all got dysentery. The meat could not have become affected in any way after the death of the pony, because it froze hard within a very short time. The manner in which we managed to keep on marching when suffering, and the speed with which we recovered when we got proper food, were rather remarkable, and the reason, no doubt, was that the dysentery was simply the result of the poison, and was not produced by organic trouble of any sort. We had a strong wind behind us day after day during this period, and this contributed in a very large measure to our safety, for in the weakened condition we had then reached we could not have made long marches against a head wind, and without long marches we would have starved between the depots. We had a sail on the sledge, formed of the floorcloth of a tent, and often the sledge would overrun us, though at other times it would catch in a drift and throw us heavily.

When we were traveling along during the early part of the journey over the level Barrier surface, we felt the heat of the sun severely, though as a matter of fact the temperature was generally very low, sometimes as low as zero F though the season was the height of summer. It was quite usual to feel one side of the face getting frozen while the other side was being sunburned. The ponies would have frozen perspiration on their coats on the sheltered side, while the sun would keep the other side hot and dry, and as the day wore on and the sun moved round the sky the frosted area on the animals would change its position in sympathy. I remember that on December 4 we were marching stripped to our shirts, and we got very much sunburned, though at noon that day the air temperature showed ten degrees of frost. When we started to climb the glacier and marched close to the rocks, we felt the heat much more, for the rocks acted as radiators, and this experience weighed with me in deciding to leave all the spare clothing and equipment at the Upper Glacier Depot, about seven thousand feet up. We did not expect to have to climb much higher, but, as the reader knows, we did not reach the plateau until we had climbed over ten thousand feet above sea level, and so we felt the cold extremely. Our wind proof Burberry clothing had become thin by this time, and had been patched in many places in consequence of having been torn on the sharp ice. The wind got in through a tear in my Burberry trousers one day and I was frost bitten on the under part of the knee. This frost bite developed into an open wound, into which the wool from my underclothing worked, and I had finally to perform a rather painful operation with a knife before the wound would heal. We were continually being frost bitten up on the plateau, and when our boots had begun to give out and we were practically marching on the sennegrass inside the finnesko, our heels got frost bitten. My heels burst when we got on to hard stuff, and for some time my socks were caked with blood at the end of every day's march. Finally Marshall put some "Newskin" on a pad, and that stuck on well until the cracks had healed. The scars are likely to remain with me. In the very cold days, when our strength had begun to decrease, we found great difficulty in hoisting the sail on our sledge, for when we lifted our arms above our heads in order to adjust the sail, the blood ran from our fingers and they promptly froze. Ten minutes or a quarter of an hour sometime elapsed before we could get the sledge properly rigged. Our troubles with frost bite were no doubt due in a measure to the lightness of our clothing, but there was compensation in the speed with which we were able to travel. I have no doubt at all that men engaged in polar exploration should be clothed as lightly as is possible, even if there is a danger of frost bite when they halt on the march.

The surface over which we traveled during the southern journey changed continually. During the first few days we found a layer of soft snow on top of a hard crust, with more soft snow underneath that again. Our weight was sufficient to break through the soft snow on top, and if we were pulling the increased pressure would cause the crust to break also, letting us through into the second layer of soft snow. This surface made the traveling very heavy. Until we had got beyond Minna Bluff we often passed over high, sharp sastrugi, and beyond that we met with ridges four to six feet high. The snow generally was dry and powdery, but some of the crystals were large, and showed in reflected light all the million colors of diamonds. After we had passed latitude 80° South the snow got softer day by day, and the ponies would often break through the upper crust and sink in right up to their bellies. When the sun was hot the traveling would be much better, for the surface snow got near the melting point and formed a slippery layer not easily broken. Then again a fall in the temperature would produce a thin crust, through which one broke very easily. Between latitude 80° South and 83° South there were hard sastrugi under the soft snow, and the hoofs of the horses suffered in consequence. The surface near the land was broken up by pressure from the glaciers, but right alongside the mountains there was a smooth plain of glassy ice, caused by the freezing of water that had run off the rocky slopes when they were warm under the rays of the sun. This process had been proceeding on the snow slopes that we had to climb in order to reach the glacier. Here at the foot of the glacier there were pools of clear water around the rocks, and we were able to drink as much as we wanted, though the contact of the cold water with our cracked lips was painful.

The glacier itself presented every variety of surface, from soft snow to cracked and riven blue ice, by-and-by the only constant feature were the crevasses, from which we were never free. Some were entirely covered with a crust of soft snow, and we discovered them only when one of us broke through, and hung by his harness from the sledge. Others occurred in mazes of rotten ice, and were even more difficult to negotiate than the other sort. The least unpleasant of the crevasses were those that were wide open and easily seen, with firm ice on either side. If these crevasses were not too wide, we would pull the sledges up to the side, then jump over, and pull them after us. This was more difficult than it sounds from the fact that the ice gave only a very uncertain footing, but we always had the harness as a safeguard in case of a fall. If the crevasses were wide we had to made a detour. The sledges, owing to their length, were not liable to slip down a crevasse, and we felt fairly safe when we were securely attached to them by the harness. When the surface was so bad that relay work became necessary we used to miss the support of a sledge on the back journeys. We would advance one sledge half a mile or a mile, put up a bamboo pole to mark the spot, and then go back for the other. We were roped together for the walk back to the second sledge, but even then we felt a great deal less secure than when harnessed to one of the long, heavy sledges. On some days we had to travel up steep slopes of smooth ice, and often it became necessary to cut steps with our ice axes, and haul the sledges after us with the alpine rope. When we had gone up about sixty feet, the length of the rope, we would haul up the sledge to which we had attached the lower end, and jamb it so that it could not slide back. Then one of us would slide down in order to fix the rope to the other sledge.

One of the curious features of the glacier was a yellow line, evidently an old moraine, extending for thirty or forty miles. The rocks of the moraine had gradually sunk in out of sight, the radiation of the sun's heat from them causing the ice to melt and let them through, and there had remained enough silt and dust to give the ice a dirty yellow appearance. The traveling along this old moraine was not so bad, but on either side of it there was a mass of pressure ice, caused by the constriction of the glacier between the mountains to the east and west. Unfortunately we brought back no photographs of this portion of the glacier. The number of plates at our disposal was limited, and on the outward march we decided not to take many photographs in case we found interesting land or mountains in the far south nearer the Pole. We thought that we would be able to secure as many photographs of the glacier as we wanted on the way back if we had the plates to spare, but as a matter of fact when we did get on to the glacier a second time we were so short of food that we could not afford the time to unpack the camera, which had to be stowed away carefully on the sledge in order to avoid damage to it.

Many nights on the glacier there was no snow on which to pitch the tents, and we had to spend perhaps an hour smoothing out a space on a rippled, sharp-pointed sea of ice. The provision bags and sledges had to be packed on the snow cloths around the tents, and it was indeed fortunate for us that we did not meet with any bad weather while we were marching up the glacier. Had a blizzard come on while we were asleep, it would have scattered our goods far and wide, and we would have been faced with a very serious position. All the time that we were climbing the glacier we had a northerly wind behind us, although the direction of the sastrugi showed clearly that the prevailing wind was from the south; when we were coming back later in the season the wind was behind us all the time. We encountered a strong wind on the outward journey when near the top of the glacier, and as the ice slopes were covered with snow it was difficult to pull the sledges up them. When we reached the same slopes on the way back, the summer sun had cleared the snow from them, leaving clear ice, and we simply glissaded down all but the steepest slopes, although one of the sledge runners was very badly torn. We had to travel carefully on the steep slopes, for if we had let the sledge get out of hand it would have run away altogether, and would probably have been smashed up hundreds of feet below.

The Upper Glacier Depot was overhung by great cliffs of rock, shattered by the frosts and storms of countless centuries, and many fragments were poised in such a fashion that scarcely more than a touch seemed needed to bring them hurtling down. All around us on the ice lay rocks that had recently fallen from the heights, and we wondered whether some boulder would come down upon us while we were in camp. We had no choice of a camping ground, as all around was rough ice. The cliffs were composed largely of weathered sandstone, and it was on the same mountains, higher up the glacier, that the coal was found, at a point where the slope was comparatively gentle. Looking down from this height, we could see the glacier stretching away to the point of junction with the Barrier, the mountains rising to east and west. Many of the mountains to the west of the glacier were more or less dome shaped, but there were some sharp conical peaks to the westward of the particular mountain under which the Upper Glacier Depot had been placed. There were three distinct peaks, and the plateau ice sweeping down made a long moraine on the west side of the glacier. To the eastward there was a long ridge of high mountains, fairly uniform in shape and without any sharp peaks, but with ridges, apparently of granite, projecting toward the west and so constricting the glacier. The mountains were distant about twenty-five miles, but well defined stratification lines could plainly be seen. Below us, as we looked from the depot, could be seen the cumulus clouds that always hung above "The Cloudmaker."

When we looked to the south from this depot we saw no clouds; there was nothing but hard clear sky. The sky gave no indication of the blizzard winds that were to assail us when we reached the plateau, and after we had gone as far south as we could and retraced our footsteps to the depot, we looked back and saw the same clear sky, with a few wisps of fleecy cloud in it. We had no doubt that below those clouds the pitiless gale was still raging across the great frozen plain, and that the wind which followed us during our march back to the coast was coming from the vicinity of the Pole. As we advanced from the Upper Glacier Depot we came upon great ice falls. The surface looked smooth from a distance, and we thought that we were actually on the plateau, but as we advanced we saw that before us lay enormous ridges rising abruptly. We had to relay our gear over these ridges, and often at the tops there would be a great crevasse, from which would radiate smaller crevasses fringed with crystals and showing ghastly depths below. We would creep forward to see what lay on the other side, and perhaps would find a fall of fifty feet, with a grade of about 1 in 3. Many times we risked our sledge on very severe slopes, allowing it to glissade down, but other times the danger of a smash was too great, and we had to lower the sledge slowly and carefully with the rope. The ice was safe enough to walk upon at this time except at the ridges, where the crevasses were severe, for the smaller crevasses in the hollows and slopes could be passed without difficulty.

The ice falls delayed us a good deal, and then we got into soft snow, over which the sledge dragged heavily. We thought that we were finally on the plateau level, but within a few days we came to fresh ridges and waves of pressure ice. The ice between the waves was very rotten, and many times we fell through when we put our weight on it. We fastened the alpine rope to the sledge harness, and the first man pulled at a distance of about eighteen feet from the sledge, while the whole party was so scattered that no two men could fall into a crevasse together. We got on to better ground by steering to the westward, but this step was rather dangerous, for by taking this course we traveled parallel with the crevasses and were not able to meet them at right angles. Many times we nearly lost the sledge and ourselves when the ice started to break away into an unseen crevasse running parallel with our course. We felt very grateful to Providence that the weather remained clear, for we could not have moved a yard over this rotten ice in thick weather without courting disaster. I do not know whether the good weather we experienced in that neighborhood was normal. We generally had about seven miles of easy going after we had passed one ridge in this area, and then another ridge would rise up ahead of us, and we would start to climb again. There were always crevasses at the top of the ridges, suggesting that the ice was moving over land at no great depth.

We passed the last ridge at last, and reached the actual plateau, but instead of hard névé, such as the *Discovery* expedition had encountered in the journey to the plateau beyond the mountains west of McMurdo Sound, we found soft snow and hard sastrugi. All the sastrugi pointed to the south, and the wind blew strongly nearly all the time from the south or southeast, with an occasional change to the southwest. Sometimes we marched on hard sastrugi, and at other times we had soft snow under our feet, but could feel the sastrugi on which the snow was lying. I formed the opinion that during the winter on the plateau the wind must blow with terrible violence from the south, and that the hard sastrugi are produced then. Still further south we kept breaking through a hard crust that underlay the soft surface snow, and we then sank in about eight inches. This surface, which made the marching heavy, continued to the point at which we planted the flag. After the long blizzard, from the night of January 6 until the morning of January 9, we had a better surface over which to make our final march southwards, for the wind had swept the soft snow away and produced a fairly hard surface, over which, unencumbered with a sledge as we were, we could advance easily.

We found the surface generally to be improved on the march back. The blizzard winds had removed the soft surface snow, and incidentally uncovered many of the crevasses. We were following our outward tracks, and often I noticed the tracks led us to the edge of a crevasse which had been covered previously and over which we had passed in ignorance of our danger on the march southwards. When we got to the head of the glacier we tried to take a short cut to the point where we had left the Upper Glacier Depot, but we got enmeshed in a maze of crevasses and pressure ridges to the eastward, and so had to steer in a westerly direction again in order to get clear. The dangers that we did know were preferable to those that we did not know. On the way down the glacier we found all the snow stripped away by the wind and sun for nearly one hundred miles, and we traveled over slippery blue ice, with innumerable cracks and sharp edges. We had many painful falls during this part of the journey. Then when about forty miles from the foot of the glacier we got into deep soft snow again, over which rapid progress was impossible. There had evidently been a heavy snowfall in this area while we were further south, and for days, while our food was running short, we could see ahead of us the rocks under which the depot had been placed. We toiled with painful slowness toward the rocks, and as the reader has already learned we were without any food at all for the last thirty hours of that march. We found the Barrier surface to be very soft when we got off the Glacier, but after we had passed Grisi Depot there was an improvement. The surface remained fairly good until we reached the winter quarters, and in view of our weakened condition it was fortunate for us that it did so.

In reviewing the experience gained on the southern journey, I do not think that I could suggest any improvement in equipment for any future expedition. The Barrier surface evidently varies in a remarkable fashion, and its condition cannot be anticipated with any degree of certainty. The traveler must be prepared for either a hard surface or a very soft one, and he may get both surfaces in the course of one day's march. The eleven foot sledge is thoroughly suitable for the work, and our method of packing the stores and hauling the sledges did not develop any weak points. We would have been glad to have had crampons for use on the glacier; what would be better still would be heavy alpine boots with nails all around, for very often the surface would give little grip to crampons, which would only touch the rough ice at one or two points. The temperature is too cold to permit of the explorer wearing ordinary leather boots, and some boot would have to be designed capable of keeping the feet warm and carrying the nails all around. A mast consisting of a bamboo lashed to the forward oil box proved as efficient as could be required for use in connection with a sail on the sledges. It was easily rigged and had no elaborate stays. I would suggest no change in the clothing, for the light woolen underclothing, with thin windproof material outside, proved most satisfactory in every way. We could certainly not have traveled so fast had we been wearing the regulation pilot cloth garment generally used in polar exploration. Our experience made it obvious that a party which hopes to reach the Pole must take more food per man than we did, but how the additional weight is to be provided for is a matter for individual consideration. I would not take cheese again; for although it is a good food, we did not find it as palatable as chocolate, which is practically as sustaining. Our other foods were all entirely satisfactory.

Each member of the Southern Party had his own particular duties to perform. Adams had charge of the meteorology, and his work involved the taking of temperatures at regular intervals, and the boiling of the hypsometer, sometimes several times in a day. He took notes during the day, and wrote up the observations at night in the sleeping bag. Marshall was the cartographer and took the angles and bearings of all the new land; he also took the meridian altitudes and the compass variation as we went south. When a meridian altitude was taken, I generally had it checked by each member of the party, so that the mean could be taken.

Marshall's work was about the most uncomfortable possible, for at the end of a day's march, and often at lunch time, he would have to stand in the biting wind handling the screws of the theodolite. The map of the journey was prepared by Marshall, who also took most of the photographs. Wild attended to the repair of the sledges and equipment, and also assisted me in the geological observations and the collection of specimens. It was he who found the coal close to the Upper Glacier Depot. I kept the courses and distances, worked out observations and laid down our directions. We all kept diaries. I had two, one my observation book, and the other the narrative diary.

CHAPTER XIX

Return of the *Nimrod*

The Ship blocked by Ice off Beaufort Island: Mails landed
Twenty-eight Miles from Cape Royds on January 3:
Mackintosh and McGillan travel over Ice to Winter Quarters:
Narrow Escapes: They reach Hut January 12

AFTER leaving us on February 22, the *Nimrod* had an
uneventful voyage back to New Zealand. Fair winds
were encountered all the way, and the ice gave no difficulty, the coast of New Zealand being sighted twelve
days after the departure from Cape Royds. During the
winter the *Nimrod* had been laid up in Port Lyttelton
waiting till the time arrived to bring us back to civilization. The little ship had been docked and thoroughly
overhauled, so that all effects of the severe treatment
she received during the first voyage down to the ice had
been removed, and she was once more ready to battle
with the floes. Toward the end of the year stores were
taken on board, for there was a possibility that a party
might have to spend a second winter at Cape Royds, if
the men comprising one of the sledging expeditions had
not returned, and, of course, there was always the possibility of the *Nimrod* herself being caught in the ice and
frozen in for the winter. Sufficient stores were taken on
board to provide for any such eventualities, and as much
coal as could be stowed away was also carried. Captain
P. F. Evans, who had commanded the *Koonya* at the time
she towed the *Nimrod* down the Antarctic Circle, was appointed master of the *Nimrod* under my power of attorney,
Captain England having resigned on account of ill health
after reaching New Zealand earlier in the year.

The *Nimrod* left Lyttelton on December 1, 1908, and
encountered fine weather for the voyage southwards. On
the evening of the 3rd, the wind being favorable, the
propeller was disconnected, and the vessel proceeded
under sail alone until the 20th, when she was in latitude
66° 30' South, longitude 178° 28' West. The "blink" of

ice was seen ahead and the ship was hove to until steam had been raised and the propeller connected. Then Captain Evans set sail again, and proceeded toward the pack. The vessel was soon in brash ice, and after pushing through this for a couple of hours reached the pack, and made her way slowly through the lanes. Numerous seals were basking on the floes, regarding the ship with their usual air of mild astonishment. On the following day the pack was more congested, and the progress southward was slow, so much so that the crew found time to kill and skin several crabeater seals. Open water was reached again that evening, and at noon on the 22nd the *Nimrod* was in latitude 68° 20' South, longitude 175° 23' East, and proceeding under sail through the open water of Ross Sea. The belt of pack ice had been about sixty miles wide.

On December 26 the *Nimrod* reached latitude 70° 42' South, longitude 173° 4' West, the position in which, in 1843, Sir James Ross sighted "compact, hummocky ice," but found only drift ice, with plenty of open water. A sounding gave no bottom with 1575 fathoms of wire, so that the theory that the ice seen by Ross was resting on land was completely disproved. At noon on the 27th the *Nimrod* which was proceeding in a southeast direction, was brought up by thick floes in latitude 72° 8' South, longitude 173° 1' West. Progress became possible again later in the day, and at four o'clock on the following morning the *Nimrod* was in open water, with the blink of pack to the eastward. Captain Evans had kept east with the hope of sighting King Edward VII Land, but the pack seemed to be continuous in that direction, and on the 30th he therefore shaped a course for Cape Bird, and on January 1, 1909, Mount Erebus was sighted. The experience of Captain Evans on this voyage confirms my own impression that, under normal conditions, the pack that stretches out from the Barrier to the eastward of the Ross Sea is not penetrable, and that the *Discovery* was able to push to within sight of King Edward VII Land in 1902 for the reason that the ice was unusually open that season.

The progress of the *Nimrod* toward the winter quarters was blocked by ice off Beaufort Island, and after maneuvering about for three hours Captain Evans made the vessel fast to a floe with ice anchors. The next morning he cast off from the floe, and with the help of the current, which seems to set constantly to the west between Cape Bird and Beaufort Island, and by taking advantage of lanes of open water, gradually proceeded in two days to a point only twenty-eight miles from Cape Royds. Some heavy bumps against the floes tested the strength of the vessel, and finally what appeared to be fast ice was encountered, so that no further progress toward the south was possible for the time.

There seemed to be no immediate possibility of the *Nimrod* reaching Cape Royds, and Captain Evans therefore decided to send Mackintosh with three men to convey a mailbag and the news of the ship's arrival to the winter quarters. The party was to travel over the sea ice with a sledge, and it did not seem that there would be any great difficulties to be encountered. A start was made at 10:15 A.M. on January 3, the party consisting of Mackintosh, McGillan, Riches, and Paton, with one sledge, a tent, sleeping bags, cooking equipment and a supply of provisions. The distance to be covered was about twenty-five miles. In the afternoon Mackintosh sent Riches and Paton back to the ship, and he reduced the load on the sledge by leaving fifty pounds of provisions in a depot. The traveling became very rough, the two men encountering both bad ice and soft snow. They camped at 7:50 P.M. and started for Cape Royds again at 1:55 A.M. on the following day. They soon got on to a better surface, and made good progress until 5:30 A.M., when they met with open water, with pressure ice floating past. This blocked the way. They walked for two hours in a westerly direction to see how far the open water extended, but did not reach the end of it. The whole of the ice to the southward seemed to be moving, and the stream at the spot at which they were then standing was traveling at the rate of about three miles an hour. They breakfasted at 7:30 A.M., and then started back for the ship, as there seemed to be no chance of reaching Cape Royds in consequence of the open water.

Presently Mackintosh found that there was open water ahead, blocking the way to the ship, and a survey of the position from a hummock revealed the unpleasant fact

that the floe ice was breaking up altogether, and that
they were in most serious danger of drifting out into the
sound. Safety lay in a hurried dash for the shore to the
east, and they proceeded to drag their sledge across
rough ice and deep snow with all possible speed. At
places they had to lift the sledge bodily over the ice
faces, and when, after an hour's very heavy work, they
arrived off the first point of land, they found an open
lane of water barring their way. "We dragged on to the
next point, which appeared to be safe," wrote Mackintosh in his diary. "The floes were small and square in
shape. Every two hundred yards we had to drag our
sledge to the edge of a floe, jump over a lane of water,
and then with a big effort pull the sledge after us. After
an hour of this kind of work our hands were cut and
bleeding, and our clothes, which, of course, froze as stiff
as boards, were wet through to the waist, for we had
frequently slipped and fallen when crossing from floe to
floe. At 2:30 P.M. we were near to the land, and came
to a piece of glacier ice that formed a bridge. The floe
that we were on was moving rapidly, so we had to make
a great effort and drag our sledge over a six-foot breach.
Our luck was in, and we pulled our sledge a little way
up the face of the fast ice, and unpacked it. We were in
a safe position again, and none too soon, for fifteen minutes later there was open water where we had gained
the land."

Mackintosh decided to go into camp near the spot
where they had landed, as a journey across the rocks
and the glaciers of the coast was not a thing to be undertaken lightly, and would probably be impossible unless
the mailbag was left behind. McGillan, moreover, had
developed snow blindness, and both men were very
tired. I will quote from Mackintosh's report on the subsequent experience of this little party.

"Early the next morning I found McGillan in great
pain," wrote Mackintosh. "His eyes were closed up completely, and his face was terribly swollen. The only rem-
edy I could apply was to bathe them, and this seemed
to give him some relief. From an elevated position I had
a good look around for the ship, and could not see a
trace of her. As the day wore on my own eyes became

painful. I fervently hoped I was not going to be as bad as my companion, for we would then be in a very difficult position. The morning of January 6 found us both blind. McGillan's face was frightfully swollen, and his eyes completely and tightly shut, so that he did not know that I was attacked too. At first I refrained from telling him, but the pain was very severe, and I had to tell him. By the painful process of forcing my eyelids apart with my fingers I could see a little, but I was not able to do this for long. I continued to bathe McGillan's eyes, and then suffered six hours' agony, ending in a good long sleep, from which I awoke refreshed and much better. I was able to see without effort. McGillan was also much better, and our relief, after the anxiety we had felt, was very great. By midnight we had improved so much that we walked to the penguin rookery, where we had great fun with the birds and found several eggs."

The men stayed in camp for several days, seeing no sign of the ship, and after their eyes were better spent a good deal of time studying the neighborhood and especially the bird life. They cut down their food to two meals a day, as their supply of food was not large. Finally, Mackintosh decided that he would leave the mailbag in the tent, it being too heavy to carry for any distance, and march in to Cape Royds. They made a start on the morning of January 11, carrying forty pounds each, including food for three meals, and expected to be able to reach the winter quarters within twenty-four hours. The first portion of the journey lay over hills of basaltic rock, at the base of Mount Bird, and they thought it best to get as high as possible in order to avoid the valleys and glaciers. They went up about five thousand feet, and had fairly easy traveling over slopes until they got well on to the glaciers. Then their troubles commenced. They were wearing ski boots without spikes, and had many heavy falls on the slippery ice. "We were walking along, each picking his own tracks, and were about fifty yards apart, foolishly not roped, when I happened to look around to speak to my companion, and found that he had disappeared," wrote Mackintosh. "Suddenly I heard my name called faintly from the bowels of the glacier, and immediately rushed

toward the place from which the sound proceeded. I
found McGillan in a yawning chasm, many feet beneath
me, and held up on a projection of ice. I took off my
straps from my pack and to them tied my waist lashing,
and lowered this extemporized rock down to him. It just
reached his hand, and with much pulling on my part and
knee climbing on his, he got safely to the surface of the
glacier again. The primus stove and our supply of food
had gone further down the crevasse. We tried to hook
them up, and in doing so I lost my straps and line which
I had attached to a ski stick, so we were left almost
without equipment. As soon as McGillan had recovered
from the shock he had received we started off again,
with the spare strap tying the two of us together. We
crossed over many snow bridges that covered the dangers underneath, but soon we were in a perfect hotbed
of crevasses. They were impassable and lay right across
our path, so that we could look down into awful depths.
We turned and climbed higher in order to get a clear
passage around the rope. We were roped together and
I was in the lead, with McGillan behind, so that when I
fell, as I often did, up to my waist in a crevasse, he could
pull me out again. We found a better surface higher up,
but when we began to descend we again got into crevassed regions. At first the crevasses were ice covered
gaps, but later we came to huge open ones, whose yawning depths made us shudder. It was not possible to cross
them. We started to ascend again, and soon came to a
bridge of ice across a huge crevasse about twenty feet
wide. We lashed up tighter, and I went off in the lead,
straddle legged across the narrow bridge. We both
reached the other side in safety, but one slip, or the
breaking of the bridge, would have precipitated us into
those black depths below."

The two men found their way blocked by crevasses in
whichever direction they turned, and at last reached a
point from which ascent was out of the question, while
below lay a steep slope running down for about three
thousand feet. They could not tell what lay at the bottom
of the slope, but their case was desperate, and they decided to glissade down. Their knives, which they attempted to use as brakes, were torn from their grasp,

but they managed to keep their heels in the snow, and although they passed crevasses, none lay directly in their path. They reached the bottom in safety at 4 P.M. on the 11th. They were very hungry and had practically no food, but they could get forward now, and at 6 P.M. they could see Cape Royds and were traveling over a smooth surface. They ate a few biscuit crumbs and half a tin of condensed milk, the only other food they had being a little chocolate. Soon snow commenced to fall, and the weather became thick, obscuring their view of the Cape. They could not see two yards ahead, and for two hours they stumbled along in blinding snow. They rested for a few minutes, but their clothes were covered with ice, icicles hung from their faces, and the temperature was very low. In a temporary clearing of the blizzard Mackintosh thought that he could make out the Cape and they dashed off, but at lunch time on the 12th they were still wandering over the rocks and snow, heavy snow cutting off all view of the surrounding country. Soon after this the snow ceased to fall, though the drift snow, borne along by the blizzard wind, still made the weather thick. Several times they thought that they saw Cape Royds, but found that they had been mistaken. As a matter of fact they were quite close to the winter quarters when, at about 7 P.M., they were found by Day. They were in a state of complete exhaustion, and were just managing to stagger along because they knew that to stop meant death. Within a few minutes they were in the hut, where warm food, dry clothes, and a good rest soon restored them. They had a narrow escape from death, and would probably have never reached the hut had not Day happened to be outside watching for the return of the ship.

Mackintosh and McGillan reached the hut on January 12, but in the meantime the *Nimrod* had arrived at Cape Royds, and had gone north again in search of the missing men. Murray had sailed in the *Nimrod*, and as events turned out, he was not able to get back to the hut for about ten days. "We were having tea on the afternoon of January 5, and Marston happened to open the door, there was the *Nimrod* already moored to the edge of the fast ice, not more than a mile away," wrote Murray in a report on the summer work. "We ran toward the ship, over the rotten sea ice, in boots or slippers as chanced, with the one idea that is uppermost in these circumstances—to get 'letters from home.' We were doomed to disappointment. Before we had finished greeting our old friends, the officers asked us, 'Has Mackintosh arrived?' and we learned to our horror that he and a companion had left the ship two days before and thirty miles north of Cape Royds, to try to bring the letters sooner to us over the sea ice, over the bay where only a few days ago we saw a broad sheet of open water to the horizon, and which was even now only filled with loose pack! So we got no home letters, and had good reason to believe that our friends had lost their lives in the endeavor to bring them. We knew that they must have embarked on a large floe, and little expected to see them again. On January 7 the *Nimrod* left Cape Royds to seek for the lost men on the chance that they might have got ashore near Cape Bird. Within a few hours she was caught by the pack which was drifting rapidly southward along the shore of Ross Island. Driven almost on shore near Horseshoe Bay, the ship, by dint of hard steaming, got a little way off the land, and was there beset by the ice and so remained from the 7th to the 15th, with only a few hours' ineffectual steaming during the first day or two. At length she was rigidly jammed and was carried helplessly by a great eddy of the pack away toward the western side of the sound, and gradually northward.

"On January 12 she was as tight as though frozen in for the winter. In the afternoon sudden pressure affected all the ice from the *Nimrod* as far as we could see. Great blocks of ice, six or eight feet in thickness, were tossed and piled on the surface of the floes. These pressure heaps were formed on each side of the ship's bow, but she took no harm, and in about an hour the pressure ceased. On the morning of January 15 there was not the slightest sign of slacking of the pack, but in the early afternoon, Harbord, from the crow's nest, saw lanes of water at no great distance to the east. Steam was got up and in a few hours we had left our prison and got into a broad lane, with only thin ice which the ship could charge, and the open water was in sight. Shortly after midnight we got clear of the ice. When released we were not very far from the Nordenskjold Ice Barrier.

"The deceptive appearance of loose pack was impressed upon us. For many hours there was blue water apparently only a mile or two ahead, but it never appeared to get any nearer for hours, and we could not be sure it was really near till we were within a few hundred yards of the edge. All this time in the pack we were in doubt as to the fate of Mackintosh, or rather, we had not much doubt about it, for we had given him up for lost, but we were helpless to do anything. On the afternoon of the 16th, on which day we cleared the ice, we had passed Beaufort Island and were approaching through very loose pack the only piece of shore on which there was any chance of finding the lost men. Near the end of this stretch of beach, where it is succeeded by hopeless cliffs, a small patch of greenish color was seen, and the telescope showed the details of a deserted camp, a tent torn to ribbons and all the camp gear lying around. A boat was sent ashore in charge of Davis, who found the bag of letters, and a note from Mackintosh pinned to the tent, telling of his risky attempt to cross the mountains nearly a week before. Knowing the frightfully crevassed character of the valley between Mount Bird and Mount Erebus, there seemed to us little hope that they would get through. The crevassed slope extends right to the top of Mount Bird, and is very steep toward the Erebus side. When we reached Cape Royds about midnight, only two men came out to meet the ship. One of the men was Mackintosh's comrade in all his adventures, and we soon learned that all had ended well."

In the meantime the Bluff Depot party had started off to place a supply of provisions off Minna Bluff in readiness for the return of the Southern Party. The crew of the *Nimrod* proceeded to take on board the geological and zoological specimens collected by the expedition and stored at the hut, so that all might be in readiness for the final departure when the parties had been picked up. Then followed weeks of uncertainty as to the fate of the men who were away.

CHAPTER XX

Bluff Depot Journey
January 15 to February 16, 1909

Dog team with Load of 500 lb: A *Discovery* Depot: Southern
Party Overdue: Sledge marks of Outward March of
Southern Party found: Good Work by Dogs

A PARTY, under Joyce, left Cape Royds on January 15
to place, at a point about fourteen miles off Minna Bluff,
a depot of stores for the use of the Southern Party on
its return journey. This work was very important as the
four members of the Southern Party would be depending
on this depot to supply them with the provisions necessary for the last 100 miles or so of the journey back to
winter quarters.

Joyce was accompanied by Mackintosh, Day, and
Marston. They took one sledge (with 500 lb. of provisions) drawn by eight dogs. They camped for the night
at Glacier Tongue, and had to remain there until the
18th owing to a blizzard. A seven foot sledge was loaded
with 300 lb. of stores from the depot at the Tongue, and
the four men took on the two sledges with a total weight
of 800 lb. The dogs pulled very well, and the party
reached Hut Point at midnight on the 18th.

Rapid progress was made over the Barrier surface,
although they had unpleasant experiences with crevasses,
and at midnight on January 25 the party reached their
destination. During the spring journey* of 1908 I had
fixed the site of this depot, and arranged all details
with Joyce.

The total height of the mound of snow, on the top of
which two bamboos lashed together carried three black
flags, was twenty-two feet. The depot could be seen at
a distance of eight miles.

The party started north again on the 27th. After they
had traveled a short way, Day sighted a pole about 8 ft.
high (with a tattered flag attached) projecting from the

*See p. 158.

snow, some distance to the west of their course. Joyce was able to identify this pole as marking the site of the depot laid out for the return of the *Discovery*'s southern party in 1902.

Rapid progress was made toward Cape Armitage until the area of crevasses was reached again, when for thirty-seven miles the party twisted and turned in order to make a course past these obstacles. Joyce reported that he had counted 127 ranging from two to thirty feet in width. On the 30th the men were held up by another blizzard, which completely buried the dogs and sledge; but they reached Hut Point at 11 P.M. on January 31.

Having secured a second load of stores from the depot (including some luxuries, such as apples and fresh mutton, brought by a party from the *Nimrod*), Joyce started again for Bluff Depot on February 2. He kept a course toward Cape Crozier for two days and then marched south. The party reached the Bluff Depot for the second time on February 8.

They found, to their surprise, that the Southern Party had not arrived. It came on to blow from the south, and the wind turned into a howling blizzard which did not cease until the 11th. The men climbed to the top of the snow mound and searched the horizon with glasses, expecting to see the Southern Party loom up out of the whiteness. As this party was now eleven days overdue, their non-arrival caused great anxiety.

After a consultation, it was decided (1) to lay depot flags in toward the Bluff, so that there would be no chance of the Southern Party missing the food depot; and (2) to march due south to look for the Southern Party.

After the flags had been laid three and a half miles apart, with directions where to find the depot, the march due south commenced. At every halt the horizon was examined, through glasses, from the top of the sledge.

On the 13th, Day found the hoof prints of the ponies made on the outward march of the Southern Party three months before; the tracks of the four sledges showed distinctly. These tracks were followed for seven hours when they were lost.

Joyce then decided to return to the Bluff Depot, and

the party arrived there at noon on the 16th. They found everything just as they had left it.

After examining the flags to the eastward, the party started on the march back to the coast, filled with gloomy thoughts as to the fate of the Southern Party, then eighteen days overdue.

CHAPTER XXI

Notes on the Western Journey

Christmas Day at Knob Head Mountain: In search of Fossils:
Adrift on a Floe: Party picked up by the *Nimrod*,
January 26

MEANWHILE the Western Party, which had left the winter quarters for the second time on December 9, had been working in the western mountains. The three men (Armytage, Priestley, and Brocklehurst) reached the stranded moraines on December 13, and on this occasion succeeded in securing a large supply of skuas' eggs. The anticipated feast was not enjoyed, however, for only about a dozen of the eggs were "good enough for eating," to quote the words of a member of the party. The other eggs were thrown on to the snow near the tent, and the result was an invasion of skuas. They not only ate the eggs, but also made themselves a general nuisance by pulling about the sledge harness and stores. At this time the men were troubled with patches of thin ice, about an eighth to a quarter of an inch thick, forming a lenticle, the top of the middle being sometimes as much as five or six inches from the actual surface. When these patches of ice were trodden on they broke down, and not infrequently disclosed a puddle of salt water an inch or two deep. Priestley thought that they were the final product of the thawing of snowdrifts, and owed their character to the fact that the salt water worked faster from below than did the sun from above.

On December 15 the party started to ascend the Ferrar Glacier, Priestley examining the rocks carefully on the way with a view to securing fossils if any were to be found. The surface was hard for the most part, soft snow being encountered where ice had been expected. On December 19 they were held up by a blizzard, and then they got on to very slippery crevassed ice. On December 20 they camped near the Solitary Rocks, at the spot where Captain Scott had camped after leaving Dry Valley. The idea of getting to Depot Nunatak had to be abandoned, for a heavy snowfall made the traveling difficult, and the time at the disposal of the expedition was short. Priestley worked under the Bluff between Dry Valley and the east fork of the glacier without success and then they moved over to Obelisk Mount. An examination of the Solitary Rocks proved that the map was incorrect at this point. The previous expedition had thought that the rocks formed an island, with the glacier flowing down on either side, but a close examination showed that the rocks were in reality a peninsula, joined to the main north wall by an isthmus of granite at least one thousand feet high. Priestley proceeded with geological and survey work in the neighborhood. On December 24 a new camp was pitched at the foot of Knob Head Mountain.

Christmas Day was spent at this camp, and, as was the case with the other sledging expeditions that were out at the time, a special feast was provided. For breakfast they had hoosh, sardines in tomato sauce and raisins; for lunch, Garibaldi biscuits and jelly; and for dinner, potted boneless chicken and a small plum pudding. Armytage picked up a piece of sandstone with fernlike markings, but Priestley was not hopeful of finding fossils in the greatly altered sandstone. The day was spent in geological work. "We lose the sun here about 9:30 P.M.," noted Priestley in his diary, "and it is curious to observe the sudden change from bright light to darkness in the tent, while outside the thin surface of ice covering the thaw water round the rocks immediately contracts with reports like a succession of pistol shots, and sometimes breaks up and flies about in all directions, making a noise like broken glass. This is the effect of the quick cooling of the ice by the cold plateau wind immediately the sun's influence is withdrawn. The plum pudding was 'top hole.' Must remember to give one of the pot holed sandstones to Wild for the New Zealand girl who gave him the plum pudding."

On December 27 the men proceeded down the glacier again in order to see whether the Northern Party had arrived at Butter Point. Priestley studied the moraines on the way down, and made an extensive collection of specimens, and on January 1 they arrived at the depot. They had constant trouble with crevasses and "potholes" on the way down the glacier, but met with no serious accident. The snow bridges many times let them through up to their knees or waists, but never broke away entirely. The weather was unpleasantly warm for the sort of work they were undertaking, since the snow was thawing, and they were constantly wet.

They found no sign of the Northern Party at Butter Point, and after waiting there until the 6th they proceeded to the "stranded moraines," a day's trek to the south, in order that geological specimens might be secured. The moraines, which were found by the *Discovery* expedition, and are relics of the days of more extensive glaciation, present a most varied collection of rocks, representative of the geological conditions to be found in the mountains to the west, and are of very great interest on that account. After spending two days at this spot, the party went back to Butter Point with about 250 lb. of specimens, and camped again till the 11th. Still there was no sign of the Northern Party, and on the 12th they went north to Dry Valley. There Priestley found a raised beach, about sixty feet above sea level, and Brocklehurst climbed the mountain known as the Harbor Heights.

They went back to the depot on the 14th, and pitched camp in order to wait for the Northern Party until the 25th, when they were to make their way back to winter quarters, or signal for the ship by means of the heliograph. On January 24–25 this party had a very narrow escape from disaster. They were camped on the sea ice at the foot of Butter Point, intending to move off on the return journey early on the morning of the 25th. Their position was apparently one of safety. Armytage had examined the tide crack along the shore, and had found no sign of more than ordinary movement, and the ice in the neighborhood seemed to be quite fast. At 7 A.M. on the 24th Priestley was first out of the tent, and a few minutes later he came running back to his companions to tell them that the ice they were on had broken away and was drifting away north to open sea. The other two men turned out promptly, and found that his statement was only too true. There were two miles of open water between the floe and the shore, and they were apparently moving steadily out to sea. "When we found that the ice had gone out," wrote Armytage in his report to me, "we struck camp, loaded up the sledge, and started away with the object of seeing whether we could get off the floe to the north. The position seemed to be rather serious, for we could not hope to cross any stretch of open water, there was no reasonable expectation of assistance from the ship, and most of our food was at Butter Point. We had not gone very far to the north before we came to an impassable lane of open water, and we decided to return to our original position. We went into camp and had breakfast at 11 A.M. Then we held a consultation and agreed that it would be best to stop where we then were for a time, at any rate, on the off chance of the ship coming along one of the lanes to pick us up on the following day, or of the current changing and the ice once more touching the shore. We waited till three o'clock in the afternoon, but there did not seem to be any improvement in the position. The killer whales were spouting in the channels, and occasionally bumping the ice under us. Then we marched north again, but met with open water in every direction, and after we had marched right round the floe we got into camp at the old position at 10 P.M. We had a small meal of hoosh and biscuit. We had only four days' provisions on the floe with us, and I decided that we would have to go on short rations. We were encouraged by the fact that we had apparently ceased to move north, and were perhaps getting nearer the fast ice again. We got into our sleeping bags in order to keep warm. At 11:30 P.M. Brocklehurst turned out to see whether the position had changed, and reported that we seemed to be within a few hundred yards of the fast ice, and still moving toward the land. I got out of my bag and put on my finnesko, and at midnight saw that we were very close to the fast ice, probably not more than two hundred yards away. I ran back as fast as I could, deciding that there was a prospect of an attempt to get ashore proving successful, and gave the other two men a shout. They struck the camp and loaded up within a very few minutes, while I went back to the edge of the floe at the spot toward which chance had first directed my steps. Just as the sledge got up to me, I felt the floe bump the fast ice. Not more than six feet of the edge touched, but we were just at that spot, and we rushed over the bridge thus formed. We had only just got over when the floe moved away again, and this time it went north to the open sea. The only place at which it touched the fast ice was that to which I had gone when I left the tent, and had I happened to go to any other spot we would not have escaped. We made our way to Butter Point, and at about three o'clock in the morning camped and had a good meal. Then we turned in and slept. When we got up for breakfast, there was open water where we had been drifting on the floe, and I sighted the *Nimrod* under sail, ten or twelve miles out. We laid the heliograph on to the vessel, and after flashing for about an hour got a reply. The *Nimrod* came alongside the fast ice at three o'clock in the afternoon of January 26, and we went on board with our equipment and specimens. We left a depot of provisions and oil at Butter Point in case the Northern Party should reach that point after our departure."

On January 22 and 23 a fresh wind blew from the south and commenced to break up the ice sheet in the neighborhood of Cape Royds, compelling the ship to refasten further to the southward. From this point Davis took a sledge party to Hut Point with despatches that the supporting party was to convey to me at the Bluff Depot. On the 25th the ice had broken up to such an extent that Captain Evans thought there would be a chance of getting far enough across McMurdo Sound to search the western coastline for the party that had been exploring the western mountains, and also for the Northern Party, which might by that time have returned from the journey to the Magnetic Pole and reached Butter Point. The *Nimrod* stood out into the sound, and from a distance of ten or twelve miles a heliograph was seen twinkling near Butter Point. The ship was able to get right alongside the fast ice, and picked up Armytage, Priestley, and Brocklehurst.

After this date fine weather was experienced only at short intervals, the season being advanced, and as a consequence the fast ice that remained in the sound commenced to break up rapidly, and took the form of pack trending northwards. When blizzards blew, as they did frequently, the *Nimrod* moored on the lee side of a stranded iceberg in the neighborhood of Cape Barne, with the object of preserving her position without the consumption of more coal than was absolutely necessary. After the ice had broken up sufficiently, shelter was found under Glacier Tongue.

The waiting was rather unpleasant for the remaining members of the shore party and for those on board the ship, for the time was approaching when it would be necessary to leave for the north unless the *Nimrod* was to be frozen in for the winter, and two of the parties were still out. I had left instructions that if the Northern Party had not returned by February 1 a search was to be made along the western coast in a northerly direction. The party was three weeks overdue, and on February 1, therefore, the *Nimrod* went north, and Captain Evans proceeded to make a close examination of the coast. The ship did not get back to the hut until February 11. During this time Murray and Priestley found work of scientific interest. Priestley tramped the country, and now that the snow had in great measure disappeared, was enabled to see various interesting geological deposits previously covered up. Beds of sponge spicules, enclosing various other fossils, were evidence of recent elevation of the sea bottom. A thick deposit of salts was found on a mound between two lakes, and some curious volcanic formations were discovered. The smaller ponds were entirely melted, and gave a chance to find some forms of life not evident in winter. The penguins continued to afford Murray material for study.

The *Nimrod*'s search for the Northern Party was both difficult and dangerous. Captain Evans had to keep close to the coast, in order to guard against the possibility of overlooking a signal, which might consist only of a small flag, and the sea was obstructed by pack ice. He was to go north as far as a sandy beach on the northern side of the Drygalski Barrier, and he performed his duty most thoroughly in the face of what he afterwards modestly described as "small navigational difficulties." The beach,

which had been marked on the chart, was found to have
no existence in fact, but the *Nimrod* reached the neighborhood indicated, and then proceeded south again, still
searching every yard of the coast. On the 4th a tent was
sighted on the edge of the Barrier, and when a double
detonator was fired the three men who had been to the
Magnetic Pole came tumbling out and ran down toward
the edge of the ice. Mawson was in such a hurry that he
fell down a crevasse, and did not get out again until a
party from the ship went to his assistance. "They were
the happiest men I have ever seen," said Davis in describing the finding of the party. Their sledge, equipment, and specimens were taken on the *Nimrod*, which
was able to moor right alongside the fast ice, and then
Captain Evans proceeded back to the winter quarters.
In the chapters that follow Professor David tells the
story of the Northern Party's journey.

CHAPTER XXII

Extracts from the Narrative of Professor David

Final Instructions: Loss of a Cooker: Camp at Butter Point:
Traveling over Sea ice heavy Relay work: Cooking with
Blubber: Seal Bouillon: Drygalski Glacier: Depot laid:
Preparations for Trek inland: Depot at Mount Larsen
New Year's Day in Latitude 74° 18': Arrival at Magnetic
Pole (mean position of) January 16, 1909, 72° 25' S.,
155° 16' E.: Union Jack hoisted at 3:30 P.M.

THE final instructions for the journey of the Northern
Party were read over to me in the presence of Mawson
and Dr. Mackay, at Cape Royds on September 19, 1908.
They were as follows:

"BRITISH ANTARCTIC EXPEDITION, 1907.
"CAPE ROYDS, *September* 19, 1908.

INSTRUCTIONS FOR NORTHERN SLEDGE-PARTY
UNDER COMMAND OF PROFESSOR E. DAVID.

"DEAR SIR,—The sledge party which you have
charge of consists of yourself, Douglas Mawson, and
Alistair Mackay.

"You will leave winter quarters on or about October 1, 1908. The main objects of your journey are to
be as follows:

"(1) To take magnetic observations at every suitable
point with a view of determining the dip and the position of the Magnetic Pole. If time permits, and your
equipment and supplies are sufficient, you will try and
reach the Magnetic Pole.

"(2) To make a general geological survey of the
coast of Victoria Land. In connection with this work
you will not sacrifice the time that might be used to
carry out the work noted in paragraph (1). It is unnecessary for me to describe or instruct you as to details

re this work, as you know so much better than I do what is requisite.

"(3) I particularly wish you to be able to work at the geology of the western mountains, and for Mawson to spend at least one fortnight at Dry Valley to prospect for minerals of economic value on your return from the north, and for this work to be carried out satisfactorily you should return to Dry Valley not later than the first week of January. I do not wish to limit you to an exact date for return to Dry Valley if you think that by lengthening your stay up north you can reach the Magnetic Pole, but you must not delay, if time is short, on your way south again to do geological work. I consider that the *thorough* investigation of Dry Valley is of supreme importance.

"(4) The *Nimrod* is expected in the sound about January 15, 1909. It is quite possible you may see her from the west. If so, you should try to attract attention by heliograph to winter quarters. You should choose the hours noon to 1 P.M. to flash your signal, and if seen at winter quarters the return signal will be flashed to you, and the *Nimrod* will steam across as far as possible to meet you and wait at the ice edge. If the ship is not in, and if she is and your signals are not seen, you will take into account your supply of provisions and proceed either to Glacier Tongue or Hut Point to replenish if there is not a sufficient amount of provision at Butter Point for you.

"(5) *Re* Butter Point. I will have a depot of at least fourteen days' food and oil cached there for you. If there is not enough in that supply you ought to return as mentioned in paragraph (4).

"(6) I shall leave instructions for the master of the *Nimrod* to proceed to the most accessible point at the west coast and there ship all your specimens. But before doing this, he must ship all the stores that are lying at winter quarters, and also keep in touch with the fast ice to the south on the lookout for the southern sledge party. The Southern Party will not be expected before February 1, so if the ship arrives in good time you may have all your work done before our arrival from the south.

"(7) If by February 1, after the arrival of the *Nimrod,* there is no evidence that your party has returned, the *Nimrod* will proceed north along the coast, keeping as close to the land as possible, on the lookout for a signal from you flashed by heliograph. The vessel will proceed very slowly. The ship will not go north of Cape Washington. This is a safeguard in event of any accident occurring to your party.

"(8) I have acquainted both Mawson and Mackay with the main facts of the proposed journey. In the event of any accident happening to you, Mawson is to be in charge of the party.

"(9) Trusting that you will have a successful journey and a safe return.

"I am, yours faithfully,
"(Sgd.) ERNEST H. SHACKLETON,
"*Commander.*

"PROFESSOR DAVID,
"CAPE ROYDS,
"ANTARCTIC."

"CAPE ROYDS,
"BRITISH ANTARCTIC EXPEDITION, *September* 20, 1907.

"PROFESSOR DAVID.

"DEAR SIR,—If you reach the Magnetic Pole, you will hoist the Union Jack on the spot, and take possession of it on behalf of the above expedition for the British nation.

"When you are in the western mountains, please do the same at one place, taking possession of Victoria Land as part of the British Empire.

"If economic minerals are found, take possession of the area in the same way on my behalf as Commander of this expedition.

"Your faithfully,
"(Sgd.) ERNEST H. SHACKLETON,
"*Commander.*"

We had a farewell dinner that night.
The following day, September 20, a strong southeasterly blizzard was blowing. In the afternoon the wind

somewhat moderated, and there was less drift. Mackay had been making a sail for our journey to the Magnetic Pole, and we now tried the sail on two sledges lashed together on the ice at Backdoor Bay. We used the tent poles of one of the sledging tents as a mast. The wind was blowing very strongly and carried off the two sledges with a weight on them of 300 lb., in addition to the weights of Mackay and myself. We considered this a successful experiment.

The weather continued bad till the night of the 24th.

On September 25 we were up at 5:30 A.M., and found that the blizzard had subsided. Priestley, Day, and I started in the motorcar, dragging behind us two sledges over the sea ice. One sledge, with its load, weighed 606 lb.; the other weighed 250 lb. At first Day traveled on his first gear; he then found that the engine became heated, and we had to stop for it to cool down. He discovered while we were waiting that one of the cylinders was not firing. This he soon fixed up all right. He then remounted the car and he put her on to the second gear. With the increased power given by the repaired cylinder we now sped over the floe ice at fourteen miles an hour, much to the admiration of the seals and penguins. When, however, we had traveled about ten miles from winter quarters, and were some five miles westerly from Tent Island, we encountered numerous sastrugi of softish snow, the car continually sticking fast in the ridges. A little low drift was flying over the ice surface, brought up by a gentle blizzard. We left the heavy sledge ten miles out, and then with only the light sledge to draw behind us, Day found that he was able to travel on his third gear at eighteen miles an hour. At this speed the sledge, whenever it took one of the snow sastrugi at right angles, leapt into the air like a flying fish and came down with a bump on the surface of the ice. We had just reached Flagstaff Point, and were taking a turn in toward the shore opposite the Penguin Rookery when the blizzard wind caught the side of the sledge nearly broadside on, and capsized it heavily. So violent was the shock that the aluminum cooking apparatus was knocked out of its straps, and the blizzard wind immediately started trundling this metal cylinder over the smooth ice. Day stopped his car as soon as possible, Priestley and I jumped off, and immediately gave chase to the runaway cooker. Meanwhile, the cooker had fallen to pieces, so to speak; the tray part came away from the big circular cover; the melter and the supports for the cooking pot and for the main outer covering also came adrift as well as the cooking pot itself. The lid of the last mentioned fell off, and immediately dumped on to the ice the three pannikins and our three spoons. These articles raced one after another over the smooth ice surface in the direction of the open water of Ross Sea. The spoons were easily captured, as also were the pannikins, but the large snow melter, the main outer casing, and the tray kept revolving in front of us at a speed which was just sufficient to outclass our own most desperate efforts. Finally, when we were nearly upon them, they took a joyous leap over the low cliff of floe ice and disappeared one after another most exasperatingly in the black waters of Ross Sea.

This was a shrewd loss, as aluminum cookers were, of course, very scarce.

The following day we had intended laying out our second depot, but as some of the piston rings of the motorcar needed repair, we decided to postpone the departure until the day after. That afternoon, after the repairs had been completed, Day and Armytage went out for a little tobogganning before dinner. Late in the evening Armytage returned dragging slowly and painfully a sledge bearing the recumbent, though not inanimate, form of Day. We crowded round to inquire what was the matter, and found that just when Armytage and Day were urging their wild career down to steep snow slope Day's foot had struck an unyielding block of kenyte lava, and the consequence had been very awkward for the foot. As no one but Day could be trusted to drive the motorcar, this accident necessitated a further postponement of the laying of our second depot.

On October 3, the weather having cleared, Day, Priestley, Mackay, and I started with two sledges to lay our second depot. All went well for about eight miles out, then the carburetor played up. Possibly there was some dirt in the nozzle. Day took it all to pieces in the cold wind, and spent three-quarters of an hour fixing it up. We then started off again gaily in good style. We crossed a large crack in the sea ice where there were numbers of seals and Emperor penguins. On the other side of this crack our wheels stuck fast in snow sastrugi. All hands got on to the spokes and started swinging the car backwards and forwards; when we got a good swing on, Day would suddenly snatch on the power and over we would go—that is, over one of the sastrugi—only to find, often, that we had just floundered into another one ahead. In performing one of these evolutions Priestley, who, as usual, was working like a Trojan, got his hand rather badly damaged through its being jammed between the spokes of the car wheel and the framework. Almost immediately afterwards one of my fingers was nearly broken, through the same cause, the flesh being torn off one of my knuckles; and then Mackay seriously damaged his wrist in manipulating what Joyce called the "thumb-breaking" starter. Still we went floundering along over the sastrugi and ice cracks, Day every now and then getting out to lighten the car and limping alongside. At last we succeeded in reaching a spot amongst the snow sastrugi on the sea ice, fifteen miles distant from our winter quarters. Here we dumped the load intended for the Northern Party, and then Day had a hard struggle to extricate the car from the tangle of sastrugi and ice cracks. At last, after two capsizes of the sledges, we got back into camp at 10 P.M., all thoroughly exhausted, all wounded and bandaged. Brocklehurst carried Day on his back for about a quarter of a mile from where we left the car up to our winter quarters.

October 4 was a Sunday, and after the morning service we took the ponies out for exercise. In the evening the gramophone discoursed appropriate music, concluding with the universal favorite, "Lead, Kindly Light."

Meanwhile, Mackay had his damaged wrist attended to, and I put the question to him as to whether or not he was prepared to undertake the long journey to the Magnetic Pole under the circumstances. He said that he was quite ready, provided Mawson and I did not object to his going with his wrist damaged and in a sling. We raised no objection, and so the matter was settled. All that night Mawson and I were occupied in writing final letters and packing little odds and ends.

The following morning, October 5, after an early breakfast, we prepared for the final start. Brocklehurst took a photograph of us just before we started, then Day, Priestley, Roberts, Mackay, Mawson and I got aboard, some on the motorcar, some on the sledges. Those remaining behind gave us three cheers, Day turned on the power, and away we went. A light wind was blowing from the southeast at the time of our start, bringing a little snow with it and another blizzard seemed impending.

After traveling a little over two miles, just beyond Cape Barne, the snow had become so thick that the coastline was almost entirely hidden from our view. Under these circumstances I did not think it prudent to take the motorcar further, so Mackay, Mawson, and I bid adieu to our good friends. Strapping on our harness, we toggled on to the sledge rope, and with a "One, two, three" and "away," started on our long journey over the sea ice.

We reached our ten mile depot at 7 P.M. and got up our tent. We slept that night on the floe ice, with about three hundred fathoms of water under our pillow.

The following morning, October 6, we started our relay work. We dragged the Christmas Tree sledge on first, as we were specially liable to lose parcels off it, for a distance of from one-third to half a mile. Then we returned and fetched up what we called the Plum Duff sledge, chiefly laden with our provisions. The weather may be described as thick, with snow falling at intervals. We camped that night amongst screw pack ice within less than a mile of our fifteen mile depot.

The following day, October 7, was beautifully fine and calm. We started about 9 A.M. and sledged over pressure ice ridges and snow sastrugi, reaching our fifteen mile depot in three-quarters of an hour. Here we camped and repacked our sledges. We took the wholemeal plasmon biscuits out of two of the biscuit tins and packed them into canvas bags. This saved us a weight of about 8 lb.

We started again in the afternoon, relaying with the two sledges. The sledging again was heavy on account of the fresh, soft snow, and small sastrugi. We had a glorious view of the western mountains, crimsoned in the light of the setting sun. We camped that night close to a seal hole which belonged to a fine specimen of Weddell seal. We were somewhat disturbed that night by the snorting and whistling of the seals as they came up for their blows . . .

On October 10, we were awakened by the chatter of some Emperor penguins who had marched down on our tent during the night to investigate us. The sounds may be described as something between the cackle of a goose and the chortle of a kookaburra. On peeping out of the Burberry spout of our tent I saw four standing by the sledges. They were much interested at the sight of me, and the conversation between them became lively. They evidently took us for penguins of an inferior type, and the tent for our nest. They watched, and took careful note of all our doings, and gave us a good sendoff when we started about 8:30 A.M. The sky was overcast, and light snow began to fall in the afternoon. A little later a mild blizzard sprang up from the southeast; we thought this a favorable opportunity for testing the sailing qualities of our sledges, and so made sail on the Plum Duff sledge. As Mackay put it, we "brought her to try with main course." As the strength of the blizzard increased, we found that we could draw both sledges simultaneously, which was, of course, a great saving in labor. We were tempted to carry on in the increasing strength of the blizzard rather longer than was wise, and consequently, when at last we decided that we must camp, had great difficulty in getting the tent up. We slipped the tent over the poles placed close to the ground in the lee of a sledge. While two of us raised the poles, the third shoveled snow on to the skirt of the tent, which we pulled out little by little, until it was finally spread to its full dimensions. We were glad to turn in and escape from the biting blast and drifting snow.

Sunday, October 11. A violent blizzard was still blowing, and we lay in our sleeping bag until past noon, by which time the snow had drifted high upon the door side of our tent. As this drift was pressing heavily on our feet and cramping us, I got up and dug it away. The cooker and primus were then brought in and we all got up and had some hoosh and tea. The temperature, as usually happens in a blizzard, had now risen considerably, being 8.5° F at 1:30 P.M. The copper wire on our sledges was polished and burnished by the prolonged blast against it of tiny ice crystals, and the surface of the sea ice was also brightly polished in places. As it was still blowing we remained in our sleeping bag for the rest of that day as well as the succeeding night.

When we rose at about 2 A.M. on Monday, October 12, the blizzard was over. We found very heavy snow-drifts on the lee side of our sledges, and it took us a considerable time to dig these away and get the hard snow raked out of all the chinks and crannies among the packages on the sledges. We made a start about 4 A.M., and all that day meandered amongst broken pack ice. It was evident that the southeast blizzards drive large belts of broken floe ice in this direction across McMurdo Sound to the western shore. The fractured masses of sea ice, inclined at all angles to the horizontal, are frozen in later, as the cold of winter becomes more intense, and, of course, constitute a very difficult surface for sledging.

October 13. We camped at the foot of a low ice cliff, about 600 yards south southeast of Butter Point. Butter Point is merely an angle in this low ice cliff near the junction of the Ferrar Glacier valley with the main shore of Victoria Land. This cliff was from fifteen to twenty feet in height, and formed of crevassed glacier ice.

During part of this day Mawson and Mackay were busy making a mast and boom for the second sledge, it being our intention to use the tent floorcloth as a sail. Meanwhile I sorted out the material to be left at the depot at Butter Point.

The following day, Wednesday, October 14, we spent the morning in resorting the loads on our sledges. We depoted two tins of wholemeal plasmon biscuits, each weighing about 27 lb., also Mackay's mountaineering nail boots, and my spare headgear material and mits. Altogether we lightened the load by about 70 lb. We sunk the two full tins of biscuits and a tin containing boots, etc., a short distance in the glacier ice to prevent the blizzards blowing them away. We then lashed to the tins a short bamboo flagpole, carrying one of our black depot flags, and securely fastened to its base one of our empty airtight milk tins, in which we placed our letters. In these letters for Lieutenant Shackleton and R. E. Priestley respectively, I stated that in consequence of our late start from Cape Royds, and also on account of the comparative slowness of our progress thence to Butter Point, it was obvious that we could not return to Butter Point until January 12, at the earliest, instead of the first week of January, as was originally anticipated. We ascertained months later that this little depot survived the blizzards, and that Armytage, Priestley, and Brocklehurst had no difficulty in finding it, and that they had read our letters.

October 14. Leaving the depot about 9 A.M., we started sledging across New Harbor in the direction of Cape Bernacchi. In the afternoon a light southerly wind sprang up bringing a little snow with it, the fall lasting from about 12:30 to 2:30 P.M. We steered in the direction of what appeared to us to be an uncharted island. On arriving at it, however, we discovered that it was a true iceberg, formed of hard blue glacier ice with a conspicuous black band near its summit formed of fine dark gravel. The iceberg was about a quarter of a mile in length, and thirty to forty feet high.

October 15. We had a glorious view up the valley of the Ferrar Glacier. The cold was now less severe; at 8 P.M. the temperature was 9.5° F.

October 16. We were up at 3:30 A.M., and got under way at 5:30. A cold wind was blowing from the south, and after some trouble we set sail on both sledges, using the green floorcloth on the Christmas Tree sledge, and Mackay's sail on the Plum Duff sledge. A short time after we set sail it fell nearly calm; thick cloud gathered; a light wind sprang up from the southeast, veering to east northeast, then back again to southeast in the afternoon. Fine snow fell for about three hours, forming a layer nearly a quarter of an inch in thickness. Toward evening we reached one of the bergs that had been miraged up the night before. It was four hundred yards long, and eighty yards wide, and was a true iceberg formed of glacier ice; Mackay, Mawson, and I explored this. Like the previous iceberg, its surface was pitted with numerous deep dust wells.

As the shore was high and rocky, and seemed not more than half a mile distant, I went over toward it after our evening meal. On the way, for the first time, I met with a structure in the sea ice known as pancake ice. The surface of the ice showed a rounded polygonal structure something like the tops of a number of large weathered basaltic columns. The edges of these polygons were slightly raised, but sufficiently rounded off by thawing or ablation to afford an easy surface for the runners of our sledge. Close in shore the pancake ice was traversed by deep tidal cracks.

October 17. Mawson, Mackay, and I landed at Cape Bernacchi, a little over a mile north of our previous camp. Here we hoisted the Union Jack just before 10 A.M. and took possession of Victoria Land for the British Empire. Cape Bernacchi is a low rocky promontory, the geology of which is extremely interesting. The dominant type of rock is a pure white coarsely crystalline marble; this has been broken through by granite rocks, the latter in places containing small red garnets. After taking possession we resumed our sledging, finding the surface of pancake ice very good.

October 18. We reached an interesting headland today about one and a quarter miles from our preceding camp. The rocks bore a general resemblance to those at Cape Bernacchi. Mawson thought that some of the quartz veins traversing this headland would prove to be auriferous. After leaving this Point the wind freshened considerably. We had previously hoisted sail, and the wind was sufficiently strong to admit of our pulling both sledges together. The total distance traveled was seven statute miles. This was the most favorable wind we experienced during the whole of our journey to and from the Magnetic Pole.

That night I experienced a rather bad attack of snow blindness through neglecting to wear my snow goggles regularly. Finding that my eyes were no better next morning, and my sight being dim I asked Mawson to take my place at the end of the long rope, the foremost position in the team. Mawson proved himself on this occasion and afterward so remarkably efficient at picking out the best track for our sledges, and steering a good course, that at my request he occupied this position throughout the rest of the journey.

The next two days were uneventful, except for the fact that we occasionally had extremely heavy sledging over screw pack ice and high and long sastrugi.

On the night of October 20, we camped on the sea ice about three-quarters of a mile off shore. To the northeast of us was an outward curve of the shoreline, shown as a promontory on the existing chart. Early the next morning I walked over to the shore to geologize, and found the rocky headland composed of curious gneissic granite veined with quartz. On ascending this headland I noticed to my surprise that what had been previously supposed to be a promontory was really an island separated by a narrow strait from the mainland.

While Mawson determined the position of this island by taking a round of angles with the theodolite, Mackay and I crossed the strait and explored the island, pacing and taking levels. The rocks of which the erratics and boulder-bearing gravels were formed were almost without exception of igneous origin. One very interesting exception was a block of weathered clayey limestone. This was soft and yellowish gray externally, but hard and blue on the freshly fractured surfaces inside. It contained traces of small fossils which appeared to be seeds of plants. Two chips of this rock were fortunately preserved, sufficient for chemical analysis and microscopic examination. There could be little doubt that this clayey limestone has been derived from the great sedimentary formation, named by H. T. Ferrar, the Beacon sandstone. The island which we had been exploring we named provisionally Terrace Island. It was approximately triangular in shape, and the side facing the strait, down which we traveled, measured one mile 1200 yards in length.

October 23. Today we held a serious council as to the future of our journey toward the Magnetic Pole. It was quite obvious that at our present rate of traveling, about four statute miles daily by the relay method, we could not get to the Pole and return to Butter Point early in

January. I suggested that the most likely means of getting to the Pole and back in the time specified by Lieutenant Shackleton would be to travel on half-rations depoting the remainder of our provisions at an early opportunity. Mawson and Mackay agreed, after some discussion, to try this expedient, and we decided to think the matter over for a few days and then make our depot.

October 24. We reached in the evening a long rocky point of gneissic granite, which we called Gneiss Point. After our evening hoosh we walked across to the point and collected a number of interesting geological specimens, including blocks of kenyte lava.

October 25 proved a very heavy day for sledging, as we had to drag the sledges over new snow from three to four inches deep. In places it had a tough top crust which we would break through up to our ankles. We met also several obstacles in the way of wide cracks in the sea ice, from six to ten feet in width, and several miles in length. The seawater between the walls of the cracks had only recently been frozen over, so that the ice was only just thick enough to bear the sledges.

In pursuing our northwesterly course we were now crossing a magnificent bay, which trended westward some five or six miles away from the course we were steering. On either side of this bay were majestic ranges of rocky mountains parted from one another at the head of the bay by an immense glacier with steep ice falls. On examining these mountains with a field glass it was evident that in their lower portions they were formed of granite and gneiss, producing reddish brown soils. At the higher levels, further inland, there were distinct traces of rocks showing horizontal stratification. The highest rock of all was black in color, and evidently very hard, apparently some three hundred feet in thickness. Below this was some softer stratified formation, approximately one thousand feet in thickness. We concluded that the hard top layer was composed of igneous rock, possibly a lava, while the horizontal stratified formation belonged in all probability to the Beacon sandstone formation. Some fine nunataks of dark rock rose from the southeast side of the great glacier. On either side of this glacier were high terraces of rock reaching back for several miles from a modern valley edge to the foot of still higher ranges. It was obvious that these terraces marked the position of the floor of the old valley at a time when the glacier ice was several thousand feet higher than it is now, and some ten miles wider than at present. The glacier trended inland in a general southwesterly direction.

We longed to turn our sledges shoreward and explore these inland rocks, but this would have involved a delay of several days—probably a week at least—and we could not afford the time. Mawson took a series of horizontal and vertical angles with the theodolite to all the upper peaks in these ranges. We were much puzzled to determine on what part of the charted coast this wide bay and great glacier valley was situated. We found out much later that the point opposite which we had now arrived was in reality Granite Harbor, and that its position was not shown correctly on the chart.

October 27. The weather was beautifully clear and sunshiny, and we had a glorious view of the great mountain ranges on either side of Granite Harbor. The rich coloring of warm sepia brown and terra cotta in these rocky hills was quite a relief to the eye. Wind springing up in the southeast, we made sail on both sledges, and this helped us a good deal over the soft snow and occasional patches of sharp edged brash ice.

Toward evening we fetched up against some high ice pressure cracks with the ice ridged up six to eight feet high in huge tumbled blocks. We seemed to have got into a labyrinth of these pressure ridges from which there was no outlet. At last, after several capsizes of the sledges and some chopping through the ice ridges by Mackay, we got the sledges through, and camped on a level piece of ice. Mawson and I at this time were still wearing finnesko, while Mackay had taken to ski boots.

October 28. The sledging was again very heavy over sticky, soft snow alternating with hard sastrugi and patches of consolidated brash ice. After our evening hoosh, Mawson and I went over to the shore, rather more than half a mile distant, in order to study the rocks. These we found were composed of coarse red granite; the top of the granite was much smoothed by glacier ice, and strewn with large erratic blocks. In places the granite was intersected by black dykes of basic rocks. One could see that the glacier ice, about a quarter of a mile inland from the rocky shore, had only recently retreated and laid bare the glaciated rocky surface. We found a little moss here amongst the crevices in the granite rock.

October 29 was beautifully fine, though a keen and fresh wind, rather unpleasantly cold, was blowing from off the high mountain plateau to our west. We were all thoroughly done up at night after completing our four miles of relay work. That evening we discussed the important question of whether it would be possible to eke out our food supplies with seal meat so as to avoid putting ourselves on half rations, and we all agreed that this should be done. We made up our minds that at the first convenient spot we would make a depot of any articles of equipment, geological specimens, etc., in order to lighten our sledges, and would at the same time, if the spot was suitable, make some experiments with seal meat. The chief problem in connection with the latter was how to cook it without the aid of paraffin oil, as we could not afford paraffin for this purpose.

October 30 was full of interest for us, as well as hard work. In the early morning, between 2:30 A.M. and 6:30 A.M., a mild blizzard was blowing. We got under way a little later and camped at about 10:30 A.M. for lunch alongside a very interesting rocky point. Mawson got a good set of theodolite angles from the top of this point.

We tried, on that day, the experiment of strengthening the brew of the tea by using the old tea leaves of a previous meal mixed with the next ones. This was Mackay's idea, and Mawson and I at the time did not appreciate the experiment. Later on, however, we were very glad to adopt it.

The weather was now daily becoming warmer and the saline snow on the sea ice became sticky in consequence. It gripped the runners of the sledges like glue, and we were only able with our greatest efforts to drag the sledges over this at a snail's pace. We were all thoroughly exhausted that evening when we camped at the base of a rocky promontory about 180 ft. high. This cliff was formed of coarse gneiss, with numerous dark streaks, and enclosures of huge masses of greenish-gray quartzite. After our evening hoosh we walked over to a very interesting small island about three-quarters of a mile distant. It was truly a most wonderful place geologically, and was a perfect elysium for the mineralogist. The island, which we afterwards called Depot Island, was accessible on the shoreward side, but rose perpendicularly to a height of 200 ft. above sea level on the other three sides. There was very little snow or ice upon it, the surface being almost entirely formed of gneissic granite. This granite was full of dark enclosures of basic rocks, rich in black mica and huge crystals of hornblende. It was in these enclosures that Mawson discovered a translucent brown mineral, which he believed to be monazite, but which has since proved to be titanium mineral.

October 31. We packed up and made for the island at 9:30 A.M. The sledging was extremely heavy, and we fell into a tide crack on the way, but the sledge was got over safely. Mackay sighted a seal about six hundred yards distant from the site of our new camp near the island, and just then, we noticed that another seal had bobbed up in the tide crack close to our old camp. Mackay and Mawson at once started off in the direction where the first seal had been sighted. It proved to be a bull seal in very good condition, and they killed it by knocking it on the head with an ice axe. Meanwhile, I unpacked the Duff sledge and took it out to them. Returning to the site of our camp I put up the tent, and on going back to Mawson and Mackay found that they had finished fletching the seal. We loaded up the empty sledge with seal blubber, resembling bars of soap in its now frozen condition, steak and liver, and returned to camp for lunch.

After lunch we took some blubber and seal meat on to the island, intending to try the experiment of making a blubber fire in order to cook the meat. We worked our way a short distance up a steep, rocky gully, and there built a fireplace out of magnificent specimens of hornblende rock. It seemed a base use for such magnificent mineralogical specimens, but necessity knows no laws. We had brought with us our primus lamp in order to start the fire. We put blubber on our iron shovel, warmed this underneath by means of the heat of the primus lamp so as to render down the oil from it, and then lit the oil. The experiment was not altogether successful. Mawson cooked for about three hours, closely and anxiously watched by Mackay and myself. Occasionally he allowed us to taste small snacks of the partly cooked seal meat, which were pronounced to be delicious.

While the experiment was at its most critical stage, at about 6 P.M., we observed sudden swirls of snowdrift high up on the western mountains, coming rapidly to lower levels. For a few minutes we did not think seriously of the phenomenon, but as the drift came nearer we saw that something serious was in the air. Mackay and I rushed down to our tent, the skirt of which was only temporarily secured with light blocks of snow. We reached it just as it was struck by the sudden blizzard which had descended from the western mountains. There was no time to dig further blocks of snow, all we could do was to seize the heavy food bags on our sledges, weighing sixty pounds each, and rush them on to the skirt of the tent. The blizzard struck our kitchen on the island simultaneously with our tent, and temporarily Mawson lost his mits and most of the tidbits of seal meat, but these were quickly recovered, and he came rushing down to join us in securing the tent. While Mawson in frantic haste chopped out blocks of snow and dumped them on to the skirt of the tent, Mackay, no less frantically, struggled with our sleeping bag, which had been turned inside out to air, and which by this time was covered with drift snow. He quickly had it turned right side in again, and dashed it inside the tent. At last everything was secured, and we found ourselves safe and sound inside the tent.

On November 1 we breakfasted off a mixture of our ordinary hoosh and seal meat. After some discussion we decided that our only hope of reaching the Magnetic Pole lay in our traveling on half rations from our present camp to the point on the coast at the Drygalski Glacier, where we might for the first time hope to be able to turn inland with reasonable prospect of reaching the Magnetic Pole. Mawson was emphatic that we must con-

serve six weeks of full rations for our inland journey to
and from the Pole. This necessitated our going on half
rations from this island to the far side of the Drygalski
Glacier, a distance of about one hundred statute miles.
In order to supplement the regular half rations we intended to take seal meat.

While I was busy in calculating the times and distances
for the remainder of our journey, and proportioning the
food rations to suit our new program, Mawson and
Mackay conducted further experiments on the cooking
of seal meat with blubber. While at our winter quarters,
Mackay had made some experiments on the use of blubber as a fuel. He had constructed a blubber lamp, the
wick of which kept alight for several hours at a time,
feeding itself on the seal oil. He had tried the experiment
of heating up water over this blubber lamp, and was
partly successful at the time when we left winter quarters
for our present sledging journey. But his experiments at
the time were not taken very seriously, and the blubber
lamp was left behind, a fact which we now much regret-
ted. An effective cooking stove was, however, evolved,
as the result of a series of experiments this day, out of
one of our large empty biscuit tins. The lid of this was
perforated with a number of circular holes for the recep-
tion of wicks. Its edges were bent down, so as to form
supports to keep the wick holder about half an inch
above the bottom of the biscuit tin. The wick holder was
put in place; wicks were made of pieces of old calico
food bags rolled in seal blubber, or with thin slices of
seal blubber enfolded in them, the calico being done up
in little rolls for the purpose of making wicks, as one
rolls a cigarette, the seal blubber taking the place of the
tobacco in this case. Lumps of blubber were laid around
the wick holder. Then, after some difficulty, the wicks
were lighted. They burned feebly at first, as seal blubber
has a good deal of water in it. After some minutes of
fitful spluttering, the wicks got fairly alight, and as soon
as the lower part of the biscuit tin was raised to a high
temperature, the big lumps of blubber at the side commenced to have the water boiled out of them and the
oil rendered down. This oil ran under the wick holder
and supplied the wicks at their base. The wicks, now fed

with warm, pure seal oil, started to burn brightly, and even fiercely, so that it became necessary occasionally to damp them down with chips of fresh blubber. We tried the experiment of using lumps of salt as wicks, and found this fairly successful, but we decided to rely for wicks chiefly on our empty food bags, and thought possibly that if these ran out we might have recourse to moss. But the empty food bags supplied sufficient wick for our need.

That day, by means of galvanized iron wires, we slung the inner pot from our aluminum cooker over the lighted wicks of our blubber cooker, thawed down snow in it, added chips of seal meat and made a delicious bouillon. This had a rich red color and seemed very nutritious, but to me was indigestible. While Mawson was still engaged on further cooking experiments, Mackay and I ascended to the highest point of the island, selected a spot for a cairn to mark our depot, and Mackay commenced building the cairn. Meanwhile, I returned to camp.

It had, of course, become clear to us, in view of our experience of the already cracking sea ice near Granite Harbor, as well as in view of our comparatively slow progress by relay, that our retreat back to camp from the direction of the Magnetic Pole would in all probability be entirely cut off through the breaking up of the sea ice. Under these circumstances we determined to take the risk of the *Nimrod* arriving safely on her return voyage at Cape Royds, where she would receive the instructions to search for us along the western coast, and also the risk of her not being able to find our depot and ourselves. We knew that there was a certain amount of danger in adopting this course, but we felt that we had got on so far with the work entrusted to us by our Commander that we could not honorably now turn back. Under these circumstances we each wrote farewell letters to those who were nearest and dearest, and the following morning, November 2, we were up at 4:30 A.M. After putting all the letters into one of our empty dried milk tins, and fitting on the airtight lid, I walked with it to the island and climbed up to the cairn. Here, after carefully depoting several bags of geological specimens at the base of the flagstaff, I lashed the little post office by means of cord and copper wire securely to the flagstaff, and then carried some large slabs of exfoliated granite to the cairn, and built them up on the leeward side of it in order to strengthen it against the southerly blizzards. A keen wind was blowing, as was usual in the early morning, off the high plateau, and one's hands got frequently frost bitten in the work of securing the tin to the flagstaff. The cairn was at the seaward end of a sheer cliff two hundred feet high.

It was later than usual when we started our sledges, and the pulling proved extremely heavy. The sun's heat was thawing the snow surface and making it extremely sticky. Our progress was so painfully slow that we decided, after with great efforts doing two miles, to camp, have our hoosh, and then turn in for six hours, having meanwhile started the blubber lamp. At the expiration of that time we intended to get out of our sleeping bag, breakfast, and start sledging about midnight. We hoped that by adopting nocturnal habits of traveling, we would avoid the sticky ice surface which by daytime formed such an obstacle to our progress. We carried out this program on the evening of November 2, and the morning of November 3. We found the experiment fairly successful, as at midnight and for a few hours afterward the temperature remained sufficiently low to keep the surface of the snow on the sea ice moderately crisp.

On November 3 and 4 the weather was fine, and we made fair progress.

On the following day, November 5, we were opposite a very interesting coastal panorama, some twenty miles north of Granite Harbor. Magnificent ranges of mountains, steep slopes free from snow and ice, stretched far to the north and far to the south of us, and finished away inland, toward the heads of long glacier cut valleys, in a vast upland snow plateau. The rocks which were exposed to view in the lower part of these ranges were mostly of warm sepia brown to terra cotta tint, and were evidently built up of a continuation of the gneissic rocks and red granites which we had previously seen. Above these crystalline rocks came a belt of greenish gray rock, apparently belonging to some stratified formation and possibly many hundreds of feet in thickness; the latter was capped with a black rock that seemed to be either a basic plateau lava or a huge sill. In the direction of the glacier valleys, the plateau was broken up into a vast number of conical hills of various shapes and heights, all showing evidence of intense glacial action in the past. The hills were here separated from the coastline by a continuous belt of piedmont glacier ice. This last terminated where it joined the sea ice in a steep slope, or low cliff, and in places was very much crevassed. Mawson, at our noon halt for lunch, continued taking the angles of all these ranges and valleys with our theodolite.

The temperature was now rising, being as high as 22° F at noon on November 5. We had a very heavy sledging surface that day, there being much consolidated brash ice, sastrugi, pie crust snow, and numerous cracks in the sea ice. As an offset to these troubles we had that night, for the first time, the use of our new frying pan, constructed by Mawson out of one of our empty paraffin tins. This tin had been cut in half down the middle parallel to its broad surfaces, and loops of iron wire being added, it was possible to suspend it inside the empty biscuit tin above the wicks of our blubber lamp. We found that in this frying pan we could rapidly render down the seal blubber into oil, and as soon as the oil boiled we dropped into the pan small slices of seal liver or seal meat. The liver took about ten minutes to cook in the boiling oil, the seal meat about twenty minutes. These facts were ascertained by the empirical method. Mawson discovered by the same method that the nicely browned and crisp residue from the seal blubber, after the oil in it had become rendered down, was good eating, and had a fine nutty flavor. We also found, as the result of later experiments, that dropping a little seal's blood into the boiling oil produced eventually a gravy of very fine flavor. If the seal's blood was poured in rapidly into the boiling oil, it made a kind of gravy pancake, which we also considered very good as a variety.

We had a magnificent view this day of fresh ranges of mountains to the north of Depot Island. At the foot of these was an extensive terrace of glacier ice, a curious type of piedmont glacier. Its surface was strongly convex near where it terminated seaward in a steep slope or low cliff. In places this ice was heavily crevassed. At a distance of several miles inland, it reached the spurs of an immense coastal range, while in the wide gaps in this range the ice trended inland as far as the eye could see until it blended in the far distance with the skyline high up on the great inland plateau.

A little before 9 P.M. on November 5 we left our sleeping bag, and found snow falling, with a fresh and chilly breeze from the south. The blubber lamp, which we had lighted before we had turned in, had got blown out. We built a chubby house for it of snow blocks to keep off the wind, and relighted it, and then turned into the sleeping bag again while we waited for the snow and chips of seal meat in our cooking pot to become converted into a hot bouillon; the latter was ready after an interval of about one hour and a half. Just before midnight we brought the cooker alight into the tent in order to protect it from the blizzard which was now blowing and bringing much falling snow with it. Mawson's cooking experiments continued to be highly successful and entirely satisfactory to the party.

We waited for the falling snow to clear sufficiently to enable us to see a short distance ahead, and then started again, the blizzard still blowing with a little low drift. After doing a stage of pulling on both sledges to keep ourselves warm in the blizzard we set sail—always a chilly business—and the wind was a distinct assistance to us. We encountered a good deal of brash ice that day, and noticed that this type of ice surface was most common in the vicinity of icebergs, which just here were very numerous. The brash ice is probably formed by the icebergs surging to and fro in heavy weather like a lot of gigantic Yermaks, and crunching up the sea ice in their vicinity. The latter, of course, refreezes, producing a surface covered with jagged edges and points.

We were now reduced to one plasmon biscuit each for breakfast and one for evening meal, and we were unanimous in the opinion that we had never before fully realized how very nice these plasmon biscuits were. We became exceedingly careful even over the crumbs. As some biscuits were thicker than others, the cook for the week would select three biscuits, place them on the outer cover of our aluminum cooker, and get one of his mates to look in an opposite direction while the messman pointed to a biscuit and said, "Whose?" The mate with averted face, or shut eyes, would then state the owner, and the biscuit was earmarked for him, and so with the other two biscuits. Grievous was the disappointment of the man to whose lot the thinnest of the three biscuits had fallen. Originally, on this sledge journey, when biscuits were more plentiful, we used to eat them regardless of the loss of crumbs, munching them boldly, with the result that occasional crumbs fell on the floorcloth. Not so now. Each man broke his biscuit over his own pannikin of hoosh, so that any crumbs produced in the process of fracture fell into the pannikin. Then, in order to make sure that there were no loose fragments adhering to the morsel we were about to transfer to our mouths, we tapped the broken chip, as well as the biscuit from which it had been broken, on the sides of the pannikin, so as to shake into it any loose crumbs. Then, and then only, was it safe to devour the previous morsel. Mackay, who adopted this practice in common with the rest of us, said it reminded him of the old days when the sailors tapped each piece of broken biscuit before eating it in order to shake out the weevils.

Mawson and I now wore our ski boots instead of finnesko, the weather being warmer, and the ski boot giving one a better grip on the snow surface of the sea ice. The rough leather took the skin off my right heel, but Mackay fixed it up later in the evening, that is, my heel, with some "Newskin."

We sledged on uneventfully for the remainder of November 6, and during the 7th, and on November 8 it came on to blow again with fresh falling snow. The blizzard was still blowing when the time came for us to pitch our tent. We had a severe struggle to get the tent up in the high wind and thick falling snow. At last the work was accomplished, and we were all able to turn into our sleeping bag, pretty tired, at about 12:30 P.M.

The weather was still bad the following day, November 9. After breakfast of seal's liver, and digging out the sledges from the snowdrift, we started in the blizzard, the snow still falling. After a little while we made sail on both sledges. The light was very bad on account of the thick falling snow, and we were constantly falling up to our knees in the cracks in the sea ice. It seemed miraculous that in spite of these very numerous accidents we never sprained an ankle.

That day we saw a snow petrel, and three skua gulls visited our camp. At last the snow stopped falling and the wind fell light, and we were much cheered by the fine, though distant, view of the Nordenskjold Ice Barrier to the north of us. We were all extremely anxious to ascertain what sort of a surface for sledging we should meet with on this great glacier. According to the Admiralty chart, prepared from observations by the *Discovery* expedition, this glacier was between twenty-four and thirty miles wide, and projected over twenty miles from the rocky shore into the sea. We hoped that we might be able to cross it without following a circuitous route along its seaward margins.

We started off on November 10, amongst very heavy sastrugi and ridges of broken pack ice. Cracks in the sea ice were extremely numerous. The temperature was up to plus 3° F at 8 A.M. That day when we pitched camp we were within half a mile of the southern edge of the Nordenskjold Ice Barrier.

The following day, November 11, as Mawson wished to get an accurate magnetic determination with the Lloyd-Creak dip circle, we decided to camp, Mackay and I exploring the glacier surface to select a suitable track for our sledges while Mawson took his observations. After breakfast we removed everything containing iron several hundred yards away from the tent, leaving Mawson alone inside it in company with the dip circle. We found that the ascent from the sea ice to the Nordenskjold Ice Barrier was a comparatively easy one. The surface was formed chiefly of hard snow glazed in places, partly through thawing and refreezing, partly through the polishing of this windward surface by particles of fresh snow driven over it by the blizzards. The surface ascended gradually to a little over one hundred feet above the level of the sea ice, passing into a wide undulating plain which stretched away to the north as far as the eye could see.

We returned to Mawson with the good news that the Nordenskjold Ice Barrier was quite practicable for sledging, and would probably afford us a much more easy surface than the sea ice over which we had previously been passing. Mawson informed us, as the result of his observations with the dip circle, that the Magnetic Pole was probably about forty miles further inland than the theoretical mean position calculated for it from the magnetic observations of the *Discovery* expedition seven years ago.

Early on the morning of November 12 we packed up, and started to cross the Nordenskjold Ice Barrier. We noticed here that there were two well-marked sets of sastrugi, one set, nearly due north and south, formed by the strong southerly blizzards, the other set, crossing nearly at right angles, coming from the west and formed by the cold land winds blowing off the high plateau at night on to the sea.

November 12 was an important one in the history of Mawson's triangulation of the coast, for he was able in the morning to sight simultaneously Mount Erebus and Mount Melbourne, as well as Mount Lister. We were fortunate in having a very bright and clear day on this occasion, and the round of angles obtained by Mawson with the theodolite were in every way satisfactory.

November 13. We were still on the Nordenskjold Ice Barrier. The temperature in the early morning, about 3 A.M., was minus 13° F. Mawson had provided an excellent dish for breakfast consisting of crumbed seal meat and seal's blood, which proved delicious. We got under way about 2 A.M. It was a beautiful sunshiny day with a gentle cold breeze off the western plateau. When we had sledged for about one thousand yards Mawson suddenly exclaimed that he could see the end of the barrier where it terminated in a white cliff only about six hundred yards ahead. We halted the sledge, and while Mawson took some more theodolite angles Mackay and I reconnoitered ahead but could find no way down the cliff. We returned to the sledge and all pulled on for another quarter of a mile. Once more we reconnoitered, and this time both Mawson and I found some steep slopes formed by drifted snow which were just practicable for a light sledge lowered by an alpine rope. We chose what seemed to be the best of these; Mackay tied the alpine rope around his body, and taking his ice axe, descended the slope cautiously, Mawson and I holding on to the rope meanwhile. The snow slope proved fairly soft, giving good foothold, and he was soon at the bottom without having needed any support from the alpine rope. He then returned to the top of the slope, and we all set to work unpacking the sledges. We made fast one of the sledges to the alpine rope, and after loading it lightly lowered it little by little down the slope, one of us guiding the sledge while the other two slacked out the alpine rope above. The man who went with the sledge to the bottom would unload it there on the sea ice and then climb up the slope, the other two meanwhile pulling up the empty sledge. This maneuver was repeated a number of times until eventually the whole of our food and equipment, including two sledges, were safely down on the sea ice below.

We were all much elated at having got across the Nordenskjold Ice Barrier so easily and so quickly. We were also fortunate in securing a seal; Mackay went off and killed this, bringing back seal steak, liver, and a considerable quantity of seal blood. From the last Mackay said he intended to manufacture a black pudding.

While Mackay had been in pursuit of the seal meat Mawson had taken a meridian attitude while I kept the time for him. After our hoosh we packed the sledges, and Mawson took a photograph showing the cliff forming the northern boundary of the Nordenskjold Ice Barrier. This cliff was about forty feet in height. There can be little doubt, I think, that the greater part of this Nordenskjold Ice Barrier is afloat.

The sun was so warm this day that I was tempted before turning in to the sleeping bag to take off my ski boots and socks and give my feet a snow bath, which was very refreshing.

The following day, November 14, we were naturally anxious to be sure of our exact position on the chart, in view of the fact that we had come to the end of the ice barrier some eighteen miles quicker than the chart led us to anticipate. Mawson accordingly worked up his meridian altitude, and I plotted out the angular distances he had found respectively, for Mount Erebus, Mount Lister, and Mount Melbourne. As the result of the application of our calculations to the chart it became evident that we had actually crossed the Nordenskjold Ice Barrier of Captain Scott's survey, and were now opposite what on this chart was termed Charcot Bay. This was good news and cheered us up very much, as it meant that we were nearly twenty miles further north than we previously thought we were. The day was calm and fine, and the surface of the sea ice was covered with patches of soft snow with nearly bare ice between, and the sledging was not quite as heavy as usual. In the evening two skua gulls went for our seal meat during the interval that we were returning for the second sledge after pulling on the first one.

We had a magnificent view of the rocky coastline, which is here most impressive. The sea ice stretched away to the west of us for several miles up to a low cliff and slope of piedmont glacier ice, with occasional black masses of rock showing at its edge. Several miles further inland the piedmont glacier ice terminated abruptly against a magnificent range of mountains, tabular for the most part but deeply intersected. In the wide gaps between this coast range were vast glaciers fairly heavily crevassed, descending by steep slopes from an inland plateau to the sea.

We were still doing our traveling by night and sleeping during the afternoon. When we arose from our sleeping bags at 8 P.M. on the night of November 15, there was a beautifully perfect "Noah's Ark" in the sky; the belts of cirrus stratus composing the ark stretched from south southwest to north northeast, converging toward the horizon in each of these directions. Fleecy sheets of frost smoke arose from over the open water on Ross Sea, and formed dense cumulus clouds. This, of course, was a certain indication to us that open water was not far distant, and impressed upon us the necessity of making every possible speed if we hoped to reach our projected point of departure on the coast for the Magnetic Pole before the sea ice entirely broke up.

The following day, November 17, after a very heavy sledging over loose powdery snow six inches deep, we reached a low glacier and ice cliff. We were able to get some really fresh snow from this barrier or glacier, the cliffs of which were from thirty to forty feet high. It was a great treat to get fresh water at last, as since we had left the Nordenskjold Ice Barrier the only snow available for cooking purposes had been brackish.

November 18 was bright and sunny, but the sledging was terribly heavy. The sun had thawed the surface of the saline snow and our sledge runners had become saturated with soft water. We were so wearied with the great effort necessary to keep the sledges moving that at the end of each halt we fell sound asleep for five minutes or so at a time across the sledges. On such occasions one of the party would wake the others up, and we would continue our journey. We were even more utterly exhausted than usual at the end of this day.

By this time, however, we were in sight of a rocky headland which we took to be Cape Irizar, and we knew that this cape was not very far to the south of the Drygalski Glacier. Indeed, already a long line was showing on the horizon which could be no other than the eastward extension of this famous and, as it afterward proved, formidable glacier.

November 19. We had another heavy day's sledging, ankle deep in the soft snow. We only did two miles of relay work this day, and yet were quite exhausted at the end of it.

November 20. Being short of meat, we killed a seal calf and cow, and so replenished our larder. At the end of the day's sledging I walked over about two miles to a cliff face, about six miles south of Cape Irizar. The rocks all along this part of the shore were formed of coarse gneissic granite, of which I was able to collect some specimens. The cliff was about one hundred feet high where it was formed of the gneiss, and above this rose a capping of from seventy to eighty feet in thickness of heavily crevassed blue glacier ice. There were here wide tide cracks between the sea ice and the foot of the sea cliff. These were so wide that it was difficult to cross them.

November 21. The sledging was painfully heavy over thawing saline snow surface and sticky sea ice. We were only able to do two and two-third miles.

November 22. On rounding the point of the low ice barrier, thirty to forty feet high, we obtained a good view of Cape Irizar, and also of the Drygalski Ice Barrier.

November 23. We found that a mild blizzard was blowing, but we traveled on through it as we could not afford to lose any time. The blizzard died down altogether about 3 A.M., and was succeeded by a gentle westerly wind off the plateau. That evening, after our tent had been put up and we had finished the day's meal, I walked over a mile to the shore. The prevailing rock was still gneissic granite with large whitish veins of aplitic granite. A little bright green moss was growing on tiny patches of sand and gravel, and in some of the cracks in the granite. The top of the cliff was capped by the blue glacier ice. With the help of steps cut by my ice axe I climbed some distance up this in order to try and get some fresh ice for cooking purposes, but close to the top of the slope I accidentally slipped and glissaded most unwillingly some distance down before I was able to check myself by means of the chisel edge of the ice axe. My hands were somewhat cut and bruised, but otherwise no damage was done.

November 24. A strong keen wind was blowing off the plateau from the west southwest. We were all suffering from want of sleep, and although the snow surface was better than it had been for some little time we still found the work of sledging very fatiguing. A three man sleeping bag, where you are wedged in more or less tightly against your mates, where all snore and shin one another and each feels on waking that he is more shinned against than shinning, is not conducive to real rest; and we rued the day that we chose the three man bag in preference to the one man bags.

On the following day, November 26, we saw on looking back that the rocky headland, where I had collected the specimens of granite and moss, was not part of the mainland but a small island.

We had some good sledging here over pancake ice nearly free from snow and traveled fast. While Mackay secured some seal meat Mawson and I ascended the rocky promontory, climbing at first over rock, then over glacier ice, to a height of about six hundred feet above the sea. The rock was a pretty red granite traversed by large dykes of black rocks. From the top of the headland to the north we had a magnificent view across the level surface of sea ice far below us. We saw that at a few miles from the shore an enormous iceberg, frozen into the floe, lay right across the path which we had intended to travel in our northerly course on the morrow. To the northwest of us was Geikie Inlet, and beyond that stretching as far as the eye could follow was the great Drygalski Glacier. Beyond the Drygalski Glacier were a series of rocky hills. One of these was identified as probably being Mount Neumayer. Several mountains could be seen further to the north of this, but the far distance was obscured from view by cloud and mist so that we were unable to make out the outline of Mount Nansen. It was evident that the Drygalski Glacier was bounded landward on the north by a steep cliff of dark, highly jointed rock, and we were not a little concerned to observe with our field glasses that the surface of the Drygalski Glacier was wholly different to that of the Nordenskjold Ice Barrier. It was clear that the surface of the Drygalski Glacier was formed of jagged surfaces of ice very heavily crevassed, and projecting in the form of immense séracs separated from one another by deep undulations or chasms; but we could see that, at the extreme eastern extension, some thirty miles from where we were standing, the surface appeared fairly smooth. It was obvious from what we had seen looking out to sea to the east of our camp that there were large bodies of open water trending shorewards in the form of long lanes at no great distance. The lanes of water were only partly frozen over, and some of these were interposed between us and the Drygalski Glacier. Clearly not a moment was to be lost if we were to reach the glacier before the sea ice broke up. A single strong blizzard would now have converted the whole of the sea ice between us and the glacier into a mass of drifting pack.

The following day, November 27, we decided to run our sledges to the east of the large berg which we had observed on the previous day, and this course apparently would enable us to avoid a wide and ugly looking tide crack extending northward from the rocky point at our previous camp. The temperature was now as high as from plus 26° to plus 28° F at midday, consequently the saline snow and ice were all day more or less sticky and slushy. We camped near the large berg.

On the morning of November 28 we packed up and started our sledges, and pulled them over a treacherous slushy tide crack, and then headed them around an open lead of water in the sea ice. At 3 A.M. we had lunch near the east end of the big berg. Near here Mackay and Mawson succeeded in catching and killing an Emperor penguin, and took the breast and liver. This bird was caught close to a lane of open water in the sea ice. We found that in the direction of the berg this was thinly frozen over, and for some time it seemed as though our progress further north was completely blocked. Eventually we found a place where the ice might just bear our sledges. We strengthened this spot by laying down on its slabs of sea ice and shovelfuls of snow, and when the causeway was completed—not without Mackay breaking through the ice in one place and very nearly getting a ducking—we rushed our sledges over safely, although the ice was so thin that it bent under their weight. We were thankful to get them both safely to the other side.

We now found ourselves amongst some very high sastrugi of hard tough snow. We had to drag the sledges over a great number of these, which were nearly at right angles to our course. This work proved extremely fatiguing. The sastrugi were from five to six feet in height. As we were having dinner at the end of our day's sledging we heard a loud report which we considered to be due to the opening of a new crack in the sea ice. We thought it was possible that this crack was caused by some movement of the great active Drygalski Glacier, now only about four miles ahead of us to the north.

We got out of our sleeping bag soon after 8 P.M. on the evening of the 28th, and started just before midnight. The ice surface over which we were sledging this day had a curious appearance resembling rippling stalagmites, or what may be termed ice marble. This opacity appeared to be due to a surface enamel of partly thawed snow. This surface kept continually cracking as we passed over it with a noise like that of a whip being cracked. It was evidently in a state of tension, being contracted by the cold which attained its maximum soon after midnight, for, although of course we had for many weeks past been having the midnight sun, it was still so low in the heavens toward midnight that there was an appreciable difference in the temperature between midnight and the afternoon.

We were now getting very short of biscuits, and as a consequence were seized with food obsessions, being unable to talk about anything but cereal foods, chiefly cakes of various kinds and fruits. Whenever we halted for a short rest we could discuss nothing but the different dishes with which we had been regaled in our former lifetime at various famous restaurants and hotels.

The plateau wind blew keenly and strongly all day on November 29. As we advanced further to the north the ice surface became more and more undulatory, rising against us in great waves like waves of the sea. Evidently these waves were due to the forward movement, and consequent pressure of the Drygalski Glacier. We had a fine view from the top of one of these ridges over the surface of the Drygalski Glacier, to the edge of the inland plateau. Far inland, perhaps forty or fifty miles away, we could see the great névé fields, which fed the Drygalski Glacier, descending in conspicuous ice falls, and beyond these loomed dim mountains. At the end of this day we hardly knew whether we were on the edge of the sea ice or on the thin edge of the Drygalski Glacier. Probably, I think, we were on very old sea ice, perhaps representing the accumulations of several successive seasons.

It fell calm at about 9 P.M., but just before midnight, November 29–30, the plateau wind returned, blowing stronger than ever. As the sun during the afternoon had now considerable heating power, we tried the experiment of putting snow into our aluminum cooking pot, the exterior of which by this time was permanently coated with greasy lamp black from the blubber lamp, and leaving the pot exposed in the evening to the direct rays of the sun. The lamp black, of course, formed an excellent absorbent of the sun's heat rays. On getting out of the sleeping bag at 9 P.M. on November 29 I found that about half the snow I had put into the cooking pot had been thawed down by the sun's heat. This, of course, saved both paraffin and blubber. It takes, of course, as much energy to thaw ice or snow at a temperature of 32° F to form a given volume of water as it does to raise that water from 32° F up to boiling point. As our snow and ice used for domestic purposes frequently had a temperature of many degrees below zero, the heat energy necessary to thaw it was greater than that required to raise the water from freezing point to boiling point.

As we advanced with our sledge on the early morning of November 30, the ice ridges fronting us became higher and steeper, and we had much ado straining with all our might on the steep ice slopes to get the sledges to move, and they skidded a good deal as we dragged them obliquely up the slopes. The plateau wind, too, had freshened, and was now blowing on our port bow at from fifteen to twenty miles an hour, bringing with it a good deal of low drift. At last, about 10 A.M., the plateau wind dropped and with it the drift, and the weather became warm and sunny.

The glacier now spread before us as a great billowy sea of pale green ice, with here and there high embankments of marble like névé resembling railway embankments. Unfortunately for our progress, the trend of the latter was nearly at right angles to our course. As we advanced still further north the undulations became more and more pronounced, the embankments higher and steeper. These embankments were now bounded by cliffs from forty to fifty feet in height, with overhanging cornices of tough snow. The cliffs faced northward. The deep chasms which they produced formed a very serious obstacle to our advance, and we had to make some long detours in order to head them off. On studying one of these chasms it seemed to me that their mode of origin was somewhat as follows: In the first place the surface of the ice had become strongly ridged through forward movement of the glacier, with perhaps differential frictional resistance, the latter causing a series of undulations; the top of each ice undulation would then be further raised by an accumulation of snow partly carried by the west northwest plateau wind, partly by the southerly blizzard wind. These two force components produced these overhanging cliffs facing the north. For some reason the snow would not lie at the bottoms of the troughs between the undulations. Probably they were swept bare by the plateau wind. It was hardly to be wondered at that we were unable to advance our sledges more than about one mile and a half that day.

The next day, December 1, the hauling of our sledges became much more laborious. For half a day we struggled over high sastrugi, hummocky ice ridges, steep undulations of bare blue ice with frequent chasms impassable for a sledge, unless it was unloaded and lowered by alpine rope. After struggling on for a little over half a mile we decided to camp, and while Mawson took magnetic observations and theodolite angles, Mackay and I reconnoitered ahead for between two and three miles to see if there was any way at all practicable for the sledge out of these mazes of chasms, undulations, and séracs. Mackay and I were roped together for this exploratory work, and fell into about a score of crevasses before we returned to camp, though in this case we never actually fell with our head and shoulders below the lids of the crevasses, as they were mostly filled at the surface with tough snow. We had left a black signal flag on top of a conspicuous ice mound as a guide to us as to the whereabouts of the camp, and we found this a welcome beacon when we started to return, as it was by no means an easy task finding one's way across this storm tossed ice sea, even when one was only a mile or two from the camp. On our return we found that Mawson was just completing his observations. He found that the dip of the needle here was 2½° off the vertical. We brought the tent down from where he had been taking magnetic observations, and treading warily, because of crevasses, set it up again close to our sledge, and had lunch.

That afternoon we discussed the situation at some

length. It appeared that the Drygalski Glacier must be at least twenty miles in width. If we were to cross it along the course which we were now following at the rate of half a mile every half day it would obviously take at least twenty days to get to the other side, and this estimate did not allow for those unforeseen delays which experience by this time had taught us were sure to occur. The view which Mackay and I had obtained of the glacier ice ahead of us showed that our difficulties, for a considerable distance, would materially increase. Under these circumstances we were reluctantly forced to the conclusion that our only hope of ultimate success lay in retreat. We accordingly determined to drag the sledges back off the glacier on to the sea ice by the way along which we had come.

Early on the morning of December 2 the retreat began. Owing to the fog, there was some difficulty in picking up our old sledge tracks.

December 3. We were still traveling eastward parallel to southern edge of the glacier.

December 4. Reconnoitering expedition.

December 5. Mackay brought back to camp a most welcome addition to our larder—over 30 lb. of seal meat. To secure this he had made a long journey over the sea ice.

December 6. We left our camp on the south side of glacier, and struck across high ridges of blue ice into the small valley which we had prospected on December 4.

December 7 and 8. We were still struggling across this glacier.

December 9. The glacier ice kept cracking from time to time with sharp reports. Possibly this may have been due to the expansion of the ice under the influence of the hot sun (the temperature at midnight being as high as plus 19° F). At one spot the sledges had to be dragged up a grade of 1 in 3 over smooth blue glacier ice. Just before camping time Mackay sighted open water on the northern edge of the Drygalski Ice Barrier, from three to four miles away. It was now clear that we could not hope for sea ice over which to sledge westward to that part of the shore where we proposed to make our final depot before attempting the ascent of the great inland plateau in order to reach the Magnetic Pole.

December 10. We were much rejoiced at the end of the day's sledging to find ourselves at last off the true glacier type of surface, and on to a surface of the undulating barrier type. This improvement in the surface enabled us to steer westward. At first we had to incline to northwest to skirt some high ice ridges, and then we were able to go nearly due west.

December 11. We had a fine view of "Terra Nova" Bay, and as far as could be judged the edge of the Drygalski Ice Barrier on the north was now scarcely a mile distant. We were much surprised at the general appearance of the outline of the ice. It did not agree, as far as we could judge, with the shape of this region as shown on the Admiralty chart, and we could see no certain indication whatever of what was called, on the chart, "the low, sloping shore." Accordingly we halted a little earlier than usual in order to reconnoiter. There was a conspicuous ice mound about half a mile to the northwest of this camp. Mackay started off with the field glasses for a general look round from this point of vantage. Mawson started changing his plates in the sleeping bag, while I prepared to go out with my sketch book and get an outline panoramic view of the grand coast ranges now in sight. Crevasses of late had been so few and far between that I thought it was an unnecessary precaution to take my ice axe with me, but I had scarcely gone more than six yards from the tent when the lid of a crevasse suddenly collapsed under me at a point where there was absolutely no outward or visible sign of its existence, and let me down suddenly nearly up to my shoulders. I only saved myself from going right down by throwing my arms out and staying myself on the snow lid on either side. The lid was so rotten that I dared not make any move to extricate myself, or I might have been precipitated into the abyss. Fortunately Mawson was close at hand, and on my calling to him, he came out of our sleeping bag, and bringing an ice axe, chipped a hole in the firm ice on the edge of the crevasse nearest to me. He then inserted the chisel edge of the ice axe in the hole and, holding on to the pick point, swung the handle toward me: grasping this, I was able to extricate myself and climbed out on to the solid ice.

It was a beautiful day, the coastline showing up very finely, and I was able to get from the ice mound a sketch of the mountains. Mawson also took three photographs, making a panoramic view of this part of the coast. He was able, also, to get a valuable series of angles with the theodolite, which showed that the shape of the coastline here necessitated serious modification of the existing chart.

Far beyond the golden mountains to the north and west lay our goal, but as yet we knew not whether we were destined to fail or succeed. Meanwhile no time was to be lost in hurrying on and preparing for a dash on to the plateau, if we were to deserve success.

The following day, December 12, we sledged on for half a mile until we were a little to the west of the conspicuous ice mound previously described. We concluded that as this ice mound commanded such a general view of the surrounding country, it must itself be a conspicuous object to any one approaching the Drygalski Glacier by sea from the north; and so we decided that as there was still no trace of the "low, sloping shore" of the chart, and that as the spot at which we had now arrived was very near to the area so named on the chart, we would make our depot. We intended to leave at this depot one of our sledges with any spare equipment, a little food, and all our geological specimens, and proceed thence shoreward and inland with one sledge only. We estimated that we still had fully 220 miles to travel from this depot on the Drygalski Glacier to the Magnetic Pole. It was, therefore, necessary now to make preparations for a journey there and back of at least 440 miles. We thought that with detours the journey might possibly amount to 500 miles.

We could see, even from our distance of from twenty to thirty miles from the shoreline, that we had no light task before us in order to win a way on to the high inland plateau.

Our first business was to lay in a stock of provisions sufficient to last us for our 500 miles for further journeying. Mackay started for a small inlet about a mile and a half distant from our camp, where he found a number of seals and Emperor and Adelie penguins. He killed some seals and Emperor penguins, and loaded a good supply of seal steak, blubber, liver, and penguin steak and liver on to the sledge. In the course of his hunting, he fell through an ice bridge, at a tide crack, up to his waist in the water. Mawson and I went out to meet him when the sledge was loaded, and helped to drag it back to camp. We found it very hot in the tent, the weather being fine and sunny. It was delightful to be able at last to rest our weary limbs after the many weeks of painful toil over the sea ice and the Drygalski Glacier.

We started cooking our meat for the sledging trip on the following day, December 13, our intention being to take with us provisions for seven weeks, in addition to equipment, including scientific instruments, etc. We estimated that the total weight would amount to about 670 lb. We were doubtful, in our then stale and weakened condition, whether we should be able to pull such a load over the deep loose snow ahead of us, and then drag it up the steep ice slopes of the great glaciers which guarded the route to the plateau.

The sun was so hot that it started melting the fat out of our pemmican bags, so that the fat actually oozed through not only the canvas of the bags themselves, but also through the thick brown canvas of the large fortnightly foodbags, which formed a sort of tank for containing the pemmican bags, and we found it necessary at once to shade the foodbags from the sun by piling our Burberry garments over them. Leather straps, tar rope, tins, sledge harness, lamp black off the blubber cooker, warmed by the rays of the sun, all commenced to sink themselves more or less rapidly into the névé.

We unpacked and examined both sledges, and found that of the two, the runners of the Duff Sledge were the less damaged. As the result of the rough treatment to which it had recently been subjected, one of the iron brackets of this sledge was broken, but we replaced it with a sound one from the discarded Christmas Tree Sledge.

The following day, December 14, we were still busy

preparing for the great trek inland. Mackay was busy cooking Emperor penguin and seal meat for the plateau journey; Mawson was employed in transferring the scientific instrument boxes and the Venesta boxes in which our primus lamp and other light gear were packed from the Christmas Tree sledge on to the Duff sledge. He also scraped the runners of the sledge with pieces of broken glass in order to make their surfaces as smooth as possible. I was busy fixing up depot flags, writing letters to the Commander of the *Nimrod,* Lieutenant Shackleton, and my family, and fixing up a milk tin to serve as a post office on to the depot flagpole. When all our preparations were completed we drew the Christmas Tree sledge with some of our spare clothing, our blubber cooker, a biscuit tin with a few broken biscuits, and all our geological specimens to the top of the ice mound, about a quarter of a mile distant. On reaching the top of the mound we cut trenches with our ice axes in which to embed the runners of the sledge, fixed the runners in these grooves, piled the chipped ice on top, then lashed to the sledge, very carefully, the flagpole about six feet high, with the black flag displayed on the top of it. The wind blew keenly off the plateau before our labors were completed. We all felt quite sorry and downcast at parting with this sledge, which by this time seemed to us like a bit of home. We then returned to camp. Just previous to depoting this sledge, Mackay fixed another small depot flag close to the open sea a few yards back from the edge of the ice cliff.

Soon after we had turned into our sleeping bags, a gentle blizzard started to blow from west by south. This continued all night, increasing in intensity in the morning. We were able to see great whale backed clouds, very much like those with which we had been familiar over Mount Erebus, forming over Mount Nansen. As this blizzard wind was blowing partly against us, we decided that we would wait until it had either slackened off or decreased in force.

The blizzard continued till midnight of December 15–16, when its force markedly decreased. We breakfasted accordingly just after midnight. I dug out the sledge from the snow which had drifted over it, and

Mackay cached some seal meat in an adjoining ice
mound. At last, about 7 A.M., we made a start, and we
were delighted to find that, chiefly as the result of the
three days' rest in camp, we were able to pull our
sledge—weighing about 670 lb.—with comparative ease.
The snow, though soft, had become crusted over the
surface through the thaw brought on by the blizzard,
followed by freezing during the succeeding cold night.
The sledging was certainly heavy, but not nearly so dis-
tressing as that which we had recently experienced in
crossing the Drygalski Glacier. We steered toward the
great black nunatak midway between Mount Nansen and
Mount Larsen, as Mawson and Mackay both considered
that in this direction lay our chief hope of finding a practical route to the high plateau.

On December 17 we had a very interesting day. The
sledging was rather heavy, being chiefly over soft snow
and pie crust snow. It was difficult to decide sometimes
whether we were on fresh-water ice or on sea ice. Here
and there we crossed ice ridges, evidently pressure ridges
of some kind. These would be traversed by crevasses
which showed the ice in such places to be at least thirty
to forty feet in thickness. Close to our final camping
ground for the day was a long shallow valley or barranca; it was from one hundred and twenty to one hundred and thirty yards in width. The near side was steep,
though not too steep for us to have let our sledge down;
but the far side was precipitous, being bounded by an
overhanging cliff from twenty to thirty feet high. The
floor of this valley was deeply and heavily crevassed.
This sunken valley, therefore, formed a serious obstacle
to our advance.

While Mackay was preparing the hoosh Mawson traveled to the right, and I to the left along this valley seek-
ing for a possible crossing place. At last Mawson found
a narrow spot where there had been an ice bridge over
the valley, but this had become cracked through at the
center. It was nevertheless strong enough to bear our
sledge. Near this ice bridge Mawson stated that he noticed muddy material containing what appeared to be
foraminifera, squeezed up from below. The day had

been calm and clear, and we were able to get detailed sketches of this part of the coast range.

The following day we made for the ice bridge with our sledge, and found that the crack crossing it had opened to a width of eighteen inches during the night. The far side had become, too, somewhat higher than the near side. We had little difficulty in getting the sledge over, and after crossing several other cracks in the ice and névé without mishap, reached once more a fairly level surface.

At lunch time, soon after midnight, we reached some very interesting glacial moraines in the form of large to small blocks, mostly of eruptive rock, embedded in the ice. It was probable, from their general distribution, that they formed part of an old moraine of Mount Nansen, though now about fifteen miles in advance of the present glacier front. We collected a number of specimens from this moraine.

Fine rolls of cumulus clouds were gathering to our northeast. The day was calm with occasional gleams of sunshine. After the plateau wind had died down about 2 P.M. it commenced to snow a little, the snow coming from between southwest and west southwest.

At midnight on December 19 we started sledging in the falling snow, guided partly by the direction of the wind, partly by that of the pressure ridges and crevasses, occasionally taking compass bearings. Before we had gone far we reached a tide crack with open water three to four feet wide. There was also a width of about eighteen feet of recently formed thin ice at this tide crack. We tasted the water in this crack and found that it was distinctly salt. It was clear then that at this part of our journey we were traveling over sea ice. About half a mile further on we reached another open tide crack, and had to make a considerable detour in order to get over it. The surface of the ice was now thawing, and we trudged through a good deal of slushy snow, with here and there shallow pools of water as blue as the Blue Grotto of Capri. On the far side of this second tide crack, and beyond the blue pools, we reached a large pressure ridge forming a high and steep scarped slope barring our progress. Its height was about eighty feet.

There was nothing for it, if we were to go forward, but to drag our heavy sledge up this steep slope. It was extremely exhausting work, and we were forced to halt a few times, and had to take the sledge occasionally somewhat obliquely up the slope where it was very steep. In such cases the sledge frequently skidded. Our troubles were increased by the fact that this ice slope was traversed by numerous crevasses, which became longer and wider the further we advanced in this direction.

At last we got to the slope, only to see in the dim light that there were a succession of similar slopes ahead of us, becoming continually higher and steeper. The ice, too, became a perfect network of crevasses, some of which were partly open, but most of them covered over with snow lids. Suddenly, when crossing one of these snow lids, just as he was about to reach the firm ice on the other side, there was a slight crash and Mawson instantly disappeared from sight. Fortunately the toggle at the end of his sledge rope held, and he was left swinging in the empty space between the walls of the crevasse, being suspended by his harness attached to the sledge rope. Mackay and I hung on to the rope in case it should part at the toggle, where it was somewhat worn. Meanwhile, Mawson called out from below to pass him down the alpine rope. Leaving Mackay to keep hold of the toggle end of Mawson's harness rope, I hurried back to the sledge, which was about ten feet behind, and just as I was trying to disengage a coil of rope Mawson called out that he felt he was going. I ran back and helped Mackay to keep a strain on Mawson's harness rope. Mawson then said that he was all right. Probably at the time he felt he was going the rope had suddenly cut back through the lid of the crevasse and let him down for a distance of about a couple of feet. Altogether he was about eight feet down below the level of the snow lid. While I now held on to Mawson's harness rope Mackay hurried back to the sledge, and with his Swedish knife, cut the lashing around the alpine rope, and started uncoiling it, making a bowline at the end in which Mawson could put his foot. Meanwhile Mawson secured some ice crystals from the side of the crevasse, and threw them up for examination. The alpine rope having been lowered, Mawson put his foot in the bowline and got Mackay to haul his leg up as high as his bent knee would allow it to go, then, calling to him to hold tight the rope, Mawson, throwing the whole weight of his body on to it, raised himself about eighteen inches by means of his arms so as to be able to straighten his right leg. Meanwhile, I took in the slack of his harness rope. He then called to me to hold tight the harness rope, as he was going to rest his whole weight on that, so as to take the strain off the alpine rope. Mackay then was able to pull the alpine rope up about eighteen inches, which had the effect of bending up Mawson's right leg as before. Mackay then held fast the alpine rope, and Mawson again straightened himself up on it, resting his whole weight on that rope. Thus little by little he was hoisted up to the under surface of the snow lid, but as his harness rope had cut back a narrow groove in this snow lid several feet from where the snow gave way under him, Mawson now found his head and shoulders pressing against the under side of the snow lid, and had some difficulty in breaking through this in order to get his head out. At last the top of his head emerged, a sight for which Mackay and I were truly thankful, and presently he was able to get his arms up, and soon his body followed, and he got safely out on the near side of the crevasse. After this episode we were extra cautious in crossing the crevasses, but the ice was simply seamed with them. Twice when our sledge was being dragged up ice pressure ridges it rolled over sideways with one runner in a crevasse, and once the whole sledge all but disappeared into a crevasse, the snow lid of which had partly collapsed under its weight. Had it gone down completely it would certainly have dragged the three of us down with it, as it weighed nearly one-third of a ton. It was clear that these high pressure ridges and numerous crevasses were caused now, not by the Drygalski, but by the Nansen Glacier.

It was just commencing to snow, and wind was freshening from the southwest. We were now in a perfect labyrinth of crevasses and pressure ridges. Snow continued falling heavily accompanied by a blizzard wind, for the rest of that day and the whole of the succeeding night. Inside the tent we experienced some discomfort through the dripping of water caused by the thawing snow. As usual during a blizzard the temperature rose, and although the sun's heat rays were partly intercepted by the falling snow, quite sufficient warmth reached the side of the tent nearest the sun to produce this thaw. Pools of water lodged on the foot of our sleeping bag, but we were able to keep the head of it fairly dry by fixing up our Burberry blouses and trousers across the poles on the inside of the tent so as to make a temporary waterproof lining just above our heads. We were all thoroughly exhausted, and slept until about 7 A.M. the following day, December 20. By that time the snow had cleared, after about six inches had fallen.

December 20. After morning hoosh we held a council of war. The question was whether we should continue pulling on in the direction of the nunatak rising from the Mount Nansen Glacier, or whether we should retreat and try some other way which might lead us to the plateau. Mackay was in favor of hauling ahead over the Mount Nansen Glacier, while Mawson and I favored retreat, and trying a passage in some other direction.

At last we decided to retreat. Our fortunes now, so far as the possibility of reaching the Magnetic Pole were concerned, seemed at a low ebb. It was already December 20, and we knew that we had to be back at our depot on the Drygalski Glacier not later than February 1 or 2, if there was to be a reasonable chance of our being picked up by the *Nimrod.* We had not yet climbed more than 100 ft. or so above sea level, and even this little altitude was due to our having climbed ice pressure ridges, which from time to time dipped down again to sea level. We knew that we had to travel at least 480 to 500 miles before we could hope to get to the Magnetic Pole and back to our depot, and there remained only six weeks in which to accomplish this journey, and at the same time we would have to pioneer a road up to the high plateau. Now that everything was buried under soft snow it was clear that sledging would be far slower and more laborious than ever.

We started off to reconnoiter in a southwesterly direction with the intention of seeing whether the Mount Bellingshausen Glacier slope would be more practicable for our sledges than the Mount Nansen Glacier. We trudged through soft thawing snow with here and there shallow pools of water on the surface of the ice. This, of course, saturated our socks, which froze as the temperature fell during the night. After proceeding about two and a half miles we observed with the field glasses that the foot of the Mount Bellingshausen Glacier was not only steep but broken and rugged. We decided to examine what appeared to be a narrow stretch of snow mantling around the base of a granite mountain, one of the off-shoots from the Mount Larsen massif. After crossing much pressure ice and many crevasses, and floundering amongst the boulders of old moraines, we reached some shallow lakes of thawed snow near the junction between the sea ice and the foot of the snow slope for which we had been steering.

After paddling, unwillingly, in the shallow lakes, we reached the foot of what proved now to be not a snow slope but a small branch glacier. This was covered with a considerable depth of soft newly drifted snow, and we found the ascent in consequence very tiring as we sunk at each step in the soft snow over our knees. At last we attained an altitude of 1200 ft. above sea level, and were then high enough to see that the upper part of this branch glacier joined the Mount Bellingshausen Glacier at about 800 ft. higher and some half-mile further on. We were well pleased with this discovery, but as the glacier front ascended about 1500 ft. in less than a mile we did not look forward to the task of getting our heavy sledge up this steep slope, encumbered as it was with soft deep thawing snow.

On our return to the shoreline down the glacier slope we discovered that it was slightly crevassed in places, though not heavily so. At the foot of the glacier, and a short distance toward our camp, we found a moraine gravel. This was intermixed with a dark marine clay containing numerous remains of serpulae, pecten shells, bryozoa, foraminifera, etc., Mackay also found a perfect specimen of a solitary coral, allied to Deltocyathus, and also a Waldheimia. All these specimens were carefully preserved and brought into camp. While we were collecting these specimens we could hear the roar of many mountain torrents descending the steep granite slopes of the great mountain mass to the south of our branch glacier. Occasionally, too, we heard the boom and crash of an avalanche descending from the high mountain top. Such sounds were strange to our ears, accustomed so long to the almost perfect solitude and silence of the Antarctic, hitherto broken only by the bleating of baby seals and the call of the penguins.

Mawson discovered in another part of the moraine, nearer to our camp, a bright green mineral forming thin crusts on a very pretty quartz and felspar porphyry. These we decided to examine more carefully on the morrow. We were all thoroughly exhausted after the day's work, and Mackay had a rather bad attack of snow blindness. For some time after we got into the sleeping bag, and before we dozed off, we could still hear the intermittent roar of avalanches like the booming of distant artillery.

The following day, December 22, we picked our way with our sledge cautiously amongst the crevasses and over the pressure mounds, the traversing of which gave us some trouble in places, and eventually reached a fairly good track along the ice parallel to the moraine from which we had been collecting the day previous.

As we skirted the foot of the small branch glacier we noticed several small puffs of snow near the top angle of the snow slope which we proposed to escalade. Just as we were pulling our sledge to the foot of this slope the puff of wind with drift snow developed suddenly into a strong blizzard. We pulled in against this with great difficulty for half an hour, then camped at the foot of the slope.

We were able now to economize fuel, as we could bale the water out of these rock pools and streams for making our hoosh, tea, and cocoa. All that night the blizzard raged, and we thought any moment that the tent would be ripped up from top to bottom. It was getting very thin by this time and had already been frequently repaired by Mackay and Mawson.

December 24. About 7 A.M I got up and dug away the drift snow from the lee side of the tent, which was cramping our feet and legs, and found that it was still snowing heavily outside, and blowing hard as well. In the afternoon the blizzard slacked off somewhat, and the drift nearly ceased. We got up accordingly and had a meal. We halved our sledge load, repacked the sledge, and by dint of great exertions dragged it up the steep snow and ice slope to a height of 800 ft. above the sea. This was done in the teeth of a mild but freshening blizzard. The blizzard at last got too strong for us, so that we left the load at the altitude mentioned and returned back to our tent with the empty sledge.

Mackay's eyes, still suffering from the effects of snow blindness, were treated with a solution of thin tabloids (laminae) of sulphate of zinc and cocaine, with the result that his eyes were much better the following day, December 25. We started shortly before noon and commenced dragging up the second part of our load to the accompaniment of the music of murmuring streams. During our interval for lunch, Mawson was able to get some theodolite angles. We had the great satisfaction, when we turned in at 10 P.M. on Christmas Eve, to find that we were above the uncomfortable zone of thaw, and everything around us was once more crisp and dry, though cold. Our spirits, too, mounted with the altitude. We were now over 1200 ft. above sea level.

The following day, December 25, was Christmas Day. When I awoke, I noticed a pile of snow on top of the sleeping bag close to my head. At first, before I was fully awake, I imagined that it was the moisture condensed from Mawson's breath. Then I heard the gentle patter of snowflakes, and, on turning my head in the direction in which the rustling proceeded, saw that the wind had undermined the skirt of our tent, and was blowing the snow in through a small opening it had made. Accordingly, I slipped out and snowed up the skirt again, trampling the snow down firmly. A plateau wind was now blowing with almost blizzard force.

About two hours later we got up, and after some trouble with the primus lamp on account of the wind, had our breakfast, but as the wind was blowing dead against us, we turned into the sleeping bag for a short time. It was nearly noon before the wind died down, and we started off with our sledge, still relaying with half loads, the day being now beautifully clear and sunny. At the 1300 ft. level we started our sledge meter again, having lifted it off the ice while we were going up the steep slope. A little further on we were able to put the whole of our load again on to the sledge and so dispense with further relay work. This, too, was a great blessing.

When we arrived at our spot for camping that night we had the satisfaction of finding that we were over 2000 ft. above sea level, and that we had, in addition to the climbing, traveled that day about four miles. The plateau wind had almost gone, and once more we reveled in being not only high, but dry. Having no other kind of Christmas gift to offer, Mawson and I presented Mackay with some sennegrass for his pipe, his tobacco having long ago given out. We slept soundly that Christmas night.

On December 26 we observed dense dark snow clouds to the northeast, and a little light snow commenced to fall, but fortunately the weather cleared toward the afternoon. Mawson lost one of his blue sweaters off the sledge, but he and Mackay went back some distance and recovered it. Toward the afternoon we found it necessary to cross a number of fairly large crevasses. These were completely snowed over, and although we frequently fell through up to our knees, we had no serious trouble from them on this occasion. Some of them were from twenty to thirty feet in width, and it was fortunate for us that the snow lids were strong enough to carry safely the sledge and ourselves. Mackay suggested, for greater security, fastening the alpine rope around Mawson, who was in the lead, and securing the other end of it to the sledge. The rope was left just slack enough to admit of the strain of hauling being taken by the harness rope, hence Mawson had two strings to his bow in case of being suddenly precipitated into a crevasse. This was a good system, which we always adopted afterward in crossing heavily crevassed ice.

The following day, December 27, we decided to make a small depot of our ski boots (as by this time it appeared we were getting off the glacier ice on to hard snow and névé where we should not require them) and also of all our geological specimens, and about one day's food supply, together with a small quantity of oil—a supply for about two days in one of our oil cans. The following is a list of the provisions: Powdered cheese (enough for two meals), tea (for four meals), twenty-five lumps of sugar, hoosh for one meal, chocolate (for one and a half meals), twelve biscuits.

We also left an empty biscuit tin into which we crammed our ski boots, and our three ice axes, using one of them stuck upright as a staff for a small blue flag to mark the depot. Mawson took some good bearings with the prismatic compass, and we then proceeded on our way. This depot we called the Larsen Depot, as it was close to one of the southern spurs of Mount Larsen.

All eyes were now strained, as we advanced with our sledge, to see whether there was still any formidable range of mountains ahead of us barring our path to the plateau. At one time it seemed as though there was a high range in the dim distance, but a careful examination with the field glasses showed that this appearance was due only to clouds. Our joy and thankfulness were unbounded when we at last realized that apparently there was now a fairly easy ascent of hard névé and snow on to the plateau. That day we sledged a little over ten miles. During the night there was a very strong radiant in the sky from about southwest to northeast, with a movement of altro stratus cloud from northwest to southeast. Therefore, probably, this radiant was due to formation of great rolls of cloud curled over by the anti-trade wind as it pressed forward in a southeasterly direction. The rolls of clouds were distinctly curved convexly toward the southeast.

The following day, December 28, we traveled on north westward in thick cloudy weather, at first quite calm. At about 10 A.M. a breeze set in from the sea, spreading westward over the top of Mount Nansen over 8000 ft. above sea level. Above Nansen it met the upper current wind and was obviously deflected by it in a southeasterly direction. Meanwhile, in the direction of the coast the sky was very dark and lowering, and probably snow was falling there. Remarkable pillars of cloud formed over the Mount Larsen group. These were photographed by

Mawson. We passed over occasional patches of nearly bare glacier ice, alternating with stretches of hard névé. When we camped that evening we had sledged a little over ten miles, and a keen, cold wind was blowing gently off the high plateau to our west.

The following day, December 28, was clear, calm, and cold, and on December 30 Mounts Larsen and Bellingshausen were disappearing below the horizon, and several mountains were showing up clearly and sharply to the north of us, the principal peaks of which were at first identified by us as Mount New Zealand and Mount Queensland of Captain Scott's chart. Later Mawson concluded that the western of the two at any rate was new and unnamed.

There was still a strong plateau wind. We were now at an altitude of about 4500 ft. Once more, as in winter time, our breath froze into lumps of ice, cementing our Burberry helmets to our beards and mustaches. Our distance traveled was eleven miles, and we were still traveling on an upgrade, being now nearly 5000 ft. above sea level.

December 31. Mawson took a fresh set of magnetic observations. We camped for this purpose at the bottom of a wide undulation in the névé surface. We were disappointed at his announcement that he made out that the Magnetic Pole was further inland than had been originally estimated. What with the observations with the Lloyd-Creak dip circle, and the time occupied in repairing the rents in the tent, we ran ourselves somewhat short of time for our sledging that day, and did not camp until a little before midnight. We were still dragging the sledge on an upgrade; the surface was softer and more powdery than before, and the sastrugi heavier. Also we had been obliged to put ourselves on somewhat shorter rations than before, as we had to take one-eighth of our rations out in order to form an emergency food supply in the event of our journey to and from the Magnetic Pole proving longer than we originally anticipated.

That night, about a mile before reaching camp, we sighted to the west of us, much to our surprise, some distinct ice falls. This showed us that the snow desert over which we were traveling had still some kind of creeping movement in it. A skua gull came to visit us this New Year's Eve. He had been following us up for some time in the distance, mistaking us, perhaps, for seals crawling inland to die, as is not infrequently the habit of these animals. We were now about eighty miles inland from the nearest open water. The run for the day was about ten miles. We felt very much exhausted when we turned into our sleeping bag that night.

January 1, 1909 (New Year's Day), was a beautiful calm day with a very light gentle plateau wind, with fairly high temperature. The sky was festooned in the direction of Mount Nansen with delicate wispy cirrus clouds converging in a northeast direction. Mawson took observations for latitude and for magnetic deviation at noon. He made our latitude at noon to be 74° 18'. That night Mawson gave us a grand hoosh and a rich pot of cocoa in celebration of New Year's Day. We all thoroughly enjoyed this meal after our exhausting march.

On January 2 we noticed that the sastrugi were gradually swinging around into a direction a little north of west. The snow was frequently soft in large patches, which made sledging very heavy. We ascended altogether about 290 ft., but we crossed a large number of broad undulations, the troughs of which were from thirty to forty feet below their crests. These undulations considerably increased the work of sledging. We were much exhausted when the time came for camping. We were beginning to suffer, too, from hunger, and would have liked more to drink if we could have afforded it. We talked of what we would have drunk if we had had the chance. Mackay said he would have liked to drink a gallon of buttermilk straight off; Mawson would have preferred a big basin of cream; while I would have chosen several pots of the best coffee with plenty of hot milk.

We were still climbing on January 3, having ascended another 500 ft. It proved the heaviest day's sledging since we reached the plateau. The snow was still softer than on the previous day, and the surface was more undulating than ever, the troughs of the undulations being about fifty feet below the crests. The sastrugi themselves were from two to three feet in height. The crests of the large undulations were usually formed of hard snow, the strong winds having blown any loose material off them. This loose material had accumulated to some depth in the troughs, and hence made the wide patches of soft snow which made our sledge drag so heavily as we crossed them. By dint of great efforts we managed to finish our ten miles for that day.

The next day, January 4, we were pleased to find that there was less upgrade than on the previous day. We were now at an altitude of over 6000 ft., and found respiration in the cold, rarefied air distinctly trying. It was not that we suffered definitely from mountain sickness, but we felt weaker than usual as the result, no doubt, of the altitude combined with the cold. On the whole the sledging was a little easier today than the preceding day, and again we managed to do our ten miles.

On the morning of January 5 we found the sky thickly overcast, except to the south and the southeast where clear strips of blue were showing. We thought that snow was coming. The weather was perfectly calm, comparatively warm, but the light dull. We could still see the new inland mountain and Mount New Zealand distinctly. The sun was so oppressively hot when it peeped out from behind the clouds that one could feel it burning the skin on one's hands. We sledged ten miles.

January 6. Today the weather was gloriously fine. Bright, warm sunshine with a crisp, cold air in the early morning and the weather almost calm. The pulling was rather heavy during the afternoon; possibly the hot sun may have somewhat softened the surface of the snow. This morning I left off my crampons and put on a new pair of finnesko. These later proved somewhat slippery, and in falling heavily this afternoon over one of the sastrugi I slightly strained some muscles on the inner side of my left leg, just below the knee. This gave me a considerable amount of pain for the rest of the journey. Mackay lost all his stockings and socks off the bamboo pole of the sledge, but was fortunate enough to recover them after walking back over a mile on our tracks.

January 7. We were up at 5 A.M., when the temperature was minus 13°F. We were anxious to arrive at the end of our first five miles in good time for Mawson to get a meridian attitude, and take theodolite angles to the new mountain and Mount New Zealand, which were now almost disappearing from view below the horizon. Mawson made our latitude today 73° 43'. This was one of the coldest days we had as yet experienced on the plateau, the wind blowing from west by north. We all felt the pulling very much today, possibly because it was still slightly uphill, and probably partly on account of mountain lassitude. The distance traveled was ten miles.

Friday, January 8. Today, also, was bitterly cold. The wind blew very fresh for some little time before noon from a direction about west by north, raising much low drift. Our hands were frostbitten several times when packing up the sledge. The cold blizzard continued for the whole day. Mawson's right cheek was frostbitten, and also the top of my nose. The wind was blowing all the time at an angle of about 45° on the port bow of our sledge. We just managed to do our ten miles and were very thankful when the time came for camping.

The following day, January 9, a very cold plateau wind was still blowing, the horizon being hazy with low drift. We were now completely out of sight of any mountain ranges, and were toiling up and down amongst the huge billows of a snow sea. The silence and solitude were most impressive. About 10:30 A.M. a well marked parhelion, or mock sun, due to floating ice crystals in the air, made its appearance. It had the form of a wide halo with two mock suns at either extremity of the equator of the halo parallel to the horizon and passing through the real sun. Mawson was able to make his magnetic deviation observation with more comfort, as toward noon the wind slackened and the day became gloriously bright and clear. In the afternoon it fell calm.

We were feeling the pinch of hunger somewhat, and as usual our talk under these circumstances turned chiefly on restaurants, and the wonderfully elaborate dinners we would have when we returned to civilization. Again we accomplished our ten miles, and were now at an altitude of over 7000 ft.

January 10 was also a lovely day, warm and clear; the snow surface was good and we traveled quickly.

January 11. We were up about 7 A.M., the temperature

at that time being minus 12°F. It was a cold day, and we had a light wind nearly southerly. Mawson had a touch of snow blindness in his right eye. Both he and Mackay suffered much through the skin of their lips peeling off, leaving the raw flesh exposed. Mawson, particularly, experienced great difficulty every morning in getting his mouth opened, as his lips were firmly glued together by congealed blood.

That day we did eleven miles, the surface being fairly firm, and there being no appreciable general upgrade now, but only long ridged undulations, with sastrugi. We noticed that these sastrugi had now changed direction, and instead of trending from nearly west, or north of west, eastward, now came more from the southeast directed toward the northwest. This warned us that we might anticipate possibly strong head winds on our return journey, as our course at the time was being directed almost northwest, following from time to time the exact bearing of the horizontal magnetic compass. The compass was now very sluggish, in fact the theodolite compass would scarcely work at all. This pleased us a good deal, and at first we all wished more power to it: then amended the sentiment and wished less power to it. The sky was clear, and Mawson got good magnetic meridian observations by means of his very delicately balanced horizontal moving needle in his Brunton transit instrument.

January 12. The sky today was overcast, the night having been calm and cloudy. A few snowflakes and fine ice crystals were falling. We sledged today ten and three-quarter miles.

That evening, after hoosh, Mawson, on carefully analyzing the results set forth in the advance copy of the Discovery Expedition Magnetic Report, decided that although the matter was not expressly so stated, the Magnetic Pole, instead of moving easterly, as it had done in the interval between Sabine's observations in 1841 and the time of the *Discovery* expedition in 1902, was likely now to be traveling somewhat to the northwest. The results of dip readings taken at intervals earlier in the journey also agreed with this decision. It would be necessary, therefore, to travel farther in that direction than we had anticipated in order to reach our goal. This was extremely disquieting news, for all of us, as we had come almost to the limit of our provisions, after making allowance for enough to take us back on short rations to the coast. In spite of the anxiety of the situation, extreme weariness after sledging enabled us to catch some sleep.

The following morning, January 13, we were up about 6 A.M. A light snow was falling, and fine ice crystals made the sky hazy. There was a light wind blowing from about south southeast. About 8 A.M. the sun peeped through with promise of a fine day. We had had much discussion during and after breakfast as to our future movements. The change in the position of the Pole necessitated, of course, a change in our plans. Mawson carefully reviewed his observations as to the position of the Magnetic Pole, and decided that in order to reach it we would need to travel for another four days. The horizontally moving needle had now almost ceased to work. We decided to go on for another four days and started our sledging. It was a cold day with a light wind. The temperature at about 10:30 A.M. being minus 6°F. At noon Mawson took a magnetic reading with the Lloyd-Creak dip circle, which was now fifty minutes off the vertical, that is, 89° 10'. At noon the latitude was just about 73° South. That day we sledged thirteen miles.

January 14. The day was gloriously clear and bright with a warm sun. A gentle wind was blowing from about south southeast, and there was a little cumulus cloud far ahead of us over the horizon. The surface of the snow over which we were sledging was sparkling with large reconstructed ice crystals, about half an inch in width and one-sixteenth of an inch in thickness. These crystals form on this plateau during warm days when the sun's heat leads to a gentle upward streaming of the cold air with a small amount of moisture in it from beneath. Under these influences, combined with the thawing of the surface snow, these large and beautiful ice crystals form rapidly in a single day. The heavy runners of our sledge rustled gently as they crushed the crystals by the thousand. It seemed a sacrilege. Our run today was twelve miles one hundred fifty yards.

January 15. We were up today at 6 A.M. and found a cold southerly breeze blowing, the temperature being minus 19°F at 6:30 A.M. Mawson got a good latitude determination today, 72° 42'.

At about twenty minutes before true noon Mawson took magnetic observations with the dip circle, and found the angle now only fifteen minutes off the vertical, the dip being 89° 45'. We were very much rejoiced to find that we were now so close to the Magnetic Pole. The observations made by Bernacchi, during the two years of the *Discovery* expedition's sojourn at their winter quarters on Ross Island, showed that the amplitude of daily swing of the magnet was sometimes considerable. The compass, at a distance from the Pole, pointing in a slightly varying direction at different times of the day, indicates that the polar center executes a daily round of wanderings about its mean position. Mawson considered that we were now practically at the Magnetic Pole, and that if we were to wait for twenty-four hours taking constant observations at this spot the Pole would, probably, during that time, come vertically beneath us. We decided, however, to go on to the spot where he concluded the approximate mean position of the Magnetic Pole would lie. That evening the dip was 89° 48'. The run for the day was fourteen miles.

From the rapid rate at which the dip had been increasing recently, as well as from a comparison of Bernacchi's magnetic observations, Mawson estimated that we were now about thirteen miles distant from the probable mean position of the South Magnetic Pole. He stated that in order to accurately locate the mean position possibly a month of continuous observation would be needed, but that the position he indicated was now as close as we could locate it. We decided accordingly, after discussing the matter fully that night, to make a forced march of thirteen miles to the approximate mean position of the Pole on the following day, put up the flag there, and return eleven miles back on our tracks the same day. Our method of procedure on this journey of twenty-four miles is described in the journal of the following day.

Saturday, January 16. We were up at about 6 A.M., and after breakfast we pulled on our sledge for two miles. We then depoted all our heavy gear and equipment with the exception of the tent, sleeping bag, primus stove, and cooker, and a small quantity of food, all of which we placed on the sledge together with the legs of the dip circle and those of the theodolite to serve as marks. We pulled on for two miles and fixed up the legs of the dip circle to guide us back on our track, the compass moving in the horizontal plane being now useless for keeping us on our course. At two miles further we fixed up the legs of the theodolite, and two miles further put up our tent, and had a light lunch. We then walked five miles in the direction of the Magnetic Pole so as to place us in the mean position calculated for it by Mawson, 72° 25' South latitude, 155° 16' East longitude. Mawson placed his camera so as to focus the whole group, and arranged a trigger which could be released by means of a string held in our hands so as to make the exposure by means of the focal plane shutter. Meanwhile, Mackay and I fixed up the flagpole. We then bared our heads and hoisted the Union Jack at 3:30 P.M. with the words uttered by myself, in conformity with Lieutenant Shackleton's instructions, "I hereby take possession of this area now containing the Magnetic Pole for the British Empire." At the same time I fired the trigger of the camera by pulling the string. Thus the group were photographed in the manner shown on the plate. The blurred line connected with my right hand represents the part of the string in focus blown from side to side by the wind. Then we gave three cheers for his Majesty the King.

There was a pretty sky at the time to the north of us with low cumulus clouds, and we speculated at the time as to whether it was possible that an arm of the sea, such as would produce the moisture to form the cumulus, might not be very far distant. In view of our subsequent discovery of a deep indent in the coastline in a southerly direction beyond Cape North, it is possible that the sea at this point is at no very considerable distance.

The temperature at the time we hoisted the flag was exactly 0° F. It was an intense satisfaction and relief to all of us to feel that at last, after so many days of toil, hardship, and danger, we had been able to carry out our leader's instructions, and to fulfill the wish of Sir James Clarke Ross that the South Magnetic Pole should be actually reached, as he had already in 1831 reached the North Magnetic Pole. At the same time we were too utterly weary to be capable of any great amount of exultation. I am sure the feeling that was uppermost in all of us was one of devout and heartfelt thankfulness to the kind Providence which had so far guided our footsteps in safety to that goal. With a fervent "Thank God" we all did a right about turn, and as quick a march as tired limbs would allow back in the direction of our little green tent in the wilderness of snow.

It was a weary tramp back over the hard and high sastrugi, and we were very thankful when at last we saw a small dark cone, which we knew was our tent, rising from above the distant snow ridges. On reaching the tent we each had a little cocoa, a biscuit and a small lump of chocolate. We then sledged slowly and wearily back, picking up first the legs of the theodolite, then those of the dip circle. We finally reached our depot a little before 10 P.M.

In honor of the event we treated ourselves that night to a hoosh, which though modest was larger in volume than usual, and was immensely enjoyed. Mawson repacked the sledge after hoosh time, and we turned into the sleeping bag faint and weary, but happy with the great load of apprehension of possible failure, that had been hanging over us for so many weeks, at last removed from our minds. We all slept soundly after twenty-four miles of travel.

CHAPTER XXIII

The Return March
January 17 to February 5

March of 250 Miles back to our Depot on Drygalski Glacier:
Sugar in the Hoosh: A Question of Route: Ice Dongas:
Nearing the Coast: A Barranca: Severe Climbing: Our
Unhappy Lot: A Double Detonator: Mawson in a
Crevasse: Afternoon Tea on board the *Nimrod*

I CALLED the camp a little before 10 A.M. the following morning. We now discussed the situation and our chances of catching the *Nimrod,* if she came in search of us along the coast in the direction of our depot on the Drygalski Glacier. We had agreed, before we decided to do the extra four days' march to the shifted position of the Magnetic Pole, that on our return journey we would do not less than thirteen miles a day. At the Magnetic Pole we were fully 260 statute miles distant, as the skua flies, from our depot on the Drygalski Glacier. As we had returned eleven of these miles on the day previous, we still had 249 miles to cover. We accordingly decided to try and get back to our Drygalski depot by February 1. This gave us fifteen days. Consequently we would have to average sixteen and two-third miles a day in order to reach the coast in the time specified. This, of course, did not allow for any delay on account of blizzards, and we had seen from the evidence of the large sastrugi that blizzards of great violence must occasionally blow in these quarters, and from the direction of the sastrugi during our last few days' march it was clear that the dominant direction of the blizzard would be exactly in our teeth. The prospect, therefore, of reaching our depot in the specified time did not appear bright. Providentially we had most beautiful and glorious weather for our start on January 17. It remained fine for the whole day, and we were greatly favored by a light wind which now blew from between northwest and west northwest— a perfectly fair wind for our journey. In fact the wind changed direction with us. It had helped us by blowing from the southeast, just before we reached the Magnetic Pole, and now it was blowing in the opposite direction, helping us home. That day, in spite of the late start, we sledged sixteen miles.

On January 18 the weather again was fine, and we had a hard day's sledging. Unfortunately Mawson's left leg became very lame and pained him a good deal. Our run for the day was sixteen miles two hundred yards. This was the end of my week's cooking, and we were able to indulge that night in a fairly abundant hoosh, also in very milky and sweet cocoa, and Mackay admitted that he actually felt moderately full after it for the first time since we had left the Drygalski Depot.

The following day, January 19, we boiled the hypsometer at our camp, and found the level to be about 7350 ft. above the sea. The boiling point was 196.75° F. That morning we had quite an unusual diversion. Mawson, who is a bold culinary experimenter, being messman for the week, tried the experiment of surreptitiously introducing a lump of sugar into the pemmican. Mackay detected an unusual flavor in the hoosh, and cross questioned Mawson severely on the subject. Mawson admitted a lump of sugar. Mackay was thereupon roused to a high pitch of indignation, and stated that this awful state of affairs was the result of going out sledging with "two foreigners." We had a great struggle that day to make our sixteen miles, but we just managed it.

Owing to some miscalculation, for which I was responsible, we discovered that we had no tea for this week, our sixth week out, unless we took it out of the tea bag for the seventh week. Accordingly we halved the tea in the seventh week bag, and determined to collect our old tea bags at each of our old camps as we passed them, and boil these bags together with the small pittance of fresh tea. And here I may mention the tastes of the party in the matter of tea somewhat differed. Mackay liked his tea thoroughly well and long boiled, whereas Mawson and I liked it made by just bringing the water to the boil; as soon as we smelt the aroma of tea coming from underneath the outer lid of the cooker we used to shut off the primus lamp immediately and decant the tea into the pannikins. Mackay had always objected to this procedure when we were sledging along the sea ice where water boils at about 212° F; now, however, he had a strong scientific argument in his favor for keeping the pot boiling for a few minutes after the tea had been put in. He pointed out that at our present altitude water boiled at just over 196° F, a temperature which he maintained was insufficient to extract the proper juices and flavor from the tea, unless the boiling was very much prolonged. Mawson, however, averred—on chemical and physical grounds—that with the diminished atmospheric pressure certain virtuous constituents of the tea could be extracted at a lower temperature. The discussion was highly scientific and exhilarating, though not very finite. It was agreed as a compromise to allow the boiling to continue for three or four minutes after the water had come to the boil before the tea was poured out. As in our progress coastward we were continually coming upon more old tea bags at our old camps, and always collected these and did not throw away any that had been used before we soon had quite an imposing collection of muslin bags with old tea leaves, and with the thorough boiling that they now got there was a strong flavor of muslin super added to that of old tea. Nevertheless the drink was nectar.

January 20. We were still able today to follow our sledge tracks, which was a great blessing, the magnetic needle being of so little use to us. We had the wind slightly against us, bringing up a little low drift. Again we made our sixteen mile run, though with great difficulty, for the wind had been blowing freshly all day on our starboard bow.

In view of the good progress that we had made, and after carefully calculating out the provisions left over, Mawson, who was at this time messman, proposed that we should return to nearly full rations, as we were becoming much exhausted through insufficient food. This proposal was, of course, hailed with delight.

On January 21 there was a light wind with low temperature, clear sky and hot sun, which combined to consolidate the surface over which we were sledging. By this time Mackay and Mawson's raw lips, which had been cracked and bleeding for about a fortnight previously, were now much better. Mawson's lame leg had also improved. Again we did our sixteen mile run.

January 22. We were up soon after 7 A.M. It was a clear day with bright sunshine. The wind started soon after 5 A.M., constantly freshening, as it usually did in this part of the plateau, till about 3 P.M. Then it gradually died down by about 10 P.M. The temperature at 7:15 A.M. was minus 20° F, and at this altitude we found the wind very trying. Today we had to sledge over a great deal of pie crust snow, which was very fatiguing. We had since the day before yesterday lost our old sledge tracks. Today we sledged fifteen miles.

January 23. The weather was bright and cold with a light southerly wind. This day was very fatiguing, the sledging being over patches of soft snow and pie crust snow. At the same time we were conscious that although we were sledging up and down wide undulations we were on the whole going down hill, and the new mountain (first seen by Mackay on January 21) was already showing up as an impressive massif. The air was cold and piercing. Mawson's right leg was still painful. That night we were all very much exhausted, and were obliged to allow ourselves fully eight hours' sleep. Our run was sixteen miles.

January 24. Today we had more heavy sledging over a lot of pie crust snow and soft snow. The wind was blowing somewhat against us at about twelve miles an hour, the temperature being minus 4 F in the afternoon. A low drift was sweeping in waves over the snow desert; it was a desolate scene. Later in the day we were cheered by the sight of Mount Baxter.

Toward evening we had some discussion as to whether we were following approximately our old outgoing tracks. Mackay thought we were nearer to the new mountain than before, I thought we were farther southwest, Mawson, who was leading, contended that we were pretty well on our old course. Just then I discovered that we were actually on our old sledge tracks, which showed up plainly for a short distance between the newly formed sastrugi. This spoke volumes for Mawson's skill as a navigator. Distance sledged sixteen miles.

January 25. It was blowing a mild blizzard. We estimated at lunch time that we were about eighty and a half miles distant now from our Mount Larsen Depot. The temperature during the afternoon was minus 3° F. We all felt, as usual, much fatigued after the day's sledging. For the past four or five days we each took an Easton syrup tablet for the last stage but one before reaching camp, and this certainly helped to keep us going. This evening the blizzard died down about 8 P.M., and Mount Nansen was sighted just before we camped.

January 26. We lost our old sledge tracks again today. The weather turned cloudy in the afternoon, and the light was very bad. We now reached a surface of hard marble-like névé, which descended by short steep slopes. We did not at first realize that we were about to descend what we had termed the Ice Falls on the outward journey. Every now and then the sledge would take charge and rush down this marble staircase, bumping very heavily over the steps. Mawson and I frequently came heavy croppers. Mawson put on crampons outside his finnesko to enable him to get a grip of the slippery surface, but my crampons were frozen so hard and so out of shape that I was unable to get them on, so I followed behind and steadied the sledge as it continued bumping its way down the marble steps. At last we reached once more a flattened surface and camped. Our run for the day was fourteen and a half miles.

January 27. This morning we all felt very slack after the night spent in the closely covered sleeping bag, the sky at the time being cloudy. During the morning fine snow fell and the weather was quite thick to the south and east of us. Mawson steered us by the trend of the sastrugi. As the day wore on, the weather cleared up and we had a good view of the new mountain, Mount New Zealand, and Mount Baxter. The pulling at first was very hard, being uphill, but later we had a good run downhill to the spot where we camped for lunch. After lunch we sledged down a still steeper slope, the sledge occasionally taking charge. At this spot Mackay partially fell into a crevasse. Today we were much cheered by the sight at last of Mount Larsen. By the time we reached the spot where we camped that night we had a good clear view of Larsen. The distance traveled was sixteen miles. We were now only about forty miles from our Mount Larsen Depot.

January 28. We turned out of the sleeping bag today at about 6:30 A.M. A blizzard was blowing, and after breakfast we had much difficulty in the cold wind in getting up the mast and sail. Mackay, who usually did the greater part of this work, got his hands rather badly frostbitten before our preparations were completed. We used the thick green canvas floor cloth as a sail; the tent poles served us for a mast, and a piece of bamboo did duty as a yard.

The wind was blowing at, perhaps, about twenty-five miles an hour, and as soon as we started the sledge, it began to travel at such a hot pace that Mackay and Mawson, with their long legs, were kept walking at the top of their speed, while I, with my shorter ones, was kept on a jog trot. Occasionally, in an extra strong puff of wind, the sledge took charge. On one of these occasions it suddenly charged into me from behind, knocked my legs from under me, and nearly juggernauted me. I was quickly rescued from this undignified position under the sledge runners by Mawson and Mackay. We had now arrived at a part of the plateau where the monotonous level or gently undulating surface gave place to sharp descents. It was necessary in these cases for one of us to untoggle from the front of the sledge and to toggle on behind, so as to steer and steady it. About noon, when we were in full career, the bow of the sledge struck one of the high sastrugi obliquely and the sledge was capsized heavily, but fortunately nothing was broken. After righting the sledge, we camped for lunch.

At lunch, with a faint hope of softening the stern heart of our messman for the week—Mackay—and inducing him to give us an extra ration of food, I mildly informed him that it was my birthday. He took the hint and we all fared sumptuously at lunch and dinner that day. The day's run was twenty miles. It had been one of the most fatiguing days that we had as yet experienced, and we were all utterly exhausted when we turned into our sleeping bag at 8:30 P.M.

January 29. We were up at about 8 A.M., and found that the plateau wind was still blowing at a speed of about fifteen miles an hour. After our experience of the preceding day we decided that we would not make sail on the sledge, and as a matter of fact, found that pulling the sledge in the ordinary way was far less wearying than the sailing had proved the preceding day. We pulled on steadily hour after hour, and Mounts Nansen and Larsen grew every moment clearer and larger, and we began to hope that we might be able to reach our depot at Mount Larsen that night. But later in the day, Mawson's sprained leg caused him a good deal of pain, and we had almost decided to camp at a point nearly twenty miles from our preceding camp, when Mackay's sharp eyes sighted, at a distance of about a mile, our little blue flag, tied to the ice axe at our depot. We soon reached the depot, fixed up the tent, had a good hoosh, and turned into the sleeping bag past midnight.

We were up at 9 A.M. on January 30. The day was sunny, but ominous clouds were gathering overhead as well as to the south. After breakfast we collected the material at our depot, chiefly ski boots, ice axes, oil, a little food, and geological specimens, and loaded these on to our sledge. We found that, owing to the alternate thawing and freezing of the snow at our depot, our ski boots were almost filled with solid ice. The work of chipping out this ice proved a slow and tedious job, and we did not get started until about 11 A.M. Soon after we got going we found ourselves for a time in a meshwork of crevasses. These were from a foot up to about twenty feet in width.

After crossing a number of crevasses, we discovered that the wheel of our sledge meter had disappeared. Probably it had got into one of the crevasses, and gone to the bottom. As we were now so close to the end of our journey, the loss of this, which earlier in our travels would have been a serious disaster, was not of much importance. We had run about eight miles before we discovered the loss of our sledge meter wheel. At lunch time Mawson compounded a wonderful new hoosh made out of seal liver, pounded up with a geological hammer, and mixed with crushed biscuit.

We had some discussion as to whether it would be better to descend on to the sea ice by the old track up which we had come, which we termed Backstairs Passage, or make down the main Larsen Glacier to the point where it junctioned with the Drygalski Glacier. Mackay was in favor of the former, Mawson and I of the latter. Had we descended by our old route, we should have had to retrace our steps and become involved in a very arduous uphill piece of sledging necessitating an ascent of at least 1000 to 1500 ft. in a distance of a little over a mile. As subsequent events proved, Mackay was right and we were wrong.

We held on down the main glacier with the imposing cliffs and slopes of dark-red granite and blackish eruptive rock intermixed with it close on our left. Mawson's leg was now so bad that it was only with considerable pain and difficulty that he could proceed, and both Mackay's and my eyes were affected a good deal by snow blindness and were painful. We found as we advanced that at about six miles easterly from our lunch camp, the surface of the Mount Larsen Glacier descended at a very steep angle. Somewhat ahead to the right it was clear that, where it junctioned with the Drygalski Glacier, it was seamed by enormous crevasses and traversed by strong pressure ridges. We held on with our sledge on a course which took us close to the north side of the glacier. At last the descent became so steep that it was with the utmost difficulty that we could hold the sledge back and prevent its charging down the slope. We halted here and Mackay went ahead to reconnoiter. Presently he came back and said that the narrow strip of snow covering the glacier ice, near its contact with the rocky cliffs on our left, was continuous right down to the bottom of the slope, and he thought it was practicable, if we made rope brakes for the runners on our sledge, to lower it down this steep slope in safety. He fixed on some brakes of brown tarred rope by just twisting the rope spirally around the sledge runners. We then cautiously started the sledge down the steepest bit of the slope, all of us ready to let go in case the sledge took charge. The rope brake worked wonders, and it was even necessary to put a slight pull on the sledge in places in order to get it down the steep snow surface. We had left the great crevasses and ice falls near the junction of the

Mount Larsen and Drygalski Glaciers a little to our right.

We now found ourselves on an ice surface quite unlike anything which we had hitherto experienced. In the foreground were some small frozen lakes close to the foot of the granite hills; on the far side of the lakes were beautiful glacial moraines. All around the lakes, and for a considerable distance up the ice slopes descending toward them, the surface of the ice was formed of a series of large thin anastomosing curved plates of ice.

After sledging for a short distance over surfaces of this kind, sloping somewhat steeply to the small lakes, we decided to camp on the pale green ice of one of these lakes. Mawson tested this ice and found that it was strong enough to hold, though evidently of no great thickness. We sledged along this lake for a few hundred yards to its northeast end. There was a little snow here which would do for loading the skirt of our tent. By this time the sky was thickly overcast. We fixed up the tent, chopping little holes in the surface of the smooth ice, in which to socket the ends of the tent poles, and while Mackay cooked, Mawson and I snowed the skirt. This was subsequent to a little reconnoitering which we each did. It was 2 A.M. before we camped on the lake ice, and 4 A.M. before we turned into our sleeping bag.

January 31. We were up about 11 A.M., having slept soundly after the very exhausting work of our previous day's sledging. During the night it had snowed heavily, there being fully from three to four inches of newly fallen snow covering everything around us, and it was still snowing while we were having breakfast. After breakfast the snow nearly ceased, and we took half the load off our sledge and started with the remainder to try and work a passage out of the ice pressure ridges of the combined Drygalski and Larsen Glaciers on to the smoother sea ice, and eventually on to the Drygalski Ice Barrier. While Mawson and Mackay pulled, I steadied the sledge on the lower side in rounding the steep sidelings. We were still sledging over the leafy or tile ice, which mostly crunched underfoot with a sharp tinkling sound. We skirted the lateral moraine for a distance of over half a mile, following a depression in the ice surface apparently produced by a stream, the outlet of the waters of the small lakes. At one spot Mawson crashed right through into the water beneath, and got wet up to his thighs. In spite of my efforts to keep it on even keel, the sledge frequently capsizes on these steep sidelings. At last, after struggling up and down heavy slopes, and over low lying areas of rotten ice, which every here and there let us through into the water beneath, we arrived at the foot of an immense ice pressure ridge. It was a romantic looking spot, though at the time we did not exactly appreciate its beauties. To our left was a huge cliff of massive granite rising up steeply to heights of about 2000 ft. The combined pressure of the Drygalski and Mount Larsen Glaciers had forced the glacier ice up into great ridges, trending somewhat obliquely to the coast cliff.

We went back to the tent where we got some hot tea, of which Mawson, particularly, was very glad, as he was somewhat cooled down as the result of his wetting. Then we packed up the remainder of our belongings on the sledge and dragged it down to where we had dumped the half load on the near side of the pressure ridge. Mackay reconnoitered ahead, and found that the large pressure ridge, which appeared to bar our progress toward our depot, gradually came nearer and nearer in to the granite cliff, until it pressed hard against the cliff face. Obviously, then, we were impounded by this huge pressure ridge, and would have to devise some means of getting over it. Taking our ice axes we smoothed a passage across part of the ridge. This proved a very tough piece of work. We then unloaded the sledge and passed each one of our packages over by hand. Finally we dragged the sledge up and hoisted it over and and lowered it down safely on the other side. After this we reloaded the sledge and dragged it for some considerable distance over more of the leafy ice surface alternating with flattish depressions of rotten ice and snow, with water just beneath. We were now troubled, not only by the tile ice surface, but also by small channels with steep banks, apparently eroded by glacial streams which had been flowing, as the result of the thaw, while we were on the Magnetic Pole plateau. We were also worried from time to time as to how to get over the vast number of intersecting crevasses which lay in our path.

Little by little the surface improved as we sledged toward our depot. After lunch, the sledging surface, though still heavy, owing to the newly fallen snow, improved a little, but we soon found our progress barred by what may be termed an ice donga, apparently an old channel formed by a river of thaw water. We encountered three such dongas that afternoon. They were from a few feet up to fifty or a hundred feet or more in width, and from ten to twenty feet deep, and bounded by precipitous or overhanging sides.

After a considerable amount of reconnoitering by Mackay and Mawson, and often making considerable detours with our sledge, we managed to cross them. Our difficulties were increased by the innumerable crevasses and steep ice ridges. Some of these crevasses were open, while others were roofed over with tough snow. We fell into these crevasses from time to time, and on one occasion, Mackay and I fell into the same crevasse simultaneously, he up to his shoulders and I up to my waist. Fortunately we were able, by throwing out our arms, to prevent ourselves from falling right through the snow lid. While we were sledging on through the night amongst this network of crevasses, the sky became heavily overcast, and it commenced to snow. At last we succeeded in getting within less than a mile of the moraine containing the boulders of remarkable sphenediorite, specimens of which we had collected at that spot on our outward journey. Here we camped and turned into our sleeping bag at 7 A.M. on February 1.

It continued snowing heavily during the day, the fall being about six inches in depth. Mawson's sprained leg pained him a great deal. We estimated that we were now only about sixteen miles, as the skua flies, from our depot on the Drygalski Glacier, but as we had only two days' food left, it became imperative to push on without delay. We started sledging in the thick driving snow on the evening of February 1. The surface was covered with a layer of soft snow, nine inches in thickness, but in the drifts it was, of course, deeper. The work of sledging under these circumstances was excessively laborious and exhausting, and besides it was impossible to keep our proper course while the blizzard lasted. Accordingly, we camped at 8 P.M., and after our evening meal we rolled into our sleeping bag and slid into the dreamless sleep that comes to the worn and weary wanderer.

At 8 A.M. on February 2 we were rejoiced to find the sun shining in a clear sky. We intended making a desperate attempt this day to reach our depot, as we knew that the *Nimrod* would be due—perhaps overdue—by the night. We saw as we looked back that our track of yesterday was about as straight as a corkscrew. Once more we pulled out over the soft snow, and although refreshed somewhat by our good sleep we found the work extremely trying and toilsome. We crossed an ice donga, and about four miles out reached the edge of a second donga. Here we decided to leave everything but our sledge, tent, sleeping bag, cooking apparatus, oil and food, and make a forced march right on to the Drygalski Depot. Accordingly we camped, had tea and two biscuits each, and fixed up our depot, including the Lloyd Creak dip circle, theodolite and legs, geological collection, etc., and marked the spot with a little blue flag tied on to an ice axe.

We now found the sledge, thus lightened, distinctly easier to pull, and after making a slight detour, crossed the donga by a snow bridge. Soon we reached another donga, and successfully crossed it. At three and a half miles further at 8 P.M. we camped again and had a little cheese and biscuit. After this short halt we pulled on again, steering north 8° east magnetic. Mawson occasionally swept the horizon with our excellent field glasses in hopes of sighting our depot. Suddenly he exclaimed that he saw the depot flag distinctly on its ice mound, apparently about seven miles distant, but it was well around on the starboard bow of our sledge on a bearing of south 38° west magnetic. Mackay and I were much excited at Mawson's discovery. Mackay seized the field glasses as soon as Mawson put them down and directed them to the spot indicated, but could see no trace of the flag; then I looked through the glasses with equally negative results. Mawson opined that we must both be snow blind. Then he looked through them again, and at once exclaimed that he could see no trace of the flag now. The horizon seemed to be walloping up and down, just as though it was boiling, evidently the result of a mirage. Mawson, however, was so confident that he had seen the flag when he first looked, that we altered course to south 38° west magnetic, and after we had gone a little over a mile, and reached the top of a slight eminence in the ice surface, we were rejoiced to hear the announcement that he could now see the depot flag distinctly. We kept on sledging for several miles further. At midnight, when the temperature had fallen to zero, I felt that the big toe of my right foot was getting frost bitten. My ski boots had all day been filled with the soft snow and the warmth of my foot had thawed the snow, so that my socks were wet through; and now, since the springing up of the wind and the sudden fall in temperature, the water in the socks had turned to ice. So we halted, got up the tent, started the primus and prepared for a midnight meal, while, with Mawson's assistance, I got off my frozen ski boots and socks and restored the circulation in my toe, and put on some socks less icy than those I had just taken off.

We were much refreshed by our supper, and then started off again, thinking that at last we should reach our depot, or at all events, the small inlet a little over a mile distant from it, but "the best laid schemes of mice and men gang aft agley." There was an ominous white streak ahead of us with a dark streak just behind it, and we soon saw that this was due to a ravine or barranca in the snow and ice surface interposing itself between ourselves and our depot. We soon reached the near cliff of the barranca.

The barranca was about two hundred yards in width, and from thirty to forty feet deep. It was bound by a vertical cliff or very steeply inclined slope on the near side, the northwest side, and by an overhanging cliff festooned with stalactites on the southeast side. To the northeast a strip of dark seawater was visible between the walls of the barranca, which evidently communicated by a long narrow channel with the ocean outside, some three miles distant. Inland, the barranca extended for many miles as far as the eye could reach. The bottom

of the barranca immediately beneath us was floored with
sea ice covered with a few inches of snow. This ice was
traversed by large tide cracks, and we were much excited
to see that there were a number of seals and Emperor
penguins dotted over the ice floor. We determined to
try and cross the barranca. We looked up and down the
near cliff for a practicable spot where we could let down
our sledge, and soon found a suitable slope, a little to
the northeast of us, formed by a steep snow drift. We
sledged on to this spot, and making fast the alpine rope
to the bow of the sledge, lowered it cautiously, stern
first, to the bottom. The oil cans in the rear of the sledge
were rattled up somewhat when it struck bottom, but no
harm was done. At the bottom we had some trouble in
getting the sledge over the gaping tide cracks, some ten
to fifteen feet deep and three to five feet wide.

Arrived at the middle of the floor of the barranca,
Mackay killed two Emperor penguins, and took their
breasts and livers to replenish our exhausted larder.
Meanwhile, Mawson crossed to the far side of the floor
of the barranca on the lookout for a possible spot where
we might swarm up. I joined him a few minutes later,
and as I was feeling much exhausted after the continuous
forced marches back from the Magnetic Pole, asked him
to take over the leadership of the expedition. I considered that under the circumstances I was justified in taking this step. We had accomplished the work assigned
to us by our leader, having reached the Magnetic Pole.
We were within two or three miles of our Drygalski
Depot, and although the only food left there was two
days' supply of broken biscuits with a little cheese, we
had a good prospect of meat supply, as the barranca
abounded in seals and penguins, so that for the present
we had no reason to apprehend the danger of starvation.
On the other hand, as regards our ultimate personal
safety, our position was somewhat critical. We were not
even certain that the Nimrod had arrived at all in Ross
Sea that season, though we thought it, of course, very
probable that she had. In the next case, on the assump-
tion that she had arrived, it was very possible that in
view of the great difficulties of making a thorough search
along the two hundred miles of coast, at any part of

which we might have been camped—difficulties arising from heavy belts of pack ice and icebergs, as well as from the deeply indented character of that bold and rugged coast—it was quite possible that the *Nimrod* would miss sighting our depot flags altogether. In the event of the *Nimrod* not appearing within a few days, it would be necessary to take immediate and strenuous action with a view either to wintering at the spot, or with a view to an attempt to sledge back around the great mountain massifs and over the many steeply crevassed glaciers for over two hundred miles to our winter quarters at Cape Royds. Even now, in the event of some immediate strenuous action being necessary, if the *Nimrod* were to suddenly appear at some point along the coast, I thought it would be best for Mawson, who was less physically exhausted than myself, to be in charge. He had, throughout the whole journey, shown excellent capacity for leadership, fully justifying the opinion held of him by Lieutenant Shackleton when providing in my instructions that in event of anything happening to myself Mawson was to assume the leadership. When I spoke to him on the subject, he at first demurred, but finally said that he would act for a time, and would think the matter over at his leisure before definitely deciding to become permanently the leader. I offered to give him authority in writing as leader, but this he declined to receive.

Meanwhile, the examination of the cliff face on the southeast side of the barranca showed that there was one very difficult but apparently possible means of ascent. We returned to where we had left Mackay, and then we three dragged the sledge around to the edge of a rather formidable tide crack, behind which lay the mound of snow up which we hoped to climb; our idea being to unpack our sledge, drag it to the top of this steep mound, and, rearing it on end at the top of the mound, use it as a ladder for scaling the overhanging cliff above. Mackay managed to cross the tide crack, using the bamboo poles of our tent as a bridge, and after some difficulty, reached the top of the snow mound under the overhanging cliff. Much to our disappointment, however, he discovered that the mound was formed of very soft snow, his ice axe sinking in to the whole depth of the handle directly he placed it on top of the mound. It was obvious that as our sledge would sink in to at least an equal depth, the top of it would then be too short to enable any of us to scale the overhanging cliff by its means. We were, therefore, reluctantly compelled to drag our sledge back again over the tide cracks to the northwest side of the barranca down which we had previously lowered our sledge. We then discovered that, as in classical times, while the descent to Avernus was easy, it was difficult and toilsome to retrace one's steps. With Mawson ahead with the ice axe and towing rope, and Mackay and I on either side of the sledge in the rear, we managed by pulling and pushing together to force the sledge up a few inches at a time. At each short halt, Mawson would stick in the ice axe, take a turn of the leading rope around it, and support the sledge in this way for a brief interval while we all got our breath. At last the forty feet of steep slope was successfully negotiated, and we found ourselves once more on the level plain at the top of the barranca, but, of course, on the wrong side in reference to our depot. As we were within three miles of the open sea we thought it would be safe to camp here, as had the *Nimrod* sighted our depot flag and stood in to the coast, we could easily have hurried down to the entrance of the inlet and made signals to her.

We had now been up since 8 A.M. on the previous day, and were very thankful to be able to enter our tent, and have a meal off a stew of minced penguin liver. We then turned into the sleeping bag at about 7 A.M. Just about a quarter of an hour after we had turned in, as we learned later, the *Nimrod* must have passed, bound north toward Mount Melbourne, within three miles of the ice cliff on which our tent was now situated. Owing, however, to a light wind with snow drift, she was unable to sight either our depot flag or tent.

February 3. After sleeping in the bag from 7 A.M. until 11 A.M. we got up and had breakfast, packed our sledge, and started along the north bank of the snow canyon. The snow and ice at the bottom were dotted with basking seals and molting Emperor penguins. Fully a hundred seals could be counted in places in a distance of as many yards along the canyon. At about one mile from the camp we reached a small branch canyon, which we had to head off by turning to our right. We now proceeded about one and a half miles further along the edge of the main canyon, and in our then tired and weak state were much dispirited to find that it still trended inland for a considerable distance. We now halted by the sledge while Mackay went ahead to try and find a crossing, and presently Mawson and I were rejoiced to hear him shout that he had discovered a snow bridge across the canyon. Presently he rejoined us, and together we pulled the sledge to the head of the snow bridge. It was a romantic spot. A large slice of the snow or névé cliff had fallen obliquely across the canyon, and its surface had then been raised and partially leveled up with soft drift snow. There was a crevasse at both the near and far ends of the bridge, and the middle was sunk a good deal below the abutments. Stepping over the crevasse at the near end, we launched the sledge with a run down to the center of the bridge, then struggled up the steep slope facing us, Mackay steadying the sledge from falling off the narrow causeway, while we all three pulled for all we were worth. In another minute or two we were safely across with our sledge, thankful that we had now surmounted the last obstacle that intervened between us and our depot.

While heading for the depot we sighted an Emperor penguin close to our track. Mackay quickly slew him, and took his flesh and liver for our cooking pot. Two miles further on we camped. Mawson minced the Emperor's flesh and liver, and after adding a little snow, I boiled it over our primus so as to make one and a half pots of soupy mincemeat for each of us. This was the most satisfying meal we had had for many a long day. After lunch we sledged on for over one and a half miles further toward the depot, and at about 10:30 P.M. reached an ice mound on the south side of the inlet in which the snow canyon terminated seawards. This camping spot was a little over a mile distant from our depot. We were now all thoroughly exhausted and decided to camp. The spot we had selected seemed specially suitable, as from the adjacent ice mound we could get a good view of the ocean beyond the Drygalski Barrier. While Mawson and I got up the tent, Mackay went to kill a seal at the shore of the inlet. He soon returned with plenty of seal meat and liver. He said that he had found two young seals, and had killed one of them; that they had both behaved in a most unusual manner, scuttling away quickly and actively at his approach, instead of waiting without moving, as did most of the Weddell seals, of which we had hitherto had experience. We discovered later that these two seals belonged to the comparatively rare variety known as Ross seal. After a delicious meal of seal blubber, blood, and oil, with fried meal and liver, cooked by Mawson, Mawson and I turned into the sleeping bag, leaving Mackay to take the first of our four hour watches on the lookout for the *Nimrod*. During his watch he walked up to our depot and dug out our biscuit tin, which had served us as a blubber lamp and cooker, together with the cut down paraffin tin which we had used as a frying pan. Both these he carried down to our tent. There he lit the blubber lamp just outside the tent and cooked some penguin meat, regaling himself at intervals, during his four hours' watch, with dainty morsels from the savory dish. When he called me up at 4 A.M. I found that he had thoughtfully put into the frying pan a junk of Emperor's breast, weighing about two pounds, for me to toy with during my watch. A chilly wind was blowing off the plateau and I was truly thankful for an occasional nibble at the hot penguin meat. After cooking some more penguin meat I called up Mawson soon after 8 A.M. on February 4, and immediately afterward turned into the bag, and at once dropped off sound asleep.

Mawson did not call Mackay and myself until after 2 P.M. We at once rolled up the sleeping bag, and Mawson cooked a generous meal of seal and penguin meat and blubber, while Mackay made a thin soupy broth on the primus. Meanwhile, I went on to the ice mound with the field glasses, but could see nothing in the way of a ship to seaward and returned to the tent. We all thoroughly enjoyed our liberal repast, and particularly relished the seal's blood, gravy, and seal oil.

After the meal we discussed our future plans. We decided that we had better move the tent that afternoon up to our old depot, where it would be a conspicuous object from the sea, and where, too, we could command a more extensive view of the ocean. We also talked over what we had best do in the event of the *Nimrod* not turning up, and decided that we ought to attempt to sledge overland to Hut Point, keeping ourselves alive on the way, as best we might, with seal meat. It must be admitted that the prospect of tackling two hundred miles of coast, formed largely of steep rocky foreshores, alternating with heavily crevassed glacier ice, was not a very bright one. We also discussed the date at which we ought to start trekking southward. Mackay thought we ought to commence making our preparations at once, and that unless the *Nimrod* arrived within a few days we ought to start down the coast with our sledge, tent, sleeping bag, cooker, and seal meat, leaving a note at the depot for the *Nimrod*, in case she should arrive later, asking her to look out for us along the coast, and if she couldn't sight us, to lay depots of food and oil for us at certain specified spots. He considered that by this method we could make sure of beginning the long journey in a sound state of health and, if fortunate, might reach Hut Point before the beginning of the equinoctial gales in March. Mawson and I, on the other hand, thought that we ought to wait on at our present camp until late in February.

From whatever point of view we looked at it, our present lot was not a happy one. The possibility of a long wait in the gloomy region of the Drygalski Glacier, with its frequent heavy snows at this season of the year, and leaden sky vaulted over the dark sea, was not pleasing to contemplate. Still less cheerful was the prospect of a long, tedious, and dangerous sledge journey toward Hut Point. Even the diet of seal and penguin, just for the moment so nice, largely because novel, would soon savor of *toujours perdrix*.

Dispirited by forebodings of much toil and trouble, we were just preparing to set our weary limbs in motion to pack up our belongings for the short trek up to the depot, when Bang! went something, seemingly close to the door of our tent; the sound thrilled us; in another instant the air reverberated with a big boom! much louder than the first sound. Mawson gave tongue first, roaring out, "A gun from the ship!" and dived for the tent door. As the latter was narrow and funnel shaped there was for the moment some congestion of traffic. I dashed my head forward to where I saw a small opening, only in time to receive a few kicks from the departing Mawson. Just as I was recovering my equilibrium, Mackay made a wild charge, rode me down, and trampled over my prostrate body. When at length I struggled to my feet, Mawson had got a lead of a hundred yards and Mackay of about fifty. "Bring something to wave," shouted Mawson, and I rushed back to the tent and seized Mackay's rucksack. As I ran forward this time, what a sight met my gaze. There was the dear old *Nimrod,* not a quarter of a mile away, steaming straight toward us up the inlet, her bows just rounding the entrance. At the sight of the three of us running frantically to meet the ship, hearty ringing cheers burst forth from all on board. How those cheers stirred every fiber of one's being! It would be hard, indeed, for any one, not situated as we had been, to realize the sudden revulsion of our feelings. In a moment, as dramatic as it was heavenly, we seemed to have passed from death into life. My first feelings were of intense relief and joy; then of fervent gratitude to the kind Providence which had so mercifully led our friends to our deliverance.

A sudden shout from Mackay called me back to earth, "Mawson's fallen into a deep crevasse. Look out, it's just in front of you!" I then saw that Mackay was kneeling on the snow near the edge of a small oblong sapphire blue hole in the névé. "Are you all right, Mawson?" he sang out, and from the depth came up the welcome word, "Yes." Mackay then told me that Mawson was about twenty feet down the crevasse. We decided to try and pull him up with the sledge harness, and hurried back to the sledge, untoggled the harness, ran back with it to the crevasse, and let one end down to Mawson. We found, however, that our combined strength was insufficient to pull him up, and that there was a risk, too, of the snow lid at the surface falling in on Mawson, if weight was put upon it, unless it was strengthened with some planking. Accordingly, we gave up the attempt to haul Mawson up, and while I remained at the crevasse holding one end of the sledge harness Mackay hurried off for help to the *Nimrod,* which was now berthing alongside the south wall of the inlet, about two hundred yards distant. Mackay shouted to those on board, "Mawson has fallen down a crevasse, and we got to the Magnetic Pole." The accident had taken place so suddenly that those on board had not realized in the least what had happened. A clear, firm, cheery voice, that was strange to me, was now heard issuing prompt orders for a rescue party. Almost in less time than it takes to write it, officers and sailors were swarming over the bows of the *Nimrod,* and dropping on to the ice barrier beneath. I called down to Mawson that help was at hand. He said that he was quite comfortable at present; that there was sea water at the bottom of the crevasse, but that he had been able to sustain himself a couple of feet above it on the small ledge that had arrested his fall. Meanwhile, the rescue party, headed by the first officer of the *Nimrod,* J. K. Davis, had arrived on the scene. The crevasse was bridged with a suitable piece of sawn timber, and Davis, with that spirit of thoroughness which characterizes all his work, promptly had himself lowered down the crevasse. On reaching the bottom he transferred the rope by which he had been lowered to Mawson, and with a long pull and a strong pull and a pull altogether, the company of the *Nimrod* soon had Mawson safe on top, none the worse for the accident with an exception that his back was slightly bruised. As soon as the rope was cast free from Mawson, it was let down again for Davis, and presently he, too, was safely on top.

And now we had a moment of leisure to see who constituted the rescue party. There were the dear old faces so well known on our voyage together the previous year, and interspersed with them were a few new faces. Here were our old comrades, Armytage and Brocklehurst, Dr. Michell, Harbord (the officer who—as we learned later—had sighted our depot flag), our good stewards Ansell and Ellis, the genial boatswain Cheetham, Paton, and a number of others. What a joyous grasping of hands and hearty all-around welcoming followed. Foremost among them all to welcome us was Captain Evans, who had commanded the S.S. *Koonya,* which towed the *Nimrod* from Lyttleton to beyond the Antarctic Circle, and it goes without saying that the fact that the *Nimrod* was now in the command of a master of such experience, so well and favorably known in the shipping world of New Zealand and Australia, gave us the greatest satisfaction. He hastened to assure me of the safety and good health of my wife and family. While willing hands packed up our sledge, tent, and other belongings, Captain Evans walked with us to the rope ladder hanging over the bows of the *Nimrod.*

Quickly as all this had taken place, Mackay had already found time to secure a pipe and some tobacco from one of our crew, and was now puffing away to his heart's content. We were soon all on the deck of the *Nimrod* once more, and were immediately stood up in a row to be photographed. As soon as the cameras had worked their wicked will upon us, for we were a sorry sight, our friends hurried us off for afternoon tea. After our one hundred twenty-two days of hard toil over the sea ice of the coast and the great snow desert of the hinterland, the little ship seemed to us as luxurious as an ocean liner. To find oneself seated once more in a comfortable chair, and to be served with new made bread, fresh butter, cake, and tea, was Elysium.

We heard of the narrow escape of Armytage, Priestley, and Brocklehurst, when they were being carried out to sea, with only two days' provisions, on a small ice floe surrounded by killer whales; and how, just after the momentary grounding of the floe, they were all just able to leap ashore at a spot where they were picked up later by the *Nimrod.* We also heard the extraordinary adventures and escape of Mackintosh and MacGillan in their forced march overland, without tent or sleeping bag, from Mount Bird to Cape Royds; of the departure of the supporting party to meet the Southern Party; and, in short, of all the doings at Cape Royds and on the *Nimrod* since we had last heard any news. Pleasantly the buzz of our friends' voices blended itself with the gentle fizzing of steam from the *Nimrod*'s boiler, and surely since the days of John Gilpin "were never folk so glad" as were we three.

After afternoon tea came the joy of reading the home letters, and finding that the news was good. Later we three had a novel experience, the first real wash for over four months. After much diligent work with hot water, soap, and towel, some of the outer casing of dirt was removed, and bits of our real selves began to show through the covering of seal oil and soot. Dinner followed at 6 P.M., and it is scarcely necessary to add that, with our raging appetites and all the new types of dainty food around us, we overate ourselves. This did not prevent us from partaking liberally of hot cocoa and gingerbread biscuits before turning in at 10 P.M. None but those whose bed for months has been on snow and ice can realize the luxury of a real bunk, blankets, and pillow, in a snug little cabin. A few minutes' happy reverie preceded sound sleep. At last our toilsome march was over, the work that had been given us to do was done, and done just in the nick of time; the safety of those nearest and dearest to us was assured, and we could now lay down our weary limbs to rest.

Under Providence one felt one owed one's life to the patient and thorough search, sound judgment, and fine seamanship of Captain Evans, and the devotion to duty of his officers and crew: and no pen can describe how that night one's heart overflowed with thankfulness for all the blessings of that day. One's last thought in the twilight that comes between wakefulness and sleep is expressed in the words of our favorite record on the gramophone, the hymn so grandly sung by Evan Williams:

"So long Thy power hath blest me, sure it still will
lead me on."

A Brief Retrospect

IF one may be permitted to take a brief retrospect of our journey, the following considerations present themselves: The total distance traveled from Cape Royds to the Magnetic Pole and back to our depot on the Drygalski Glacier was about 1260 miles. Of this, 740 miles was relay work, and we dragged a weight of, at first, a little over half a ton, and finally somewhat under half a ton for the whole of this distance. For the remaining 520 miles from the Drygalski Depot to the Magnetic Pole and back we dragged a weight, at first, of 670 lb., but this finally became reduced to about 450 lb., owing to consumption of food and oil, by the time that we returned to our depot.

We were absent on our sledge journey for one hundred twenty-two days, of which five days were spent in our tent during heavy blizzards, and five days partly in experimenting in cooking with blubber and partly in preparing supplies of seal meat for the journey from the sea ice over the high plateau, and three days in addition were taken up in reconnoitering, taking magnetic observations, etc. We therefore covered this distance of 1260 miles in 109 traveling days, an average of about eleven and a half miles a day.

We had laid two depots before our final start, but as these were distant only ten miles and fifteen miles respectively from our winter quarters, they did not materially help us. We had no supporting party, and with the exception of help from the motorcar in laying out these short depots, we pulled the sledges for the whole distance without assistance except, on rare occasions, from the wind.

The traveling over the sea ice was at first pretty good,

but from Cape Bernacchi to the Nordenskjold Ice Barrier we were much hampered by screwed pack ice with accompanying high and hard snow ridges. Toward the latter part of October and during November and part of December the thawing surface of saline snow, clogging and otherwise impeding our runners, made the work of sledging extremely laborious. Moreover, on the sea ice—especially toward the last part of our journey over it—we had ever present the risk of a blizzard breaking the ice up suddenly all around us, and drifting us out to sea. There can be no doubt, in view of the wide lanes of open water in the sea ice on the south side of the Drygalski Glacier, when we reached it on November 30, that we got to *glacies firma* only in the nick of time.

Then there was the formidable obstacle of the Drygalski Glacier, with its wide and deep chasms, its steep ridges and crevasses, the passage of this glacier proving so difficult that, although only a little over twenty miles in width, it took us a fortnight to get across. On the far side of the Drygalski was the open sea forcing us to travel shoreward over the glacier surface. Then had come the difficult task of pioneering a way up to the high plateau—the attempt to force a passage up the Mount Nansen Glacier—our narrow escapes from having our sledge engulfed in crevasses—the heavy blizzard with deep new fallen snow and then our retreat from that region of high pressure ridges and crevasse entanglements—our abandonment of the proposed route up the snout of the Bellingshausen Glacier, and finally our successful ascent up the small tributary glacier, the "backstairs passage," to the south of Mount Larsen.

On the high plateau were: the difficulty of respiration, biting winds with low temperatures, difficult sledging—sometimes against blizzards—over broad undulations and high sastrugi, the cracking of our lips, fingers, and feet, exhaustion from insufficient rations, disappointment at finding that the Magnetic Pole had shifted further inland than the position previously assigned to it. Then, after we had just succeeded by dint of great efforts in reaching the Pole of verticity, came the necessity for forced marches, with our sledge, of from sixteen to twenty miles a day in order to reach the coast with any reasonable prospect of our being picked up by the *Nimrod*.

Then came our choice of the difficult route down the snout of the Bellingshausen Glacier, and our consequent difficulties in surmounting the ice pressure ridges; then the difficulty of sledging over the "tile ice" surface, the opposing ice barrancas formed by the thaw water while we were on the high plateau; the final heavy snow blizzard; our loss of direction when sledging in bad light and falling snow, and finally our arrest by the deep barranca of what afterward was known as Relief Inlet.

But ours were not the only, nor the greatest, difficulties connected with our journey. There were many disappointments, dangers, and hardships for the captain, officers, and crew of the *Nimrod* in their search for us along that two hundred miles of desolate and, for the great part, inaccessible coastline. How often black spots ashore, proving on nearer view to be seals or penguins, had been mistaken for depot flags; how often the glint of sunlight off brightly reflecting facets of ice had been thought to be "helios," only the disappointed ones can tell; how often, too, the ship was all but aground, at other times all but beset in the ice pack in the efforts to get a clearer view of the shoreline in order to discover our depot! This is a tale that the brave men who risked their lives to save ours will scorn to tell, but it is nevertheless true.

As the result of our journey to the Magnetic Pole and back, Mawson was able to join up in his continuous triangulation survey, Mount Erebus with Mount Melbourne, and to show with approximate accuracy the outline of the coastline, and the position and height of several new mountains. He and I obtained geological collections, sketches, and notes—especially on glacial geology—along the coastline, and he also took a series of photographs; while Mackay determined our altitudes on the plateau by means of the hypsometer. Mawson also made magnetic determinations, and I was able to gather some meteorological information.

Unfortunately the time available during our journey was too short for detailed magnetic, geological, or meteorological observations. Nevertheless, we trust that the information obtained has justified the journey. At all events we have pioneered a route to the Magnetic Pole, and we hope that the path thus found will prove of use to future observers.

It is easy, of course, to be wise after the event, but there is no doubt that had we known that there was going to be an abundance of seals all along the coast, and had we had an efficient team of dogs, we could have accomplished our journey in probably half the time that it actually occupied. Future expeditions to the South Magnetic Pole would probably do well to land a strong and well equipped party, either at Relief Inlet or, better, as near to Backstairs Passage as the ship can be taken, and as early in December as the state of the sea ice makes navigation possible. A party of three, with a supporting party also of three, with good dog teams and plenty of fresh seal meat, could travel together for about seventy miles inland; then the supporting party might diverge and ascend Mount Nansen from its inland extremity. The other party, meanwhile, might proceed to the Magnetic Pole at not less than fifteen miles a day. This should admit of their spending from a week to a fortnight at the Pole, and they should then be able to return to the coast early in February. Meanwhile, there would be plenty of scope for a third party to explore the foothills of Mount Larsen and Mount Nansen, search and map their wonderful moraines, and examine the deeply indented rocky coastline from Nansen to the—as yet untrodden—volcano Mount Melbourne.

CHAPTER XXV

All Aboard: The Return to New Zealand

An Oar Breaks: Disaster Averted: Last View of Winter
Quarters: Supplies left at Cape Royds: New Coastline:
Anchored at Mouth of Lord's River, Stewart Island,
March 22: Arrived Lyttelton, March 25, 1909

THE *Nimrod,* with the members of the Northern Party aboard, got back to the winter quarters on February 11 and landed Mawson. The hut party at this period consisted of Murray, Priestley, Mawson, Day, and Roberts. No news had been heard of the Southern Party, and the depot party, commanded by Joyce, was still out. The ship lay under Glacier Tongue most of the time, making occasional visits to Hut Point in case some of the men should have returned. On February 20 it was found that the depot party had reached Hut Point, and had not seen the Southern Party. The temperature was becoming lower, and the blizzards were more frequent.

The instructions left by me had provided that if we had not returned by February 25, a party was to be landed at Hut Point, with a team of dogs, and on March 1 a search party was to go south. In connection with the landing party, Murray showed Captain Evans my full instructions that the party was to be landed on the 25th, and on this being understood the *Nimrod* left Cape Royds on the 21st with the party, whilst Murray remained in charge at Cape Royds, which was now cut off by sea from Hut Point. Murray was in no way responsible for the failure of that party to be landed, and this is a point I did not make clear in the first edition of my book; it is therefore due to Murray to make this explanation. All arrangements being completed, most of the members of the expedition then on board went ashore at Cape Royds to get the last of their property packed ready for departure. The ship was lying under Glacier Tongue when I arrived at Hut Point with Wild on February 28 and after I had been landed with the relief party in order to bring in Adams and Marshall, it proceeded to Cape Royds in order to take on board the remaining members of the shore party and some specimens and stores.

The *Nimrod* anchored a short distance from the shore, and two boats were launched. The only spot convenient for embarkation near the ship's anchorage was at a low ice cliff in Backdoor Bay. Everything had to be lowered by ropes over the cliff into the boats. Some hours were spent in taking on board the last of the collections, the private property, and various stores.

A stiff breeze was blowing, making work with the boats difficult, but by 6 A.M. on March 2 there remained to be taken on board only the men and dogs. The operation of lowering the dogs one by one into the boats was necessarily slow, and while it was in progress the wind freshened to blizzard force, and the sea began to run dangerously. The waves had deeply undercut the ice cliff, leaving a projecting shelf. One boat, in charge of Davis, succeeded in reaching the ship, but a second boat, commanded by Harbord, was less fortunate. It was heavily loaded with twelve men and a number of dogs, and before it had proceeded many yards from the shore an oar broke. The *Nimrod* was forced to slip her moorings and steam out of the bay, as the storm had become so severe that she was in danger of dragging her anchors and going on the rocks. An attempt to float a buoy to the boat was not successful, and for some time Harbord and the men with him were in danger. They could not get out of the bay owing to the force of the sea, and the projecting shelf of ice threatened disaster if they approached the shore. The flying spray had encased the men in ice, and their hands were numb and half frozen. At the end of an hour they managed to make fast to a line stretched from an anchor a few yards from the cliff, the men who had remained on shore pulling this line taut. The position was still dangerous, but all the men and dogs were hauled up the slippery ice face into safety before the boat sank. Hot drinks were soon ready in the hut, and the men dried their clothes as best they could before the fire. Nearly all the bedding had been sent on board, and the temperature was low, but they were thankful to have escaped with their lives.

The weather was bitter on the following morning (March 3), and the *Nimrod,* which had been sheltering under Glacier Tongue, came back to Cape Royds. A heavy sea was still running, but a new landing place was selected in the shelter of the cape, and all the men and dogs were got aboard. The ship went back to the Glacier Tongue anchorage to wait for the relief party.

About ten o'clock that night Mackintosh was walking the deck engaged in conversation with some other members of the expedition. Suddenly he became excited and said, "I feel that Shackleton has arrived at Hut Point." He was very anxious that the ship should go up to the Point, but nobody gave much attention to him. Then Dunlop advised him to go up to the crow's nest if he was sure about it, and look for a signal. Mackintosh went aloft, and immediately saw our flare at Hut Point. The ship at once left for Hut Point, reaching it at midnight, and by 2 A.M. on March 4 the entire expedition was safe on board.

There was now no time to be lost if we were to attempt to complete our work. The season was far advanced, and the condition of the ice was a matter for anxiety, but I was most anxious to undertake exploration with the ship to the westward, toward Adelie Land, with the idea of mapping the coastline in that direction. As soon as all the members of the expedition were on board the *Nimrod,* therefore, I gave orders to steam north, and in a very short time we were under way. It was evident that the sea in our neighborhood would be frozen over before many hours had passed, and although I had foreseen the possibility of having to spend a second winter in the Antarctic when making my arrangements, we were all very much disinclined to face the long wait if it could be avoided. I wished first to round Cape Armitage and pick up the geological specimens and gear that had been left at Pram Point, but there was heavy ice coming out from the south, and this meant imminent risk of the ship being caught and perhaps "nipped." I decided to go into shelter under Glacier Tongue in the little inlet on the north side for a few hours, in the hope that the southern wind, that was bringing out the ice, would cease and that we would then be able to return and secure the specimens and gear. This was about two o'clock on the morning of March 4, and we members of the Southern Party turned in for a much needed rest.

At eight o'clock on the morning of the 4th we again went down the sound. Young ice was forming over the sea, which was now calm, the wind having entirely dropped, and it was evident that we must be very quick if we were to escape that year. We brought the *Nimrod* right alongside the pressure ice at Pram Point, and I pointed out the little depot on the hillside. Mackintosh at once went off with a party of men to bring the gear and specimens down, while another party went out to the seal rookery to see if they could find a peculiar seal that we had noticed on our way to the hut on the previous night. The seal was either a new species or the female of the Ross seal. It was a small animal, about four feet six inches long, with a broad white band from its throat right down to its tail on the underside. If we had been equipped with knives on the previous night we would have dispatched it, but we had no knives and were, moreover, very tired, and we therefore left it. The search for the seal proved fruitless, and as the sea was freezing over behind us I ordered all the men on board directly the stuff from the depot had been got on to the deck, and the *Nimrod* once more steamed north. The breeze soon began to freshen, and it was blowing hard from the south when we passed the winter quarters at Cape Royds. We all turned out to give three cheers and to take a last look at the place where we had spent so many happy days. The hut was not exactly a palatial residence, and during our period of residence in it we had suffered many discomforts, not to say hardships, but, on the other hand, it had been our home for a year that would always live in our memories. We had been a very happy little party within its walls, and often when we were far away from even its measure of civilization it had been the Mecca of all our hopes and dreams. We watched the little hut fade away in the distance with feelings almost of sadness, and there were few men aboard who did not cherish a hope that some day they would once more live strenuous days under the shadow of mighty Erebus.

I left at the winter quarters on Cape Royds a supply of stores sufficient to last fifteen men for one year. The vicissitudes of life in the Antarctic are such that such a supply might prove of the greatest value to some future expedition. The hut was locked up and the key hung up outside where it would be easily found, and we read-justed the lashing of the hut so that it might be able to withstand the attacks of the blizzards during the years to come. Inside the hut I left a letter stating what had been accomplished by the expedition, and giving some other information that might be useful to a future party of explorers. The stores left in the hut included oil, flour, jams, dried vegetables, biscuits, pemmican, plasmon, matches, and various tinned meats, as well as tea, cocoa, and necessary articles of equipment. If any party has to make use of our hut in the future, it will find there everything required to sustain life.

The wind was still freshening as we went north under steam and sail on March 4, and it was fortunate for us that this was so, for the ice that had formed on the sea water in the sound was thickening rapidly, assisted by the old pack, of which a large amount lay across our course. I was anxious to pick up a depot of geological specimens on Depot Island, left there by the Northern Party, and with this end in view the Nimrod was taken on a more westerly course than would otherwise have been the case. The wind, however, was freshening to a gale, and we were passing through streams of ice, which seemed to thicken as we neared the shore. I decided that it would be too risky to send a party off for the specimens, as there was no proper lee to this small island, and the consequences of even a short delay might be serious. I therefore gave instructions that the course should be altered to due north. The following wind helped us, and on the morning of March 6 we were off Cape Adare. I wanted to push between the Balleny Islands and the mainland, and make an attempt to follow the coastline from Cape North westward, so as to link it up with Adelie Land. No ship had ever succeeded in penetrating to the westward of Cape North, heavy pack having been encountered on the occasion of each attempt. The *Discovery* had passed through the Balleny Islands and sailed over part of the so called Wilkes Land of the maps, but the question of the existence of this land in any other position had been left open.

We steamed along the pack ice, which was beginning to thicken, and although we did not manage to do all that I had hoped, we had the satisfaction of pushing our little vessel along that coast to longitude 166° 14' East, latitude 69° 47' South, a point further west than had been reached by any previous expedition. On the morning of March 8 we saw, beyond Cape North, a new coastline extending first to the southward and then to the west for a distance of over forty-five miles. We took angles and bearings, and Marston sketched the main outlines. We were too far away to take any photographs that would have been of value, but the sketches show very clearly the type of the land. Professor David was of the opinion that it was the northern edge of the polar plateau. The coast seemed to consist of cliffs, with a few bays in the distance. We would all have been glad of an opportunity to explore the coast thoroughly, but that was out of the question; the ice was getting thicker all the time, and it was becoming imperative that we should escape to clear water without further delay. There was no chance of getting farther west at that point, and as the new ice was forming between the old pack of the previous year and the land, we were in serious danger of being frozen in for the winter at a place where we could not have done any geological work of importance. We therefore moved north along the edge of the pack, making as much westing as possible, in the direction of the Balleny Islands. I still hoped that it might be possible to skirt them and find Wilkes Land. It was awkward work, and at times the ship could hardly move at all.

Finally, about midnight on March 9, I saw that we must go north, and the course was set in that direction. We were almost too late, for the ice was closing in and before long we were held up, the ship being unable to move at all. The situation looked black, but we discovered a lane through which progress could be made, and in the afternoon of the 10th we were in fairly open water, passing through occasional lines of pack. Our troubles were over, for we had a good voyage up to New Zealand, and on March 22 dropped anchor at the mouth of Lord's River, on the south side of Stewart Island. I did not go to a port because I wished to get the news of the expedition's work through to London before we faced the energetic newspaper men.

That was a wonderful day to all of us. For over a year we had seen nothing but rocks, ice, snow, and sea. There had been no color and no softness in the scenery of the Antarctic; no green growth had gladdened our eyes, no musical notes of birds had come to our ears. We had had our work, but we had been cut off from most of the lesser things that go to make life worthwhile. No person who has not spent a period of his life in those "stark and sullen solitudes that sentinel the Pole" will understand fully what trees and flowers, sun flecked turf and running streams mean to the soul of a man. We landed on the stretch of beach that separated the sea from the luxuriant growth of the forest, and scampered about like children in the sheer joy of being alive. I did not wish to dispatch my cablegrams from Half Moon Bay until an hour previously arranged, and in the meantime we reveled in the warm sand on the beach, bathed in the sea, and climbed amongst the trees. We lit a fire and made tea on the beach, and while we were having our meal the wekas, the remarkable flightless birds found only in New Zealand, came out from the bush for their share of the good things. These quaint birds, with their long bills, brown plumage and quick, inquisitive eyes, have no fear of men, and their friendliness seemed to us like a welcome from that sunny land that had always treated us with such open hearted kindliness. The clear, musical notes of other birds came to us from the trees, and we felt that we needed only good news from home to make our happiness and contentment absolutely complete. One of the scientific men found a cave showing signs of native occupation in some period of the past, and was fortunate enough to discover a stone adze made of the rare pounamu, or greenstone.

Early next morning we hove up the anchor, and at 10 A.M. we entered Half Moon Bay. I went ashore to dispatch my cablegrams, and it was strange to see new faces on the wharf after fifteen months during which we had met no one outside the circle of our little party. There were girls on the wharf, too, and every one was glad to see us in the hearty New Zealand way. I dispatched my cablegrams from the little office, and then went on board again and ordered the course to be set for Lyttelton, the port from which we had sailed on the first day of the previous year. We arrived there on March 25 late in the afternoon.

The people of New Zealand would have welcomed us, I think, whatever had been the result of our efforts, for their keen interest in Antarctic exploration has never faltered since the early days of the *Discovery* expedition, and their attitude toward us was always that of warm personal friendship. But the news of the measure of success we had achieved had been published in London and flashed back to the southern countries, and we were met out in the harbor and on the wharves by cheering crowds. Enthusiastic friends boarded the *Nimrod* almost as soon as she entered the heads, and when our little vessel came alongside the quay, the crowd on deck became so great that movement was almost impossible. Then I was handed great bundles of letters and cablegrams. The loved ones at home were well, the world was pleased with our work, and it seemed as though nothing but happiness could ever enter life again.

Some Notes by James Murray, Biologist to the Expedition

PENGUINS

THOUGH so much has been written about them, the penguins always excite fresh interest in every one who sees them for the first time. There is endless interest in watching them, the dignified Emperor, dignified notwithstanding his clumsy waddle, going along with his wife (or wives) by his side, the very picture of a successful, self-satisfied, happy, unsuspicious countryman, gravely bowing like a Chinaman before a yelping dog and the little undignified matter of fact Adelie, minding his own business in a way worthy of emulation. They are perfectly adapted to a narrow round of life, and when compelled to face matters outside of their experience they often behave with apparent stupidity, but sometimes show a good deal of intelligence.

Their resemblance to human beings is always noticed. This is partly due to the habit of walking erect, but there are truly a great many human traits about them. They are the civilized nations of these regions, and their civilization, if much simpler than ours, is in some respects higher and more worthy of the name. But there is a good deal of human nature in them too. As in the human race, their gathering in colonies does not show any true social instinct. They are merely gregarious; each penguin is in the rookery for his own ends, there is no thought of the general good. You might exterminate an Adelie rookery with the exception of one bird, and he would be in no way concerned so long as you left him alone.

SOME NOTES BY JAMES MURRAY   383

Some little suggestion of altruism will appear in dealing with the nesting habits of the Adelie. Thieving is known, among the Adelies at least. One very pleasing trait is shown, which they have in common with man. Eating is not with them the prime business in life, as it is with the common fowl and most animals. Both Emperors and Adelies, when the serious business of nesting is off their minds, show a legitimate curiosity. Having fed and got into good condition they leave the sea and go off in parties, apparently to see the country, and travel for days and weeks.

THE EMPEROR

We saw the Emperor only as a summer visitor. Having finished nesting, fed up and become glossy and beautiful, they came up out of the sea in large or small parties, apparently to have a good time before molting. While the Adelies were nesting they began to come in numbers to inspect the camp. Passing among the Adelies, the two kinds usually paid no attention to one another, but sometimes an Adelie would think an Emperor came too close to her nest, and a curious unequal quarrel would ensue, the little impudence pecking and scolding, and the Emperor scolding back, with some loss of dignity. Though more than able to hold her own with the tongue, the Adelie knew the value of discretion whenever the Emperor raised his flipper.

They were curious about any unusual object and would come a long way to see a motorcar or a man. When out on these excursions the leader of a party keeps them together by a long shrill squawk. Distant parties salute in this way and continue calling till they get pretty close. A party could be made to approach by imitating this call. The first party to arrive inspected the boat, then crossed the lake to the camp. Soon they discovered the dogs, and thereafter all other interests were swallowed up in the interest excited by them. After the first discovery crowds came every day for a long time, and from the manner in which they went straight to the kennels one was tempted to believe that the fame of them had been noised abroad.

CEREMONIES OF MEETING

Emperors are very ceremonious in meeting other Emperors or men or dogs. They come up to a party of strangers in a straggling procession, some big important aldermanic fellow leading. At a respectful distance from the man or dog they halt, the old male waddles close up and bows gravely till his beak is almost touching his breast. Keeping his head bowed he makes a long speech, in a muttering manner, short sounds following in groups of four or five. Having finished the speech, the head is still kept bowed a few seconds for politeness' sake, then it is raised and he describes with his bill as large a circle as the joints of his neck will allow, looking in your face at last to see if you have understood. If you have not comprehended, as is usually the case, he tries again. He is very patient with your stupidity, and feels sure that he will get it into your dull brain if he keeps at it long enough. By this time his followers are getting impatient. They are sure he is making a mess of it. Another male will waddle forward with dignity, elbow the first aside as if to say, "I'll show you how it ought to be done," and goes through the whole business again. Their most solemn ceremonies were used toward the dogs, and three old fellows have been seen calmly bowing and speaking simultaneously to a dog, which for its part was yelping and straining at its chain in the effort to get at them.

Left to themselves the Emperor penguins seem perfectly peaceable, and no sign of quarreling was ever noticed. When a party of them was driven into a narrow space they resented the jostling, and flippers were freely used, making resounding whacks, which apparently are not felt through the dense feathery fur. The flipper strikes with equal facility forward or backward.

They seem to regard men as penguins like themselves. They are quite unsuspicious and slow to take alarm, so long as you stay still or move very slowly. If you walk too fast among them, or if you touch them, they get frightened and run away, only fighting when closely pressed. As one slowly retreats, fighting, he has a ludicrous resemblance to a small boy being bullied by a big one, his flipper toward the foe elevated in defense, and making quick blows at the bully. It is well to keep clear of that flipper when he strikes, for it is very powerful, and might break an arm.

Emperors were killed by the dogs, but it is likely that the animals hunted in couples to do this. A long fight was witnessed between an Emperor and the dog Ambrose, the largest of our dogs native to the Antarctic. The penguin was quick enough in movement to keep always facing the dog, and the flipper and long sharp bill were efficient weapons, as Ambrose seemed to appreciate. Only the bill was used, and it appeared to be due to short sight that the blow always fell short. Many of the apparently stupid acts of both kinds of penguins are doubtless to be traced to their very defective sight in air.

The Emperor can hardly be said to migrate since he remains to breed during the winter darkness, and spends the summer among the ice or on shore in the same region. Yet he travels a good deal, and the meaning of some of his journeyings remains a mystery. The visits of touring parties to the camp have been described. At the same season (early summer), when the motorcar was making frequent journeys southward to Glacier Tongue with stores for depot laying, we crossed on the way a great many penguin tracks. Many of these were beaten roads, where large parties had passed, some walking, some tobogganning. They all trended roughly to the southeast, and the wing marks and footmarks showed that they were all outward bound from the open sea toward the shore of Ross Island. Some of the roads were twelve miles or more from the open sea. There were no return tracks.

We expected to find that they had gone in to seek sheltered molting places, but on a motor trip to the Turk's Head we skirted a long stretch of the coast and found no Emperors.

On journeys they often travel many miles walking erect, when they get along at a very slow shuffle, making only a few inches at each step. In walking thus they keep their balance by the assistance of the tail, which forms a tripod with the legs. When on a suitable snow surface they progress rapidly by tobogganning, a very graceful motion, when they make sledges of their breasts and propel themselves by the powerful legs, balancing and perhaps improving their speed by means of the wings.

Eight of them visited the motorcar one day, near Tent Island, sledging swiftly toward us. Two of them were very determined fighters and refused to be driven away. One obstinate, phlegmatic old fellow, who wasn't going to be hurried by anybody, did learn to hustle as the car bore down upon him.

THE ADELIE

The Adelie is always comical. He pops out of the water with startling suddenness, like a jack in the box, alights on his feet, gives his tail a shake, and toddles off about his business. He always knows where he wants to go, and what he wants to do, and isn't easily turned aside from his purpose.

In the water the Adelie penguins move rapidly and circle in the same way as a porpoise or a dolphin, for which they are easily mistaken at a little distance. On level ice or snow they can run pretty fast, getting along about as fast as a man at a smart walk. They find even a small crack a serious obstruction, and pause and measure with the eye one of a few inches before very cautiously hopping it. They flop down and toboggan over any opening more than a few inches wide. They can climb hills of a very steep angle, but on uneven ground they use their flippers as balancers. They toboggan with great speed on snow or ice, or even on the bare rocks when scared, but in that case their flippers are soon bleeding. Very rarely they swim in the water like ducks. They lie much lower in the water than the duck. The neck is below the surface and the head is just showing.

The Adelie is very brave in the breeding season. His is true courage, not the courage of ignorance, for after he has learned to know man, and fear him, he remains to defend the nest against any odds. When walking among the nests one is assailed on all sides by powerful bills. Most of the birds sit still on the nests, but the more pugnacious ones run at you from a distance and often take you unawares. We wore for protection long felt boots reaching well above the knee. Some of the clever ones knew that they were wasting their efforts on the felt boots, and would come up behind, hop up and seize the skin above the boot, and hang on tight, beating with their wings. One of these little furies, hanging to your flesh and flapping his strong flippers so fast that you can hardly see them move, is no joke. A man once stumbled and fell into a colony of Adelies, and before he could recover himself and scramble out they were upon him, and he bore the marks of their fury for some time.

Some birds became greatly interested in the camp, and wanted to nest there. One bird (we believe it was always the same one) couldn't be kept away, and came daily, sometimes bringing some friends. As he passed among the dogs, which were barking and trying to get at him, he stood and defied them all, and when we turned out to try to drive him away, he offered to take us all on too, and was finally saved against his will, and carried away by Brocklehurst, a wildly struggling, unconquerable being.

The old birds enjoy play, while the young ones have no leisure for play, being engrossed in satisfying the enormous appetites they have when growing. Four or five Adelies were playing on the ice floe. One acted as leader, advanced to the edge of the floe, waited for the others to line up, raised his flipper, when they all dived in. In a few seconds they all popped out again, and repeated the performance, always apparently directed by the one. And so they went on for hours. While the *Nimrod* was frozen in the pack, some dozens of them were disporting themselves in a sea pool alongside. They swam together in the duck fashion, then at a squawk from one they all dived and came up at the other side of the pool.

Early in October they began to arrive at the rookery, singly or in pairs. The first to come were males, and they at once began to scrape up the frozen ground to make hollows for their nests, and to collect stones for the walls with which they surround them. The digging is hard work and is done by the feet, the bird lying prone and kicking out backward. As soon as any apology for a nest is ready the males begin displaying. He points his bill vertically upward, flaps his wings slowly, inflates his chest, and makes a series of low booming sounds, which increase in loudness, then die away again, the throat vibrating strongly. Then he slowly subsides into the usual attitude. We supposed this to be a part of his courtship, or as some phrased it "advertising for a wife," but there is good reason to suppose that the pairing is done before the birds leave the sea. Generally the male's displaying passes entirely disregarded. He continues it all through the nesting season, till the chicks are nearly fledged and the molting time is near. An epidemic of displaying often took the whole rookery at once, when the hens were mostly away disporting themselves in the sea.

When the rookery is pretty well filled, and the nest building is in full swing, the birds have a busy and anxious time. To get enough of suitable small stones is a matter of difficulty, and may involve long journeys for each single stone. The temptation is too strong for some of them, and they become habitual thieves. The majority remain stupidly honest. Amusing complications result. The bearing of the thief clearly shows that he knows he is doing wrong. He has a conscience, at least a human conscience, i.e. the fear of being found out. Very different is the furtive look of the thief, long after he is out of danger of pursuit, from the expression of the honest penguin coming home with a hard earned stone.

An honest one was bringing stones from a long distance. Each stone was removed by a thief as soon as the owner's back was turned. The honest one looked greatly troubled as he found that his heap didn't grow, but he seemed incapable of suspecting the cause.

A thief, sitting on its own nest, was stealing from an adjacent nest, whose honest owner was also at home, but looking unsuspectingly in another direction. Casually he turned his head and caught the thief in the act. The thief dropped the stone and pretended to be busy picking up an infinitesimal crumb from the neutral ground.

The stone gathering is a very strong part of the nesting

instinct. It was kept up while sitting on the eggs, and if at a late stage they lost their eggs or young, they reverted to the heaping of stones, which they did in a half-hearted way. Unmated birds occupied the fringe of the rookery, and amused themselves piling and stealing till the chicks began to hatch out.

After the two eggs were laid the males appeared to do most of the work. At any hour the males predominated, a very few pairs were at the nests, and relieving guard was rarely noticed. The females were never seen in the majority. Those which had been recently down to feed could be recognized by the fresh crustacea around the nests. Judging by this sign, it would seem that some birds never leave the nest to feed during the whole period of incubation. Many birds lost their mates through the occasional breaking loose of a dog. These birds couldn't leave the nests.

REARING THE CHICKS

The rookery is most interesting after the chicks arrive. Many curious things happen as they grow. The young chicks are silvery or slaty gray, with darker heads, which are for the first day or so heavy and hang down helplessly. As soon as they are hatched the mothers take equal share in tending them, whatever they may have been doing before that. For some weeks the nest cannot be left untended or the chicks would perish of cold or fall victims to the skuas. The parents keep regular watches, going down in turn to feed, and relieving guard is an interesting ceremony. The bird just arrived from the sea hurries to the nest. It is anxious to see the chick, and to feed it; the other is unwilling to resign, but at last reluctantly gets off the nest, evidently very stiff, stretches itself, and hangs about for a while before going down to the sea.

When the young ones can hold up their heads the feeding begins. At first the parent tries to induce its offspring to feed by tickling its bill and throat. The old bird opens its mouth and the chick puts its head right in and picks the food out of the throat. The bird can be seen bringing it up into the throat by an effort. If the young is unwilling to feed some food is thrown right up on to the ground and a little of it picked up again and placed on the chick's bill. After learning the way there is no need for such inducement, and the parents are taxed to satisfy the clamoring for more.

For some weeks after the young are hatched life in the rookery goes smoothly along. One parent is always on the nest and the young birds do not wander. Then the trouble begins. The young begin to move about and if anything disturbs the colony they run about in panic. As they don't know nest or parent they cannot return home. They meet the case by adopting parents, and run under any bird they come to. The old birds resent this and a chick is often pecked away from nest after nest till exhausted. The skuas get some at this time, but it is surprising how few. Most of the chicks take some old one unawares and get in the nest. She may have a chick already, or chicks, but as she doesn't know which is her own she cannot drive the intruder away. A sorely puzzled bird may be seen trying to cover four gigantic chicks. Some of the less precocious youngsters stay at home long enough to get to know the nest, and can find their way home after wandering a few yards. Such homes keep together a little longer.

The time comes when both parents must be absent together to get enough food for the growing chicks. Then the social order of the rookery breaks down and chaos begins. The social condition which is evolved out of the chaos is one of the most remarkable in nature, yet it serves its purpose and saves the race. A kind of communism is established, but the old birds have no part in it. They cherish the fiction that they have nests and children, and when they come up from the sea after feeding it is their intention to find the nest and feed their own young only. The young ones, for their part, establish a community of parents, and yet it isn't exactly that either, though it works out as if it were. It is each bird for itself. The chick assumes the first old one that comes within its reach to be its parent. Perhaps it really thinks so, as they are all alike.

An old bird, coming up full of shrimps, is met by clam-

orous youngsters before it has time to begin the search
for its hypothetical home. They order it to stand and
deliver. It objects and scolds, and runs off. It may be by
the irony of fate that it is its own young which accost it,
but it can't know that. The chickens are both imperative
and wheedling. Then begins one of those parent hunts
which were so familiar at the end of the season. The
end is never in doubt from the first. Every now and
again the old one stops and expostulates. This shows
weakness. There is no indecision on the part of the
young one. It never seems anxious as to the result, but
in the most matter of fact and persistent manner hunts
the old one down. The hunts are often long and exhausting. One chase was witnessed at Pony Lake beside
the camp. Nine times they circled the lake, and the hunt
was not over when the watcher had to leave. On that
occasion they must have traveled miles. At the end the
old one stops, and still spluttering and protesting, deliv-
ers up. One would think that in these circumstances the
weaker chicks would go to the wall, but it does not appear to be so. There are no ill nourished young ones
to be seen. Perhaps the hunts take so long that all get
a chance.

A few days after the eggs began to hatch there was a
severe blizzard, which lasted several days. Snow was
banked up around most of the birds. A snowdrift crossed
the densest part of the rookery, partly burying many
birds. In the deepest part nests and birds were covered
out of sight, and the only indication of the whereabouts
of a bird was a little funnel in the snow, at the bottom
of which an anxious eye could be seen. Many less deeply
buried birds had freed one wing or both, which became
stiff with cold, as they could not be got back again. The
snow, melting by the heat of their bodies, and refreezing,
made walls of ice around the birds. Many got alarmed
and left the nests, when the snow fell in and buried
them. In the warm sunny weather that followed the melting snow filled many nests with pools of water. Some
birds showed ingenuity in dealing with these floods.
They moved their nests, stone by stone (always keeping
a hollow for the eggs or chicks), as much as their own
width till they reached dry ground. While the snowdrift

remained some birds whose nests were buried scraped hollows in the snow and collected a few stones. On a moderate estimate about half the young perished in this blizzard.

The old Adelies do not mind the cold. Their thick blubber and dense fur sufficiently protect them. In a blizzard they will lie still and let the snow cover them. Going to the rookery once after a blizzard I could see no penguins; they had entirely disappeared. Suddenly at some movement or noise I was surrounded by them; they had sprung up out of the snow.

DOMESTIC ENTANGLEMENTS

While the Adelie appears to be entirely moral in his domestic arrangements, his stupidity (or his short sightedness, which causes him to seem stupid) gives rise to many domestic complications. No doubt the presence of our camp upset the social economy, and probably when undisturbed nothing of the kind would occur. He has little sense of locality, and one little heap of stones is very like another, yet pairs seem to have no means of recognizing one another but by the rendezvous of the nest. Husbands and wives, parents and children, do not know one another, but if found at the nest are accepted as bona fide.

All the birds go to their nests without hesitation when they come from the sea by the familiar route, but if taken from their nests to some other part of the rookery some find their way back without difficulty, others are quite lost. They are most puzzled when moved only a little away from home, and they will fight to keep another bird's nest while their own is only a couple of feet away. A bird will defend an egg or chick in the nest, but if it is removed just outside it will peck at it and destroy it.

Considering these facts it will be evident that if the rookery be disturbed confusion follows. A mere walk among the nests caused innumerable entanglements. One bird would leave the nest in fright, flop down a yard away beside a nest already occupied, or on a nest left exposed by another scared bird. Then one-sided fights would begin, one bird attacking another under the impression that it had usurped its nest, the rightful owner troubling little about the vicious pecking he was receiving, sitting calmly in conscious rectitude. A fight of this kind has been watched for an hour at a time, three neighboring nests having been disturbed. One bird had got into another's nest, a second was trying to establish a claim to the occupied nest of a third, and meanwhile the chicks of number one were neglected in the cold. A bird which had no family came and covered the chicks, but looked conscious of wrongdoing and kept ready to bolt on a second's notice. All these birds but the last wanted their own nests and were within a yard of them without knowing it.

In all such cases, even when a bird got established on the wrong nest, there was always an adjustment afterward. When they calmed down they became uneasy, probably observing the landmarks more critically, and would even leave a nest with chicks for their own empty nest. A chick removed from the nest and put alongside was not recognized, and the old bird never seemed to connect the facts of the empty nest and the chick beside it. If a chick were taken from the nest under the old bird's very eyes and held in front of it, it was always the chick that was viciously attacked, not the aggressor.

Some experiments were tried on them in order to trace the workings of the penguin mind. If a man stood between a bird and its nest so as to prevent it from getting on to it, the bird would make many attempts to reach home, rushing furiously at the man. After a time it would appear to meditate, and then walk off rather disconsolately, make a tour of the colony to which it belonged, and approach the nest from another side. It appeared greatly astonished that the intruder was still there. This curious trait was often seen. It is like the ostrich burying its head in the sand and imagining it is safe, or like a man refusing to believe his own eyes. It appears to think that if it takes a turn around, or comes to its nest from the other side, the horrible vision will disappear.

A bird was taken from a nest which had a chick in it and put down at a little distance. Meantime the chick was put in a neighbor's nest. Presently the bird came running up. It started back on seeing the empty nest, not in alarm or fear, but exactly as if thinking, "I've come to the wrong house!" and trotted off to a distant part of the rookery. Her reasoning seemed to be this: "There was a chick in my nest, therefore this empty nest cannot be mine." She couldn't imagine the chick leaving the nest, and so never searched for it. It was only a yard from the nest all the time. After half an hour's searching in vain for any place like home she returned to the nest, and accepted the restored chick as a matter of course.

A lost chick was never sought for. There would be no use; it couldn't be recognized. On account of this peculiarity we were able to make many readjustments of the family arrangements. When the blizzard destroyed so many chicks we distributed the young from nests where there were two to nests where there were none. They were usually adopted eagerly and the plan was quite successful.

When both birds are at a nest that is disturbed, or when the mate comes up from feeding to relieve guard, there is an interchange of civilities in the form of a loud squawking in unison, accompanied by a curious movement. The birds' necks are crossed, and at each squawk they are changed from side to side, first right then left. The harsh complaining clamor which they make was for long mistaken for quarreling.

A bird returning from the sea came to the wrong nest and tried to enter into conversation with the occupant, who would have nothing to do with him. She knew her mate had just gone off for the day, and wouldn't be such a fool as to come back too early, so she sat still, indifferent to the squawking of the other. A look of distress came into his face as he failed to get any response, and he was slow to realize that he had made a mistake.

A small colony was found with about two dozen large chicks, unattended by any old birds. They were driven across the lake to a larger colony. Halfway over a few old birds were squatted, enjoying a rest. When the chicks saw them they ran up to them joyfully, saying: "Here's pa and ma, hooray!" To their surprise they got the reverse of a cordial welcome, being driven away with vicious peckings. They were driven on to the larger colony and were swallowed up in it.

The Adelies are not demonstrative of their affections. It is difficult to discover if they have any beyond the instinctive affection for the young. The pairing appears to be a purely business matter, and the mates don't even show any power to recognize one another. A penguin was injured by the dogs, but it seemed possible that it might recover, so we did not at once put it out of pain. In a couple of days it died. Shortly after we noticed a live penguin standing by it. We removed the dead bird to a distance, and after a while found the other standing beside it as before. It was the general opinion that it was the dead bird's mate which had found it out. Such an action is entirely opposed to what we expect after a long study of their habits. There are always plenty of dead birds about a rookery, and the living go about entirely indifferent to them. It is puzzling in any point of view, but it is less difficult to believe that the bird found its dead mate than that it took an interest in a dead stranger.

ALTRUISM

When the young birds are well grown, if there is an alarm they flock together, and any old birds present in the colony form a wall of defense between the young and the enemy. This habit has given rise to the belief that they are somewhat communistic in their social order, and that the defense of the colony is a concerted action. It is not so. Each bird is defending its own young one only, and will often fight with another of the defending birds, or peck at any young one which comes in its way.

There are real instances of altruism or kindness to strangers. Our passage through the rookery frightened away the parents of a very young chick. A bird passing at the distance of a few yards noticed it and came over to it. He cocked his head on one side and looked at it, as if saying: Hullo! this little beggar's deserted; must do something for him." He tickled its bill, as the parents do when coaxing the very young chicks to feed, but it was too much frightened to feed. After coaxing it in this way for some time he turned away and put some food upon the ground, and, lifting a little in his bill, he put some on each side of the chick's bill. Just then the rightful parent returned and the helper ran off. This was not an isolated case, but was observed on several occasions.

One incident seemed to reveal true social instincts. From a small colony of about two dozen nests all the eggs but one were taken in order to find out if the birds would lay again. As it turned out they did not. The birds sat on their empty nests for some time, then they disappeared. When the time came for the solitary egg to hatch, about a dozen of the nests were reoccupied and the birds took their share in defending the one chick.

DEPARTURE OF THE YOUNG

When they have shed most of their down the young birds congregate at the edge of the sea. They cease from hunting the old ones for food, and appear to be waiting for something. When the right time comes, which they seem to know perfectly, they dive into the sea, sometimes in small parties, sometimes singly, disappear for a time, and may be seen popping up far out to sea. They dive and come up very awkwardly, but swim well.

It is marvelous how fully instinct makes these birds independent. The parents do not take them to the water and teach them to swim. They haven't even the example of the old birds, which stay behind to molt. At an early age they become independent of their own parents, and earn their living by hunting any old bird they find. Though they have spent their lives on land, and only know that food is something found in an old bird's throat, when the time comes they leave the land and plunge boldly into the sea, untaught, to get their living by straining crustacea out of the water in the same way as the whale does.

Some of our party reported that they saw penguins teaching the young to swim, but if this ever happens it is not general. Time and again the young have been watched leaving as described, entirely on their own. At that season nearly all the old birds are in the molt and never venture into the water.

Like the Emperor, the Adelie is fond of traveling when family cares are off his mind. The great blizzard which wiped our half the rookery left hundreds of old birds free. They began to explore the adjacent country in bands. The round of the lakes was a favorite trip and broad beaten roads marked this route. Tracks also led to the summits of some of the hills, though the short-sighted Adelie could hardly go there for the view.

There was no general trek southward, such as the Emperors made, yet the Southern Party found tracks of two at a distance of some eighty miles from the sea.

NEBUCHADNEZZAR AND NICODEMUS

These names dignified two penguin chicks. While chaos reigned in the rookery I found them exhausted and covered with mire, having been hunted and pecked through the rookery. They were taken to the house, put in a large cage in the porch, and fed by hand with sardines and fish cakes. The feeding was disagreeable. They didn't like the food and shook it out of their bills in disgust. So it was necessary to force it down their throats till it was beyond their reach.

In a few days they became quite tame and recognized those who fed them. Familiar only with our peculiar method of feeding them, one of them indicated when he was hungry by taking my finger into his bill. We shortened their names to Nebby and Nicky, and they answered to them, but they answered equally readily to the common name of Bill. The sounds of the rookery reached them and sometimes greatly excited them and they made desperate efforts to get through the netting of their cage. At these times we would take them out for a walk. They made no attempt to go to the rookery, and were rather frightened.

Nebuchadnezzar was a very friendly little fellow, and would follow me about outside, and come running when called. The feeding was unnatural, and for this reason, doubtless, in a few weeks they died.

THE RINGED PENGUIN

A single ringed penguin appeared at Cape Royds at the end of the breeding season, just as the Adelies were beginning to molt. No ringed penguin had been seen in this part of the Antarctic before. It was evidently a stray one which had come ashore to molt. It is about the same size as the Adelie, but is more agile. It was at the season when the young Adelies go off to sea. At a little distance the ringed penguin, among a crowd of old Adelies, looked somewhat like a young Adelie with the white throat. I picked him up by the legs to investigate. To my surprise he curled round and bit me on the hand. An Adelie could not do so. A closer examination showed what he was.

Southern Journey Distances

By the Commander of the Expedition

THE following Table gives detailed information regarding the distances traveled day by day on the Southern Journey.

The number of geographical miles given in the first column covers the period from November 15, 1908, to January 9, 1909. The distances have been taken from the chart after all corrections have been made, and represent a direct line from camp to camp.

In the second column will be found the noon latitudes, calculated from observations taken as opportunity offered.

The last column shows the distances traveled day by day according to the sledge meter, and these figures take into account all deviations and detours so often rendered necessary by the condition of the surface. The reliability of the sledge meter is proved by the fact that on the homeward journey we were able to determine our positions without taking latitude observations. Only one observation was taken on the return journey (January 31, 1909), and on that occasion the theodolite confirmed the record of the sledge meter.

The latitude observations noted in this Table were taken with a three inch theodolite, which was carefully adjusted before the start for the southern journey. An observation taken on the return journey, in February, when the position was known from bearings, showed that the instrument was correct. The observations were only taken with the theodolite "face left," but as the instrument was in good adjustment this was sufficient.

On the outward journey the last latitude observation was taken in latitude 87° 22' South. The remainder of the distance marched toward the south was calculated by sledge meter and dead reckoning. The accuracy of the sledge meters used was proved by the fact that on the return journey we were able to pick up the depots without taking observations. The "slip" was ascertained by careful tests before the start of the journey.

The chronometer watches taken were rated before leaving and on the return, and the error was only eight seconds. All bearings, angles, and azimuths were taken with the theodolite. Variation was ascertained by means of a compass attached to the theodolite, and the steering compasses were checked accordingly. At noon each day the prismatic compasses were placed in the true meridian, and checked against the theodolite compass and the steering compasses.

Date.	Geographical miles.	Noon latitudes.	Statute miles.	Yards.	Relay.
1908					
October 29 . . .	—	—	14	880	—
" 30 (Hut Point) .	—	—	9	880	—
" 31 (back to Royds)	—	—	23	—	—
November 1 (to Hut Point)	—	—	23	—	—
" 2 (blizzard) .	—	—	no march	—	
" 3 . . .	—	—	12	300	—
" 4 . . .	—	—	16	500	—
" 5 . . .	—	—	9	1200	—
" 6 (blizzard) .	—	—	no march	—	
" 7 . . .	—	—	1	—	—
" 8 (blizzard) .	—	—	no march	—	
" 9 . . .	—	—	14	600	—
" 10 . . .	—	—	15	1550	—
" 11 . . .	—	—	15	—	—
" 12 . . .	—	—	15	1650	—
" 13 . . .	—	—	15	1550	—
" 14 . . .	—	—	15	100	—
" 15 . . .	7.39 (from noon)	79° 36' S.	12	1500	—
" 16 . . .	14.91	—	17	200	—
" 17 . . .	13.3	—	16	200	—
" 18 . . .	13	—	15	500	—
" 19 . . .	13.7	—	15	200	—
" 20 . . .	13.6	—	15	800	—
" 21 . . .	13.3	—	15	500	—
" 22 . . .	16	—	15	250	—
" 23 . . .	14	—	17	1650	—
" 24 . . .	15.4	—	17	680	—
" 25 . . .	14.6	—	17	1600	—
" 26 . . .	13.2	82° 12' S.	16	1700	—
" 27 . . .	15.5	—	16	1200	—
" 28 . . .	13.6	82° 39' S.	15	1500	—
" 29 . . .	11.7	—	14	900	—
" 30 . . .	11	—	12	150	—
December 1 . . .	10.5	—	12	200	—

Date.				Geographical miles.	Noon latitudes.	Statute miles.	Yards.	Relay.
1908								
December	2	.	.	10.3	—	11	1450	—
,,	3 (Mount Hope)			—	—	20	—	—
,,	4	.	.	10.5	83° 33' S.	10	—	—
,,	5	.	.	3.1	—	5	—	4
,,	6	.	.	4.1	—	4	—	3
,,	7	.	.	9.1	—	10	570	—
,,	8	.	.	7.7	—	12	150	—
,,	9	.	.	9.8	84° 2' S.	11	1450	2
,,	10	.	.	9.8	—	11	860	—
,,	11	.	.	7.2	—	8	900	—
,,	12	.	.	3.1	—	3	500	6 1000
,,	13	.	.	4.5	—	5	—	6
,,	14	.	.	8	—	7	880	2
,,	15	.	.	11.5	—	13	200	—
,,	16	.	.	12	84° 53' S.	13	1650	—
,,	17	.	.	9.1	—	12	250	1
,,	18	.	.	3	—	6	600	12
,,	19	.	.	7.4	—	10	—	1 880
,,	20	.	.	10	85° 19' S.	11	950	1
,,	21	.	.	7	—	6	—	3
,,	22	.	.	7	—	4	—	6
,,	23	.	.	6.2	—	13	—	—
,,	24	.	.	9.2	—	11	250	—
,,	25	.	.	9.2	—	10	650	—
,,	26	.	.	11.4	—	14	480	—
,,	27	.	.	12	—	14	930	—
,,	28	.	.	11.7	—	14	450	—
,,	29	.	.	10.1	—	12	600	—
,,	30	.	.	3.7	—	4	100	—
,,	31	.	.	8.5	—	11	—	—
1909								
January	1	.	.	9.7	86° 59' S.	11	900	—
,,	2	.	.	9.1	—	10	450	—
,,	3	.	.	12.6	87° 22' S	11	1680	—
,,	4	.	.	12.2	—	14	660	—
,,	5	.	.	13.4	—	15	480	—
,,	6	.	.	13.2	(88° 7 camp)	15	313	—
,,	7 (blizzard)		.	—	—	no march	—	—
,,	8 (blizzard)		.	—	—	no march	—	—
,,	9	.	.	16.5	88° 23' S.	18	704 from camp	—
					(farthest south) {	18	704 back	—
						4	40 to camp	—

Date.	Geographical miles.	Noon latitudes.	Statute miles.	Yards.	Relay.
1909					
January 10	—	—	21	308	—
,, 11	—	—	19	1580	—
,, 12	—	—	14	100	—
,, 13	—	—	15	1560	—
,, 14	—	—	20	1600	—
,, 15	—	—	20	—	—
,, 16	—	—	18	800	—
,, 17	—	—	22	850	—
,, 18	—	—	26	900	—
,, 19	—	—	29	—	—
,, 20	—	—	15·	800	—
,, 21	—	—	17	—	—
,, 22	—	—	15	900	—
,, 23	—	—	14	100	—
,, 24	—	—	16	—	—
,, 25	—	—	26	—	—
,, 26	—	— }	16	{ —	—
,, 27	—	—		—	—
,, 28	—	—	14	890	—
,, 29 (blizzard)	—	—	2	—	—
,, 30	—	—	13	—	—
,, 31	—	82° 58'	13	850	—
February 1	—	—	13	1400	—
,, 2	—	—	13	900	—
,, 3	—	—	5	900	—
,, 4 (dysentery)	—	—	no march	—	—
,, 5	—	—	8	—	—
,, 6	—	—	10	—	—
,, 7	—	—	12	—	—
,, 8	—	—	12	—	—
,, 9	—	—	14	900	—
,, 10	—	—	20	300	—
,, 11	—	—	16	1320	—
,, 12	—	—	14	450	—
,, 13	—	—	12	—	—
,, 14	—	—	11	1400	—
,, 15	—	—	12	440	—
,, 16	—	—	13	—	—
,, 17	—	—	19	200	—
,, 18	—	—	15	400	—
,, 19	—	—	14	440	—
,, 20	—	—	14	—	—
,, 21	—	—	20	—	—
,, 22	—	—	20	800	—
,, 23	—	—	14	500	—
,, 24	—	—	15	—	—
,, 25 (blizzard)	—	—	no march	—	—
,, 26 (left A. and M.)	—	—	24	—	—
,, 27	—	— }	39	{ —	—
,, 28	—	—		—	—

Date.				Geographical miles.	Noon latitudes.	Statute miles.	Yards.	Relay.
March 1	.	.	.	—	—		—	—
,, 2	.	.	.	—	—	63	—	—
,, 3	.	.	.	—	—	30 out	—	—
,, 4	.	.	.	—	—	33 back	—	—

The total distance marched, from October 29 to March 4, as recorded on the sledge meters, was 1755 miles 209 yards statute, this including relay work and back marches.

INDEX